ESSAYS HONORING
JACK W. HAYFORD

The
Pastor &
The
Kingdom

EDITED BY JON HUNTZINGER, PhD
& S. DAVID MOORE, PhD

Gateway Academic, an imprint of Gateway Publishing, exists to advance the Kingdom of God by providing
biblically and theologically sound resources to the Church and the Academy. We affirm the Spirit-empowered
calling of vocational and lay ministers and seek to create materials that shape the mind and form the spirit.

We hope you hear from the Holy Spirit and receive God's richest blessings from this book by Gateway Academic.
We want to provide the highest quality resources that take the messages, music, and media of Gateway Church
to the world. For more information on other resources from Gateway Publishing, go to gatewaypublishing.com.

Gateway Academic, an imprint of Gateway Publishing
700 Blessed Way
Southlake, Texas 76092
gatewaypublishing.com

Contents

Foreword

A Spiritual Father: Jack Hayford's Influence on My Life

WHEN JACK HAYFORD was five years old, he received his first allowance—10 cents as payment for a chore. Instead of giving him a dime, his father gave him a nickel and five pennies. Then he sat down with Jack, showed him Scriptures on tithing, and explained that one penny out of every 10 cents belongs to God. Jack took out one penny and gave his first tithe.

Years later, when Jack and his wife, Anna, received a paycheck for more than $1,000, he realized the tithe would be triple digits for the first time in his life. When he went to write the check, he paused for just a moment and thought, "Lord, this is *a lot* of money." The Lord spoke to him and said, "It's still only one penny on every dime." And Jack has tithed one penny on every dime he has made his entire life.

That's just one of the things that stands out to me about Jack—his life of faithfulness in the big and the small. Yet, there are so many other things about him that I admire and that have influenced my life.

Pastor Jack began influencing me years before I ever met him. The first time I heard him speak was at a James Robison Bible Conference in the early 1980s. He taught on the beauty of spiritual language. As a young Baptist minister, I hadn't heard anything like it. But Jack had a very nonconfrontational way of humbly presenting Scripture. He didn't try to defend or argue a position; he simply presented his belief. He didn't say, "This is the *only* way. Either I'm right, or you're wrong." His presentation, mannerisms, Christlikeness, and humility, not to mention his knowledge of Scripture and theological soundness, caused me to open up to this man with a Pentecostal background. He caused me to start thinking about Scripture differently, and I began reading his books and watching him on television.

In 2001, a year after I founded Gateway Church, I went to a small pastors' gathering to hear Pastor Jack share about how we could help Messianic Jews. I met him in the parking lot and told him how much he ministered to me and how much I appreciated him. He was very kind and gracious. He took an interest in me and asked about the church. We only had 200 people attending at the time, yet he treated me like an equal. In fact, he treats all pastors that way. Pastor Jack once made a statement that it takes as much character, time, and energy to prepare a message for 200 people as it does for 2,000. He doesn't see pastors at different levels or hierarchies. He sees us as shepherds of God's sheep no matter how many we're pastoring. And I felt that from the first time I met him.

A couple of years later, I sent Pastor Jack an invitation to speak at our first pastors' conference. He responded by saying he wanted to talk over the phone before he accepted. During our conversation, he asked who was coming and what our focus was so that he could be a good steward of his time while he prepared. It didn't matter to him that we didn't have many people coming (maybe a few hundred); he wanted to know how he could best help and serve the pastors. When he arrived, it was like being with family. As we spent time together and got to know one another better, I absolutely fell in love with his character and his fatherly nature, and he seemed to immediately fall in love with me as a teachable son he could pour into. As that spiritual father/son relationship began to develop, we started spending more and more time together.

Not long after that, I went to Pastor Jack's week-long school of pastoral nurture with about 40 other pastors. As he poured into us, I began to realize that in addition to his vast knowledge of theology, he had a practical pastoral wisdom I'd never heard before. That week, he shared why he preached series instead of just stand-alone messages, how he arranged his series, how he used his study times, and how he spent his off times—so many practical subjects that Bible college didn't teach me. He helped prepare me for the everyday things I'd experience in ministry.

Watching how Pastor Jack handles being a well-known author and pastor helps me understand how I should steward the influence God has given me. Even with all the books he has written and all the songs he has composed, it hasn't changed his personality. He's never thought of himself as a celebrity. He doesn't have "yes people" around him. He doesn't have an entourage when he travels. He doesn't think more highly of himself than he should. When he talks, there's no pride in him; there's just a recognition that God's given him influence in the body of Christ, and he wants to steward that influence well. Jack has talked to me about times when a church or a pastor really honored and received him. It was as though he was shocked! I would think to myself, *Well, of course, they honored you! You're Jack Hayford.* But he never thinks of himself that way. He is *just* Jack, and he has always remained just Jack.

Several times, I've looked at the influence God has given me in the kingdom and thought, *Can I handle this? Can I be the good example God wants me to be? Can I be the pastor God wants me to be?* But then I look at Jack and feel encouraged because he is an example of a normal person whom God uses to do great, extraordinary, supernatural things for Him. He's a very humble, transparent person who never puts on airs. He never comes across as prideful in what he's done, yet he has a confidence knowing that God uses him. It encourages me to know I can walk with God and God can use me to part Red Seas because He's done that with Jack.

I've often joked that I have a WWJD bracelet: "What would *Jack* do?" Not to take anything away from "What would Jesus do?" because, of course, we want to be like Christ. God gives us earthly examples too, though, and Pastor Jack is one of those examples. There are times when I am leading the church to embrace a new vision, and I think to myself, *What would Jack do?* Or if I feel like I need to bring a corrective word, I think, *How would Jack say this?* Or if I'm trying to lead the elders in something I believe the Lord has spoken to me, I ask them, "How would Jack do it?"

However, this isn't just about "What would Jack do?" when it comes to ministry but also "What would Jack do?" when it comes to marriage. A few years ago, we had a celebration to honor Pastor Jack's decades of ministry and 60 years of marriage to his college sweetheart, Anna. The first time he saw her from across the gym, he decided he wanted to get to know her. He was the big man on campus, and all of Anna's friends had told her, "Just wait until you meet Jack Hayford!" Later, she said that when she met him, her first thought was, "Oh, he's not such a big deal!" But they obviously fell in love, and they remained deeply in love until her recent passing. The way Jack honored and loved Anna and the way she honored and loved him is an example to us all.

I've said many times that Pastor Jack is the Apostle Paul of our generation. Paul was a man of the Spirit and a man who knew the power of God, yet at the same time, he was a man who knew the Scriptures. He was a brilliant man who could communicate to different people and different churches in many ways, which is represented by the letters he wrote. So, when I think of the Apostle Paul, I think of a man who has a diverse and rich background. A man who is an effective teacher of the Scriptures. A man who is of the Spirit, yet a man of intellect. A man who's seen the power of God work within him. A man like Pastor Jack.

Pastor Jack is a man of the Spirit and a man of the Scriptures. When I think of him, I'm often reminded of John 4:23–24, "But the hour is coming, and now is, when the true worshipers will worship the Father in spirit and truth; for the Father is seeking such to worship Him. God *is* Spirit, and those who worship Him must worship in spirit and truth" (NKJV). Some people put more emphasis on the truth of Scripture while others may put more emphasis on life in the Spirit. Pastor Jack is the perfect blend and balance of both. He teaches people how to worship God in the life of the Holy Spirit and the truth of God's Word. He doesn't try to put them at odds with each other; instead, he emphasizes both in wonderful balance.

Pastor Jack helps all of us to yield unashamedly to the Holy Spirit. For years, it seemed like you had to be weird or melodramatic to be filled with the Holy Spirit. He came along as this soft-spoken, kind, humble, theologically sound pastor who was completely yielded to the Holy Spirit. He helped people understand that a person who is "normal" can fully believe in the work of the Holy Spirit. After years of leaders projecting "weirdness" related to "Spirit-filledness," Pastor Jack came along and modeled "normalness" and "Spirit-yieldedness."

Pastor Jack fully believes in the Holy Spirit, yet he is *normal*. When he was on TV, he never said things like, "If you send money to my ministry or if you pray for my ministry, I'm going to pray for you, and your problem is going to be solved." He never tries to draw people to himself. He *always* draws people to Christ. He is one of the first leaders I saw who influenced a large part of the body of Christ—both those who believed doctrine the way he did *and* those who might not have shared the same views doctrinally but respected his academic accomplishments, his approach to the Word, and his normalcy of life.

For years, there has been a division in the body of Christ between those who believe in the person and work of the Holy Spirit for today and those who don't. Pastor Jack bridges those gaps. In fact, many of the people who attended the James Robison Bible Conference, where I first heard Pastor Jack, were from a Baptist background. It was because of the way he presented the Word and didn't try to force it down people's throats that James Robison invited him back to speak on the gift of tongues at the conference. That message became the basis for his best-selling book, *The Beauty of Spiritual Language*.

It's amazing, really. Pastor Jack is able to speak about a very controversial gift in the body of Christ with such grace and humility that people who might not have the same doctrinal view listen to him without a competitive or argumentative spirit. It's because of his influence that the body of Christ is less splintered and in greater unity today—the greatest unity it's ever been in.

Pastor Jack has also had a tremendous influence in the area of worship—not just through the songs he's written but also through his teachings on worship. The resurgence of worship in the body of Christ today is largely due to the seeds Pastor Jack sowed in the '60s, '70s, and '80s. His teachings on worship, along with his extravagant yet genuine expressions of worship, have helped me as well as people of all faiths and in all nations learn to express their love to God. I can't think of anyone who has a greater influence in this area than Pastor Jack.

I once heard someone say, "For years the Church has been over-mothered and under-fathered." Mothers nurture us. They're the ones we run to when we fall off our bikes and scrape our knees. It's not that fathers aren't nurturing, but fathers are responsible for calling out the destiny of God in our lives. A father will say, "Get over it! Get up! Let's do it again! I know you fell and scraped your knees, but get up. Let's go for it again!" We need more fathering in the Church today. Pastor Jack is a tremendous example of a father who's loving and nurturing but also one who will encourage you and call out your destiny.

In 2 Kings 2:8–10, Elisha asked Elijah for a double portion of the spirit that was on him. And Elijah said, "If you see me *when I am* taken from you, it shall be so for you … " (v. 10 NKJV). He was saying, "If you'll stay with me to the end." We need to stay with our spiritual mothers and fathers until the end. They have something to contribute to the kingdom, and they have something to teach us. They have impartations and anointing for us. I, along with many other pastors, have experienced the benefit of this by spending time with Pastor Jack. The results of his influence are evident in my life and in churches all over the world.

Paul told the church at Corinth, "For though you might have ten thousand instructors in Christ, yet *you do* not *have* many fathers" (1 Corinthians 4:15 NKJV). We are blessed today with many wonderful teachers and instructors but just a few spiritual fathers and even fewer Jack Hayfords. Really, there's just one—and he's great!

ROBERT MORRIS
Founding Senior Pastor
Gateway Church, Dallas/Fort Worth, Texas
Best-selling Author of *The Blessed Life*,
The God I Never Knew, *Truly Free*, and *Frequency*

Acknowledgments

THIS PROJECT WOULD have been impossible without the gifts and talents of so many. Thank you to the incredible team at Gateway Publishing under the leadership of Craig Dunnagan, Executive Director, for their professionalism and unqualified support. This first publication by TKU Press, an imprint of The King's University (TKU), was on an extremely short timeline so that it could be presented to Jack Hayford at the 20th anniversary of The King's University in the Fall of 2017. We would not have met the deadline without the guidance and editorial expertise of Dr. John Andersen, Director of Book Publishing, whose unflagging support was above and beyond the call of duty. A special thank you as well to Kathy Krenzien for her gracious help in keeping things on track and also for her kind patience with the book's editors in meeting deadlines. Jenny Morgan reviewed manuscripts and attended to many details.

We are especially grateful to Pastor Robert Morris for not only contributing the book's Foreword but also for dedicating special time at the Fall 2017 Gateway Conference to present to book to TKU's founder, Dr. Jack Hayford. Pastor Morris' love and respect for Pastor Jack is evident and his support of the project was essential.

Thank you to Dr. John Spurling, former president of TKU, for endorsing the idea early on and allowing the editors to devote time to project. A thank you also to Dr. David Cole, TKU's interim president, for cheering on the project in these last months. Finally, we wish to express our gratitude to the trustees, faculty, administration, staff, and all the TKU community who have served so faithfully over the last 20 years making our 2017 anniversary celebration possible. The lives of hundreds of students have been changed because of you!

Contributors

Jim W. Adams (PhD, Fuller Theological Seminary) is Professor at Life Pacific College in San Dimas, California.

Kimberly Ervin Alexander (PhD, PhD, Open University/St. John's College) is Associate Professor in the History of Christianity at Regent University School of Divinity in Virginia Beach, Virginia.

Jon Huntzinger (PhD, Fuller Theological Seminary) is Distinguished Professor of Bible and Ministry at The King's University in Southlake, Texas.

John Jackson (PhD, University of California, Santa Barbara) is President of William Jessup University in Rocklin, California.

Veli-Matti Kärkkäinen (Dr. Theol. Habil., University of Helsinki) is Professor of Systematic Theology at Fuller Theological Seminary in Pasadena, California.

Frank D. Macchia (D. Theol., University of Basel) is Professor of Systematic and Pentecostal Theology at Vanguard University, Costa Mesa, California, and Associate Director of the Centre for Pentecostal and Charismatic Studies at Bangor University.

Susan Maros (PhD, Fuller Theological Seminary) is Affiliate Assistant Professor of Christian Leadership at Fuller Theological Seminary in Pasadena, California.

S. David Moore (PhD, Regent University) is the M.G. Robertson Professor of Pneumatology at The King's University in Southlake, Texas.

Richard Mouw (PhD, University of Chicago) is President Emeritus and Professor of Faith and Public Life at Fuller Theological Seminary in Pasadena, California.

Lloyd John Ogilvie (D.D., University of Edinburgh) is the former Chaplain (61st) to the U.S. Senate and President of Leadership Unlimited.

Cecil M. Robeck (PhD, Fuller Theological Seminary) is Senior Professor of Church History and Ecumenics and Special Assistant to the President for Ecumenical Relations at Fuller Theological Seminary School of Theology in Pasadena, California.

David Rudolph (PhD, Cambridge University) is Director of Messianic Jewish Studies and Professor of New Testament and Jewish Studies at The King's University in Southlake, Texas.

H. Vinson Synan (PhD, University of Georgia) is Dean Emeritus at Regent University School of Divinity in Virginia Beach, Virginia and Scholar in Residence at Oral Roberts University in Tulsa, Oklahoma.

Kenneth C. Ulmer (DMin, United Theological Seminary; PhD, Grace Graduate School of Theology) is Senior Pastor of Faithful Central Bible Church in Inglewood, California and is Presiding Bishop of Macedonia International Bible Fellowship.

Amos Yong (PhD, Boston University) is Director of the Center for Missiological Research (CMR) and Professor of Theology and Mission at Fuller Theological Seminary School of Intercultural Studies in Pasadena, California.

Introduction

Jack Williams Hayford, Jr. is arguably the most respected Pentecostal pastor/leader of his generation. His sane, sensible, and scriptural appeal for Spirit-filled living has garnered him a wide audience across the spectrum of contemporary Christianity. This was perhaps best epitomized in July 2005 when *Christianity Today* carried a cover photo of Hayford along with the banner headline, "Jack Hayford: The Pentecostal Gold Standard."

In February 1996, Jack Hayford was flying back to Los Angeles the day after speaking to nearly 40,000 pastors at the Promise Keepers National Clergy Conference in Atlanta. An hour or so into the flight, Hayford was looking out the window at the bright white cumulus clouds below when he heard God say, "Found a seminary."[1] Startled, Jack found himself arguing in his mind, "If I did that, people would laugh at me." Holding no advanced degrees beyond the bachelor's level, he did not think he possessed the "academic respectability" for such an endeavor. Nevertheless, he obeyed and, along with his son-in-law, Scott Bauer, just months later invited Dr. Paul Chappell, an experienced leader in academic administration, to help establish The King's College and Seminary. The school formally opened in the fall of 1997.

While he may not have held advanced degrees and despite his initial reaction to God's prompting, Jack Hayford was not a novice in the world of higher education. He served The Foursquare Church's primary ministry training institution, Life Pacific College

---

[1] Jack Hayford, Kings College/Seminary Chapel, Van Nuys, n.d., transcript, 1; Jack W. Hayford, letter to Fellow Servants and Shepherds, July 2006, The King's College and Seminary, 2.

xvi | THE PASTOR & THE KINGDOM

(then L.I.F.E. Bible College), in a number of roles over the years. From 1965 to 1969, he was the Dean of Students and a faculty member at the college, and from 1977 to 1982, while serving as the senior pastor of The Church On The Way, he served as the college's president and helped lead the school into national accreditation with the American Association of Bible Colleges (now Association of Biblical Higher Education).

From the early 1970s with "School On The Way," Jack had emphasized church-based ministerial training at The Church On The Way. The School On The Way was later formalized in 1987 and renamed The King's Institute. Led over the years by several capable academic leaders, including Sam Middlebrook and Don McKensie, the institute provided high-quality training to church members and others seeking ministerial training and enrichment. The Church On The Way also served as an extension site from 1991 to 1996 for the Oral Roberts University School of Theology, offering graduate-level courses.

Despite his sense of inadequacy to start a seminary, Jack is a man highly esteemed by all who know of his life and ministry, something that will be evident in reading this book of essays. Taking a tiny Southern California pastorate with eighteen members in 1969 and seeing it grow into one of America's flagship mega-churches with over 10,000 members, the church's growth and Hayford's balanced ministry provided a remarkable platform that helped him achieve national and international attention. Widely recognized as a pastor of pastors, for two decades he spoke to some 20,000 pastors annually at various conferences and events. As a Pentecostal, Jack Hayford's biblical fidelity and articulate preaching defied the stereo-types some people associate with Pentecostalism. His theolog-ical acumen and ecumenical generosity were also important in helping him become what could be described as a "statesman" for Pentecostal/charismatic Christianity.

This collection of essays celebrates the life and ministry of Jack W. Hayford at the 20th anniversary of the founding of The King's

University and presents the work of highly regarded scholars, educators, and practitioners across a broad spectrum of the Christian tradition. When the invitation to participate was extended, they heartily responded out of their respect and admiration for the contributions Jack has made not only to the contemporary church but to the academy as well. Although no specific theme was given them, the essays highlight themes that have characterized Jack Hayford's ministry.

Jack's advocacy for the fullness of the Holy Spirit was never strident or sectarian, and while he was never ashamed to identify with and affirm his Classical Pentecostal heritage in the Foursquare Church, he sought a mediating position regarding Spirit baptism and its relationship to speaking in tongues. Jim W. Adams' essay, "Jesus Christ the Baptizer in the Holy Spirit," explores exegetically a way forward in understanding Spirit baptism in an ecumenically sensitive way while David Moore's essay, "Discerning the 'Spirit' of the Word," draws attention to Hayford's emphasis on the centrality of the Holy Spirit in both interpreting and teaching the Bible.

A central emphasis in Hayford's ministry over the years has been the foundational role of worship in the life of the church. Three essays address that theme. In "Magnify, Come Glorify," Richard Mouw provides an insightful pathway through the debates that surround contemporary worship practices today and emphasizes the central importance of experiencing the presence of God. Ken Ulmer's essay, "Authenticity and Attractiveness in Christian Worship," complements this piece by reminding pastors and church leaders that their primary calling is to lift up Jesus in their faithful proclamation of God's Word and in their commitment to celebratory praise. Related to these two articles, in an exegetical study of the Second Gospel, "Purity and Worship: Malachi's Message in the Gospel of Mark," Jon Huntzinger shows how Mark depicts Jesus in his Gospel as one who purifies God's people by God's Spirit so that they might worship Him.

Jack Hayford's roles as an ecumenical bridge builder and peacemaker have been key features of his ministry for over four decades. He has

xviii | <small>The Pastor & The Kingdom</small>

been a constructive player in healing the racial divide between black and white Pentecostals, which reaches back to the first decade of the twentieth century. In honor of this, Cecil (Mel) Robeck contributed *"The Quiet Game*, Racism, and the Azusa Street Revival," an essay that many have hoped would one day be published. It originated with his highly regarded plenary address in 2006 at the 35th Annual Meeting of the Society for Pentecostal Studies in Pasadena, California. David Rudolph's historical essay, "Count Zinzendorf, Pastor Jack, and Messianic Jewish Revival," puts in perspective Hayford's advocacy for the Messianic Jewish community and highlights their appreciation of his vision for the people of God as the "One New Man," comprised of Jews and Gentiles. Lloyd Ogilvie's very personal reflection on Jack's role in establishing "Love LA" is a chronicle that demonstrates the power of Christian unity and brotherhood.

Many have been grateful for Jack Hayford's belief that women are rightfully called to ordained Christian ministry without restriction and are welcome partners in all spheres of leadership, including as senior/lead pastors of congregations. Kimberly Alexander's essay, "Girl Talk: A Feminist Re-Imagination of Pentecostal Theological Discourse and Experience," looks at the unique contributions women bring to the theological task. An example of such a contribution is the work of Susan Maros in the field of pastoral leadership. Her essay, "Presence, Providence, and the Calling of God," encourages Pentecostals to consider the different ways that pastoral calling may be identified and valued within the church today.

Although Jack Hayford would never think of himself as a theologian, his life and ministry have exemplified the results of a life devoted to living out in practical ways a Spirit-empowered biblical theology. He stands very much in the tradition of pastoral scholarship that dates back to the early centuries of the Church when pastors and bishops addressed the primary concerns and issues of their day with keen understanding of Scripture and effective rhetorical technique. His awareness of theological issues and debates, along with his love for the church, helped him become an articulate pastoral voice in contemporary Christianity, something evident in his over 50 published books and the accumulated treasure chest of thousands of audio, video, and print sermons. His commitment to biblical fidelity and sound spiritual formation motivated his commitment to theological education. It is no wonder that three leading Pentecostal theologians generously contributed to this volume. Veli-Matti Kärkkäinen's essay, "The Discernment of the Spirit(s) in Pentecostal Practice and Theology," addresses the topic of discernment, a critical pastoral issue facing Pentecostal pastors in the oversight of their congregations. Frank Macchia's "An Expanding Light? Pentecostals and the Protestant Reformation" looks at Pentecostalism, particularly Classical Pentecostals (those Pentecostals who trace their origin to the 1906 Azusa Street Revival in Los Angeles) as a Protestant movement and gives helpful introduction to the theological challenges inherent to modern Pentecostal movements. Given Hayford's interest in the Book of Revelation, it was serendipitous that Amos Yong contributed his 2017 plenary address from the 46th Annual Meeting of the Society for Pentecostal Studies, "Kings, Nations, and Cultures on The Way to the New Jerusalem: A Pentecostal Witness to an Apocalyptic Vision." Yong's essay carries a resonance to Hayford's conviction that the revelation to John is fundamentally about worship.

When Pastor Jack first learned about this project, he expressed his hope that two friends, John Jackson and Vinson Synan, might be invited to participate. Both men happily joined the project. Jack developed a friendship in the last few years with Dr. Jackson, president of William Jessup University, and spoke at the university's 2014 commencement. Jackson's "Jesus, Our Center of Gravity in the Church and the Academy: An Isaiah 61 Declaration for Our Time," reflects on the centrality of Jesus in both the church and the academy and how they partner together to serve God's purposes, themes that echo Jack Hayford's motivation in establishing The King's University. Vinson Synan and Jack Hayford have been friends for nearly half a century. Synan, himself a bridge builder and churchman, is best known for his contributions as a Pentecostal historian. His essay, "The Many Lives of Benjamin Hardin Irwin (1854–1926)," is a highly readable biographical sketch of one of the most idiosyncratic, radical evangelical leaders who helped birth modern Pentecostalism in the United States early in the twentieth century.

All of these essays easily fit under the umbrella title for this volume, *The Pastor and The Kingdom*. The man who is known as "Pastor Jack" to tens of thousands of people has long viewed his ministry as The Lord's ministry, refracted in and through him by the Holy Spirit, and has seen his work as an expression of the will and rule of God—God's kingdom—manifested in his submitted life lived in the presence of Jesus. How does Jack Hayford talk about God's kingdom? He speaks of God's Spirit and the free worship of God's people before Him. He speaks of peacemaking, reconciliation, and the "One New Man" described by the Apostle Paul. He speaks of calling, empowerment, and the release to serve without discrimination. And he speaks of discernment, courage, and engagement with culture in the future-present time in which we live.

The editors are especially grateful to each of these distinguished and respected contributors. Their essays speak for their scholarship. We want to also express our appreciation for their gracious cooperation in this project that came together rather quickly. We were encouraged by their kind words of regard for Jack Hayford as we corresponded regarding the project. Their participation made this project a delight.

A word as to terminology used in these essays in naming the modern Pentecostal and charismatic movements. Because of the short period of time in which this project had to be completed in order to present the book to Jack Hayford in the fall of 2017, the editors did not prescribe a uniform use of the terms in naming different expressions of renewal Christianity. Given the remarkable growth of Pentecostalism over the last century and that it is still a relatively young movement, a common terminology is still in development by scholars researching its diverse and varied expressions. Therefore, the term Pentecostal or Pentecostalism will be used at times in different ways by different contributors. We trust our readers to determine by context how the author intends the terms to be understood. Sometimes the terms Pentecostal and Pentecostalism may be capitalized, and other times they may not, depending on the authors' preferences. Our apologies in advance for any confusion this may bring.

Finally, both editors were honored to serve this project, and we make no claim of objectivity in our contributions to this volume. We also acknowledge the profound influence Pastor Jack has had on our own lives, helping shape our understanding of "Spirit-formed" Christianity. We both serve on the faculty of The King's University and have endeavored, along with the administration, staff, and the entire faculty, to see the vision of our institution's founder realized as fully as possible. Those of us who serve at The King's University are entrusted with a great responsibility in preparing new generations for faithful service to Jesus our Lord. The life and ministry of Jack Williams Hayford, Jr. is a continuing inspiration to that work.

Jon Huntzinger
David Moore
August 2017

Section One

Bible

1

Jesus Christ the Baptizer in the Holy Spirit

An Exegetical and Theological Analysis of the Spirit-Baptized Phrase[1]

Jim W. Adams

I AM EXTREMELY grateful to contribute to this festschrift for Pastor Jack Hayford. Pastor Jack has been exactly that—my Pastor. It is virtually impossible for me to articulate what Pastor Jack means to me. He has occupied a truly monumental place in my life, especially during my time as an attending church member and staff member of The Church On The Way as well as a proud graduate of The King's College. In fact, it is quite surreal to have even been asked to participate in this work. During all my time watching, listening, and talking with Pastor Jack, what has always struck me is his unquenching pursuit of the Holy Spirit's dynamic presence as well as his unflinching commitment to ecumenism. If anyone has demonstrated the gift of the Spirit as a prophetic witness to Christ as well as embracing the Church as a diverse unity, it is Pastor Jack. In this essay, I address these ideas and hope that he will find my proposals both helpful and honoring.

---

[1] This essay represents a condensed version of a much larger work, the essential part of which I presented to the Foursquare Scholars Fellowship on May 30, 2012.

Introduction

I am addressing one of the core theological positions of Pentecostal doctrine: Jesus Christ the Baptizer *in/with/by* (ἐν) the Holy Spirit.[2] The modern scholarly discussion on this theme is often marked by the publication of James D. G. Dunn's dissertation *Baptism in the Holy Spirit* in 1977.[3] But in 1964, John R. W. Stott published a pamphlet entitled *The Baptism and Fullness of the Holy Spirit*, wherein he described the ongoing blessing of the Spirit.[4] Regarding Spirit-Baptism, the current debate is nothing new as it centers on (1) is charismatic empowerment a biblically legitimate phenomenon for Christians to expect to experience today? And, (2) if the answer to the first question is "Yes," then *when* and *how* does this empowerment occur? In relation to these two questions, the Classical Pentecostal conception of Spirit-Baptism surely comes with exegetical and theological difficulties; yet, this is true for the Traditional position[5] as well. From my perspective, both schools of thought need to carefully reevaluate the contexts of the phrase "baptized ἐν the Holy Spirit," which I propose should cause each to make certain concessions, all the while not dismissing their interpretive position in total. With this in mind, my goal is to demonstrate how the Spirit-Baptized phrase is a polysemous or multivalent expression, or a "fluid metaphor," as Frank D. Macchia suggests.[6]

Diversity within Scripture is not a new topic among biblical scholars and theologians. There are varied and diverse perspectives and emphases presented across its pages, but our interpretive

---

[2] I want to thank Michael Salmeier and David Moore for their helpful critiques and suggestions of earlier drafts of this work.

[3] Dunn, *Baptism in the Holy Spirit* (Philadelphia: Westminster, 1977).

[4] Stott, *The Baptism and Fullness of the Holy Spirit* (Downers Grove: InterVarsity, 1964).

[5] I am using Traditional in this essay to refer to any person or community that does not accept or embrace an ongoing charismatic empowering and gifting of the Holy Spirit distinct from conversion/regeneration.

[6] Frank D. Macchia, *Baptized in the Spirit* (Grand Rapids: Zondervan, 2006), 58.

tendencies typically lead us to choose particular texts over others. We also often use certain texts considered normative as lenses to interpret other texts. Such an approach is formally known as *The Analogy of Faith* principle, which essentially employs a *Scripture interprets Scripture* methodology.[7] This interpretive angle can provide some insights into some texts but also possesses intrinsic problems as one's interpretation of a text tends to become the sole grid whereby one reads another text, thus becoming entrapped in a hermeneutical circle. Such a method does not allow for the writers of the Bible to speak on her/his own terms while consequently suppressing any diversity in emphasis and/or perspective. In addition, the biblical text, as with any literary work, has inherent ambiguities, some unintentional and others intentional. No more so than when the biblical writers describe the presence of God (e.g., Genesis 18; Exodus 19) with the רוח "Spirit" of God/Yahweh being one of the central ways the Old/First Testament (O/FT) refers to the presence and activity of God.

All these matters materialize when it comes to the phrase and topic of "baptized ἐν the Holy Spirit." Generally speaking, those who hold to a Traditional point of view identify this phrase as strictly referring to conversion-initiation and prefer to utilize the didactic—or assertive—type texts such as those in Paul's letters, whereas those who hold to a Classical Pentecostal position understand this as an empowering experience subsequent to conversion, while focusing on the narrative examples in the Book of Acts. These preferences also coincide with one's pneumatological concerns as they often relate to one's experience as well as what a convert should or should not expect to experience post-Pentecost. Moreover, these schools of thought use their favored texts that reflect their own theological biases while reading the less preferred texts through that lens. Most

---

[7] On this method see Daniel P. Fuller, "Biblical Theology and the Analogy of Faith," in *Unity and Diversity in New Testament Theology*. FS G. E. Ladd; ed. R. A. Guelich; (Grand Rapids: Eerdmans, 1978), 195–213.

egregiously and perhaps more so with Pentecostals, when it comes
to describing Spirit-Baptism, we often dedivinize and/or deper-
sonalize the Spirit as we attempt to create formulaic patterns to
describe predictable experience(s) of the Spirit. As with the presence
of God, such systematic attempts ultimately fail and often violate
the mystery and autonomy of the Spirit. Jesus himself compares the
πνεῦμα "Spirit" to the wind, indicating that he is both mysterious
and unpredictable (John 3:8).[8] Thus, to organize and force the Spirit
into systematic categories is as futile as attempting to capture and
control the wind.[9] As no person can completely master the wind, we
should not expect to comprehensively and formulaically explain the
workings and movements of the Spirit.

The writers of Scripture intensify this reality as they do not
present an orderly, formulaic depiction of the activity of the Spirit.
For instance, John in his Gospel presents Jesus' promise that out
of his followers will flow rivers of living water (7:37–38) and then
explicitly comments:

> And he said this concerning the Spirit whom those who
> believed in him were about to receive; for the Spirit was
> not yet because Jesus was not yet glorified (v. 39).[10]

Viewed in isolation, John's statement represents for most Christian
traditions that the Spirit was given on the Day of Pentecost as
described in Acts 2. John's comment has raised several interpretive issues, which is also reflected among the Greek manuscripts[11];
however, he could not have meant that the Spirit did not exist

---

[8] This description is enhanced by the fact that the terms רוח and πνεῦμα can also be
used for "wind" or "breath" (see e.g., 1 Kings 18:45a; 2 Kings 3:17a; Isaiah 7:2b; 11:4b; 41:16a;
2 Thessalonians 2:8; Hebrews 1:7).

[9] See Macchia, *Baptized*, 18.

[10] All translations mine.

[11] For the phrase οὔπω γὰρ ἦν πνεῦμα "for the Spirit was not yet," some MSS add
ἅγιον "holy" while others additionally include ἐπ αὐτούς "upon them." A few add δεδομένον
"given," perhaps to counter any notion of the nonexistence of the Holy Spirit for John.

nor that he was not active prior to Pentecost because of his own inclusion of John the Baptist's report of the Spirit descending and remaining upon Christ (1:32–33). Luke goes well beyond John as he describes the activity of the Spirit long before Acts 2. Early in his first volume, Luke reports both women and men "filled" (πληρόω) with the Spirit or him leading, coming upon them, and enabling them to prophesy (e.g., John the Baptist [1:15]; Elizabeth [1:41]; Zacharias [1:67]; Simeon [2:25–35]; also Anna [2:36–38]), which also coincides with Joel's prophecy of Yahweh pouring out his Spirit on all humankind (2:28–29 [Heb 3:1–2]). Luke's descriptions here reflect typical experiences occurring in the O/FT, where in fact the Spirit appears right at the beginning of Scripture and creation (Genesis 1:2; Job 26:13). For example, Yahweh took the רוח from upon Moses, and when the רוח rested upon the seventy elders, they prophesied (Numbers 11:25). Moses subsequently hoped that all of Yahweh's people were prophets and that Yahweh would place his רוח upon them (v. 29b). Similar to Moses and the seventy elders as well as the Judges (e.g., Judges 3:10; 6:34; 11:29; 13:25; 15:14), the רוח of Yahweh is put on King Saul, which results in him prophesying and being found among prophets (1 Samuel 10:6–12). Following the king's rebellion, the רוח of Yahweh came upon David (1 Samuel 16:13) while departing from Saul and was replaced with an evil רוח (vv. 14–15). Isaiah envisions a future Davidic ruler with the רוח of Yahweh resting upon him, providing wisdom, counsel, strength, knowledge, and delight for the fear of Yahweh (11:2). In Isaiah 61, an anonymous prophet declares in the first person that the רוח of Yahweh is upon *me* because he has anointed *me* to bring good news (v. 1). Finally, Micah announces that he has been "filled" (מלא) with power, with the רוח of Yahweh (LXX: ἐν πνεύματι κυρίου) to declare Israel's sin (3:8).

In sum, we must not only accept but also embrace the diversity within Scripture as well as its ambiguities. Further, we must acknowledge our own preferred texts and methods in the development of our theology that may not allow each biblical writer to have her/his own voice. If we consider the contents of Scripture as canonical and thus in its entirety authoritative, then we must follow suit and treat each book and passage equally. This does not mean, though, that we should interpret each biblical book and text in isolation from one another; rather, in the development of our theological positions, we should engage with each book and text intertextually and dialectically, all the while listening carefully to each particular voice.

Dunn's seminal and ongoing research on the Holy Spirit continues to find its way into the center of the initiation/subsequence debate. Over the years, Dunn has clearly nuanced his understanding of the dynamic role of the Spirit, which was perhaps most profoundly prompted by the doctoral work of Robert P. Menzies.[12] In his later reflections, Dunn acknowledges that the "Spirit for Luke is indeed preeminently the *Spirit of prophecy*, the Spirit that inspires speech and witness."[13] Yet, Dunn does *not* see two distinct experiences of the Holy Spirit. His reasoning for this is the potential danger "of speaking as though there were two completely dissociated functions of the Spirit, as though, in effect, the Spirit of prophecy was a different Spirit from the Spirit of salvation." In the end, for Dunn, Luke only understands "*one decisive coming of the Spirit*" (cf. Acts 1:5; 2:38–39). It is inconceivable that the one coming of the Spirit is "only a *donum superadditum* [or a charismatic gift], that is, in effect, a dispensable extra."[14] "Surely the proper deduction is rather that the coming of the one Spirit in conversion-initiation is *also* a commissioning for witness and ministry, that entrance into the new age is *also* empowering for service in the new age (Luke 3:16; Acts 1:5, 8)." This is additionally true of Paul in both Acts and his own letters as

---

[12] Menzies, *The Development of Early Christian Pneumatology with Special Reference to Luke-Acts, JSNT*:Supp 54 (Sheffield: Sheffield Academic Press, 1991).

[13] Dunn, "Baptism in the Spirit: A Response to Pentecostal Scholarship on Luke-Acts," *JPT* 3 (1993): 8 (italics mine).

[14] Here, Dunn is directly challenging Menzies' thesis (see, e.g., *Pneumatology*, 48, 112, 279, 316–18).

"conversion is *also* commissioning for life and mission (Acts 9:15–18; 22:15–16; 26:12, 18)."[15] For the NT writers, "the decisive factor" in the conversion-initiation of the Christian "was the gift of the Spirit."[16] Further, Paul provides the closest definition of a Christian, specifically expressed in Romans 8:9: "It is 'having the Spirit' which defines and determines someone as being 'of Christ'; it was by receiving the Spirit that one became a Christian."[17] Concerning the Spirit-Baptized phrase itself, Dunn's more recent research on the Book of Acts reflects his refined views all the while maintaining his one decisive gift of the Spirit position. In Luke's second volume, the metaphor emphasizes "the inauguration of a decisive new stage in the purpose and mission of God." Specifically, in the Cornelius narrative, the metaphor is "for God's initial acceptance, *not* for some second experience subsequent to conversion. … At the same time, as 1 Corinthians 12:13 makes still more clear, that initial acceptance was *also* understood to be an empowering for ministry within the body of Christ."[18]

When it comes to the concept of Spirit-Baptism, Dunn has provided a significant corrective to the Traditional view in the sense that for the NT writers, all converts should *experience* the Spirit along with expecting to be empowered for witness and service.[19] However, critics of Dunn have consistently and correctly pointed out his preference for Paul's pneumatology over all other NT writers, which has caused Dunn to use it as a lens to then describe in particular Luke's pneumatology.[20] Dunn continues to display this in his later

---

[15] Dunn, "Baptism," 25–26 (italics mine).

[16] Dunn, "Baptism and the Unity of the Church in the New Testament," in *Baptism and the Unity of the Church*, ed. M. Root and R. Saarinen (Grand Rapids: Eerdmans, 1998), 82.

[17] Dunn, "Unity," 83. See also Dunn, *The Theology of Paul the Apostle* (Grand Rapids: Eerdmans, 1998), 419–25. Dunn's claims here remain much the same as in his original research (see *Baptism*, 226).

[18] Dunn, *The Acts of the Apostles* (Valley Forge: Trinity Press International, 2009), 9, 151 (italics mine); see also Dunn, "Baptism," 19–20.

[19] See Dunn, *Baptism*, 225.

[20] See e.g., Roger Stronstad, *The Charismatic Theology of St. Luke* (Peabody: Hendrickson, 1984), 9.

research as he claims that from the earliest stages of Paul's writing, he understands that "the soteriological Spirit is *also* the Spirit of prophecy" (1 Thessalonians 1:6; 4:8; 5:19–20),[21] which are the exact same terms he uses when describing Luke's pneumatology. Overall, Dunn's own developed pneumatology remains more theologically driven than exegetical, with his primary source for these conclusions deriving from Paul's writings.[22] Pentecostal scholars have demonstrated for some time now that Luke presents a unique pneumatology. In response, Dunn, who ironically has characteristically affirmed and valued diversity within the NT,[23] does not find any merit in the interpretive angle of a Lukan *diversity*, as this requires a narrowing of "Luke's concept of the Spirit to that of charismatic phenomena," thus transforming "a Lukan *emphasis* into a dogmatic distinction, indeed, into a different Spirit."[24]

For some Pentecostal and Charismatic scholars, Luke's pneumatology does not include any soteriological aspects in distinction to the other NT writers and, in particular, Paul. Menzies remains the strongest proponent of this position as he claims that the "Spirit in Luke-Acts is *never* presented as a soteriological agent." Rather, Luke's pneumatology is "a prophetic enabling that empowers one for participation in the mission of God." The "gift of the Spirit in Luke-Acts is nonsoteriological (or charismatic), prophetic, and missiological"; it is, in fact, a *donum superadditum*.[25] Following this same line of thought, Roger Stronstad claims "that Luke, in contrast to both John and Paul, never explicitly reports that the Holy Spirit effects salvation." Thus, "(1) Luke often explicitly relates the Spirit

---

[21] Dunn, *Paul*, 419–20 (italics mine).

[22] For a more extensive analysis of the various opinions on Spirit-Baptism in relation to Dunn's work, see William P. Atkinson, *Baptism in the Spirit* (Eugene: Pickwick, 2001); Max Turner, *Power from on High*, JPT:Supp 9 (Sheffield: Sheffield Academic Press, 1996), 38–79.

[23] See e.g., Dunn, *Unity and Diversity in the New Testament*, 3rd ed. (London: SCM Press, 2006).

[24] Dunn, "Baptism," 26.

[25] William W. Menzies and Robert P. Menzies, *Spirit and Power* (Grand Rapids: Zondervan, 2000), 89; see also Menzies, *Pneumatology*, 275, 264–67.

to vocation; and (2) he never unambiguously describes the Spirit to be the agent of salvation."[26] James B. Shelton offers another angle on Luke's pneumatology as he claims that Luke "does not show *as much interest as* Paul in the Spirit's role in conversion …; rather, power for mission catches the majority of Luke's attention."[27] According to Shelton, Luke's second volume records Jesus' *reinterpretation* of John's Spirit-Baptized prophecy (1:5; 11:16) "in terms of empowerment to witness (1:8)."[28] "Just as Jesus corrected his disciples' understanding of John's prophecy, so too he corrected John's, emphasizing to him that the true nature of the Spirit baptism is empowerment to witness through word and deed."[29] Craig Keener draws some similar conclusions to Shelton as he asserts that "Luke's writings focus *almost exclusively* on prophetic empowerment." In direct contrast to Paul's view of baptism and reception of the Spirit occurring at conversion, "Luke seems to identify this initial filling of the prophetic Spirit with the baptism in the Spirit (Acts 2:4 fulfills 1:4–5; see 2:33, 39) and 'receiving the Spirit' (2:38–39)."[30] The association of the reception of the Holy Spirit with conversion occurs at the theological level as with Acts 2:38. Thus, "in the narratives, even when the Spirit is received at conversion, this reception is often expressed in a charismatic-prophetic way (10:44–48)."[31]

Luke's Pentecost description in Acts 2 presents for a number of scholars and theologians the unrepeatable historical event of the outpouring of the Spirit. According to Dunn, this Day represents "a watershed in salvation-history." Luke's Pentecost is not "merely a continuation of what went before. Pentecost is a new beginning— the inauguration of the new age, the age of the Spirit—that which

---

[26] Stronstad, *The Prophethood of All Believers* (Cleveland: CPT Press, 2010), 2–3.

[27] Shelton, *Mighty in Word and Deed* (Eugene: Wipf and Stock, 2000), 6 (italics mine).

[28] Shelton, *Word*, 37 (italics mine).

[29] Shelton, *Word*, 43.

[30] Craig Keener, *Gift Giver* (Grand Rapids: Baker Academic, 2001), 158 (italics mine). See also Keener, *Acts: An Exegetical Commentary. Volume I: Introduction and 1:1–2:47* (Grand Rapids: Baker Academic, 2012), 523.

[31] Keener, *Acts*, 522 n198; see also pages 680–81.

had not been before."[32] There is no denying that, for Luke, the Day of Pentecost represents a significant historical phenomenon (e.g., no other day involving the Spirit is identified as Pentecost; no more descriptions of wind and fire [Acts 2:1–3]). However, at least three issues arise with seeing this event as the definitive inauguration of the age of the Spirit. First, the activity of the Spirit of Yahweh is displayed explicitly and implicitly across the pages of the O/FT, which characteristically continues into the NT prior to Pentecost.[33] Second, John begins to end his Gospel reporting that the resurrected Jesus ἐνεφύσησεν "breathes" out the Spirit (20:22). Finally, there are Luke's diverse depictions and emphases of the Spirit's activity.

Looking at Acts 2, Luke describes the outpouring of the Spirit on Pentecost following Christ's resurrection (1:3), ascension (1:9–11), and, in particular, his exaltation (2:33). On this Day, the promise of being baptized ἐν the Holy Spirit is fulfilled (1:5) as Jesus "pours out" (ἐκχέω) the Spirit (2:33) and his followers are "filled" (πληρόω) with the Spirit and speak with other "tongues" (γλῶσσα) (v. 4). Luke, though, points the reader to draw a *parallel* with this Day and the Cornelius episode (10:1–11:18)[34] explicitly through the mouth of Peter (11:15–17). To enhance this correspondence, Luke implicitly plays with the number *two* in connection with the gift of the Spirit (e.g., *two* Gentile reports [10:34–48//11:1–18][35]; Peter teaches *twice* [2:14–36//10:34–46]; *both* Spirit-Baptized phrases

---

[32] Dunn, *Baptism*, 40, 44; see further Dunn, "Baptism," 16–22.

[33] See further John Goldingay, "Was the Holy Spirit Active in the Old Testament Times? What was New About the Christian Experience of God?" *Ex Auditu* 12 (1996): 14–28.

[34] On repetition in the Cornelius narrative, see Ronald D. Witherup, "Cornelius Over and Over and Over Again: 'Functional Redundancy' in the Acts of the Apostles," *JSNT* 49 (1993): 45–66.

[35] As Luke highlights Paul's conversion by repeating it three times (9:1–18; 22:3–21; 26:8–18), he comparatively elevates the Gentiles reception of the Holy Spirit to a central place in his second volume as he repeats it a third time (15:7–11), which also parallels the report of three clean/unclean visions given to Peter (10:16). See further Ronald D. Witherup, "Functional Redundancy in the Acts of the Apostles: A Case Study," *JSNT* 48 (1992): 67–86.

[1:5//11:16] and the terms ἐκχέω [2:17, 18, 33//10:45][36] and (γλῶσσα) [2:3, 4, 11, 26//10:46][37] selectively occur in the *two* narrative sections). The literary effect of Luke's parallel sequencing highlights one of the central themes of both his volumes: the democratization of the people of God. Yet, with his repetition of *twos*, Luke undoubtedly leads his readers to identify the Gentiles reception of the Spirit as a *second* Pentecost. Moreover, Luke narrates additional Pentecostal type empowerments throughout his second volume (8:15–17; 19:6).[38] Consequently, the Day of Pentecost, as Keener claims, functions paradigmatically,[39] but due to the clear *parallels*, so also does the Cornelius episode. Alongside this paradigmatic idea as presented above, Luke describes Pentecostal type empowerment *fillings* long before Acts 2. Further, some of the ones *filled* in Acts 2 are *filled* again with the Spirit (4:31). Luke describes Peter *filled* with the Spirit when he teaches (4:8). Luke also narrates Ananias commanding Paul to be *filled* with the Spirit, which apparently occurs (9:17), and later describes Paul *filled* with the Spirit (13:9) when he confronts the magician Elymas. For Luke, then, the initial Day of Pentecost has historical and theological significance but at the same time does not appear as the single definitive Day for the activity, reception, and filling of the Spirit. Perhaps if Paul wrote a narrative similar to Acts, he might have described the gift of the Spirit differently, but obviously only Luke wrote his second volume wherein he highlights the Spirit's dynamic activity while also focusing predominantly on the empowerment dimension of the gift of the Spirit.

---

[36] Luke uses ἐκχέω five times in Acts (1:18; 2:17, 18, 33; 10:45).

[37] The term γλῶσσα occurs one last time in Acts 19:6.

[38] A. T. Lincoln sees the Day of Pentecost as unrepeatable in the sense that it inaugurates a new age of God's saving purposes, but he also recognizes that "there are references back to Pentecost or mini-Pentecosts at key points in the narrative's depiction of the church's expansion—in Samaria, with Cornelius, at the Jerusalem council and in Paul's work at Ephesus (Acts 8:14–17; 10:44–48; 11:15–17; 15:7–9; 19:1–7)." A. T. Lincoln, "Pentecost," in *Dictionary of the Latter New Testament & Its Development*, eds. R. P. Martin and P. H. Davids, (Downers Grove: InterVarsity, 1997), 903.

[39] Keener, *Acts*, 793–94.

From Menzies and Stronstad's work, Macchia observes that the Spirit-Baptized phrase "is a fluid metaphor in the narrative witness of Scripture, taking on different nuances of meaning."[40] However, Macchia also notices that neither of these two scholars spend any significant amount of time exploring this idea. Menzies, in particular, recognizes that Paul and Luke's pneumatology perspectives "complement one another: together they lead us into a deeper and fuller understanding of the truth," but he does not go any further.[41] Along these lines, Macchia laments: *For all of their talk about the importance of pneumatology, Pentecostals have yet to couch their narrow pneumatological interest in charismatic/missionary empowerment within a broader pneumatological framework.*"[42] My aim here is to explore further Macchia's observations and Pentecostal theological concerns but in a much narrower sense by focusing on the seven Spirit-Baptized phrases. From my perspective, both the Traditional and Classical Pentecostal views have demonstrated an accurate aspectual meaning of this phrase; however, each has appealed to their preferred instances of it to interpret the other occurrences, thereby suppressing any diversity. Keener recognizes the varied use of the Spirit-Baptized phrase by stating, "It appears that the New Testament teaches both views—because different texts appear to employ the phrase 'baptism in the Holy Spirit' in different ways. The fact that the phrase 'baptism in the Spirit' could emphasize a different aspect of the Spirit's work in different biblical passages is not difficult to affirm once we recognize that these different emphases are all part of the work of the same Spirit."[43] In his latest work on Acts, Keener footnotes that "John the Baptist's original phrase encompasses the entire sphere of the Spirit's eschatological work."[44] Keener's conclusions concur with Macchia's and his proposal that "Spirit baptism is somewhat ambiguous as a metaphor and fluid in its

40 Macchia, *Baptized*, 58.
41 Menzies, *Empowered for Witness* (New York: T&T Clark, 2004), 242.
42 Macchia, *Baptized*, 18.
43 Keener, *Gift*, 150.
44 Keener, *Acts*, 522 n198.

meaning throughout the New Testament, because it is an eschatological metaphor that depicts the various ways in which we participate through the Spirit in the rich blessings of Christ located in the heavenly places (Ephesians 1:3, 12)."[45] Following Macchia and Keener while also differing from Shelton's reinterpretation suggestion, my thesis is as follows: *Within the NT the Spirit-Baptized phrase governs a constellation of distinct dimensions and experiences of the one Holy Spirit poured out by the one Spirit-Baptizer, Jesus Christ.*

Analysis of the Seven NT Spirit-Baptized Phrases

Paul and 1 Corinthians 12:13

The doctrinal theme of Jesus the Baptizer in the Holy Spirit comes with several interpretive difficulties that relate to how Pentecostals have typically understood this concept. Viewing the phrase "baptizes ἐν the Holy Spirit" to exclusively refer to a subsequent empowerment of the Spirit has seemingly forced some interpreters to adopt the Classical Pentecostal line of thought that there are actually two Spirit-Baptizers: Jesus Christ and the Holy Spirit. Paul's description in 1 Corinthians 12:13 is the lone text typically appealed to when attempting to distinguish two such Baptizers. Ironically, this same text is used by those holding to a Traditional position to support that the Spirit-Baptized phrase solely refers to conversion. Thus, Dunn asserts that this verse "is crucial for the Pentecostal,"[46] but as Howard M. Ervin retorts, it is equally "crucial for the conversion-initiation hypothesis."[47]

---

[45] Macchia, *Baptized*, 87. Larry Hart also points to a multifaceted function of the Spirit-Baptized phrase and the gift of the Spirit. Larry Hart, "Spirit Baptism: A Dimensional Charismatic Perspective," in *Perspectives on Spirit Baptism*, ed. C. W. Brand (Nashville: Broadman & Holman, 2004), 127–42.

[46] Dunn, *Baptism*, 127.

[47] Howard M. Ervin, *Conversion-Initiation and the Baptism in the Holy Spirit* (Peabody: Hendrickson, 1984), 98.

Guy P. Duffield and Nathaniel M. Van Cleave defend the Classical Pentecostal view as they assert: "The Holy Spirit baptizes the believer into the Body of Christ."[48] These two theologians follow suit and use 1 Corinthians 12:12–13a to support their claim. To evaluate this interpretation, it is important to look carefully at Paul's Spirit-Baptized phrase, which includes the entirety of verse 13:

[12]καθάπερ γὰρ τὸ σῶμα ἕν ἐστιν καὶ μέλη πολλὰ ἔχει, πάντα δὲ τὰ μέλη τοῦ σώματος πολλὰ ὄντα ἕν ἐστιν σῶμα, οὕτως καὶ ὁ Χριστός
[13]καὶ γὰρ ἐν ἑνὶ πνεύματι ἡμεῖς πάντες εἰς ἓν σῶμα ἐβαπτίσθημεν, εἴτε Ἰουδαῖοι εἴτε Ἕλληνες εἴτε δοῦλοι εἴτε ἐλεύθεροι, καὶ πάντες ἓν πνεῦμα ἐποτίσθημεν

[12]For just as the body is one and has many parts, and all the parts of the body, though being many, are one body; just as with Christ.
[13]For also *in/with/by* (ἐν) one Spirit we all ourselves have been baptized into one body, whether Judeans or Gentiles, slaves or free-persons, and we all have been given to drink one Spirit.

Duffield/Van Cleave contrast this baptism with the Pentecostal idea of the "Baptism in the Holy Spirit" chiefly depicted in the words of John the Baptist.[49] They assert that there

is a *vital difference* between the Holy Spirit baptizing believers into the Body of Christ, an operation of the Holy Spirit, and being Baptized with the Holy Ghost

---

[48] Duffield/Van Cleave, *Foundations of Pentecostal Theology* (Los Angeles: L.I.F.E. Bible College, 1987), 277–78.

[49] See Duffield/Van Cleave, *Pentecostal*, (304–25) (italics mine).

which is an operation of Jesus … the baptism spoke of in
1 Corinthians 12:13 is conducted *by* the Holy Spirit, and
has to do with the believer's position in Christ; while
the baptism spoken of by John in Mark 1:8 is conducted
by Jesus Christ, and has to do with the power for
service.[50]

Thus, the believer is baptized *by* the Holy Spirit apparently in
himself whereas Jesus baptizes the believer *in/with* the Holy Spirit.
So, following this semantic *in, with, by* interpretation of the preposition ἐν, two Spirit-Baptizers appear. It seems to me that because
the doctrinal position "Jesus Christ is the Baptizer in the Holy
Spirit" became strictly identified as the subsequent empowerment
event and that Paul's description in 1 Corinthians 12:13 did not
quite fit with this interpretation, this two Baptizers idea was
produced. That said, the majority of English versions translate the
first line of v. 13 ἐν ἑνὶ πνεύματι … ἐβαπτίσθημεν as "*by* one
Spirit … we have been baptized" (KJV; NKJV; RSV; NASB;
NASBU; NIV; the NRSV translates "*in* the one Spirit"),
conveying the Spirit's agency of this baptism, which Duffield/Van
Cleave obviously also follow.

In order to assess what Paul is saying here, I need to first carefully
examine the other six Spirit-Baptized texts in the Gospels and
Luke-Acts (Matt 3:11; Mark 1:8; John 1:33; Luke 3:16; Acts 1:5;
11:16). The fullest expression of this phrase is found in Matthew's
Gospel, which is closely mirrored by Luke in his Gospel:

[11]ἐγὼ μὲν ὑμᾶς βαπτίζω ἐν ὕδατι εἰς μετάνοιαν ὁ
δὲ ὀπίσω μου ἐρχόμενος ἰσχυρότερός μού ἐστιν,
οὗ οὐκ εἰμὶ ἰκανὸς τὰ ὑποδήματα βαστάσαι· αὐτὸς
ὑμᾶς βαπτίσει ἐν πνεύματι ἁγίῳ καὶ πυρί.

---

[50] Duffield/Van Cleave, *Pentecostal*, 277–78 (italics mine). Duffield/Van Cleave go on to
argue that the medium of the Holy Spirit's baptism is the Church, but this is quite illogical
and not typically suggested by other Pentecostal scholars.

[11]I myself baptize you *in/with/by* (ἐν) water for repentance, but the one coming after me is mightier than I, whose sandals I am not worthy to carry; he himself will baptize you *in/with/by* (ἐν) the Holy Spirit and fire.

Using this occurrence as a template as well as with the other five instances in mind, I offer the following observations:

- variations of the phrase βαπτίσει ὑμᾶς ἐν πνεύματι ἁγίω occur in direct contrast to John's initiatory baptizing ἐν ὕδατι or ὕδατι
- all six occurrences of the phrase include the verb βαπτίζω
- all six texts contain the prepositional phrase ἐν πνεύματι ἁγίω with Matthew and Luke including καὶ πυρί
- four instances of βαπτίζω modified by ἐν πνεύματι ἁγίω occur in the active voice with Jesus Christ clearly the subject of the verb or participle
- the two passive voice occurrences of βαπτίζω modified by ἐν πνεύματι ἁγίω in Acts point to Jesus as the agent of the action due to the clear and explicit parallels with the Gospel texts

Turning now to Paul's Spirit-Baptized version, my observations are as follows:

- he does not contrast his description with John's baptism with water
- he uses a passive form of βαπτίζω
- he uses the same basic prepositional phrase ἐν πνεύματι while adding ἑνὶ but does not include ἁγίω
- the subject of βαπτίζω is anyone who believes
- there is no explicit agent of the action of βαπτίζω
- Paul adds the line καὶ πάντες ἐν πνεῦμα ἐποτίσθημεν

Drawing all these observations together, as most interpreters agree, Paul's Spirit-Baptized phrase closely resembles the other six.[51] In addition to this, Paul's final line is quite significant, which Duffield/Van Cleave unfortunately fail to take into consideration. With each line of this verse, Paul creates a parallel concentric structure:

A καὶ γὰρ ἐν ἑνὶ πνεύματι ἡμεῖς πάντες εἰς ἓν σῶμα ἐβαπτίσθημεν
B   εἴτε Ἰουδαῖοι εἴτε Ἕλληνες
B' εἴτε δοῦλοι εἴτε ἐλεύθεροι
A' καὶ πάντες ἓν πνεῦμα ἐποτίσθημεν

With this poetical device, Paul parallels ἐν ἑνὶ πνεύματι and ἓν πνεῦμα as well as the two verbs ἐβαπτίσθημεν and ἐποτίσθημεν which he places at the end of each clause and morphologically forms identically, thereby creating an explicit paronomasia, a play on words.[52] All these literary factors point to Paul intentionally using line A' in direct parallel to line A to clarify his overall baptismal point.[53] It is certainly possible to translate ἐν ἑνὶ πνεύματι as "by the one Spirit"[54] with Paul's similar uses of the preposition ἐν in this chapter (vv. 3, 9)[55]; however, Paul's parallelism points the interpreter in a different direction.[56] The most straightforward way of understanding ἐποτίσθημεν is a passive with Christ as the obvious agent

---

[51] Stott drew this same conclusion early on (*Fullness*, 21–29).

[52] Fee sees v. 12 forming a concentric structure. Gordon D. Fee, *God's Empowering Presence*, (Peabody: Hendrickson, 1994), 176.

[53] Similarly Fee, *Presence*, 180, see further 178–82; followed by Hart, "Charismatic," 126.

[54] See Matthew Brook O'Donnell's analysis in his "Two Opposing Views of Baptism With/By the Holy Spirit and of 1 Corinthians 12:13: Can Grammatical Investigation Bring Clarity?," in *Baptism, the New Testament and the Church*. FS R. E. O. White; *JSNT:Supp* 171 (Sheffield: Sheffield Academic Press, 1999), 311–36.

[55] So cf. Ervin, *Conversion-Initiation*, 98–99.

[56] Turner, following Alistair Brown, argues exegetically for the "Spirit's agency" here in v. 13, but he does not account for the parallel structure. Max Turner, "Receiving Christ and Receiving the Spirit: In Dialogue with David Pawson," *JPT* 15 (1999): 15, see 11–15. Stanley M. Horton recently also concluded that there is "a distinction between the Spirit baptizing believers into the one body and being 'given the one Spirit to drink.'" Stanley M. Horton,

with ἐν πνεῦμα functioning as the clear direct object, and because of Paul's parallelism, ἐβαπτίσθημεν would most naturally match this function. Thus, as believers are made to drink one Spirit provided *by* Jesus Christ, so in the same way believers are baptized ἐν the Holy Spirit into the one body *by* Jesus Christ.

In Titus 3:4–6, Paul[57] presents a fuller description of the role of the Trinity in the regenerative-conversion of the believer:

> [4]ὅτε δὲ ἡ χρηστότης καὶ ἡ φιλανθρωπία ἐπεφάνη
> τοῦ σωτῆρος ἡμῶν θεοῦ
> [5]οὐκ ἐξ ἔργων τῶν ἐν δικαιοσύνῃ ἃ ἐποιήσαμεν
> ἡμεῖς ἀλλὰ κατὰ τὸ αὐτοῦ ἔλεος ἔσωσεν ἡμᾶς διὰ
> λουτροῦ παλιγγενεσίας καὶ ἀνακαινώσεως
> πνεύματος ἁγίου
> [6]οὗ ἐξέχεεν ἐφ᾽ ἡμᾶς πλουσίως διὰ Ἰησοῦ Χριστοῦ
> τοῦ σωτῆρος ἡμῶν

> [4]but when the goodness and benevolence of our Savior God appeared [5]not because of works done in righteousness which we ourselves did, but according to his mercy he saved us through the washing of regeneration and renewal of the Holy Spirit[58] [6]whom he poured out upon us richly through Jesus Christ our Savior

In typical fashion in the Pastoral Letters, Paul identifies both God the Father and Jesus Christ as σωτήρ "Savior" (see 1 Timothy 1:1; 2:3; 4:10; 2 Timothy 1:10; Titus 1:3–4; 2:10, 13;

"Spirit Baptism: A Pentecostal Perspective," in *Perspectives on Spirit Baptism*, ed. C. O. Brand (Nashville: Broadman & Holman, 2004), 69.

[57] I am assuming here that Paul wrote the Letter to Titus as well as 1 and 2 Timothy. For a defense of this position, see in particular William D. Mounce, *Pastoral Epistles*, WBC 46 (Nashville: Thomas Nelson, 2000), xlvi–cxxix.

[58] The texts D*, F, G, b, and vg^mss insert διὰ before πνεύματος ἁγίου. The addition of δια is unnecessary as it is best to see the preposition governing two parallel clauses which describe two dimensions of the single conversion event (cf. Fee, *Presence*, 781–83; Mounce, *Pastoral*, 441–43, 448–50).

see also 1 Timothy 2:4, 5–6; 2 Timothy 1:8–9; 2:10). These
identical descriptors literarily surround the work of the Spirit
which thereby highlights his own role in salvation. Looking at the
roles of the Godhead, the Father is orchestrator and provider of
this salvific conversion, Jesus Christ is the agent as God pours out
the Spirit through him, and the Spirit is the instrument; yet, at
the same time, the Spirit functions as the agent or actuator of the
believer's conversion in his transformative work. Paul describes this
work of the Spirit as a single cleansing event characterized by both
παλιγγενεσία "regeneration" and ἀνακαίνωσις "renewal" which
the Spirit actuates.[59] Paul's depiction here closely reflects Yahweh's
promise in Ezekiel 36, which also depicts a single event:

וְזָרַקְתִּי עֲלֵיכֶם מַיִם טְהוֹרִים "and I will sprinkle clean
water on you"

וְאֶת־רוּחִי אֶתֵּן בְּקִרְבְּכֶם... "and I will put my Spirit within
you" ...

וְהוֹשַׁעְתִּי אֶתְכֶם מִכֹּל טֻמְאוֹתֵיכֶם "and I will save you from
all your uncleanness" (vv. 25a, 27a, 29a).

Looking to Paul's choice of the term ἐξέχεεν, it is intertextually
significant that Peter in his sermon on Pentecost uses the same
term ἐκχέω ("pour out") three times. The first two instances occur
in his quote of the prophecy of Joel (Acts 2:17, 18), while the third
occurs in the identical form as in the above Titus passage when Peter
describes how Jesus, upon his exaltation, *has poured out* the Spirit
(v. 33). So, Paul describes this *pouring out* of the Spirit in conversion
terms whereas for Luke, this *pouring out* of the Spirit is evidenced
by charismatic empowerment. In Paul's descriptions, then, of the
salvific conversion work of the Spirit in 1 Corinthians 12:13 and
Titus 3:4–6, he remains consistent: the Spirit creatively transforms

---

[59] Some scholars have understood παλιγγενεσία "regeneration" and ἀνακαίνωσις
"renewal" as two distinct events; however, it is best to see one event of λουτροῦ "washing"
depicted or characterized by παλιγγενεσία and ἀνακαίνωσις; see further Fee, *Presence*,
782; Mounce, *Pastoral*, 443, 448.

the convert, but it is the Father through the Son who pours out the Spirit upon and baptizes believers ἐν the Spirit.

In light of all this analysis and specifically with the parallel clauses of 12:13, Paul's fuller description of Spirit conversion in Titus and the clear linguistic parallels with the Gospels and Lukan Spirit-Baptized texts show that he would most assuredly understand Jesus Christ as the one who pours out the Spirit, gives believers to drink one Spirit, and baptizes believers ἐν the one Spirit; converts are not baptized *by* the Holy Spirit. Therefore, as the overwhelming majority of interpreters agree, Paul uses his Spirit-Baptized phrase to refer to initiation-conversion.[60] So, on the one hand, Duffield/Van Cleave correctly interpret Paul's overall baptismal point of regeneration in 1 Corinthians 12; however, on the other hand, they incorrectly claim that this experience occurs *by* the Spirit. This is not to say, though, that the Spirit does not function in any way as the agent of the believer's conversion; he is, rather, simultaneously the *instrument* of Christ's baptism as well as the *actuator* of the believer's transformative conversion. Like water constitutes the instrument of John's baptism, water itself also naturally functions as the cleansing agent; so comparatively the Spirit constitutes the instrument of Jesus's baptism while it also naturally operates as the agent who cleanses, empowers, and transforms. The Spirit obviously functions in a much greater capacity as an *active* agent than inanimate water as he is the Third Person of the Godhead. In this sense, I agree with Duffield/Van Cleave and others who argue for the Spirit's agency role in 1 Corinthians 12:13. For

---

[60] Ervin most recently conceded that Paul's description of "baptized in one Spirit" in v. 13 refers to conversion, but the last line refers to Pentecostal empowerment (*Conversion-Initiation*, 98–102); so also earlier Ronald E. Cottle, "All Were Baptized," *JETS* 17 (1974): 75–80. Horton similarly concludes that the last line of v. 13 "implies not only the initial baptism in the Spirit but a continuing experience with the Spirit" ("Pentecostal," 69). Most contemporary scholars, though, concur that such a conclusion is most improbable, and even Ervin's colleague Hart agrees that Fee's analysis has the exegetical upper hand (Hart, "Charismatic," 126).

me, this cannot be substantiated exegetically from Paul's Spirit-Baptized phrase but in light of the apostle's other descriptions of the role of the Spirit in conversion (cf. Titus 3:4–6) and thus on intertextual and theological grounds. In the end, it is the entire work of the Trinity who together orchestrates, provides for, and accomplishes the salvation and empowerment of converts. The NT writers only conceive of one Spirit-Baptizer, the only one who pours out the Spirit as promised by the Father, while the Spirit himself functions in a crucial and indispensable capacity in the life of the believer. The semantically flexible preposition ἐν allows for as well as conveys the multidimensional, active work of the Holy Spirit. The Third Person of the Trinity, then, operates as the *instrument* (ἐν *in/with*) of Jesus' Spirit-Baptism as well as the *actuator* (ἐν *by*) of the believer's conversion, empowerment, and transformation.

Interpretive Consequences of Paul's Spirit-Baptized Phrase

From my analysis, then, the NT writers conceive of only *one* Spirit-Baptizer, Jesus Christ, and *one* instrument or medium of his baptizing, the Holy Spirit. Consequently, the interpreter, and, in particular, the Pentecostal, must face head on:

1) Jesus Christ baptizes believers ἐν the Holy Spirit into the body of Christ in an initiatory-conversion sense, and
2) the untenable Classical Pentecostal position that the expression "Baptism in the Holy Spirit" is the "scriptural name" *solely* referring to the subsequent charismatic empowerment of believers.[61]

The question now is: *Where does the interpreter go from here?* To begin, I strongly suggest that some of us Pentecostals (1) eliminate

[61] Duffield/Van Cleave, *Pentecostal*, 305.

this *in, with, by* semantic, interpretive dance with the Spirit-Baptized phrase to draw definitive demarcations between two Spirit-Baptizers and (2) carefully reevaluate how the NT writers *use* the Spirit-Baptized expression in order to develop a way to articulate the doctrinal concept "Baptism in the Holy Spirit" that is exegetically, theologically, and experientially sound and as ecumenical as possible.

Towards this reevaluation, I would like to offer a few ways forward. First and foremost, we must acknowledge the obvious: at conversion, every believer is regenerated—born again—as a result of the indwelling of the Spirit. The NT writers present this truth either explicitly or as a theological assumption. Jesus himself proclaimed one must be born anew, born of water and the Spirit to see and enter into the kingdom of God (John 3:3, 5). For Paul, humanity falls into two groups: those who have the Spirit and those who do not (1 Corinthians 2:10–16). The distinctive mark of the new Messianic people of God is the Spirit (Romans 2:28–29). The Spirit is the quintessential and universal characteristic of *all* those "in Christ"; those who belong to Christ in contrast to those "outside Christ." I believe with this biblical fact, though, comes a central theological problem of the Classical Pentecostal view of Spirit-Baptism: how can one receive the Spirit at conversion and thus be born anew and yet need to receive again this same, one Spirit for additional empowerment?

Regarding the conversion/subsequence debate, most recently Walter C. Kaiser Jr. proposed his definition of the Spirit-Baptized phrase that corresponds closely to Dunn and Stott's earlier conclusions.[62] Kaiser is no Cessationist and also concedes that Luke has a different pneumatological emphasis. Still, the Spirit's work as depicted in Acts cannot "be linked to the promise of the Father about the baptizing in the Holy Spirit and fire. Those are separate topics that have incorrectly been linked by way of the approach of 'an analogy

---

[62] Stott, *Fullness*, 22–23.

of faith' rather than by way of solid exegesis."[63] Yet, Kaiser inexplicably implements this same methodological principle when he claims that it is "best to go with Paul's inspired statement of purpose in 1 Corinthians 12:13 that this baptism was the initial work of God of incorporating all believers, first at Pentecost, then at Samaria, and again at Caesarea, into one unified body of Christ in the Holy Spirit."[64] Turner, the once self-identified Classical Pentecostal, is perhaps the primary NT scholar who not only endorses Dunn's thesis but has also rigorously developed and expanded upon it.[65] Turner, like Dunn, sees the pouring out of the Spirit as definitive while simultaneously including all the aspects of the Spirit.[66] Turner also acknowledges that "Luke shows *relatively little interest* in the Spirit as the power of spiritual, ethical, and religious renewal of the individual."[67] Still, "Paul's conception of the gift of the Spirit is simply *broader* than Luke's, *while nevertheless containing everything Luke implies* … Paul's comprehensive understanding of the gift of the Spirit granted to Christians at conversion does not leave anything for Luke's to 'add.'"[68] The Reformed/ Charismatic theologian Wayne Grudem follows closely this line of thought as he concludes that "when we become Christians we are

---

[63] Walter C. Kaiser, "The Baptism in the Holy Spirit as the Promise of the Father: A Reformed Perspective," in *Perspectives on Spirit Baptism*, ed. C. O. Brand (Nashville: Broadman & Holman, 2004), 29.

[64] Kaiser, "Reformed," 31. For his understanding of this method, Kaiser points his readers to his own essay, "Hermeneutics and the Theological Task," *TrinJ* 12 (1990): 3–14.

[65] In his dissertation, Turner often takes Dunn to task but has since recanted and declared that "Dunn is right." Max Turner, "James Dunn's *Baptism in the Holy Spirit*: Appreciation and Response," *JPT* 19 (2010): 31. See also Turner, "The Spirit and Salvation in Luke-Acts," in *The Holy Spirit and Christian Origins*. FS James D. G. Dunn; eds. G. N. Stanton et al. (Grand Rapids: Eerdmans, 2004), 103–16.

[66] Turner, *Power*, 86–137; see also Turner, "Luke and the Spirit: Renewing Theological Interpretation of Biblical Pneumatology," in *Reading Luke*, SHS 6, eds. C. G. Bartholomew et al. (Grand Rapids: Eerdmans, 2005), 279–81; Turner, "Salvation," 111–13; Turner, *The Holy Spirit and Spiritual Gifts* (Carlisle: Paternoster Press, 1996), 43–45; see also Dunn, "Baptism," 7–22.

[67] Turner, "Salvation," 105 (italics mine).

[68] Turner, *Spirit*, 151–52.

all 'baptized in one Spirit into one body' (1 Corinthians 12:13)," and this phrase is not what the NT "authors would use to speak of any post-conversion experience of empowering by the Holy Spirit."[69] Interestingly, the highly regarded Pentecostal scholar Gordon D. Fee also sees Spirit-Baptism as conversion that naturally accompanies charismatic empowerment.[70] It is important to note that Fee, along with his co-author Douglas Stuart, takes a hard hermeneutical line when interpreting narrative as he asserts *that unless Scripture explicitly tells us we must do something, what is merely narrated or described can never function in a normative way.*[71] Consequently, Fee's interpretive strategy symptomatically forces him to prefer Paul's Spirit-Baptized expression over and against any Lukan material. As with Dunn, each of these scholars make important contributions to understanding Spirit-Baptism and especially the ongoing experience of the Spirit for the contemporary convert; unfortunately, they do not allow the NT writers, and particularly Luke, any autonomy when describing Spirit-Baptized experiences.

The question now is: *Do these other six Spirit-Baptized texts describe something different from Paul's conversion-initiation view?* To begin, this expression never occurs as a noun clause ("Baptism in the Holy Spirit") but always as a verbal clause indicating more of a dynamic experience. Upon hearing this phrase from the mouth of John the Baptist and Jesus, first century Palestinians would have associated it with several ideas. First, the verb βαπτίζω would have naturally conveyed two ideas: *conversion* and *immersion*, as Judeans of the

---

[69] Wayne Grudem, *Systematic Theology* (Grand Rapids: Zondervan, 1994), 772–73.

[70] Gordon D. Fee, "Hermeneutics and Historical Precedent—A Major Problem in Pentecostal Hermeneutics," in *Perspectives on the New Pentecostalism*, ed. R. P. Spittler (Grand Rapids: Baker, 1976), 119–32; Fee, "Baptism in the Holy Spirit: The Issue of Separability and Subsequence," in Fee, *Gospel and Spirit* (Peabody: Hendrickson, 1991), 105–19.

[71] Gordon D. Fee and Douglas Stuart, *How to Read the Bible for All Its Worth*, 2nd ed. (Grand Rapids: Zondervan, 1982), 97. Fee/Stuart later revised this statement by adding a qualifying clause: *"unless it can be demonstrated on other grounds that the author intended it to function in this way."* Fee/Stuart, *How to Read the Bible for All Its Worth*, 3rd ed. (Grand Rapids: Zondervan, 2003), 119; see also Stott, *Fullness*, 8–9.

day regularly baptized with water unclean Gentile converts into Judaism.[72] The phrase πνεύματι ἁγίῳ would have also conjured up a number of notions for John and Jesus' contemporaries but especially that of *purification* (cf. Ezekiel 36:26–27; see also 18:31; 37:14) and *prophecy* (see Numbers 11:25–29; 1 Samuel 10:6, 10–12; 19:19–24; 2 Samuel 23:2; 2 Chronicles 15:1–7; 18:23; Micah 3:8).[73] The NT confirms these central features of the Spirit as it clearly connects the Spirit with *prophecy* (e.g., Matthew 22:43; Luke 1:17; 2:27; 4:18; Acts 11:28; 21:4; 1 Corinthians 7:40; 1 Thessalonians 5:19–20; 1 Peter 1:11; 1 John 4:1–6; Revelation 1:10; 2:7), which also included demonstrations of power (Romans 15:19)[74] as well as with giving *life* and transforming *purification* (e.g., John 3:5–8; 1 Corinthians 6:11; Galatians 4:29; 5:17–18, 22–23; 6:8; Jude 19).

The Gospels of Matthew, Mark, and John

I suggest that if we carefully examine the contexts of John's Spirit-Baptized phrase, it becomes apparent that the NT writers, while acknowledging other dimensional experiences, emphasize a particular dimension of being baptized ἐν the Holy Spirit. From my analysis, the phrase as it is found in Matthew, Mark, and John corresponds with Paul's initiation-conversion point. For Matthew and Mark, the primary message of the Baptist was repentance and the forgiveness of sins in preparation for the soon-arriving kingdom of God (Matthew 3:2; Mark 1:4) while Jesus' opening proclamation is much the same (Matthew 4:17; Mark 1:15). Similar to Matthew (see above) and according to Mark as well as Luke, John preached "a

---

[72] Most NT scholars see this as the most natural background for John's baptism. See, e.g., G. R. Beasley-Murray, *Baptism in the New Testament* (Grand Rapids: Eerdmans, 1962), 1–44; Oscar Cullmann, *Baptism in the New Testament*, SBT 1 (London: SCM Press, 1950), 62; Albrecht Oepke, "Βάπτω," *TDNT* 1: 535–40; Robert L. Webb, *John the Baptizer and Prophet*, JSNT:Supp 62 (Sheffield: JSOT, 1991), cf. 95–162.

[73] See further Craig S. Keener, *The Spirit in the Gospels and Acts* (Peabody: Hendrickson, 1997), 8–48; Keener, *Gift*, 152–54; Keener, *Acts*, 532–37.

[74] See further Turner, *Power*, 105–18.

baptism of repentance for the forgiveness of sins" (Mark 1:4; Luke 3:3) while the Gospel writers and Luke parallel John's baptism with Jesus Christ's. Particularly for Matthew and Mark, as John baptizes repentant initiates ἐν water in preparation for God's kingdom, so Jesus baptizes repentant converts ἐν the Holy Spirit into the kingdom of God.[75]

This initiation-conversion theme becomes most evident in the Fourth Gospel. Close to the beginning, the Baptist identifies Jesus Christ as the Spirit-Baptizer (1:32–33). In his narrative, John creates a literary bracket or *inclusio*[76] around this designation with another identity marker of Jesus as the Baptist announces, "Behold the Lamb of God who takes away the sin of the world!" (vv. 29 and 36). With this *inclusio*, John intentionally creates a continuity between Jesus as the Lamb of God and Spirit-Baptizer. Further, John often describes the Spirit as water (see 3:5; 7:37–39; see also 1 John 5:6–8) who cleanses and purifies as well as provides life.[77] Literarily, John presents salvation and being baptized ἐν the Holy Spirit as intrinsically bound.[78] Yet, in this same Gospel, Jesus talks about the Father giving another παράκλητος "Paraclete, Helper," the Spirit of truth (14:16–17). Jesus further says that the Father will send the Spirit in my name, who will remain with and be in his disciples to teach and bring to remembrance all of Jesus' teachings (v. 26). Jesus again promises that he himself will send the Paraclete from the Father who will "bear witness" (μαρτυρέω) of him, which in turn the disciples will "bear witness" (μαρτυρέω) of Jesus (15:26–27). Significantly, John here does not associate the Paraclete with salvation or conversion but with empowerment and especially for witness.

---

[75] For the link between the Spirit of Yahweh and the kingdom of God as well as the other motifs I describe above, see e.g., Isaiah 11:1–10; 32:9–20; 42:1–4; 59:15b–21; 61:1–11; Ezekiel 36:22–29; 37:1–14; 39:25–29; Joel 2:28–29; see also Jeremiah 31:31–34; 32:38–40.

[76] For example see Psalm 8:1 and 9.

[77] On the theme of water in John, see Keener, *Gift*, 138–43.

[78] Similarly Hart, "Charismatic," 129.

As I touched on above, John begins to close his Gospel with Jesus breathing and commanding his disciples to "Receive the Holy Spirit" (20:22). Much has been written on this short verse and especially concerning its relationship with Acts 2. Numerous scholars have typically conflated these two narrative depictions of the giving of the Spirit in one way or another.[79] This is especially true with the highly influential idea that John 20:22 presents a "Johannine Pentecost."[80] For numerous interpreters, Acts 2 functions as the lens whereby to interpret John 20,[81] and relatedly, the NT writers envision only one definitive gift of the Spirit.[82] More specifically, it is the Pauline conversion-initiation interpretation of Acts 2 that functions as this lens! Thus, in the case of John 20:22, the disciples simultaneously are created new, are baptized in the Spirit, have drank living waters, and are given the Paraclete.

Towards evaluating this interpretation, a clear and widely recognized semantic intertextual link occurs between Jesus breathing on his disciples and Yahweh breathing into the first human. This is evidenced by the use of ἐνεφύσησεν "he breathed" in John 20 and the Septuagint version of Genesis 2:7. Yahweh breathing into the

---

[79] For example, D. A. Carson sees Jesus breathing as an "acted parable," symbolically pointing to Acts 2. D. A. Carson, *The Gospel According to John* (Grand Rapids: Eerdmans, 1991), 651, 655; so also Andreas J. Köstenberger, *John*, BECNT (Grand Rapids: Baker Academic, 2004), 574.

[80] Cf. Raymond Brown, *The Gospel According to John XIII–XXI*, Anchor Bible vol. 29A (New York: Doubleday, 1970), 1022–24, 1036–39. For similar ideas see, e.g., George Beasley-Murray, *John*, WBC 36, rev. ed. (Nashville: Thomas Nelson, 1999), 381; Thomas R. Hatina, "John 20,22 in Its Eschatological Context: Promise or Fulfillment?," *Bib* 74 (1993): 196–219; Robert W. Lyon, "John 20:22, Once More," *ATJ* 41 (1988): 73–85; This idea is somewhat anticipated by C. K. Barret, *The Gospel According to St. John*, 2nd ed. (Philadelphia: Westminster, 1978), 570. For the main arguments of a "Johannine Pentecost," see Turner, *Spirit*, 91–93.

[81] For a different view of a "Johannine Pentecost," see Rudolf Schnackenburg, *The Gospel According to St. John*, HTCNT; 3 vols. (New York: Crossroad, 1982), 3:325–26.

[82] See Marianne Meye Thompson, "The Breath of Life: John 20:22–23 Once More," in *The Holy Spirit and Christian Origins*, FS James D. G. Dunn, eds. G. N. Stanton et al. (Grand Rapids: Eerdmans, 2004), 70.

first human the πνοὴν ζωῆς "breath of life" recalls Jesus' likening the Spirit to wind (3:8) and specifically to his recreating work (vv. 3–6).[83] Another important intertextual use of the term occurs in Ezekiel's vision of the valley of dry bones (37).[84] Here, the dead bones are "breathed" (ἐνεφύσησεν) into (v. 9b), resulting in the πνεῦμα entering into them and thereby coming back to life (vv. 10a, 14a). Thus, two interrelated ideas occur here and with John 20: life after death and the Spirit. In connection with Ezekiel 36, Yahweh's Spirit within his people also promises to create an inner capacity to obey Yahweh (v. 27) and to realize the covenantal goal: "you shall be my people and I will be your God" (v. 28b; 37:27b).[85]

In the first parts of John's Gospel, as described above, the Spirit is consistently depicted as providing purification and life (3:5–8; 4:10–14; 6:63; 7:37–39). Related to this, Jesus breathes after he presented himself alive eternally! Following Jesus' breathing, he gives the disciples authority to forgive sins (v. 23) in a similar manner to Matt 16:19 and 18:15–18.[86] In his Gospel, John rarely includes the idea of forgiveness of sin. The single explicit reference occurs here, along with the only other related instance of Jesus identified as the Lamb of God (1:29).[87] John's minimal space given to the forgiveness of sin ironically highlights its significance and, specifically, its undeniable association with the giving of the Spirit. John creates a larger *inclusio* with his use of the Spirit-Baptized phrase, and John 20:22 makes it even clearer that Jesus' baptism provides the forgiveness of sins.

Drawing all this together, in John 20 the disciples experience recreation as Jesus breathes out the Spirit.[88] With Christ's resur-

---

[83] So, e.g., Craig S. Keener, *The Gospel According to John*, 2 vols. (Peabody: Hendrickson, 2003), 2: 1204.

[84] The term ἐμφυσάω also occurs in 1 Kings 17:21 and Wisdom of Solomon 15:11.

[85] See further, Thompson, "Breath," 73–75.

[86] See Keener, *John*, 2: 1207–08.

[87] See further, Thompson, "Breath," 75.

[88] Numerous scholars over the years have recognized these semantic links, which Dunn himself saw early on while also drawing similar recreation conclusions (see Dunn, *Baptism*, 180; see most recently Thompson, "Breath," 69–78).

rection, the Spirit is now given (7:39) as Jesus baptizes converts
ἐν the Holy Spirit (1:33), resulting in the forgiveness of sins
(1:29; 20:23) and being born of the Spirit and water (3:3, 5), not
flesh (1:12–13). Prior to Jesus' breathing, he declares that he is
now sending them as he was sent by the Father (20:21), which
implicitly parallels Matthew 28:18–20. John associates sending,
empowerment, and the Spirit three times in his Gospel: God
sent John the Baptist to baptize with water (1:33), the Father will
send the Paraclete to teach and remind (14:26), and here Jesus
sends his disciples to continue on his own mission.[89] Beyond this,
though, John never expands upon nor narrates the impact of the
Paraclete. What John explicitly emphasizes is Jesus as the Baptizer
ἐν the Holy Spirit for conversion-initiation while including in
his Gospel the dimension of empowerment. John, then, sees two
distinct dimensions of the gift of the Spirit: regeneration and
empowerment.[90]

Luke-Acts

Looking to Luke-Acts, as I introduced above, it has been
Pentecostal scholars in particular who have convincingly demonstrated that Luke emphasizes the charismatic, prophetic empowerment of the Spirit. This can be especially seen in Luke's narrative
focus and structuring. In particular, and in contrast to the other
Gospels, Luke describes and presents Jesus as an eschatological,
Spirit-anointed προφήτης "prophet." Luke's first instance of John's
Spirit-Baptized phrase (3:16) is not explicitly associated with
conversion as it is in John's Gospel but rather with the empowering
dimension of the Spirit. Following Luke's use of the phrase, the
Spirit descends upon Jesus as he rises out of the waters of

---

[89] F. F. Bruce, *The Gospel of John* (Grand Rapids: Eerdmans, 1983), 392 and Shelton
(*Word*, 160) claim that John 20:22 depicts a bestowal of empowerment, not rebirth.

[90] Keener draws similar conclusions theologically (*John*, 2: 1204–05; see also Hart,
"Charismatic," 133).

baptism (3:22). The next description of the Spirit occurs when
Luke uniquely narrates Jesus being "full" (πλήρης) of and led by
the Spirit into the wilderness (4:1) and successfully withstanding
forty days of temptation (4:2–12). Luke describes Jesus returning
"in the *power* (δύναμις) of the Spirit" to Galilee (v. 14) and then
exclusively presents Jesus' very first teaching instance as he audibly
reads from the "scroll of the *prophet* Isaiah." Jesus purposefully turns
to and reads a version of 61:1–2 and then announces that these
words of an anonymous Spirit-anointed *prophet* are now fulfilled
(4:16–21). Following this, Jesus explicitly identifies himself as a
prophet who has no honor in his hometown (vv. 22–30) while Mark
places this saying much later in his Gospel (6:1–6). Throughout his
Gospel, Luke reports others identifying Jesus as a *prophet* (e.g.,
7:16). Very near the close of his first volume, Luke includes the
report on the road to Emmaus that this Jesus of Nazareth was a
prophet "mighty (δύναμις) in deed and word" (24:19), which forms
a larger type of *inclusio* highlighting again Luke's emphasis. Thus,
from beginning to end, Jesus is identified as a man full of the Spirit
who is a charismatically anointed *prophet*.[91] In his second volume,
Luke particularly accents how the same Spirit that rested upon the
Anointed One has now been poured out by this Spirit-Baptizer
upon his followers. In his narrative work, Luke creates an undeniable literary parallel between Jesus' anointing (*never* baptized ἐν the
Holy Spirit![92]) and the disciples being baptized ἐν the Holy Spirit:
both Jesus and his disciples are praying (Luke 3:21–22//Acts 1:14);
the Spirit descends upon both while resembling something physical
(Luke 3:22//Acts 2:3, 33); this endowment is particularly for
proclaiming Good News (Luke 4:18–21; 24:47–49//Acts 1:8; 2:1);
and resulting in the public ministries of both commenced with
programmatic sermons (Luke 4:16–28//Acts 2:14–40).[93]

---

91 Stronstad, *Prophethood*, 38.
92 Contra Dunn, *Baptism*, 24.
93 Similarly Ervin, *Conversion-Initiation*, cf. 161; Keener, *Acts*, 678–79; Menzies, *Pneumatology*, 201 note 2, 206–07; Menzies, *Empowered*, 168–72; Walt Russell, "The Anointing with the Holy Spirit in Luke-Acts," *TrinJ* 7NS (1986): 47–63; Stronstad,

Luke ends his first volume with resurrection appearances of Christ (24), quite similar to John 20. Rather than the typical conflation of John 20 and Acts 2, I agree with Marianne Meye Thompson that John 20 parallels Luke 24 and, in particular, vv. 36–40.[94] Both narratives include a peace greeting (Luke 24:36//John 20:19, 21)[95], appearances of the risen Christ (Luke 24:13–36//John 20:16–29) with physical evidence (Luke 24:39//John 20:27–29), and instructions concerning the forgiveness of sins (Luke 24:47//John 20:23). Regarding the Spirit, where Luke differs from John is with the continuance of his empowerment emphasis. Towards the close of Luke's first volume, Jesus begins by declaring that his disciples are μάρτυρες "witnesses" (v. 48) to his death and resurrection (v. 46) and that he is sending τὴν ἐπαγγελίαν τοῦ πατρός "the promise of the Father" upon them, and they are to wait in the city until they are clothed ἐξ ὕψους δύναμιν "from on high with power" (v. 49).[96] Luke repeats these ideas in Acts 1:4–8 and directly links τὴν ἐπαγγελίαν τοῦ πατρὸς to John's Spirit-Baptized phrase (vv. 4–5).[97] Jesus explicitly defines the phrase as empowerment while identifying himself as the Spirit-Baptizer (v. 5). Jesus then declares that his apostles will receive δύναμιν when the Spirit comes upon them to successfully operate as his μάρτυρες (v. 8). Jesus' baptizing ἐν the Holy Spirit, then, will create a charismatic community of *prophets* as envisioned by Joel, who will *witness* about the Messiah, the Savior, to the ends of the earth. This directly contrasts John's

---

Charismatic, 50–52; Charles H. Talbert, *Literary Patterns*, SBLMS 20 (Missoula, MT: Scholars Press, 1974), 16; Turner, *Power*, 343–44.

[94] Thompson, "Breath," 76.

[95] The peace greeting in Luke is found in all MSS except D it.

[96] Luke's phrase ἐξ ὕψους δύναμιν vaguely alludes to Isaiah 32:15a, which Turner places quite a bit of interpretive weight on (including vv. 15–20 and relatedly 44:3–5) to support his comprehensive Spirit of prophecy view (see "Salvation," 110). One problem with this stance is the glaring differences between the lxx and Luke (ἕως ἂν ἐπέλθη ἐφ' ὑμᾶς πνεῦμα ἀφ' ὑψηλοῦ "until the Spirit comes upon you from on high").

[97] On the relationship between the close of Luke's first volume and the opening of his second, see Keener, *Acts*, 647–49.

narrative wherein he describes Jesus recreating his disciples. Thus, "John tells of one gift of the Spirit and Luke of another."[98]

There have been numerous attempts to reconcile the chronological and theological differences between John 20 and Acts 2. For most Pentecostals, the disciples were obviously regenerated in the former narrative and then subsequently received the "Baptism in the Holy Spirit" in the latter. Dunn does not interpretively combine these two narratives nor see a Johannine Pentecost; rather, he recognizes "two bestowals of the Spirit" in John's Gospel.[99] However, Dunn, followed closely by Turner, argues that what the first disciples experienced is "unique and unrepeatable."[100] Whether or not this argument has any merit is not important for my purposes here,[101] only that John presents two distinct dimensions of the gift of the Holy Spirit: one narrated and the other not. Viewed sequentially, John 20 and Acts 2 present an appealing Classical Pentecostal chronology[102]; however, the empowering dimension of the Spirit described in the O/FT and the Gospels prior to Pentecost poses serious challenges to such a successive configuration—especially when Luke reports in his first volume individuals *filled* with the Spirit with no reference to conversion, initiation, or regeneration. What becomes quite evident is that when it comes to the activity of the Spirit, the writers of Scripture do not present a uniform, formulaic pattern, and this is most clearly displayed in Luke and John.

All this said, Luke's depictions of the Spirit are not devoid of any soteriological aspects.[103] It seems quite clear that Luke, through the mouth of Peter, associates the gift of the Spirit with repentance and the forgiveness of sins in Acts 2:38 and this promise of the Spirit with being "*saved* (σῴζω) from this perverse generation"

[98] Leon Morris, *The Gospel According to John*, rev. ed. (Grand Rapids: Eerdmans, 1995), 748.

[99] Dunn, *Baptism*, 177.

[100] See Dunn, *Baptism*, 178–82; Turner, *Spirit*, 98–100.

[101] For critiques see, e.g., Ervin, *Conversion-Initiation*, 133–41; Keener, *John*, 2: 1198–1200 (Keener specifically addresses Turner's version); see also Atkinson, *Baptism*, 111–20.

[102] So, e.g., Ervin, *Conversion-Initiation*, 139–40.

[103] So, e.g., Macchia, *Baptized*, 68.

(vv. 39–40). Peter similarly describes the Spirit falling upon Gentiles in the Cornelius narrative (10:1–11:18). Peter associates the Gentiles' experience and John's Spirit-Baptized phrase (11:16) with conversion. Peter speaks words to Cornelius whereby he and his household would σωθήσῃ "be saved" (v. 14), and he explains how the Spirit fell upon these Gentiles as upon them at the beginning (v. 15) and how God gave them the same gift of the Spirit as they received on Pentecost (v. 17). The charismatic gifting of the Spirit on Cornelius and his household is direct evidence for Peter that "God therefore has also granted repentance for *life* (ζωή) to the Gentiles" (v. 18b). In his report to the Jerusalem council in 15:7–11, Peter repeats these same connections of the "giving of the Holy Spirit" (v. 8), τῇ πίστει καθαρίσας τὰς καρδίας αὐτῶν "by faith cleansing their hearts" (v. 9), and σωθῆναι "being saved" (v. 11).

In correlation to all this, it is the charismatic empowerment of the Spirit that gives Jesus' followers bold confidence to witness about the Good News (e.g., Acts 4:13; 13:46; 14:3; 18:26; 19:8; 26:26). In fact, Luke consistently shows how it is the Spirit who directs these disciples to proclaim the Gospel and thus actively initiates the salvation of future converts to Christ (e.g., Acts 8:29; 11:12; 13:2). Thus, while almost concentrating entirely on the gift of the Spirit for empowerment throughout his two-volume work, Luke understands and utilizes the Spirit-Baptized phrase with an eye on conversion-regeneration.

Paul Again

As I discussed above, Paul uses his version of the Spirit-Baptized phrase to refer to initiation-conversion. However, Paul places this phrase squarely within his larger and most comprehensive discussion on charismatic gifts (1 Corinthians 12–14). Thus, Paul literarily and directly connects his regenerative Spirit-Baptized description with the charismatic endowment of the Spirit while focusing on the prophetic gift (14:1, 3–4, 22, 24–25, 29–33, 39; see also

1 Thessalonians 5:19–20). Paul's larger point in these chapters (especially chapter 12) is that each person within the Body of Christ plays an equally vital and charismatic role for the building up of the whole because each one is used by the *one* Spirit, and Jesus Christ has baptized each individual ἐν this *same* Spirit. Importantly, Paul also describes the work of the *Holy* Spirit in a purification sense. In the very center of his discussion on charismatic gifting, he sets his now famous chapter on love. Although Paul does not explicitly describe the Spirit's role in this section, it is a natural conclusion that the work of this one Spirit also includes love. In fact, the gifts of the Spirit working without love are meaningless (13:1–2)! Significantly, Paul unites the Spirit with love explicitly in his letter to the Galatians as it is the first fruit (5:22). Expanding upon this, Paul commands his Ephesian readers "to be continually filled with the Spirit" (5:18), which enables them to exhort one another with songs, being thankful as well as living out the Gospel in relationship with others (5:19–6:9).[104] Paul then includes in the work of the Holy Spirit the purification of the believer (e.g., 1 Corinthians 6:11), which, for Paul, is a primary role of the Spirit within the Trinity (e.g., Romans 15:16; 2 Corinthians 3:15–18; 2 Thessalonians 2:13; see also 1 Peter 1:2).[105] Thus, while emphasizing the Spirit-Baptized experience as conversion-initiation, Paul also has in view the charismatic and transformative dimensions of the gift of the one Spirit.

Conclusion

From my investigation, the NT writers present multidimensional experiences of being baptized ἐν (*in/with*) the one Holy Spirit ἐν (*by*) the one Baptizer, Jesus Christ. To rehearse, in John's Gospel two

---

[104] I am assuming here that Paul wrote the Letter to the Ephesians. For a defense of this position, see Clinton E. Arnold, *Ephesians*, ZECS:NT (Grand Rapids: Zondervan, 2010), 46–50.

[105] See Hart, "Charismatic," 135–39.

distinct dimensions of the Spirit appear: regeneration and empowerment. John concentrates on narrating the former dimension and
linking it directly with the Spirit-Baptized phrase while narratively
including the other but never explicitly reporting the impact of this
dimension nor associating it with conversion. Luke clearly recognizes
the salvific dimension of the gift of the Spirit, but he uses the Spirit-
Baptized phrase in direct reference to empowerment for witness. Paul
follows along similar lines as John and explicitly identifies his Spirit-
Baptized phrase with conversion-initiation. Still, Paul associates the
gift of the Spirit with the dimension of charismatic empowerment as
well as transforming power. The typical Traditional position, as well
as Dunn and others, reads the Spirit-Baptized phrase through the
lens of Paul's central use of it, whereas Classical Pentecostals read the
phrase through the grid of Luke's emphasis, while some also propose
two Spirit-Baptizers. However, from my observations, each NT
writer uses the phrase to underscore his specific dimensional emphasis while assuming and/or touching upon the experiential reality of
additional aspects accented by the other authors. For me, these
distinct descriptions are not evidence that the NT writers conflict
with or contradict each other, but rather reflect the dynamic, sovereign, and mysterious activity of the Holy Spirit.

In the final analysis, believers are clearly baptized ἐν the Holy
Spirit at conversion in line with Paul's primary use of the Spirit-
Baptized phrase. Yet, converts should expect to be additionally
baptized ἐν the Holy Spirit for charismatic empowerment distinct
from regeneration following the primary Lukan use. Significantly,
from a biblical perspective, the typical and consistent dimension of
the Spirit has always been empowerment—often for prophecy—and
it is primarily Luke who follows along this charismatic continuum,
beginning with the opening pages of his Gospel. The distinct aspect
of this empowerment dimension is the pouring out of the Spirit
upon women, men, and children, Jew and Gentile, slave and free!
For Luke as well as the other NT writers, while also anticipated by
Moses and others in the writing the O/FT, it appears unthinkable

that this empowerment dimension could ever be considered a "dispensable extra" but rather embraced as an essential experience of being baptized ἐν the Holy Spirit. What emerges as truly unique, though, is the regeneration-conversion dimension of the gift of the Spirit envisioned by the O/FT prophets.

As I have attempted to demonstrate, *the Spirit-Baptized phrase in the NT governs a constellation of distinct dimensions and experiences in/with the one Holy Spirit poured out by the one Spirit-Baptizer, Jesus Christ.* These dimensional experiences of the one Holy Spirit include (1) initiation-conversion-regeneration, (2) charismatic empowerment, and (3) purification towards a transformed life. It is historically and theologically significant that these three dimensions reflect how the Church has traditionally understood the work of the Spirit. As already stated, the Traditional position has emphasized the regeneration dimension while Wesleyans have focused on sanctification identified as the "second blessing" or "second work of grace," with Pentecostals obviously emphasizing charismatic empowerment. For the first Pentecostals, this endowment was identified as a "third blessing" subsequent to conversion and sanctification.[106] Overall, the Classical Pentecostal expression "Baptism in the Holy Spirit" cannot *solely* refer to charismatic empowerment; nevertheless, the Spirit-Baptized phrase clearly refers to distinct charismatic empowerment experience(s) (Luke's emphasis). We Pentecostals must concede, though, that the phrase also identifies the conversion of the believer (Paul's emphasis). This *both/and*, rather than *either/or*, view of the Spirit-Baptized phrase derives from how I see the NT writers using the expression to encompass distinct dimensional experiences when the believer is baptized ἐν (*by*) Jesus Christ alone ἐν (*in/with*) the one Holy Spirit.

---

[106] See Veli-Matti Kärkkäinen, *Pneumatology* (Grand Rapids: Baker Academic, 2002), 87–90; Keener, *Gift*, 149–50.

2

Purity and Worship
Malachi's Message in the Gospel of Mark[1]
Jon Huntzinger

The Book of Malachi

MARK INTRODUCES HIS good news about Jesus Christ, the son of God, with a quote combining Malachi 3:1, Exodus 23:20, and Isaiah 40:3:

> "Behold, I send my messenger before your face,
>   who will prepare your way,
> the voice of one crying in the wilderness;
>   'Prepare the way of the Lord, make his paths straight'"
> (Mark 1:2–3 ESV).

From Isaiah, he develops the theme of Jesus on the way to the temple and the cross, and from Exodus he shows the significance of the wilderness for understanding Jesus' ministry.[2] Rather than looking at

---

[1] I have observed both purity and worship in Jack Hayford's life and ministry over 30 years at The Church On the Way and at The King's University.

[2] Regarding Isaiah, see Rikki E. Watts, *Isaiah's New Exodus in Mark*. WUNT 2/88 (Tübingen: Mohr Siebeck, 1997), and Joel Marcus, *The Way of the Lord: Christological Exegesis of the Old Testament in the Gospel of Mark* (Louisville: Westminster John Knox, 1992). Regarding Exodus, see Ulrich Mauser, *Christ in the Wilderness: The Wilderness Theme in the Second Gospel and Its Basis in the Biblical Tradition*. SBT 39 (London: SCM Press, 1963). Also, Timothy C. Gray, *The Temple in the Gospel of Mark: A Study in Its Narrative Role* (Grand Rapids: Baker Academic, 2008).

the importance of Isaiah or Exodus for Mark, however, this essay builds upon studies that see Malachi and its message as informative for understanding his portrait of Jesus.[3]

The Post-Exilic Background of Malachi

The book of Malachi is dated to the early/mid-fifth century BCE during the reign of Xerxes (486–465 BCE). At that time, Xerxes slashed government funding from what it had been under the previous king (Darius). These reductions included building and renovation projects throughout the Persian realm, such as the refurbishment of the temple in Jerusalem. The burden for these expenses shifted responsibility to local peoples. "The temple during Xerxes' time existed as an institution without support from the imperial powers. Religion became much more of a voluntary part of a pluralistic lifestyle within a huge and diverse empire."[4]

In view of the reduction in funding for the temple, Malachi portrays a people who struggle with disappointment, a disappointment foreshadowed by Haggai when he comments on the dismay of many in the refurbished temple during his time (520 BCE): "Who is left among you who saw this house [the temple] in its former glory? How do you see it now? Is it not as nothing in your eyes?" (Haggai 2:3 ESV).

---

[3] For example, Richard Hicks, "Markan Discipleship According to Malachi," *JBL* 132/1, 179–199, where he studies the "broader intertextual relationship between Malachi 3 and Mark 10:17–22" (181). In the conclusion to his article, Hicks recognizes the overall influence of Malachi on Mark when he writes, "The Gospel of Mark characterizes Jesus in terms of the Lord in Malachi, who recognizes unfaithfulness on the way to the temple." (195).

[4] Jon L. Berquist, *Judaism in Persia's Shadow: A Social and Historical Approach* (Minneapolis: Fortress Press, 1995), 87.

Malachi's Message

Malachi addresses a disenchanted Judah coming to terms with a new financial reality and dubious of the words they had received from prophets like Malachi. In their flagging faith, priests and people had begun to question those words.[5] Thus, to God's affirmation of love, they ask, "How have you loved us?" To God's assertion of being despised and polluted, they demand, "How have we despised your name?… How have we polluted you?" To God's complaint of weariness, they frown, "How have we wearied you?" To God's claim of being robbed, both priests and people retort, "How have we robbed you?" And to God's insistence that they persistently contradict Him, they say with remarkable irony, "How have we spoken against you?" (1:2; 1:6–7; 2:17; 3:8; 3:13)[6]

Not only have priests and people grown cynical toward God's words, but they have become complacent in their worship of Him as well. As Judah thought back to Solomon's temple and its renowned glory and at the same time thought forward to the glorious temple envisioned by Ezekiel, they saw in the present temple a symbol of inglorious failure. Rather than responding to their present social and economic situation by giving the best of their flocks as required by the law (Leviticus 22:17–25) and filling up the treasury of the temple with their tithes,[7] those with sufficient means are content to give blind, lame, and sick animals for sacrifice instead and to withhold their gifts from

---

[5] Both priests and people are culpable in Malachi's estimation. "The laity who withhold funds and goods from the temple worship receive the same harshness of condemnation as the priests. The laity become the objects of Malachi's wrath because of their bringing inadequate animals to the temple; the temple priests receive the same derision because of their willingness to offer such animals in the worship service" (Berquist, 96).

[6] "This disputational form allows for the depiction of social debate not only through the content of the prophecies but through the medium as well" (Berquist, 94). The questions highlight the tension between the priests and people and God.

[7] Without financial support from Xerxes, responsibility for maintaining the worship at the temple fell to the people. "Now the temple had to collect its own funds, and voluntarism was the only plausible means" (Berquist, 101).

the storehouse (1:6–8; 3:8).[8] From Malachi's perspective, the primary issue is that the people no longer fear God ("Where is my honor, where is my fear?" God laments [1:6]), and, because they no longer fear Him, they no longer worship Him by giving what the law requires.[9]

Malachi believes that the consequences of such failed worship are far-reaching. Because the people are giving, and the priests are accepting, impure sacrifices in the form of blind, lame, and sick animals, God's name is not honored among the nations. If God's own people will not lift His name in worship by giving pure sacrifices, the nations have no example to do so either.

God's response to this current state of worship is recorded by Malachi in the passage Mark quotes at the beginning of his Gospel. In it God declares that He himself will suddenly appear at the temple to the "sons of Levi" like "refiner's fire" and "fuller's soap" to refine and purify them to "bring offerings in righteousness to the Lord" (3:1–4). God promises to be present to His people and enable them to worship Him once again with their sacrifices and offerings. The result of this intervention, Malachi observes, is that the nations will call Judah "blessed" and, in that way, lift the name of the Lord in worship (3:12).

The Influence of Malachi on Mark

When Mark quotes from Malachi at the beginning of his Gospel, he does so with full knowledge of the prophet's message, even though he does not quote him elsewhere. Richard Hicks remarks, "[Malachi] would not have to be cited explicitly to be programmatic for Mark."[10] Mark's Gospel shows awareness of (1) the skeptical and questioning

---

[8] Based on his reading of the Hebrew text in Malachi 1:10, Jonathan Klawans argues that the sacrifices are rejected because they represented "no cost" to the worshippers (*Purity, Sacrifice, and the Temple: Symbolism and Supersessionism in the Study of Ancient Judaism* [Oxford: Oxford University Press, 2006], 87).

[9] Berquist writes, "The key issue throughout this unit [Malachi 1:1–2:9] is the opportunity to restore proper worship and the character of the community that engages in such worship.... [The] issue is at root one of respect" (95).

[10] Hicks, 186.

nature of the people's interaction with their God; (2) the inadequacy of the worship they were giving to Him at that time and the need for them to be purified so they could, indeed, give pure worship; (3) God's promise to appear suddenly at His temple to renew the worship given there; and (4) God's ultimate ambition to see His name feared among His people and lifted high before the nations. Mark draws all these themes together in his unique depiction of Jesus.

Questioning Jesus

Questions from Religious Leaders

The narrative of Mark is filled with questions that religious leaders and others ask of Jesus in the same way the narrative of Malachi is framed by the disputations between priests/people and God. Many of these questions reveal an undertow of disbelief in and rejection of Jesus' teaching and ministry[11] not unlike the critical attitude toward God's words by the people of Judah at the time of Malachi. Mark shows that the religious leaders of the people, scribes and Pharisees particularly, are nonplussed by Jesus' teaching and behavior.

Jesus' behavior is perplexing to many leaders. When he eats with tax-collecting Levi, "the scribes of the Pharisees" wonder, "Why does he eat with tax collectors and sinners?" (2:16). They do not understand why Jesus would defile himself by sharing table fellowship with such people. Not only does Jesus eat with sinners, but his disciples do not wash their hands before meals. The same scribes and Pharisees do not understand the neglect of this practice: "Why do your disciples not walk after the tradition of the elders, but eat with defiled hands?" (7:5). As if this were not enough, Jesus and his disciples do not fast

---

[11] The nature of the dispute that existed between Jesus and religious leaders as plotted by Mark is discussed by Jack Dean Kingsbury in *Conflict in Mark: Jesus, Authorities, Disciples* (Minneapolis: Fortress Press, 1989). He summarizes, "The force driving the story forward is the element of conflict" (28).

as others do. This leads people to ask, "Why do John's disciples and the disciples of the Pharisees fast, but your disciples do not fast?" (2:18). Particularly disturbing, however, is the fact that Jesus allows his disciples to eat the heads of grain on the Sabbath. This excites Pharisees to insist, "Why are they doing what is not lawful on the Sabbath?" (2:24). Finally, when Jesus overturns tables in the temple, chief priests demand, "By what authority are you doing these things?" (11:28). And, with this disturbance fresh in his mind, the high priest orders Jesus to answer, "Are you the Christ, the Son of the Blessed?" apprehensive of the answer he fears he might hear (14:61).

Jesus' teaching is equally troubling. Mark reports the story of a lame man brought to Jesus for healing. When Jesus sees the man, he pronounces forgiveness for his sins, causing the scribes who are present to ask themselves, "Who can forgive sins but God alone?" (2:7). They clearly reject Jesus' right to make such a pronouncement. Mark goes on to record several encounters in which pointed questions are posed to Jesus on matters concerning the law: "Is it lawful for a man to divorce his wife?" (10:2) "Is it lawful to pay taxes to Caesar?" (12:14). "Whose wife will she [a woman married seven times] be?" (12:23).

The questions posed to Jesus by scribes, Pharisees, and temple authorities reflect deep concerns about defiling behavior, improper interpretation of the law, illegitimate authority, and blasphemy. In their view, Jesus has become unclean by eating with people who are unclean; he and his disciples are so indifferent to the traditions of the people that they are in violation of the law of Moses; he assumes a right to forgive that does not belong to him; and, most egregiously, he has interfered with worship at the temple.

Questions from Townspeople

Not only do religious leaders show their opposition to Jesus in the questions they ask of him but also those who are closest to Jesus do the same. The disciples accuse Jesus of ignoring their danger when a storm threatens to sink their boat. They wake him from his sleep and shout, "Teacher, do you not care that we are perishing?" (4:38). And when Jesus tells them to give the crowd something to eat, they respond with incredulity, "Shall we go and buy two hundred denarii worth of bread and give it to them to eat?" (6:37). Family and friends resist Jesus when he returns to Nazareth and ask suspiciously, "Where did this man get these things? What is the wisdom given to him? How are such mighty works done by his hands?" (6:2). So great is their doubt concerning this carpenter and son of Mary that he cannot perform many works among them (6:5).

All these questions concerning Jesus' behavior and teaching reflect resistance that religious leaders and others have toward his authority and judgment. By advancing his narrative through such questions, Mark shows awareness of the debate recorded by Malachi and casts Jesus' ministry in a similar light. Just as priests and people doubted God's words to them through prophets like Malachi, so also scribes, Pharisees, family, and friends respond with cynicism to Jesus' own words and ministry. That Mark intentionally frames Jesus' ministry in this way is seen in the special note he adds to the conclusion to his narrative about the scribe who questions Jesus over the greatest commandment: "After that no one dared to ask him any more questions" (12:34).[12]

Purifying for Worship

Purity and impurity codes at the time of Jesus essentially represented boundaries.[13] These boundaries helped the people define the world in

---

[12] The scribe's question does not indicate any doubt on his part. The only questions that remain will be asked by the high priest and by Pontius Pilate who probes Jesus' mindset when he asks, "Are you the king of the Jews?" (15:2).

[13] Colin Brown writes, "Mark's Jesus repeatedly appears to cross the boundaries of purity." He says that whereas the Pharisees practiced "defensive" purity by protecting themselves from that which was impure, Mark's Jesus engages in "offensive" purity by "[making] the impure pure." "The Jesus of Mark's Gospel" in *Jesus Then & Now: Images of Jesus in History and Christology*, eds. Marvin Meyer and Charles Hughes (Harrisburg, PA: Trinity Press International, 2001), 26–27. The point to be noted is that both Jesus and the Pharisees

which they lived as well as determine their place in it. Such codes identified what was proper or improper behavior for people at specific times and in specific places. There was life and blessing associated with purity; and death, weakness, and loss associated with impurity.[14]

Not only did these codes establish the boundaries in which people lived, but also they prescribed the people's worship at the temple. Jonathan Klawans states, "In Leviticus, it becomes clear that ritual purity is the prerequisite for those who would come to the sanctuary to offer sacrifices, for those priests who regularly officiate at sacrifices, and for any animals that are to be offered as sacrifices." He observes that "the two ritual structures of purity and sacrifice are virtually inseparable."[15]

Mark begins his narrative of Jesus' ministry of purity with the descent of the Spirit at the Jordan and proceeds to dramatize that ministry as a fulfillment of John the Baptist's prophecy of one who would come later and "baptize with the Holy Spirit." Just as John baptized with water for the forgiveness of sins, so also Jesus is presented by Mark as baptizing with the Spirit for purification for worship.[16] This correlates with Malachi's prophecy that the Lord would refine and wash with fuller's soap the sons of Levi so they might give righteous offerings to Him (3:2–3).[17]

upheld purity boundaries, though they had different was of understanding and responding to those boundaries.

[14] See Jerome Neyrey, "The Idea of Purity in Mark's Gospel," *Semeia* 35 (1986). Neyrey writes, "Ancient Israel had a keen sense of purity and pollution" (93), so much so that the land was divided into spheres of holiness with the temple at the center (95). Likewise, society was divided into groups of people who were permitted into those different spheres. He writes, "Geography replicates social structure" (97), and identifies tax collectors, prostitutes, lepers, menstruating women, and blind and lame people on the very margins of purity. "One can and should know one's place in the purity system at all times" (98).

[15] Klawans, 4.

[16] Brown observes, "Mark intends us to understand that the prophecy ["he will baptize you with the Holy Spirit" (1:8)] was fulfilled in the activity of Jesus" (28). He continues, "Baptism is a rite of purification and consecration. The activities of Mark's Jesus were directed at the purification and consecration of Israel through 'baptism' with the Holy Spirit" (29; also 32).

[17] Mark does not describe Jesus' baptism as occurring by the Spirit and fire as do Matthew (3:11) and Luke (3:16), which we might expect if he were drawing on Malachi who says the

Purity for Worship

Mark draws attention to the purifying ministry of Jesus in the stories he narrates. In the first story, Jesus delivers a man from a spirit in the synagogue on the Sabbath. Mark's emphasis on the unclean nature of the spirit is evident by the fact he identifies the man as one *with an unclean spirit (en pneumati akatharto)*.[18] Moreover, Mark reports that the spirit responds to Jesus as "the holy one of God" and, thus, distinguishes him from all that is common and unclean (1:21–26). By making this story the first act of Jesus' ministry, Mark signals its descriptive function for his understanding of Jesus. Jerome Neyrey writes, "The exorcism is Jesus' first public action, and so can be considered programmatic for Mark's presentation of him."[19]

Mark follows this story with one in which Jesus heals a leper of his disease. It is significant that the leper does not ask Jesus to heal him but to cleanse him: "If you will, you can make me clean" (*dunasai me katharisai*). Jesus touches the man, declares him to be clean, and orders that he go to the priests for their pronouncement of purity: "Go, show yourself to the priest and offer for your cleansing (*tou katharismou sou*) what Moses commanded" (1:40–44).

In the following story, Jesus declares the sins of a lame man

---

Lord will come like a "refiner's fire" (3:2), as is being argued here. Brown answers, "Prophecy rarely has the exact, literal fulfillment. Subsequent reality modifies and defines the way in which it is fulfilled. Mark omitted the words 'and fire' because he saw *the primary fulfillment* of the prophecy in Jesus' endeavor to purify and renew the people of Israel" (31–32, his emphasis). Ulrich Mauser writes, "Fire is a symbol of judgment and the Spirit can well be understood in the same way. It is striking that Mark ... preserves no allusion to the judging function of the Lord.... The Spirit in Mark is consistently understood as the agent of purification.... Baptism with Holy Spirit is, therefore, to be regarded as the process of purification which begins with the ministry of Jesus (1.14), reveals its most obvious manifestation in the exorcisms of Jesus (3:29), and comes to its head in his death" (90–91).

[18] "While the normal term for the Satanic powers which possess humans is 'demons,' Mark insists on calling them 'unclean spirits' (1:23, 26–27; 3:11; 5:2, 8, 13; 6:7; 7:25; 9:25)" (Neyrey, 111).

[19] Neyrey, 106.

forgiven, which Colin Brown says is "another aspect of cleansing."[20] The friends have brought the man to Jesus to have his strength restored, not to have his sins forgiven. Yet, Jesus pronounces cleansing from sin which, in his estimation, is the man's greater need so that he might be restored in his relationship with God (2:1–12).

In these stories, Jesus cleanses three Jewish men and restores them in their ability to worship. The man in the synagogue is delivered from an unclean spirit and freed to participate in the synagogue service without hindrance; the leper is cleansed and freed to participate in worship at the temple; and the lame man is forgiven of sinful impurity and freed to live in a worshipful relationship with God. Mark's point is not to show that each man engages in worship at the synagogue or the temple or with God in some personal way, but to show that they have been cleansed and the possibility exists for them to do so.

Extreme Purity

After recounting these initial stories of purification, Mark presents three others that feature people outside the circle of male Jewish life—a Gentile man, an unclean Jewish woman, and a young Jewish girl—to show the continuation of Jesus' ministry of purity to a wider sphere. The first of these depicts a man whose condition is the epitome of impurity. The unnamed man lives in "the country of the Gerasenes . . . among the tombs." Mark describes him as having an unclean spirit (*pneumatic akatharto*) with the name "legion." When Jesus exerts his authority to expel the demons, they beg to be sent into a nearby herd of pigs. The entire story highlights the man's utterly unclean condition. He is a Gentile afflicted by unclean spirits, living among tombs near an area where pigs are raised. Mark shows that this man lives in a state of utter impurity and Jesus' ministry to him is an example of extreme purification.[21]

---

[20] Brown, 33.

[21] Mark specifically depicts the man's deliverance in a way that recalls the deliverance of the Israelites in Egypt when God brought them out of bondage and cleansed them for

Mark follows this story with one about the healing and cleansing of a chronically sick woman and a recently deceased girl.[22] The woman has suffered with a flow of blood for twelve years and, according to the standard of Leviticus (15:25–30), has been unclean all that time, isolated from her community (Numbers 5:1–4) and prohibited from worshipping with others at the temple (12:4). By touching Jesus' garment, her long ordeal of impurity ends, and she is made whole.

Mark also tells of a young girl who dies from an unspecified ailment. Even after hearing news of the girl's death, Jesus goes to the child, takes her by the hand, and raises her. In that death was regarded as the most conclusive manifestation of impurity, the girl's restoration is a profound example of purification. Neyrey states, "Death is the ultimate sign of the power of sin and Satan. It means irrevocable uncleanness."[23] By being restored to life, the girl is wrested from the realm of death's impurity to life's purity.

In these three stories, Mark describes people on the far verges of community life because of extreme impurity restored to their communities. Not only is each one made pure through Jesus' ministry—the man is released from the realm of utmost depravity, the woman is released from a long life of impurity, and the young girl is released from the finality of death's impurity—but also each is restored to their community, making the community whole. The man returns to his people in the Decapolis (5:20), the woman goes

---

worship. Five points to note: The man lives among the tombs (pyramids); he cannot be bound and cuts himself (the Israelites were enslaved yet continued to grow in number and could not be controlled); Jesus struggles to expel the demons from him (Moses struggles with Pharaoh to release the people); Jesus sends the demons into the pigs that rush into the sea where they drown (Pharaoh and his soldiers rush into the Red Sea in pursuit of the Israelites and drown); and Jesus directs the man to tell others of God's mercy (the Song of Moses in Exodus 15 describes the deliverance as an act of God's mercy).

[22] Mark's use of intercalation (placing one story inside another) in these two purity stories balances that of the demoniac, which represents, as noted above, an example of extreme impurity.

[23] Neyrey, 114.

"in wholeness" with others (5:34), and the girl is restored to her family.

Purity of Heart, God's Heart, and Jesus' Pure Offerings

Mark includes further accounts of purification. One involves a Syrian woman from the region of Tyre and Sidon, who approaches Jesus on behalf of her demon-afflicted daughter. Jesus' response to her is unsettling: "It is not right to take the children's bread and throw it to the dogs" (7:27). Why would he reply to the woman in this way and compare her and her daughter to dogs that were regarded as unclean animals? The answer is that Jesus is testing her to see how she responds so he can determine the attitude of her heart. Mark recounts this exchange after summarizing Jesus' teaching in the previous passage about the nature of impurity. There Jesus says, "What comes out of a person is what defiles him. For from within, out of the heart of man, [comes defiling behavior]" (7:20–21). The response of the Gentile woman, "Yes, Lord, yet even the dogs under the table eat the children's crumbs" (7:28) shows that her heart is pure by the words she speaks to Jesus. There is nothing she can do about the boundaries that would exclude her as unclean, but her response to Jesus shows that she is pure of heart.

This story of a mother who approaches Jesus for her daughter is followed by another in which a father brings his mute son to the disciples for deliverance (9:14–29). Not only does Mark describe the boy as mute, but also he says he has an unclean spirit. That he is mute means he cannot speak and, thus, cannot read the Scriptures aloud or give vocal praise to God. The unclean spirit is preventing the boy from sharing in basic worship. In fact, by throwing him to the ground, the spirit forces him to engage in a parody of true worship. In recounting this story, Mark compares the father's attitude with that of the mother described above. "Help my unbelief," he says, by which Mark means to show that he desires the type of faith/heart the Syrian woman possesses. With these two stories, Mark shows the importance of a pure heart for deliverance and worship.

Before either of these two stories, Mark reports the healing of two lame men. Both would have been regarded as impure and unqualified to give offerings because of their condition. In the first, Jesus strengthens the man's legs so he can walk as a sign of forgiveness (2:1–12). In the second, Jesus strengthens a "withered hand" as a sign of God's desire to do good and make the man whole (3:1–6). With these two stories Mark shows that God's desire—His heart—is to forgive and to do good for His people.

It is also God's desire for His people to understand His ways and know Him, which is why Mark reports two blind men who have their sight restored by Jesus (8:22–26; 10:46–52). As in the case of lame people, blind people were regarded as impaired and unqualified to give offerings to God. Jesus rubs spit over the eyes of the man from Bethsaida to renew his sight and then gives sight to Blind Bartimaeus when he comes running/stumbling to him. By restoring the sight of these two men, Jesus makes it possible for them to worship God with new understanding.

Through the stories of the desperate Syrian mother and distressed Jewish father, Mark highlights the role of the heart (faith) in deliverance and restoration. In the stories of the lame men, Mark shows that God's heart is to forgive and restore people so they might be strengthened in their relationship with Him and enabled to worship in purity. And, in the stories of the blind men, Mark makes it clear that God opens eyes, which is a sign of understanding, so people might know who He is and what He is doing through His son Jesus and, thereby, worship with that knowledge. Moreover, given Mark's knowledge of Malachi, who complains about the blind and lame sacrifices that are being given to God, it is apparent that he sees the healing of the lame and blind men as examples of pure offerings that Jesus himself is giving to his Father through his ministry.

Robbing God and Purifying the Temple

A significant way that Mark draws upon Malachi in his depiction of purity and worship is his account of Jesus in the temple. Though most scholars object to the description of Jesus' action in the temple as a cleansing,[24] it seems apposite based on Mark's overall depiction of Jesus' ministry as one of cleansing and purification.[25] Much has been written about Jesus' actions and most scholars agree that it is unlikely Jesus objected to the practical business provided by money changers and vendors. Nonetheless, it is evident from Mark's account that something disturbed him.[26]

Jesus accuses the priests of turning the temple into a den of robbers.[27] In addition to recalling Isaiah and Jeremiah, his remarks

[24] Hans Dieter Betz, "Jesus and the Purity of the Temple (Mark 11:15–18): A Comparative Religion Approach," *JBL* 116/3 (1997): 459. Klawans objects to the notion of cleansing by saying, "The term is … inappropriate, for it implies that something practical was achieved by Jesus' act, that some filth was cleansed or some sin purged" (224). Garland, too, "As the fig tree is not cleansed but cursed, so the temple is not cleansed but, in effect, cursed by a prophetic gesture that betokens God's wrathful displeasure." *A Theology of Mark's Gospel: Good News about Jesus the Messiah, the Son of God* (Grand Rapids: Zondervan, 2015), 489–490. Timothy Gray argues that Jesus' action should be interpreted as a condemnation of the temple for its failure to serve the nations: "Mark does not intend to portray Jesus' demonstration simply as a social protest but rather as a prophetic gesture foretelling the eschatological end of the temple" (29). My support for *cleansing* is based on considerations related to Mark's overall presentation of Jesus' ministry as one of purification and restoration. What is being prophetically acted out by Jesus is the removal of obstacles to Gentile worship in the outer courts of the temple.

[25] Brown offers, "Jesus' action in the temple appears as the climatic act of his program of purification…. Jesus' action in the Temple could be described as *the baptism of the Temple*" (39, his emphasis).

[26] Klawans surveys different possibilities for Jesus' actions at the temple (225–241). His own view is that Jesus was upset by the tax burden that had been placed upon the poor to pay for their own offerings or those of the community, and, thus, he drove out those who were directly involved in this imposition (238–239). See Garland's summary and response to the various interpretations of Jesus' actions (485–496), which he views as prophetic of a "new means of atonement" (490). Also, William Domeris, "The enigma of Jesus' temple intervention: Four essential keys," *Hervormde Teologiese Studies* 71.1 (2015), 1–8.

[27] Gray contends that Mark's focus here is on the temple and not temple leadership: "The target of [Jesus'] teaching, just as with [his] actions, is the temple itself. Too often, because of

reprise Malachi[28] where the prophet accuses the priests and people of robbing God by failing to bring tithes to the temple and, as a result, depriving themselves of His blessing of the opened windows of heaven and depriving the nations of a testimony to His generosity and faithfulness. By reporting Jesus' words, "Is it not written, 'My house shall be called a house of prayer for all the nations'? But you have made it a den of robbers" (11:17 ESV),[29] Mark draws attention to this very issue. In his view, the presence of money changers and vendors in the outer courts of the temple interfered with the worship by Gentiles.[30] The concern for Mark, as it was for Malachi, is that the nations be given a testimony by Israel of their God and the opportunity to know and worship Him. Both Malachi and Mark saw imposing obstacles to this worship. For the prophet, the people were not giving their best offerings to God and, thus, were unable to testify to the nations of His great provision; for the evangelist, the efficiency of temple ministry outweighed worship considerations and compelled Jesus to demonstrate against it. In Jesus' mind, temple leaders were robbing God of the worship He wanted to have from them and from the nations at His temple. Mark shows that Jesus acts against those things that interfere with such worship, even as he has previously acted to expel unclean spirits from people so that they might be free to worship God without hindrance.

---

the culpability of the temple establishment, interpreters focus on the Jewish leadership and miss the thrust of the narrative—the corruption and self-serving leadership is poignantly judged by bringing the temple institution to an end" (34). Nonetheless, following Malachi, I believe Mark shows Jesus addressing the practices of leadership and not the ritual of the temple itself.

[28] While Gray notes the connection that Mark makes with Malachi in this passage, he draws a different conclusion than the one in this essay. "For Malachi warns about the Lord's coming to the temple (Mal 3:2) as he will come in judgment (3:5), a judgment particularly focused upon the priests (3:3). The charge against them is that they are robbing God (Mal 3:8–9), a charge that resonates with the accusations Jesus will make against the temple authorities" (44). He sees Malachi's reference to God's appearance at the temple in terms of judgment, while I see it in terms of purification.

[29] Of the Gospel writers, Mark is the only one to include the phrase "for all nations" (Gray, 33).

[30] Garland disagrees based on the Herodian expansion of the temple (488).

The Urgency of the Spirit

Mark not only draws on Malachi to show Jesus' ministry as one of purity of worship but also to show it as one of urgency. He takes Malachi's declaration that the Lord "will suddenly (LXX *exaiphnes*) come to his temple" to refine and wash the sons of Levi (3:1–3)[31] and applies the prophecy to Jesus' own ministry.

After receiving the Spirit, Jesus is compelled (*ekballo*) into the wilderness only to return with a message about the immanence of the kingdom of God: "The time is fulfilled and the kingdom of God is at hand" (1:15). Mark highlights the dramatic nature of Jesus' ministry by using the word *immediately* (*euthys*) more than 40 times.[32] Though Mark does not say that Jesus went immediately to Jerusalem and the temple, the fact that everything he does or is done to him is done promptly or rapidly infuses the narrative with a sense of urgency.[33] Thus, Jesus sees the heavens opened to him as

---

[31] Though *exaiphnes* is generally used in the context of judgment, Malachi uses it to emphasize the urgency God feels over the unclean condition of the people. David Daube observes that when the Lord's presence is described as occurring suddenly, some experience it as judgment but others experience it as blessing. "The ambiguity to which we have repeatedly adverted [that suddenly points to judgment and blessing] is not absent [in Malachi's use]: the judgment, 'sudden' and terrible as it is for the haughty sinners, will at the same time vindicate those oppressed by them, the fatherless, the widows, the strangers." *The Sudden in the Scriptures* (Leiden: E.J. Brill, 1964), 5.

[32] Daube, 46. It is true that Mark chooses *euthys* rather than *exaiphnes* to describe the imperative nature of Jesus' ministry; nonetheless he uses *exaiphnes* when he reports Jesus' Olivet Discourse (13:36). There Jesus exhorts the disciples to stay awake and watch for the coming of the Son of Man: "Concerning that day or that hour, [of the coming of the Son of Man] no one knows.... Therefore stay awake ... lest he come suddenly and find you asleep" (13:32–36 ESV). Likely, Mark wants the reader to connect these remarks with the failure of the disciples to remain awake in the Garden of Gethsemane that he reports in the following passage. He sees Jesus' exhortation to the disciples to remain awake for the soon coming of the Son of Man to be realized in the events of his passion. Brown states: "Some of the phenomena described in Mark 13 occur already in Mark 14–16" (40).

[33] Though Daube argues that *euthys* in Mark sometimes means less than "at once," nonetheless "in not a few texts the literal force of 'at once' is clear. . . . Mark had a reason to choose

soon as he comes up out of the water at his baptism (1:10), and the Spirit then drives him into the wilderness without delay (1:12). After Jesus returns, he says that the time for the kingdom of God is at hand, meaning it is now present in Jesus himself (1:15). Then, upon entering the synagogue on the Sabbath, Jesus begins to teach and is interrupted right away by a man with an unclean spirit (1:23). When Jesus delivers the man, his fame goes out at once to the surrounding land (1:28).

Mark reports that all cases of deliverance and healing occur immediately. Jesus takes the hand of Peter's mother-in-law, and her fever leaves at that time (1:31);[34] he touches a leper, and the man is immediately cured (1:42); he commands the lame man to get up, and he does so right away (2:12). The woman with the issue of blood is healed the moment she touches Jesus' garment, and the little girl gets up from her deathbed instantly when Jesus takes her by the hand (5:29; 5:42). And Mark reports that Bartimaeus regains his sight as soon as Jesus speaks to him (10:52). What is unusual, in Mark's telling, is when a man or woman is not healed immediately. So, when Jesus struggles with Legion[35] or must pray twice for the blind man to gain his vision, it is apparent that Mark is drawing particular attention to that fact.

The rapid pacing of the narrative does slow once Jesus arrives in Jerusalem at the temple, after which time the events of his arrest, trial, and death are recounted in deliberate fashion.[36] Even so, Jesus is quickly arrested in the garden after praying to his Father (14:43), and as soon as Peter denies Jesus a second time, the rooster crows (14:72).

---

just this connecting particle where he did—the reason being that it does express the inevitable one-after-the-other succession of events, from the first temptation to the final delivering over to Pilate" (60).

[34] See Daube's note on the Greek text (49).

[35] "For [Jesus] *was saying* to him, 'Come out of the man, you unclean spirit'" (5:8 ESV, my emphasis; an iterative imperfect in my reading).

[36] Gray, 11.

Fearing Jesus and Worshipping God

A primary theme in Malachi is the fear of the Lord. The people display their lack of fear by presenting unworthy offerings to God, even as He desires to be revered by them and known to the nations. Malachi draws attention to this problem by having God ask, "Where is my fear?" (LXX *pou estin ho phobos mou;*) to indifferent people (1:6). He desires for His people to fear Him and hold Him in reverence so that He can be present to them and the nations will glorify His name (LXX *to onoma mou epiphanes en tois ethnesin*) (1:11–14; 3:16). He wants His people to be like Levi and keep a covenant of fear with Him (LXX *edoka auto en phobo phobeisthai me*) (2:5) because such a covenant offers blessing and healing in the light of the sun of righteousness (4:2).

The Fear of the People

Mark appraises the response of the people to the purifying ministry of Jesus as one of fear and amazement. Time and again the people marvel over Jesus' miracles: A ruler of the synagogue is "overcome with amazement" (*exestesan eksastasi megalen*) when his daughter is raised to life after being pronounced dead (5:42); when townsmen see a man formerly possessed by demons sitting with Jesus "in his right mind," they are "afraid" (*ephobethesan*) of what they see (5:15); and when Jesus heals a deaf man in the region of the Decapolis, enabling him to speak, the people "were astonished beyond measure" (*hyperperissos exeplessonto*) at the miracle (7:37).

Those closest to Jesus experience fear and amazement as well. The disciples are "filled with great fear" (*ephobethesan*) when Jesus speaks to the churning sea, causing it to calm (4:41). Mark's description of the event is ironic in that he does not describe the disciples as fearing the wind and waves, but he describes their fear in response to Jesus' power over the sea. Mark portrays Peter, James, and John as "terrified" (*ekphoboi*) when Jesus is transfigured before their eyes on the mountain (9:6), and he reports that the disciples are "amazed" at his teaching about the kingdom of God when he says, "How difficult it will be for those who have wealth to enter the kingdom of God!... It is easier for a camel to go through the eye of a needle than for a rich person to enter the kingdom of God" (10:23–26 ESV).[37]

The Fear of the Women

Mark concludes his Gospel by describing three women fleeing from the tomb in fear (*ephobounto*) of what they have heard and not seen (16:8).[38] Their behavior is best understood in view of Malachi, who brings his prophecy to a close by describing the Day of the Lord (4:1–3). For some, that day will be destructive like a hot oven that sets them ablaze while for others who fear God, it will be restorative like a warm day that causes them to go about leaping like calves: "But for you who fear my name, the sun of righteousness shall rise with healing in its wings. You shall go out leaping like calves from the stall" (4:2). Calves leap about when they're afraid. The fear described by Malachi, then, isn't one of resignation and dread but one of hope due to the relationship the people have with God. Mark's overall dependence on Malachi concludes when he describes the women fleeing from the tomb in fear. Their fear is not one of abject terror but of excited anticipation. Their fear is one of trembling and excitement (*tromos kai ekstatsis*). Like calves bounding, the women go bounding from the tomb with hope that exceeds their greatest dreams.[39]

Throughout the Gospel of Mark, people are amazed by Jesus' teaching and miracles. The disciples are filled with wonder at the calmed sea. The women are filled with expectation at the empty

---

[37] There are occasions when the people or the disciples are afraid for their lives, such as when Mark reports a young man running from the soldiers who have come to arrest Jesus (14:51–52).

[38] "The final irony is that death, the ultimate pollution, serves as the very source of purity for Jesus' followers" (Neyrey, 115).

[39] A note of appreciation to Joe Wainer (TKU alumnus and Foursquare Foundation CEO) for this insight gained from his experience on his family's Florida ranch.

tomb. Mark says they all experienced fear, by which he means reverence for and acknowledgement of the power of God manifested in Jesus' Spirit-enabled teaching and healing ministry. He means they experienced deep gratitude and hard-to-suppress excitement for the kingdom breaking into their midst through Jesus. He means appreciation for the mighty cleansing power exercised by Jesus to release people to worship God. Mark answers the question found in Malachi, "Where is my fear?" by showing that the fear of the Lord is everywhere Jesus ministers through the power of the Spirit. It is a fear that leads to the recognition of His name among the nations.

The Testimony of the Nations

In Malachi, God laments the lack of honor His people are giving Him. Not only is their behavior an affront to Him, but it is also a sad testimony to the nations about His worthiness to receive honor. Without an example to follow from God's own people, the peoples of the earth do not know how to lift His name in worship. However, if God's people will show honor to Him by giving their best offerings and filling the temple storehouse with their tithes, then the nations will notice and call them blessed. To do this is to acknowledge the power of God to bless them with abundance. It is a form of lifting God's name.

In Mark's Gospel, Jesus is depicted as moving quickly to purify God's people to give worship to Him. The response of amazement and fear to Jesus' teaching and ministry is proof that the Lord is present in their midst, and Mark is careful to show the response of the nations. The stories of the Gerasene man, the Syrophoenician woman, and the Roman centurion at the cross all portray the nations responding to the purifying work of God in Jesus. The man from Gerasa responds to his deliverance by declaring the mercy of God among the people of the Gentile Decapolis; the woman whose daughter is afflicted by a demon responds to Jesus with a word of faith; and the centurion upon seeing Jesus breathe his last breath declares, "This man was the son of God!" (5:19–20; 7:24–30; 15:39) In these three people who represent the nations—a man, a woman, and a Roman—the power of God is displayed in their lives, and the goodness of God is recognized in their own different ways.

Conclusion

This essay has outlined several ways that Mark drew upon Malachi's message in his Gospel. Just as the prophet depicts a priesthood and people who have come to doubt the words of God, so also Mark shows Jesus confronted by religious leaders and others who question his actions and teachings. While Malachi reports that God will appear suddenly at His temple to purify the sons of Levi so that righteous sacrifices will once again be offered, Mark shows that Jesus moves with readiness in his ministry to take away uncleanness from the people so they might be made whole in their lives and free to give worship to God. Not only are they freed to give worship to God, but in the cases of the lame and blind men, they themselves become pure offerings that Jesus offers his Father through his purifying ministry by the Spirit. Just so, Jesus moves quickly to the temple where he reacts to what he sees to be an obstacle to worship by the nations and prophetically cleanses the Gentile precincts. Finally, Malachi under-scores God's desire to be feared both by His people and by the nations. For this reason, Mark records the fear and amazement of people to Jesus' teaching, deliverance, and miracles throughout his Gospel, even as he makes a point to emphasize the fear of the women to Jesus' great victory of purity over death by concluding his Gospel in a dramatic and abrupt way. He concludes his Gospel by recording the women running in fear—not helpless and confused but in awe of the empty tomb and the harbinger of hope it promises. Not only this, but Mark also highlights the fear of the nations in the great work of God in Jesus through the words of a Roman soldier who, as a repre-sentative of those nations, says, "Truly, this man was the son of God."

Section Two

History

3

The Quiet Game, Racism, and the Azusa Street Revival[1]

Cecil M. Robeck, Jr.

SOME YEARS AGO, I picked up a mystery by Greg Iles titled *The Quiet Game*.[2] It is set in Natchez, Mississippi, and it revolves around the unsolved civil rights murder of a young black man killed in 1968. Everyone in Natchez *knows* who killed him. Everyone presumes that they know *why* he was killed. But no one is willing to dig into the facts or talk about his murder to the person intent upon solving it. It remains unsolved 40 years later because they refuse to talk; hence the title, *The Quiet Game*.

As I read this book, I found the following lines, and I wondered whether they might not also apply to us.

> This is a small town. In small towns there are sometimes truths that everyone knows but no one mentions. Open secrets, if you will. No one really wants to probe the details, because it forces us to face too many uncomfortable realities. We'd rather turn away than acknowledge the primitive forces working beneath the surface of society.[3]

---

[1] This is a shortened and slightly revised version of a plenary address given at the annual meeting of the Society for Pentecostal Studies in 2006. I offer it here in honor of Dr. Jack Hayford's efforts in racial reconciliation.

[2] Greg Iles, *The Quiet Game* (New York, NY: Signet, 1999).

[3] Iles, *The Quiet Game*, 358.

I believe that within the "small town" of American Pentecostalism we have some open secrets, uncomfortable realities, and primitive forces at work among us. I wonder whether many of us in the Pentecostal community have not been playing *The Quiet Game* for over a century. I wonder whether racism has not been an open secret since the time of the Azusa Street revival in Los Angeles.[4] We all *know* about it, and we have formed opinions about it based on our limited knowledge of that "event." We *know* the primary players. We *know* what went on in its services. We *know* about its impact. But I have come to realize that our knowledge of the subject has been extremely limited. In fact, I have wondered if we have not been afraid to plumb its depths because "Azusa Street" forces us to face our "uncomfortable realities." We'd rather turn away from a thorough analysis of the subject than to acknowledge the "primitive forces working beneath the surface" of our "small town."

I have been deeply troubled that it has taken us an entire century to come anywhere close to telling the story of "Azusa Street" in a way that takes seriously the social, political, spiritual, and ecclesial contexts in which it emerged.[5] I have also been astonished at our

---

[4] My original work, Cecil M. Robeck, Jr., *The Azusa Street Mission and Revival: The Birth of the Global Pentecostal Movement* (Nashville, TN: Nelson Reference & Electronic, 2006), was written for the average layperson. I have a much longer, fully documented work intended for the academic community nearing completion.

[5] Since 1925, Pentecostals have cited Frank Bartleman, *How Pentecost Came to Los Angeles: As It Was in the Beginning* (Los Angeles, CA: F. Bartleman, 1925) as the primary eyewitness of the Azusa Street Mission and revival. In 1981, Douglas J. Nelson completed a dissertation on the subject, "FOR SUCH A TIME AS THIS: The Story of Bishop William J. Seymour and the Azusa Street Revival, A Search for Pentecostal/Charismatic Roots," unpublished Ph.D. dissertation (Birmingham, England: Faculty of Arts, Department of Theology, University of Birmingham, 1981). More recently, Robert R. Owens, *Speak to the Rock: The Azusa Street Revival: Its Roots and Its Message* (Lanham, MD: University Press of America, 1998), and Larry Martin, *The Life and Ministry of William J. Seymour and a History of the Azusa Street Revival* The Complete Azusa Street Library CASL 1 (Joplin, MO: Christian Life Books, 1999) have attempted to fill gaps in our knowledge of the revival.

willingness to allow the story to be told so poorly for so long.[6]
The Pentecostal Movement has seldom given much credibility to
history. It is a restoration movement that has dismissed much of
the history of the Church as having little value. Our emphases have
been on what we read in the New Testament and what we experience today.

One of my concerns has been to determine the nature of the
relationship between Charles F. Parham, a white man, and the
revival to which he gave form, and William J. Seymour, a black
man, and the revival that made the Azusa Street Mission a global
household name. Through this, I have come to believe that the story
of "Azusa Street" is the story of our small town.

I have been astonished to find over a thousand new sources that
shed light on the Azusa Street revival. Almost all of these sources
have been available in libraries across the country for a century, yet
no historian, Pentecostal or otherwise, has taken the time to locate
or study them until now.[7] My question is, "Why is this so?" Could
it be that the "open secret" that we know as "Azusa Street" scares us
because we know that just below the surface lie "too many uncomfortable realities" and too many "primitive forces" that we would just as
soon forget? What is it about Azusa Street that seems to draw so many
of us to it as a kind of "Ur" event, a myth that helps to explain our
Pentecostal origins? What is it that keeps us from addressing the open
secrets that we find there?

I know that these are pointed and painful questions, but what
I have tried to do is to take a deeper look at this "open secret" that
we share, hoping that we can address the "uncomfortable realities"
and the "primitive forces" still at work beneath the surface of the
Pentecostal Movement. It is time to move past the simplistic "Azusa

---

[6] I am thinking of the many famous retellings of the events that allegedly surrounded the
Azusa Street revival, especially in our popular denominational magazines and in several very
popular books.

[7] The two exceptions to this are Douglas Nelson and Larry Martin. Both did considerable
groundbreaking work in locating sources.

myth." It is time for us to move beyond our fears and the anger that confronts us when we look at our origins.

Most of us know the basic storyline of Azusa Street, but for the sake of those who may be new to Pentecostalism or to this discussion, let me review a few of the basic facts. In December 1900, a white man, Charles Fox Parham, conducted a short-term Bible school in Topeka, Kansas, in which they discussed how the Apostles had "turned the world upside down."[8] They concluded that the Apostles had been baptized in the Holy Spirit. Their discussion regarding this baptism in the Spirit led to the conclusion that it was accompanied by what Parham called the "Bible evidence" of speaking in tongues observed in Acts 2:1–4. By January 1, 1901, a white woman named Agnes Ozman and then others in the class began to do just that. Charles Parham formed what he called the Apostolic Faith Movement, with him as its "Projector," and over the next half dozen years, he sought to expand his movement in Kansas, Missouri, Texas, and California.

In January 1906, at the encouragement of African American preacher Lucy W. Farrow, William Joseph Seymour (Farrow's associate)[9] enrolled in a short-term Bible school that Charles Parham was then conducting in Houston, Texas. Seymour accepted Parham's theory regarding baptism in the Spirit. Six weeks later, Seymour left Houston in response to an invitation to serve as pastor of a small Holiness Church in Los Angeles founded by an African American woman named Mrs. Julia Hutchins. Within days, Mrs. Hutchins decided that Seymour held a heretical view on the doctrine

---

[8] Parham's story is best told in James R. Goff, Jr., *Fields White unto Harvest: Charles F. Parham and the Missionary Origins of Pentecostalism* (Fayetteville, AR: The University of Arkansas Press, 1988), although one can still learn much from reading Sarah E. Parham, ed., *The Life of Charles F. Parham: Founder of the Apostolic Faith Movement* (Joplin, MO: Hunter Printing Co., *circa* 1930; Reprint New York, NY: Garland Publishing, 1985). The size of Parham's movement is still very much a question in need of documentation.

[9] Larry Martin, *The Life and Ministry of William J. Seymour and a History of the Azusa Street Revival*; Rufus G. W. Sanders, *William J. Seymour: Black Father of the Twentieth Century Pentecostal/Charismatic Movement* (Sandusky, OH: Alexandria Publications, 2001).

of baptism in the Holy Spirit, which she, like most Holiness people, equated with sanctification. Seymour was allowed to explain himself to the denomination's leaders. After being told that there was no room in the Holiness Church for his teachings, he was fired.

In the ensuing days, Seymour began a cottage prayer meeting, first at the home of Edward and Mattie Lee and then at the home of another African American couple, Richard and Ruth Asberry, at 214 North Bonnie Brae Street. On April 9, 1906, the Spirit fell on that small prayer meeting, and people began to speak and sing in other tongues. Within a week, they had leased the former home of First AME Church at 312 Azusa Street. On or about Easter Sunday, April 15, they began meetings there.

By April 18, 1906, the same day as the San Francisco earthquake, nine days after the initial outpouring of the Spirit at the Asberry home, and four days after the mission opened its doors, Seymour and his congregation were the subject of a *Los Angeles Daily Times* article titled "Weird Babel of Tongues."[10] As news of this new Apostolic Faith congregation on Azusa Street spread across the country and throughout the world, thousands of people came to see for themselves whether the reports of what God was doing in that church were true. That church became known popularly as the "Azusa Street Mission," and the services conducted there through 1909 were called the "Azusa Street Revival." From that mission, scores of evangelists, church planters, and missionaries departed, taking the message of Pentecost to the world in ways that were unprecedented.

We now know much more about the people who actually attended the meetings, and we have a relatively good estimate of the total numbers served by the mission in the three years of the revival. Several local newspapers repeatedly reported between 500 and 700 worshippers inside the building during services.[11] Others

---

[10] "Weird Babble of Tongues," *Los Angeles Daily Times*, April 18, 1906.

[11] "Rolling and Diving Fanatics 'Confess,'" *Los Angeles Daily Times*, June 23, 1906; "Religious Fanaticism Creates Wild Scenes," *Los Angeles Record*, July 14, 1906; "Women with Men Embrace," *Los Angeles Daily Times*, September 3, 1906.

reported large crowds of people standing outside the Mission's windows, trying to see and hear what was going on inside.[12] Many people worshipped on the ground floor, then made their way into other parts of the building throughout the day and well into the night, making Arthur Osterberg's estimate of 1500 people served there on any given Sunday a realistic possibility.[13] These facts suggest that for a time "Azusa Street" was the largest black church in Los Angeles.[14]

The Azusa Street Mission was very much like any other church in its political makeup. It had a stable congregation of roughly 200 voting members whose names we have, drawn from half a dozen different neighborhoods. We also know the names of over 500 people who attended the Mission during the critical years of 1906–1909. We know what many of them did for a living, and by looking at their neighborhoods and their occupations, we are much closer to evaluating their specific social and economic locations.[15] We know that the Mission had a statement of faith, held regular business meetings, and had an elected board of trustees, articles of incorporation, regularly scheduled services, a large staff including full and

---

[12] "Negroes at Revival Meeting Talk in Strange Tongues," *Los Angeles Examiner*, June 11, 1906.

[13] Arthur Osterberg, "I Was There," Full Gospel Business Men's Fellowship International: *Voice*, (May 1966): 18.

[14] G. R. Bryant, "Religious Life of Los Angeles Negroes," *Los Angeles Daily Times*, February 12, 1909. See Cecil M. Robeck, Jr., "The Azusa Street Mission and the Historic Black Churches: Two Worlds in Conflict in Los Angeles' African American Community," in Amos Yong and Estrelda Alexander, eds., *Afro-Pentecostalism: Black Pentecostal and Charismatic Christianity in History and Culture* (New York, NY: New York University Press, 2011), 21–41.

[15] Robert Mapes Anderson, *Vision of the Disinherited: The Making of American Pentecostalism* (New York, NY: Oxford University Press, 1979), 114–136 argues that early Pentecostals were among the disinherited. Grant Wacker, *Heaven Below: Early Pentecostals and American Culture* (Cambridge, MA: Harvard University Press, 2001), 208 has provided a much-needed corrective to this assumption. My work strongly supports Wacker's conclusions.

part time employees, and its own publication, *The Apostolic Faith* [Los Angeles, CA]. It even held a regular children's church.

It was common knowledge among the black leaders in Los Angeles that Pastor Seymour envisioned his church as a multiracial, multiethnic congregation from the time it came into existence.[16] That point, explicitly stated in the leading African American newspaper in Los Angeles, may put a very different slant on the way we read the rest of the texts we have. Frank Bartleman, for instance, mentions that the "colorline" was essentially meaningless at the Mission, but if you don't pay close attention to his ongoing narrative, you might be lulled into thinking that it was a dominantly white congregation led by a black man.[17] On the other hand, if you were to pay attention only to the local press, you could miss the fact that the mission was not simply a black church that some foolish white people attended.[18] And if these two sources were all you had, you could still miss the extent to which other ethnic groups were present, especially various kinds of Latinos.[19]

The Mission's newspaper, *The Apostolic Faith* [Los Angeles, CA], which had a circulation high of 50,000 copies per issue, accurately

---

[16] "Church Members Riot," *California Eagle*, January 5, 1931.

[17] Bartleman, *How Pentecost Came to Los Angeles*, 54.

[18] "Weird Babel of Tongues," *Los Angeles Daily Times*, April 18, 1906; "Negroes at Revival Meeting Talk in Strange Tongues," *Los Angeles Examiner*, June 11, 1906; "Women with Men Embrace," *Los Angeles Daily Times*, September 3, 1906.

[19] While little has been written about Latino involvement at the Azusa Street Mission to date, they were clearly present from the time the Mission opened its doors in April 1906. Cf. Manuel Gaxiola, *La Serpiente y La Paloma: Historia, Teología y Análisis de la Iglesia Apostólica de la Fe en Cristo Jesús (1914–1994)* (1970, Mexico City, Mexico: Libros PYROS, 2nd ed., revised and corrected, 1994), 117; Cecil M. Robeck, Jr., "Evangelization or Proselytism of Hispanics? A Pentecostal Perspective," *Journal of Hispanic/Latino Theology* 4:4 (1997): 42–64; Gastón Espinosa, "Borderland Religion: Los Angeles and the Origins of the Latino Pentecostal Movement in the U.S., Mexico, and Puerto Rico, 1900–1945," (unpublished PhD dissertation, University of California, Santa Barbara, 1999); Arlene M. Sánchez Walsh, *Latino Pentecostal Identity: Evangelical Faith, Self, and Society* (New York, NY: Columbia University Press, 2003), 12–13, 15–21.

reflected the Mission's earliest history as well as its racial and ethnic makeup when it announced,

> The work began among the colored people. God baptized several sanctified wash women with the Holy Ghost, who have been much used of Him. The first white woman to receive the Pentecost and gift of tongues in Los Angeles was Mrs. Evans who is now in the work in Oakland. Since then multitudes have come. God makes no difference in nationality, Ethiopians, Chinese, Indians, Mexicans, and other nationalities worship together.[20]

That same month, the paper made another announcement that can only be labeled an understatement.

> The secular papers have been stirred and published reports against the movement, but it has only resulted in drawing hungry souls who understand that the devil would not fight a thing unless God was in it. So they have come and found it was indeed the power of God.[21]

Secular reporters attended the Mission and then ridiculed its faithful. It was a free-for-all as reporters exploited euphemisms like "Holy Rollers," "Holy Kickers," "Holy Jumpers," "Holy Ghosters," and "Tangled Tonguers." Such bywords quickly caught the public's attention, inflamed their imagination, and, what ultimately counted, sold papers. They conjured up visions of freewheeling ecstasy, unbridled emotionalism, seething spirituality, jarring gymnastics, fanatical abandonment, and radical wildfire. More "sophisticated" worshippers labeled it general pandemonium or bedlam. The sweat-drenched passion of the "Holy Roller" worshippers was easily visualized, quickly given over to ridicule, and dismissed just as quickly

---

[20] "The Same Old Way," *The Apostolic Faith* [Los Angeles, CA] 1.1 (September 1906), 3.2.
[21] Untitled item, *The Apostolic Faith* [Los Angeles, CA] 1.1 (September 1906), 1.3.

because it held little more than cheap, vulgar, primitive entertainment value for the run of the mill observer.

From the first known article that introduced the Azusa Street Mission to the public, "Weird Babel of Tongues," with lurid subtitles that cautioned, "New Sect of Fanatics Is Breaking Loose," or gossiped, "Wild Scene Last Night on Azusa Street" and "Gurgle of Wordless Talk by a Sister," the die was cast.[22] Other titillating titles would follow. "Rolling and Diving Fanatics 'Confess,'" clamored the *Times* three months later.[23] "'Holy Kickers' Baffle Police," it barked. "Hold High Carnival in Azusa Street Until Midnight." "Authorities Put Stop to High Kicking Feats of Women but Have Not Been Able to Break Up Meetings." "Frenzied Woman Embraces Man on Street." These were the types of alluring subtitles that still grab the "inquiring minds" of tabloid readers today.[24]

The result of such reporting served several ends. For some, it pointed toward the ridiculous nature of such carryings on in the name of religion. From the perspective of the Mission, it demonstrated that the faithful were being persecuted for the sake of righteousness. At the same time, the Mission could not have paid for the amount of free advertising that it gave to their message.[25]

Another criticism high on the list that was constantly brought forward by the press came from the degree of interracial mixing that took place there. In recent years, a number of scholars have openly doubted Frank Bartleman when he noted that the color line had been "washed away in the blood" in the minds of the Azusa Street faithful or that the interracial character had been reproduced

---

[22] "Weird Babel of Tongues," *Los Angeles Daily Times*, April 18, 1906.

[23] "Rolling and Diving Fanatics 'Confess,'" *Los Angeles Daily Times*, June 23, 1906.

[24] "'Holy Kickers' Baffle Police," *Los Angeles Daily Times*, July 12, 1906.

[25] *The Apostolic Faith* [Los Angeles, CA] 1.1 (September 1906): 1.3; William F. Manley, "True Pentecostal Power, with Signs Following," *Household of God* 2.9 (September 1906): 7; Cf. *The Apostolic Faith* [Portland, OR] 2.15 (July–August 1908): 1–2; Cf. Nils Bloch-Hoell, *The Pentecostal Movement: Its Origin, Development, and Distinctive Character* (Oslo, Norway: Universitetsforlaget, 1964), 41.

anywhere else.[26] But local news reporters bear profound witness to the fact that the racial lines that were in place, even in progressive era Los Angeles, were no competition when placed next to the reality of racial mixing that was clearly evident at the Mission and in many other congregations that were products of, or heavily influenced by, the Mission in Los Angeles; for example, Long Beach, Portland, and Indianapolis. Indeed, many of the local news reports suggested that the familiarity among people of different races that they witnessed at these churches was nothing less than scandalous by society's standards.[27]

Urged on by the press, a number of public offices, such as the Los Angeles Police Department, the Humane Society responsible for child welfare, the Health Department, the City Prosecutor's Office, mayors and city councils in the local area, and members of the local judiciary all figured into the conflict. Many people were simply arrested, both inside and outside the Mission. Charges against them varied from "disturbing the peace" to being a "public nuisance" and from "child endangerment" to "interfering with a police officer in the conduct of his duty." More were arrested and jailed on charges of "insanity." Tensions ran high as people debated public policy and the limits of free speech and argued over the limits of religious freedom under the US Constitution.[28] For those of us who have been

---

[26] Edith Blumhofer has argued repeatedly that while the races mingled at the mission, "interracial acceptance was at best imperfect and soon broken," in the Azusa Street Revival. Edith Blumhofer, "Azusa Street revival," *The Christian Century* 123.5 (March 7, 2006): 21.

[27] "Small Boy Evangelist," *Daily Telegram* (Long Beach, CA), January 29, 1907; "Exhorters Arrested," *Daily Telegram*, February 18, 1907; "Judge Frazer Issues Ukase," *Evening Telegram*, January 3, 1907; "'Bride of the Lord' Now Has A Severe Cold," *Evening Telegram*, January 4, 1907; "Bluks Divide Home," *Indianapolis Star*, June 4, 1907; "Woman Sticks to Bluks; Husband Asks Divorce," *Indianapolis News*, June 5, 1907; "Police after Bluks," *Indianapolis Star*, June 11, 1907.

[28] "Head of Sect Is Disturber," *Pasadena Daily News*, July 13, 1906; "News Forum," *Whittier Daily News*, September 8, 1906; "Broken Arm Unattended," *Los Angeles Herald*, July 14, 1907; "Doctor Sets Child's Arm," *Los Angeles Herald*, July 15, 1907; "Rollers Neglect A Child," *Los Angeles Express*, August 20, 1907; "'Holy Roller' Girl Suffers from Serious Form of Fever," *Los Angeles Express*, August 23, 1907; "Only Prayers for Afflicted

CECIL M. ROBECK, JR. | 73

upwardly mobile, who have sought respectability while disguised as "evangelicals," these facts must surely be numbered among the "primitive forces" that give way to our "uncomfortable realities."

In its second issue, *The Apostolic Faith* [Los Angeles, CA] reported, "In California, where there has been no unity among churches, they are becoming one against this Pentecostal movement."[29] That is an extremely enigmatic sentence that says nothing about which churches were involved, what issues concerned them, or the intensity of the conflict. We now know the answers to these questions.

In April 1906, the pastors of 31 Protestant churches formed the Los Angeles Church Federation. Within three months, the churches that made up its membership locked horns with the Azusa Street Mission. They did their best to destabilize the Mission over two broad issues. The first revolved around the claims of the Mission's faithful to have new theological insight into the nature and purpose of baptism in the Spirit and the role it might play in the Christian life. In the second, the historic churches criticized the Mission for claiming to allow the Spirit to work outside of traditional structures and in more emotional ways, rendering the revival's participants vulnerable to charges of "fanaticism." The Reverend Edwin P. Ryland, President of the Federation and Pastor of Trinity Methodist Episcopal Church (South), attended the Azusa Street Mission in mid-July 1906. He stated succinctly to the local press that the meetings were marked by "enthusiastic fanaticism."[30] He worried that "certain of the enthusiasts might lose their reason through over zeal and become dangerous."[31]

Ryland scheduled a meeting of Federation members where he expressed various concerns. People were being "drawn away from

---

Girl," *Los Angeles Record*, August 26, 1907; "Hysterics vs. Religion," *Highland Park Herald*, July 27, 1907; "In Arms against Holy Rollerism," *Los Angeles Herald*, July 29, 1907; "Insane Religions," *Los Angeles Herald*, August 9, 1907.

[29] "Spreads the Fire," *The Apostolic Faith* [Los Angeles CA] 1:2 (October 1906): 4.2.

[30] "Churches Aroused to Action," *Los Angeles Express*, July 18, 1906.

[31] "Young Girl Given Gift of Tongues," *Los Angeles Express*, July 20, 1906.

the beaten paths of established faith" by the evangelistic methods of these newer groups. While his comments were clearly aimed at the Azusa Street Mission and, to a lesser extent, the nearby First New Testament Church led by Joseph Smale, Ryland cautioned the press against reading into the actions of the Federation any animosity toward these "new creeds." "The workers in these so-called new religious departures," he went on,

> have set us a good example in missionary effort, and we will seek to profit by it. New creeds are springing up here and there, and the promoters are embued [sic] with the spirit of missionary work to such an extent that they never rest. On the other hand the orthodox churches in many cases are content with enjoying the light which they have received.[32]

Despite Ryland's request that the public not read into the Federation's actions anything that would suggest it was responding directly to the challenges of the Azusa Street Mission or First New Testament Church, the reporter remained unconvinced. The public should be clear, the reporter announced, "These and other demonstrations have aroused the federation to action."[33] On September 23, 1906, Dr. R. J. Burdette, pastor of the Temple Baptist Church, leveled his charge that the Mission was nothing more than "a disgusting amalgamation of African voudou superstition and Caucasian insanity."[34]

At the same time that Dr. Burdette made this charge, Pastor Smale's congregation was subjected to public ridicule in a different way. A prominent member of Smale's congregation, Dr. Henry Sheridan Keyes, and his sixteen-year-old daughter, Lillian, created

[32] "Churches Aroused to Action," *Los Angeles Express*, July 18, 1906.
[33] Ibid.
[34] "New Religions Come, Then Go," *Los Angeles Herald*, September 24, 1906; "Denounces New Denominations," *Los Angeles Express*, September 24, 1906.

a huge stir on two occasions: first, when Dr. Keyes wrote in tongues for the *Los Angeles Daily Times*[35] and second, in an unrelated series of events, when he defended the actions of his daughter who, claiming to be inspired by the Holy Spirit, wrote a letter to Pastor Smale and informed him that the Spirit was grieved that he was not allowing the Spirit sufficient freedom to work in First New Testament Church. Smale, who had been extremely generous to those who had gone to Azusa Street, where many had been baptized in the Spirit, asked Keyes to keep his daughter in check since it was clearly not the Holy Spirit who had told her to criticize him. When Dr. Keyes refused to do so and Lillian attempted to interrupt a subsequent service, Smale moved to stop her.[36] In the end, Smale and the Keyes broke fellowship. Smale repudiated their claims, and Keyes began a new congregation that came to be known as the Upper Room Mission, choosing as its pastor Smale's primary assistant, Elmer Kirk Fisher.[37]

Until I began my work, all we really had to go on was the following little note left by Frank Bartleman to explain this explosive series of incidents.

> Pastor Smale never received the "baptism" with the "speaking in tongues." He was in a trying position. It was all new to him. Then the devil did his worst, to bring the work into disrepute and destroy it. He sent wicked spirits among us to frighten the pastor and cause him to reject it.[38]

---

[35] "Baba Bharati Says Not A Language," *Los Angeles Daily Times*, September 19, 1906.

[36] "Girl's Message From God Devil's Work, Says Pastor," *Los Angeles Express*, September 20, 1906; "Girl Is A Christian, Not Devil," *Los Angeles Express*, September 27, 1906.

[37] Joseph Smale, "The Gift of Tongues," *Living Truths: A Periodical of Present Truth, Deeper Life, and Neglected Work* 7:1 (January 1907), 38; "Sift [sic] Of Tongues Splits Flock?" *Los Angeles Herald*, September 23, 1906; "Claim Power to Raise Dead," *Los Angeles Daily Times*, September 24, 1906.

[38] Frank Bartleman, *How Pentecost Came to Los Angeles: As It Was in the Beginning* (Los Angeles, CA: F. Bartleman, 1925), 61–62.

We now know many of the details that help us understand what Bartleman merely scribbled in cryptic form. We can understand what caused Smale's desertion of Pentecostalism, and we might even be able to sympathize with him. And this was the perplexing context into which Charles Parham entered when he arrived in Los Angeles for a series of meetings he had been invited to hold at the Azusa Street Mission. But what do we know about the relationship between Parham and Seymour prior to Parham's arrival? What were Seymour's expectations upon Parham's arrival? Why did Parham reject Seymour's work? And how did Seymour respond?

Prior to Parham's arrival in Los Angeles, both Parham and Seymour viewed Seymour's work as having a direct relationship to that of Parham. This can be easily demonstrated. First, Seymour had attended Parham's school in Houston. While very selective about which of Parham's teachings he embraced, Seymour was in general sympathy with Parham's basic teaching regarding the restoration of the "Apostolic Faith." Seymour formally named the Azusa Street Mission the Apostolic Faith Mission, and he adopted a statement of faith, some or all of which had been penned by Parham.[39]

Second, three months after the Mission opened, Seymour wrote two letters, one to Warren Faye Carothers, the State Director for Parham's work in Texas, and the other to Charles Parham. He asked Carothers for the ministerial credential that Parham and Carothers had promised to him, identifying Seymour as an Apostolic Faith minister, and he asked for a supply of lapel buttons that identified Seymour's followers as members of Parham's Apostolic Faith Movement. Carothers approved the shipment to Seymour.[40] In the second letter, Seymour invited Parham to hold a series of meetings in Los Angeles. Seymour promised that he would work to bring

---

[39] "The Apostolic Faith Movement," *The Apostolic Faith* [Los Angeles, CA] 1.1 September 1906): 2.1. This statement is quoted in "Declare Parham Is Gaining," *Waukegan Daily Gazette* (Waukegan, IL), September 28, 1906, as coming from a "circular" distributed by Charles F. Parham, Projector.

[40] Personal correspondence from W. J. Seymour to W. F. Carothers, July 12, 1906.

other like-minded pastors together for that series of meetings,[41] and Parham accepted the invitation.[42]

Third, with the aid of Clara Lum, Seymour began a newspaper called *The Apostolic Faith* that was patterned after Parham's paper by the same name. In the first issue, Seymour introduced Parham to his readers and recorded his hopes for the success of Parham's visit. Pastor Seymour gave a short version of his personal call to Los Angeles, noting that he had come from Houston, Texas.[43] Furthermore, it included an article in which the opening sentence read, "This work began about five years ago last January, where a company of people under the leadership of Chas. Parham, who were studying God's word, tarried for Pentecost in Topeka, Kan."[44] In another article the following month, Parham's name was placed alongside that of Martin Luther, who was credited with restoring the doctrine of justification by faith; John Wesley, who had restored the doctrine of sanctification; and Dr. Charles Cullis, who had brought the teaching of divine healing back to the Church. Parham's contribution was listed as having restored "the Pentecostal Baptism to the Church."[45] Clearly, William Seymour held Charles Parham in high esteem, and he publicly outlined his debt to Parham.

Fourth, Parham sent several of his own people from Houston to Los Angeles to prepare for the upcoming revival. Seymour acknowledged their arrival and integrated one of them, Mrs. Anna Hall, into his work.[46] These workers reported favorably back to

41 Sarah E. Parham, *The Life of Charles F. Parham*, 154.

42 "Letter from Bro. Parham," *The Apostolic Faith* [Los Angeles, CA] 1.1 (September 1906): 1.1–2.

43 "Bro. Seymour's Call," *The Apostolic Faith* [Los Angeles, CA] 1.1 (September 1906): 1.1.

44 "The Old-Time Pentecost," *The Apostolic Faith* [Los Angeles, CA] 1.1 (September 1906): 1.2.

45 "The Pentecostal Baptism Restored," *The Apostolic Faith* [Los Angeles, CA] 1.2 (October 1906): 1.1.

46 "Jesus Is Coming," *The Apostolic Faith* [Los Angeles, CA] 1.1 (September 1906): 4.3; "Russians Hear in Their Own Tongue," *The Apostolic Faith* [Los Angeles, CA] 1.1 (September 1906): 4.3. "Enthusiasm High At This Meeting," *Whittier Daily News* 2:190

Parham regarding Seymour's work, and Parham acknowledged
these favorable reports.[47] When Parham arrived in Los Angeles, he
attended the Azusa Street Mission, where he was given a seat of
honor beside Seymour. At the appropriate time, Seymour proudly
introduced Charles Parham to the congregation as his "Father in this
gospel of the Kingdom," and Parham preached to the congregation,
by his own recollection, at least "two or three times."[48]

All of these documented facts point to a cordial relationship
between the two men. So, why did Parham reject Seymour's work?
According to Seymour, Parham began his final sermon to the Azusa
Street crowd by announcing, "God is sick at His stomach!"[49] We
do not have Parham's sermon, though we do have a number of
texts written by Charles Parham in which he outlined his reasons
for rejecting Seymour and the Azusa Street revival. *I will use his
statement rhetorically to indicate the six issues that Charles Parham
alleged made God sick at His stomach.*

First, God was sick at His stomach because Glenn Cook was a
fanatic who had brought fanaticism into the Mission. According
to Parham, Seymour had been doing a reasonable job leading
the Azusa Street Mission when "a Holy Roller religious meeting
[the local Burning Bush]… dismissed and came down to Azusa
Street."[50] From that time on, the revival had deteriorated. Cook
had been a member of the Burning Bush, and subsequently

(September 14, 1906), 1; Sarah E. Parham, *The Life of Charles F. Parham*, 154; Untitled Item,
The Apostolic Faith [Los Angeles, CA] 1.3 (November 1906): 1.2.

[47] Charles F. Parham, "The Latter Rain," *The Apostolic Faith* [Baxter Springs, KS] 2.7 (July
1926): 5; Cf. Sarah E. Parham, *The Life of Charles F. Parham*, 161–162.

[48] On the nature of his introduction see K. Brower, "Origen [*sic*] of the Apostolic Faith
Movement on the Pacific Coast," in *The Apostolic Faith* [Goose Creek, TX], (May 1921): 6.
On the number of times Parham preached, see Charles F. Parham, "The Latter Rain," *The
Apostolic Faith* [Baxter Springs, KS] 2.7 (July 1926): 6; cf. Sarah E. Parham, *The Life of
Charles F. Parham*, 163.

[49] Shumway, "A Study of the 'Gift of Tongues,'" 178.

[50] "Sermon by Chas. F. Parham, Portland, OR, Nov. 15, 1924," *The Apostolic Faith* [Baxter
Springs, KS] Number 3 (April 1925): 10.

Parham viewed him as the leader of a sect of "Holy Rollers" and a "confessed hypnotist." Assisted by a group of other "fanatics," Parham charged that Cook had turned the Azusa Street Mission into "a hotbed of wildfire." "Religious orgies outrivaling scenes in devil or fetish worship took place in the Upper Room," Parham later informed his readers,

> where deluded victims by the score were thrown into a hypnotic trance, out of which they came chattering and jabbering. While up to the advent of this man Cook, many received the Pentecost and spoke in real languages, very little real was known afterward, but barking like dogs, crowing like roosters, etc., trances, shhkes [sic], fits and all kinds of fleshly contortions with wind-sucking and jabbering resulted, until I exposed him; after he left but few new so called Pentecosts were reported at Azuza [sic].[51]

It appears, then, that Parham's first criticism was aimed at the role of a specific man, Glenn Cook, that Seymour had engaged to serve as the Mission's business manager and the style of worship that Parham believed Cook brought into the Azusa Street meetings.

Second, God was sick at His stomach because some of Seymour's altar workers allegedly resorted to mechanical techniques to lead people into baptism in the Holy Spirit. If you have spent any time in Pentecostal churches or praying around Pentecostal altars, you have seen them too. Parham routinely contended that all genuine manifestations of speaking in tongues

---

[51] [Charles F. Parham], "Leadership," *The Apostolic Faith* [Baxter Springs, KS] 1.4 (June 1912): 7–9. A portion of this passage is summarized in Sarah E. Parham, *The Life of Charles F. Parham*, 164. The term "wind-sucking" is a veterinary term used to describe the rapid swallowing of air sometimes done by horses, resulting in a hissing sound. A room on the second floor of the Mission, where seekers for baptism in the Holy Spirit prayed, was designated the "Upper Room." It is not to be confused with the nearby Upper Room Mission.

could be validated as foreign languages. The "speaking in tongues" he witnessed at the Mission was not definable language. As a result, he judged these tongues as counterfeit.

According to Parham, Seymour's well-meaning altar workers were "over-zealous, ignorant helpers" who laid hands on their victims, jerked their chins, massaged their throats, and told them to repeat certain sounds over and over or faster and faster until they spoke in tongues. "O, how many have been deceived by the Azuza [sic] mess," Parham later lamented,

> and by those workers who get the poor seekers to yell "glory, glory," until they can no longer say it in English, but in a half hypnotized condition, they cry, "glug, glug," or some other peculiar sound, and one more is counted to have his Pentecost, when only worked into a frenzy.[52]

Some were still receiving "the real baptism of the Holy Ghost" at the altar of the Mission no doubt,[53] but these techniques led to "counterfeit" results. They were nothing more than "hypnotism, sympathetic magnetism, spiritism and animalism," and Parham condemned the "chattering or jabbering accompanied by fits, spasms, jerks and uncontrollable actions of the body" that he claimed characterized the Azusa Street meetings.[54]

Third, God was sick at His stomach because the basic laws of decorum had broken down at the Mission. Seymour did not segregate his people by race. Men and women, blacks, browns, and whites mingled freely with one another. According to Parham, the Holy Spirit would be ineffective in such a situation. W. F. Carothers, Parham's chief lieutenant in the Apostolic Faith Movement to this point, had already influenced Parham in this

---

[52] [Charles F. Parham], "Baptism of the Holy Ghost," *The Apostolic Faith* [Baxter Springs, KS] 1.8 (October 1912): 9–10.

[53] Sarah E. Parham, *The Life of Charles F. Parham*, 163–164.

[54] Charles F. Parham, "Review," *The Apostolic Faith* 5 (June 1925): 8; Sarah E. Parham, *The Life of Charles F. Parham*, 163–164.

regard when he worked in Texas. While Parham was initially more moderate on racial issues than was Carothers, he was already showing a growing contempt for African Americans. Here is where the scandal of the local press and the Los Angeles Church Federation came into play.

When Parham arrived in Los Angeles, the city had already been scandalized by the freedom with which the races mingled at "Azusa Street." The newspapers consistently criticized the freedom and ease with which the customary racial taboos long embraced by polite, white American society and culture, taboos such as touching, embracing, and kissing across racial lines, were being violated at the Mission. Dr. Burdette had labeled the Mission's activities as a compromise between African voodoo superstition and Caucasian insanity.[55] Yet Seymour and many of his congregation had not blinked at these artificial standards. They failed to see what others were content to preserve, namely, the segregation of worshippers along racial lines.

Even if Parham could have reconciled the mixing of the races with his own practice, he was deeply troubled by the mixing of women and men in times of prayer. What was especially galling to him was any situation in which black men touched white women, even accidentally. Parham claimed that he was scandalized by the familiarity with which men and women interacted in the Mission's "Upper Room." In their "ecstatic" state, he charged them with unseemly behavior that he believed no person in her right mind would tolerate. He reported,

> men and women, whites and blacks, knelt together or fell
> across one another; frequently, a white woman, perhaps
> of wealth and culture, could be seen thrown back in the

---

[55] "Weird Babel of Tongues," *Los Angeles Daily Times*, April 18, 1906; "'Holy Kickers' Baffle Police," *Los Angeles Daily Times*, July 12, 1906; "Religious Fanaticism Creates Wild Scenes," *Los Angeles Record*, July 14, 1906, 1; "Women with Men Embrace," *Los Angeles Daily Times*, September 3, 1906; "How Holy Roller Gets Religion," *Los Angeles Herald*, September 10, 1906; "Woman, in Religious Frenzy, Remains Rigid an Hour," *Los Angeles Record*, September 24, 1906.

arms of a big "buck nigger," and held tightly thus as she shivered and shook in freak imitation of Pentecost. Horrible, awful shame! Many of the missions on the Pacific coast are permeated with this foolishness, and, in fact, it follows the Azuza [sic] work everywhere.[56]

What is impossible to determine is whether Parham ever observed such a scene or whether he was intentionally engaged in a ploy to etch in graphic imagery a picture designed to inflame his reader's outrage while addressing his own racial and sexual demons. Parham was no purist in this matter if Howard Goss is to be believed. Parham allowed black women and white men to mix in prayer at his Brunner, Texas, encampment, for Mrs. Lucy F. Farrow, an African American woman ministering on Parham's behalf, laid hands on him.[57] At Parham's Houston Bible School, at least one white woman shamelessly announced that she had repeatedly laid her hands on William J. Seymour when he was seeking his baptism in the Spirit.[58]

If the full integration of the races that Parham met at the Azusa Street Mission violated his own segregationist stance, issues of sexuality were also clearly in his mind. He believed that there was a direct link between men and women praying together at an altar and their inevitable entry into sexual promiscuity. "One of the fruitful sources of this cancerous condition," he wrote in a 1912 article on "Free-love,"

is the promiscuous gathering of men and women around the altars of prayer. The wild, weird prayer services in

---

[56] Charles F. Parham, "Free-Love," *The Apostolic Faith* [Baxter Springs, KS] 1.10 (December 1912): 4–5.

[57] Ethel E. Goss, *The Winds of God*, 98; H. A. Goss, "Reminiscences of an Eyewitness," 66.

[58] Stanley Wayne, "Early Revivals," in Bill Newby, James E. Griggs, and Steve D. Eutsler, *Perpetuating Pentecost: A Look at the Formation and Development of the Southern Missouri District of the Assemblies of God* (Springfield, MO: Southern Missouri District Council of the Assemblies of God, 1989), 7.

many of these fanatical meetings, where the contact of bodies in motion is as certain and damning as in the dance hall, leads to free-love, affinity-foolism and soul-mating.[59]

Parham described shaking, falling, rolling, or engaging in other spiritual acrobatics, as well as "monkey chattering" and "jabbering," as "animalistic" behaviors. From his point of view, all such practices led to promiscuous sexual behavior. As a result, Parham argued that "All meetings should have two altars, one for men and one for women; then let the men work with the men and the women with the women, and this rule should not be varied from except in rare cases."[60] In the end, Parham failed to provide evidence for even a single case of what he called "free-lovism, affinity-foolism, and soul-mating" that he found at the Mission. None!

Fourth, God was sick at His stomach because the nature of worship at the Azusa Street Mission was too dependent upon the example of the traditional worship patterns of African Americans and what Parham described as "Holy Rollers." What was taking place at Azusa Street, Parham contended, was a counterfeit form of Pentecost. In language reminiscent of Dr. Burdette, Parham was quick to label Azusa's worship as nothing more than "a cross between the Negro and Holy Roller form of worship."[61]

The reference to "Holy Roller" worship was undoubtedly aimed at the highly energetic and vocal worship style of Glenn Cook and others

---

[59] Charles F. Parham, "Free-Love," *The Apostolic Faith* [Baxter Springs, KS] 1.10 (December 1912): 4; Cf. Braude, *Radical Spirits*, 119; Ira L. Mandelker, *Religion, Society, and Utopia in Nineteenth Century America* (Amherst, MA: The University of Massachusetts Press, 1984), 102–103; John C. Spurlock, *Free Love: Marriage and Middle-Class Radicalism in America, 1825–1869* (New York, NY: New York University Press, 1988), 95–98.

[60] Charles F. Parham, "Free-Love," *The Apostolic Faith* [Baxter Springs, KS] 1.10 (December 1912): 4.

[61] Untitled Item, *The Apostolic Faith* [Baxter Springs, KS], January 1912: 6–7. Cf. "New Religions Come, Then Go," *Los Angeles Herald*, September 24, 1906; Cf. "Denounces New Denominations," *Los Angeles Express*, September 24, 1906.

who had previously affiliated with local Burning Bush and Pillar of Fire congregations. His reference to "Negro" worship, however, was likely informed by his experiences in Texas and Baxter Springs, Kansas. Baxter Springs, where Parham lived, was founded and populated by African Americans who migrated there as part of an organized exodus from the South during the period of Reconstruction.[62]

Parham claimed that what he called the "trances, falling under the power, holy-rolling-dancing-jumping, shaking, jabbering, chattering, wind-sucking and giving vent to meaningless sounds and noises" that he saw at the Mission were practices in which "the Negroes of the Southland" regularly engaged.[63] He charged Azusa's worshippers with the same "stunts" as one could find in the "old camp meetings among colored folks. If you have not seen an old-fashioned darky camp meeting in the south," he would later quip, "you have missed half of your life."[64]

Parham maintained that those who sang in tongues were merely engaged in "a modification of the Negro chanting of the Southland."[65] Parham could tolerate such activities among African Americans. It was part of their culture, the way they worshipped God. But Parham rejected out of hand that white folks, who should obviously know better, could act "after a Negro fashion," thereby "making themselves ridiculous in the sight of all sane and reasonable people [read: white folk],"[66] especially when they claimed that it was God who was at work in them.[67]

God may not have been sick at His stomach, but Parham certainly was. "What makes my soul sick, and makes me sick at my stomach," Parham openly complained, "is to see white people

---

[62] Daniel M. Johnson and Rex R. Campbell, *Black Migration in America*, 55.

[63] Untitled Item, *The Apostolic Faith* [Baxter Springs, KS] 1.8 (October 1912): 6.

[64] "Sermon by Chas. F. Parham, Portland, OR, Nov. 15, 1924," *The Apostolic Faith* [Baxter Springs, KS] 3 (April 1925): 10.

[65] Untitled Item, *The Apostolic Faith* [Baxter Springs, KS], January 1912: 6–7.

[66] Untitled Item, *The Apostolic Faith* [Baxter Springs, KS] 1.8 (October 1912): 2.

[67] Untitled Item, *The Apostolic Faith* [Baxter Springs, KS] 1.8 (October 1912): 6.

imitating unintelligent crude negroism of the Southland, and laying it on the Holy Ghost. I am sorry for the Holy Ghost for the things that are blamed on Him."[68] One couldn't expect anything more from black folks, it seems, but for white folks to follow their lead was an embarrassment to Charles Parham. He was not going to tolerate any accommodation to African American culture in *his* Apostolic Faith Movement. Primitive forces! Uncomfortable realities!

Fifth, God was sick at His stomach because the Mission had authorized and sent evangelists and missionaries around the world that Parham believed were completely unprepared and ill-equipped to carry on such a ministry. And, once again, it had been done in the name of the Apostolic Faith Movement. He believed that most of them were victims of "spiritism, hypnotism and unconscious cerubration [sic] as taught in psychic phenomena."[69] He clearly had folks like Glenn Cook and A.G. and Lillian Garr in mind. From his perspective, they would go about their evangelistic and missionary activities, only to "disgrace the cause" and bring "world-wide shame on the work of God."[70]

Sixth, God was sick at His stomach because Pastor Seymour was not capable of providing the leadership that was necessary to control the revival. He was incompetent. The revival had gotten away from him. For several months, Parham had watched from afar, writing about how pleased he was with what he was hearing from his own staff regarding Seymour's work.[71] When he arrived in Los Angeles, his story changed immediately. Parham claimed that Seymour came running to him, as though he were helplessly unable to "stem the

---

[68] "Sermon by Chas. F. Parham, Portland, OR, Nov. 15, 1924," *The Apostolic Faith* [Baxter Springs, KS] 3 (April 1925): 10.

[69] Charles F. Parham, "Unity," *The Apostolic Faith* [Baxter Springs, KS] 1.4 (June 1912): 9–10.

[70] Untitled Item, *The Apostolic Faith* [Baxter Springs, KS], January 1912: 6–7.

[71] [Charles F. Parham], "Leadership," *The Apostolic Faith* [Baxter Springs, KS] 1.4 (June 1912): 7–9. A portion of this passage is summarized in Sarah E. Parham, *The Life of Charles F. Parham*, 164.

tide" against the "hypnotism" that had emerged in the Mission.[72] We are left to wonder at Parham's credibility at this point. Seymour did not respond to Parham's criticisms in print, so we have only one side of the story.

By the time Parham arrived in Los Angeles, a number of congregations had identified with the Azusa Street revival. The Full Gospel Assembly, two Nazarene congregations, William Pendleton's Holiness Church, and Thomas Atteberry's People's Church all converted to the Pentecostal position. Frank Bartleman facilitated Pendleton's congregation transfer through Azusa Street to the Assembly at 8th and Maple. The Upper Room Mission, founded by Elmer Kirk Fisher and Dr. Henry S. Keyes, split from First New Testament Church. Swedish, German, Spanish, Russian, and Armenian congregations were all established within the first seven months of the revival, based solely on language needs. It is not the case that any of their founders had been among Seymour's "enthusiasts, who broke away to form … rival congregations nearby."[73] Pendleton's 8th and Maple Assembly, the Spanish language congregation at God's Detective Mission led by Abundio de López, and Fisher's Upper Room Mission all maintained long term relationships with Pastor Seymour, and Seymour advertised all their meetings in his paper.

Furthermore, Seymour had no control over A. H. Post's Pasadena meetings; Glenn Cook's meetings at the Monrovia Holiness Church; Henry Prentiss' forays into Whittier and Santa Ana; or those of Edward McCauley in Long Beach, most of which were clearly multiethnic in nature. It was unfair for Parham to paint Pastor Seymour with the brush of incompetence once the revival had moved beyond the doors of Azusa Street. These other works were independent of Seymour, though they had found impetus in

[72] Charles F. Parham, "The Latter Rain," *The Apostolic Faith* [Baxter Springs, KS] 2.7 (July 1926): 5; cf. Sarah E. Parham, *The Life of Charles F. Parham*, 163.
[73] Blumhofer, "For Pentecostals, A Move toward Racial Reconciliation," 444–46.

the revival. Why should Seymour be held responsible for what took place in those congregations?

What Seymour could control was the way in which services were conducted at the Azusa Street Mission. But what Seymour had ruled to be decent and orderly behavior at the Azusa Street Mission—and he had done so in full sight of Parham's aides who had previously praised him to Parham—did not fit the definitions of decency and order that Parham had brought with him. Seymour did not share either the same theological or the same cultural expectations that Parham embraced. In fact, Seymour was conducting the meetings at the Mission in ways that he believed were more consistent with New Testament practice than those ways by which Parham acted. Seymour's congregation sat in a circle with the pulpit and the altar at the center, allowing everyone to have a face to face encounter with others in the community. He included men and women as well as the old and young as full participants in his services, in prayer, music, testimonies, and sermons. He held that the culturally based class, racial, and ethnic distinctions embraced by much of American society were not consistent with what the Bible taught and therefore had no place for any such division in this radical experiment of Pentecost at the Azusa Street Mission.

From this survey, it is apparent that Parham's criticisms were not primarily theological; they were personal, and they were cultural. Let me summarize them for you. God was sick at His stomach because (1) Seymour supported the ministry of Glenn Cook, who Parham rejected; (2) Seymour's altar workers, while well-meaning, were not well prepared; (3) white folk and black folk as well as men and women were mixing in a way that Parham believed violated the basic laws of decorum; (4) Azusa's worship was too black, and white folk shouldn't act like black folk when they worship; (5) Seymour had sent out evangelists and missionaries of whom Parham did not approve; and (6) in Parham's mind, Seymour was incompetent to lead the revival. In short, Parham was not in control and was embarrassed by the fact that the revival valued people in ways that Parham did not.

Many of the Mission's faithful were heirs to an African American religious heritage. Others could rightfully be identified with a Wesleyan-Holiness or a frontier revivalism heritage. When they came together, something new came into being, in which Charles Parham introduced the "primitive force" and "uncomfortable reality" of racism. Parham thought that the Azusa Street Mission needed to be brought into conformity with the practices with which *he* was most comfortable. He went so far as to claim that Pastor Seymour had not even received the real baptism in the Spirit, claiming that Pastor Seymour merely "made up a few gutterals [*sic*]" as a ruse "to hold his sway over his followers." Seymour was not teaching that the "Bible evidence" of baptism in the Spirit was speaking in tongues in a language that could be used for missionary purposes. He would ultimately charge Seymour with teaching that any of the charisms mentioned in 1 Corinthians 12:8–10 were valid as evidences.[74]

The split that took place when Parham and Seymour severed their relationship was both real and decisive. By mid-December 1906, Parham was telling the local press that he had nothing to do with Seymour's Apostolic Faith Movement, and he criticized it forcefully.

> We conduct dignified religious services, and have no connection with the sort which is characterized by trances, fits and spasms, jerks, shakes and contortions. We are wholly foreign to the religious anarchy, which marks the Los Angeles Azusa Street meetings, and expect to do good ... along proper and profound Christian lines.[75]

Pastor Seymour did not stoop to this level, merely pointing out that the Mission had moved beyond Parham. When asked

---

[74] Untitled Item, *The Apostolic Faith* [Baxter Springs, KS] 1.6 (August 1912): 6.
[75] "Apostolic Faith People Here Again," *Whittier Daily News*, December 14, 1906.

whether Charles Parham was the leader of the Azusa Street revival, Seymour's paper carried the following response.

> We thought of having him to be our leader and so stated in our paper, before waiting on the Lord. We can be rather hasty, especially when we are very young in the power of the Holy Spirit. We are just like a baby—full of love—and were willing to accept anyone that had the baptism with the Holy Spirit as our leader. But the Lord commenced settling us down, and we saw that the Lord should be our leader. So we honor Jesus as the great Shepherd of the sheep. He is our model.[76]

One month later, Parham went on to Zion, Illinois, and then to Cleveland, Ohio. Ivey Campbell, an evangelist sent to Ohio from Azusa Street in December 1906, had been holding meetings in which scores were being baptized in the Spirit. When a popular Holiness evangelist was converted in one of Miss Campbell's services and subsequently preached on tongues at First Friends Church in Cleveland, Ohio, Charles Parham stood up and told the congregation that the Azusa Street form of the Apostolic Faith was all wrong, and his approach was right.

> The real gift of tongues is never accompanied by spasms, jerks, or foolishness of any sort. This Pentecost is never accompanied by rolling on the floor or falling on the back or in spasms. It is a dignified gift and comes to uplift. The Holy Ghost does not send fits and monkeyshines.
> There is no jabbering in the real gift of tongues. A genuine language comes. At first it may be a babble, but later it is a real living language which one can talk in. No physical manifestation is necessary beyond an expression

---

[76] "Pentecost with Signs Following," *The Apostolic Faith* [Los Angeles, CA] 1.4 (November 1906): 1.1–2.

of joy, when the gift of tongues is bestowed. The devil
conflicts it with spiritualism, clairvoyance and hypnotism and they enter the flesh and cause these
demonstrations.[77]

If Parham could not control the Azusa Street revival, he seems to
have been intent upon destroying its impact wherever he could.
Ultimately, the Friends rejected both messages.

Further evidence shows that the division between the two was
now complete. In January 1907, Glenn Cook took the Pentecostal
message to Indianapolis, and in the following June, Pastor Seymour
spoke there for two weeks. The *Indianapolis News* announced as
a matter of course and with clear reference to William J. Seymour
that it was a Negro who was the "founder" of this new faith that
had come from Los Angeles.[78] Six weeks later, the *Los Angeles Daily
Times* published an article on the Azusa Street camp meeting in
which it claimed that the camp was set up along racially segregated
lines.[79] Four days later, the *Pasadena Star* contradicted the *Times*,
noting that "no distinction has been made on account of race, color
or previous condition of servitude," and the African Americans who
had come from various Southern states were clearly evident.[80] It
would be August 3 before Robert J. Scott, the chief spokesperson for
the camp, would respond to this charge of segregation, and it would
be forcefully denied in the *Highland Park Herald*. "The Negroes are
not kept separate; indeed, we give preference to them over the whites.
The movement originated with a Negro, and it is their peculiar work,"
he reported.[81]

These statements would not have carried any clout had the folks
related to the Azusa Street Mission seen themselves as simply

---

[77] "Gift of Tongues without Babble," *Cleveland Plain Dealer*, January 11, 1907.
[78] "Woman Sticks to Bluks; Husband Asks Divorce," *Indianapolis News*, June 5, 1907.
[79] "Loud Prayers Stir Protest," *Los Angeles Daily Times*, July 18, 1907.
[80] "Holy Rollers at Camp Have a Gala Day," *Pasadena Star*, July 22, 1907.
[81] "Not 'Holy Rollers,' Says Leader," *Highland Park Herald*, August 3, 1907.

continuing Parham's work. They understood themselves to be part of something new under the leadership of William Seymour. Since that time, our "uncomfortable realities" have been routinized, our "primitive forces" have been tamed, and sides have been drawn along color lines. The story of Azusa Street has remained an "open secret" among us, one that has festered for many years. In too many cases, our statements and actions have been undertaken without having all the facts before us.

There is plenty of work to be done towards racial reconciliation if we are to understand our "Azusa Street" heritage. We must be willing to undertake the hard work that many of our predecessors have failed to conduct if we are going to face the primitive racial forces and uncomfortable racial realities that emanate from this story and continue to threaten the churches that we serve. Only when we have done this can we truly and adequately address the racial and racist biases that our denominations, cultures, and politically correct guilds raise when they look at this story. Only then can we speak with one voice about this story that for a century has been merely an "open secret" among us. Only then will we fully appreciate the wonderful contribution towards racial reconciliation that was made by William J. Seymour and his flock at the Azusa Street Mission.

4

Count Zinzendorf, Pastor Jack, and Messianic Jewish Revival

David Rudolph

THE MESSIANIC MOVEMENT is made up of thousands of Messianic Jews who have devoted their lives to lifting up the name of Yeshua (Jesus) within the Jewish world. At the same time, the Messianic community would not exist without the many Gentile Christians who have come alongside Messianic Jews to serve as champions of the movement. This essay profiles two such individuals—Nikolaus Ludwig von Zinzendorf and Jack Hayford—and aims to detail how each has served as a catalyst for Messianic Jewish revival.

Count Zinzendorf and the Restoration of Messianic Jews in the Eighteenth Century

When we speak of Messianic Judaism in antiquity and the modern era, we are referring to a religious tradition in which Jews have claimed to follow Jesus as the Messiah of Israel while continuing to live within the orbit of Judaism. Communities of such Jews existed in the first four centuries of the Common Era in the Land of Israel, Syria, and beyond.[1]

---

[1] See David Rudolph, "Messianic Judaism in Antiquity and in the Modern Era," in *Introduction to Messianic Judaism: Its Ecclesial Context and Biblical Foundations* (Grand Rapids: Zondervan, 2013), 21–24.

92

From the fifth century until the eighteenth century—for 1300 years—Messianic Jews disappeared from the world scene. The "parting of the ways" between the Church and the Synagogue precluded Messianic Judaism.[2] To put it another way, Christian and Jewish leaders banned Messianic Jews to maintain the myth that Christianity was a separate and distinct religion from Judaism.[3]

In the eighteenth century, a new era dawned. Through the spiritual leadership of Count Zinzendorf, the Moravian Brethren in Herrnhut, Germany (1735) caught a vision for the restoration of Messianic Jews.[4] Zinzendorf established in the *Brüdergemeine* (Brethren community) a congregation in which Jesus-believing Jews were encouraged to live out Jewish life and identity. He called this congregation a *Judenkehille* (Jewish community):

---

[2] The view that Jews could not become Christians and remain Jews was backed by canon law and Constantine's sword. The Second Council of Nicaea in 787 CE was the first ecumenical council to ban Messianic Jews from the church.

[3] Jewish believers in Jesus were required to renounce all ties to Judaism through professions of faith like the one from the Church of Constantinople ("I renounce absolutely everything Jewish, every law, rite and custom" [Assemani, *Cod. Lit.* 1:105]). From the fourth century until the modern period, millions of Jews converted to Christianity and left behind their Jewish identity.

[4] See Lutz Greisiger, "Israel in the Church and the Church in Israel: The Formation of Jewish Christian Communities as a Proselytising Strategy Within and Outside the German Pietist Mission to the Jews of the Eighteenth Century," in *Pietism and Community in Europe and North America 1650–1850* (ed. Jonathan Strom; Leiden: Brill, 2010), 133–34; Lutz Greisinger, "Recent Publications on the German Pietists' Mission to the Jews," *European Journal of Jewish Studies* 2:1 (2008): 135–64; Peter Vogt, *Zwischen Bekehrungseifer und Philosemitismus: Texte zur Stellung des Pietismus zum Judentum* (Leipzig: Evangelische Verlagsanstalt, 2007); Lutz Greisiger, "Chiliasten und 'Judentzer': Judenmission und Eschatologie im protestantischen Deutschland des 17. und 18. Jahrhunderts," *Kwartalnik Historii Żydów—Jewish History Quarterly* 4 (2006): 535–75; Christiane Dithmar, *Zinzendorfs nonkonformistische Haltung zum Judentum* (Heidelberg: Universitätsverlag C. Winter, 2000); Hans-Jürgen Schrader, "Sulamiths verheißene Wiederkehr. Hinweise zu Programm und Praxis der pietistischen Begegnung mit dem Judentum," in *Conditio Judaica: Judentum, Antisemitismus und deutschsprachige Literatur vom 18. Jahrhundert bis zum Ersten Weltkrieg* (ed. Hans Otto Horch and Horst Denkler; Tübingen: Max Niemeyer, 1988), 71–107.

Soon the program of "gathering firstlings" emerged. The program aimed at integrating individual Jews into the *Brüdergemeine* without encouraging them to abandon their identity....The new converts were intended to be gathered in a Jewish-Christian congregation within the *Brüdergemeine*, the *Judenkehille* ("Jews' Qehillah," the latter part of the word being derived from the Hebrew word for "community").[5]

The *Judenkehille* was to be a Torah-observant Messianic Jewish community:

> Zinzendorf and Lieberkühn believed that Jewish converts should continue to observe the Mosaic laws. Their plan to establish a *Judenkehille* of Jewish-Christian believers within the Moravian movement reflected their appreciation for the Jewish tradition and recognition of its continuing value. Moreover, it offered a pastoral response to the precarious situation of proselytes, who usually found themselves "displaced"—cut off from their Jewish roots and yet not quite at home in Christianity.[6]

As the years passed, Zinzendorf reassessed his approach and concluded that it would be better for *Judenkehille* congregations to exist autonomously within the Jewish community rather than within Gentile Christian churches. He thus redirected Moravian efforts toward this end:

> In the early 1750s, Zinzendorf reacted by modifying the project of the *Judenkehille* to the effect that he now aimed

---

[5] Greisiger, "Israel in the Church and the Church in Israel," 137–38. See Peter Vogt, "Connectedness in Hope: German Pietism and the Jews," in *A Companion to German Pietism, 1660–1800* [Leiden: Brill, 2014], 106–107).

[6] Vogt, "Connectedness in Hope: German Pietism and the Jews," 112. See also, Anke Költsch, "Foundations, Institutes, Charities, and Proselytes in the Early Modern Holy Roman Empire," *Jewish History* 24:1 (2010): 87–104; Elisheva Carlebach, *Divided Souls: Converts from Judaism in Germany, 1500–1750* (New Haven: Yale University Press, 2001).

at establishing it *within* the Jewish communities. The converted Jews should, as an autonomous community, remain in their Jewish environment and form a sort of nucleus of the converted Israel. By this time Zinzendorf had moved to London to apply himself to the organization of the local branch of the *Brüdergemeine*. At that point, the new *Judenkehille* was also intended to be based in London and to be supervised by Lieberkühn and the convert Benjamin David Kirchhof (1716–1784).[7]

By as late as the 1770s, the Moravian Brethren were facilitating the establishment of fully autonomous *Judenkehille* congregations in Germany, England, and Switzerland.[8]

Zinzendorf's success in reviving Messianic Jewish congregations after 13 centuries of suppression raises the question, "What was it about his leadership that made this reemergence possible?" Among the various reasons that one could point to, there are at least 10 that help to explain why he was such a force for change in the eighteenth century when it came to making room for Messianic Jews:

(1)   Zinzendorf had vision for the national and spiritual resto-
        ration of Israel in the land, according to the Scriptures, and
        a desire to see the "firstfruits" (Rev 14:4) of Israel's renewal
        (a vibrant Messianic Jewish community) in his own day.[9]
        He remained committed to this vision for fifty years.[10]

---

[7] Greisiger, "Israel in the Church and the Church in Israel," 139–40. Cf. Greisiger, "Recent Publications on the German Pietists' Mission to the Jews," 162-63; Dithmar, *Zinzendorfs nonkonformistische Haltung zum Judentum*, ch. 7.

[8] See Greisiger, "Israel in the Church and the Church in Israel," 140; Rudolph, "Messianic Judaism in Antiquity and in the Modern Era," 25–26.

[9] Rolf G. Heitmann, "The Global Messianic Movement," in *Chosen to Follow: Jewish Believers Through History and Today* (ed. Knut H. Høyland and Jakob W. Nielsen; Jerusalem: Caspari Center for Biblical and Jewish Studies, 2012), 116. See Oskar Skarsaune, *Israels Venner* (Oslo: Luther forlag, 1994), 23.

[10] J. E. Hutton, *A History of the Moravian Missions* (London: Moravian Publication Office, 1922), 146; Peter Vogt, "The Attitude of Eighteenth Century German Pietism toward Jews and Judaism: A Case of Philo-Semitism?" *The Covenant Quarterly* (November 1998):

(2) Zinzendorf was a highly influential Christian leader in
      Europe, North America and Africa (e.g., the impact he
      had on John Wesley with whom he corresponded). This
      gave credibility to the nascent Messianic community.

(3) As a bishop of the Moravian Church, Zinzendorf was
      able to influence his own denomination to support and
      nurture the establishment of *Judenkehille* congregations.

(4) The count used the material resources of his estate to
      bless the budding Messianic movement and the wider
      Jewish community.[11]

(5) Zinzendorf had a high regard for Jewish people on a
      convictional level. He explains in *Sonderbare Gespräche*
      (1739)[12] that this was because: (a) Jesus is a Jew (pres-
      ent tense); (b) Most of the Scriptures came from
      the Jewish people; (c) They are "direct offspring" of
      Abraham whereas Gentile Christians are "grafted in"
      (Romans 11:17–24);[13] (d) Gentile believers are "explic-
      itly prohibited to boast against them, for (i) they bear
      us and not we them (Romans 11:18), and (ii) God
      is well able to graft them in again and to cut us off
      (Romans 11:21–24);"[14] (e) When Jewish people turn to
      their Messiah, they turn wholeheartedly; and (f) The
      Jewish people "have for the most part a sense that most
      of us lack, a sense of honor for God."[15]

(6) He actively opposed Christian anti-Semitism.[16]

22; Gustav Dalman, "Graf Zinzendorfs jüdisches Patenkind," *Herrnhut* 13 (1889): 28–30;
Greisiger, "Recent Publications on the German Pietists' Mission to the Jews," 158; Arthur
Glasser, "Zinzendorf and the Jewish People," *Jews for Jesus Newsletter* (November 1994): 1.

[11] Hutton, *A History of the Moravian Missions*, 147.

[12] Nikolaus Ludwig von Zinzendorf, *Sonderbare Gespräche* (ed. Hans Schneider; Leipzig:
Evangelische Verlagsanstalt, 2005).

[13] See Peter Vogt, "Count Zinzendorf's Encounter with Judaism and the Jews: A
Fictitious Dialogue from 1739," *Journal of Moravian History* 6 (2009): 109.

[14] Vogt, "Count Zinzendorf's Encounter with Judaism and the Jews," 109.

[15] Vogt, "Count Zinzendorf's Encounter with Judaism and the Jews," 110.

[16] Vogt, "Count Zinzendorf's Encounter with Judaism and the Jews," 109–110.

(7) Zinzendorf developed close relationships with Jewish people who did not believe in Jesus. He did not impose his faith on Jews but invited Jewish friends and acquaintances to dialogue with him about matters of faith. If they were not open to dialogue, he did not press the matter and maintained that the witness of one's walk with Jesus was more important than what one said.[17] Zinzendorf's love for Jesus and the Jewish people was known in the Jewish world.[18]

(8) He prayed for Israel and the reestablishment of a vibrant Messianic Jewish movement and introduced this priority into the Moravian liturgy.[19]

(9) As a German Pietist, Zinzendorf held an ecumenical vision that celebrated unity and diversity in the body of Messiah. "Zinzendorf enjoined his followers to remember the following triad of values: 'in essentials unity; in non-essentials diversity; in all things charity.'"[20]

(10) Zinzendorf appointed leaders over the *Judenkehille* congregations who passionately loved Jesus, loved the Jewish people,[21] and affirmed the importance of Jewish life and identity for Jesus-believing Jews.[22] Their training

---

[17] Vogt, "The Attitude of Eighteenth Century German Pietism toward Jews and Judaism," 24; Vogt, "Connectedness in Hope," 103.

[18] See Eugen Isolani, "Graf Ludwig von Zinzendorf und die Juden," *Allgemeine Zeitung des Judenthums* 64 (1900): 260–61.

[19] Vogt, "The Attitude of Eighteenth Century German Pietism toward Jews and Judaism," 25; Greisiger, "Recent Publications on the German Pietists' Mission to the Jews," 162.

[20] Chris Beneke, *Beyond Toleration: The Religious Origins of American Pluralism* (Oxford: Oxford University Press, 2006), 85.

[21] See *Periodical Accounts Relating to the Missions of the Church of the United Brethren, Established Among the Heathen* (vol. 12; London: Brethren's Society for Furtherance of the Gospel Among the Heathen, 1831), 346.

[22] Lieberkühn affirmed the continuing role of Torah observance for Jesus-believing Jews, "The first followers who were all Jews, continued to observe the ritual law, as is plain from Acts xxi. 20; and, consequently, the Jews who shall believe on Jesus in the latter days, may do the same, till God shall teach them otherwise." *Periodical Accounts Relating to the Missions of the Church of the United Brethren, Established Among the Heathen* vol. 15; (London: Brethren's

reflected the value that Zinzendorf placed on higher education and Jewish studies in particular. Two of his appointed leaders were Benjamin David Kirchhof, a Messianic Jew, and Samuel Lieberkühn, a Messianic Gentile who studied theology and biblical languages at the Pietist University of Halle and the University of Jena, and had been offered a Professorship of Oriental Languages at the University of Königsberg.[23] Though Lieberkühn was not Jewish, he was conversant in Yiddish, able to read Hebrew and Aramaic texts, and was fully at home in the Jewish community, "During his stay in Amsterdam from 1739 to 1741, he studied together with a rabbi, ate kosher food, and visited each day the services at the synagogue. Thus, he soon gained considerable knowledge of Judaism and Jewish culture. After some initial difficulties, Lieberkühn enjoyed the trust and friendship of many Jews and was commonly called 'Rabbi Shmuel.'"[24]

To sum up these traits that contributed to Zinzendorf's revival of Messianic congregations in the eighteenth century, it may be said that he had a continuing vision for Israel's restoration and its " firstfruits," international influence, denominational backing to plant Messianic Jewish communities, resources he used to bless Messianic Jews and the wider Jewish community, high regard for

---

Society for Furtherance of the Gospel Among the Heathen, 1839), 157–58. Translated from *Beyträge zur Erbauung, aus der Brüdergemeine* 2 (1817): 84. Zinzendorf maintained a similar view (Dithmar, *Zinzendorfs nonkonformistische Haltung zum Judentum*, 109–115).

[23] See Yaakov Ariel, "A New Model of Christian Interaction with the Jews: The Institutum Judaicum and Missions to the Jews in the Atlantic World," *Journal of Early Modern History* 21 (2017): 117; *Periodical Accounts Relating to the Missions of the Church of the United Brethren, Established Among the Heathen*, 153; Greisiger, "Recent Publications on the German Pietists' Mission to the Jews," 158.

[24] Vogt, "The Attitude of Eighteenth Century German Pietism toward Jews and Judaism," 24.

Jewish people, opposition to Christian anti-Semitism, a witness among Jews characterized by love and respect, commitment to prayer for Israel, an ecumenical heart, and involvement in raising up Messianic leaders.

Pastor Jack and the Messianic Movement in the Late Twentieth Century

Count Zinzendorf (1700–1760) opened the door to Messianic Jews and Messianic Judaism in the eighteenth century, but it was not until two hundred years after his death, in the late twentieth century, that Messianic synagogues, reflecting the *Judenkehille* model, began to dot the landscape of major cities around the world.

In the 1960s and 1970s, many Jews in their twenties became believers in Jesus and refused to assimilate into Gentile churches. They wanted to maintain their Jewish identity, live as Jews, and lift up the name of Jesus within their local Jewish communities, and they established Messianic Jewish congregations to make this possible. Within a decade, the Messianic Jewish movement went from being a blip on the North American religious scene to being a grassroots congregational movement fueled by a new generation of Messianic Jews.[25]

It was during this time that Pastor Jack Hayford began leading The Church On The Way in Van Nuys, California (1969–). The Jesus Movement was in full swing and hundreds of Jewish followers of Jesus began attending Hayford's church. In addition to teaching in a way that affirmed Jesus-believing Jews as Jews, at The Church On The Way,

---

[25] The Union of Messianic Jewish Congregations (UMJC) was formed in 1979 with nineteen member congregations, and the International Alliance of Messianic Congregations and Synagogues (IAMCS) followed in 1986 with fifteen member congregations. In 2017, these two umbrella organizations represent more than two hundred Messianic synagogues. There are an additional three-hundred-plus congregations around the world that are independent or linked to smaller Messianic Jewish networks. See Rudolph, "Messianic Judaism in Antiquity and in the Modern Era," 30–31.

Hayford backed the planting of Messianic synagogues in Los Angeles. Dr. Ray Gannon, who established one of these synagogues, remembers Hayford's staunch support for the growing Messianic community:

> The Church On The Way was just taking off when we started doing Jewish evangelism in greater Los Angeles. About half of the Jewish people we discipled were culturally comfortable to attend churches. For the balance we provided Messianic synagogues to meet their spiritual, cultural and social needs. Many of our Beth Emanuel regulars in our chain of multiplied Jewish home Bible studies across Los Angeles attended The Church On The Way, particularly before we moved into the synagogue model (November 1973). Jack was always supportive of me and the Jewish expression of our commonly shared Jewish saints.... He was very happy to have many hundreds of Jewish believers in his church but always was supportive of our Temple Beth Emanuel Messianic Synagogue located just 5 miles away. When I introduced Jack as a speaker for the (Mike Evans) Shechinah 1976 conference at USC, I introduced him as the man with the largest Jewish ministry in America. At that time some thought perhaps 500–1,000 Jewish people visited his congregation each week.... Ari and Shira Sorko-Ram had met at The Church On The Way.... David Stern likewise attended Jack's teachings at The Church On The Way in those early days until he finished Fuller (MDiv) and went to work with Jews for Jesus.... Jack has been nothing but a great friend to Jewish ministry in all the 45 years I have known him.[26]

Why did Hayford become a champion of the Messianic community? He addresses this question in his essay "Allowing

---

[26] From personal correspondence with Ray Gannon, 10 May 2017.

the Spirit to Refocus Our Identity" (2011),[27] published in *Unity: Awakening the One New Man* (a volume representing a collaboration of Gentile Christians and Messianic Jews).[28] Here Hayford offers three insights that contributed to his "introduction to" and "approach in partnering with" Messianic Jews:[29] (1) Gentile believers have a primary mission to love, affirm, and stand with the Jewish people; (2) The whole body of Christ needs to embrace Messianic Jews in order to become One New Man; and (3) One must be awakened by the Holy Spirit to these spiritual truths.

A Primary Mission to the Jewish People

The Church On The Way is situated in an area where almost half a million Jewish people live. Consequently, many Jewish people have visited the church, and Hayford has invited them to "open their hearts" to Jesus the Messiah:

> For more than three decades, the context of my life was localized at The Church On The Way. It is still where I attend, as well as where I occasionally speak. Over the years, I have watched a lot happen. There are 400,000 Jews within a 25-mile radius of the church. Among the 75,000 decisions made for Christ at The Church On The Way, I know that hundreds have been made by Jews.... It might be a surprise to learn that during those years, I never asked anyone to "become a Christian" when I gave an invitation. I never said I wasn't asking that; I think most Gentile Christians presume that was what I was doing because they know I am not ashamed to be called

[27] Jack Hayford, "Allowing the Spirit to Refocus Our Identity," 2011. Online: http://www.jackhayford.org.

[28] Jack Hayford, "Allowing the Spirit to Refocus Our Identity," in *Unity: Awakening the One New Man* (eds. Robert F. Wolff and Don Enevoldsen; Chambersburg: Drawbaugh, 2011), 17–32. First published as *Awakening the One New Man* (Shippensburg: Destiny Image, 2011).

[29] Hayford, "Allowing the Spirit to Refocus Our Identity," 20.

that. The reason I didn't use those words was because I knew that there were always Jews who came to our church—they might be brought by people with whom they work, or by other Jews, perhaps relatives. In the Jewish mindset, "becoming a Christian" means something it doesn't mean to the average Gentile. While for Gentiles, it is an issue of faith, to a Jew, it can seem to be an issue of sacrificing one's individuality, heritage, and ethnicity.[30]

Hayford developed a profound sense of mission to love and care for the Jewish people in this ecclesial setting where he pastored hundreds of Jews.[31] Moreover, during the course of his Jew-Gentile ministry at The Church On The Way, he came to a growing awareness that Jewish people were in a unique covenant relationship with the God of Israel that required affirmation by the Gentile Christian world: "The heart of God is clearly committed to all peoples, but there is a distinct covenant commitment of His love and purpose for Israel."[32] In addition to God's irrevocable covenant with the Jewish people, Hayford understood from Romans 11:17–21 that Gentile believers were dependent on the descendants of Abraham, Isaac, and Jacob. The Jewish people were the "root system" on which Gentile believers stood:

> "And if some of the branches were broken off, and you, being a wild olive tree, were grafted in among them, and with them became a partaker of the root and fatness of the olive tree, do not boast against the branches. But if you do boast, *remember that* you do not support the root, but the root *supports* you. You will say then, 'Branches were broken off that I might be grafted in.' Well *said*. Because of unbelief they were broken off, and

---

[30] Jack Hayford, "Ready for the Wedding" (2014), 1. Online: http://www.jackhayford.org.

[31] Jack Hayford, "Seeing Israel and the Jews Through the Eyes of God" (26 April 1995), 11. Online: http://www.jackhayford.org.

[32] Jack Hayford, "Understanding God's Purposes for Israel" (2 July 2000), 1. Online: http://www.jackhayford.org; cf. Jack Hayford, "The Jews: God's Chosen People" (29 April 2001), 3, 6–7. Online: http://www.jackhayford.org.

you stand by faith. Do not be haughty, but fear. For if God did not spare the natural branches, He may not spare you either" (Romans 11:17–21 NKJV). Verses 17 through 21 of Romans 11 says, in effect: You would be wise, then, as a Gentile believer, to note that your root system comes from the Jews. It would be both foolish and mindless not to acknowledge that there is an accountability in that relationship that holds you dutiful to care, to pray for, and to support them. Not because of their perfection (any more than God has loved you or me because of our perfection), but because it is of a divine order of things.[33]

For these reasons, Hayford came to regard love and care for the Jewish people as a "primary mission" of The Church On The Way and The King's University. This ethic in turn became part of the DNA of these institutions:

I hold *all* Jews in deep respect, no matter what their spiritual convictions may be. My belief is that our primary mission as a local congregation as well as an educational center training leaders for ministry in today's Church, is to love, affirm, and stand with the Jewish people and Israel.[34]

Hayford has asserted for more than forty years that love for the Jewish people should lead to condemning anti-Semitism of all kinds, including replacement theology:

Many Christians are subconsciously, if not consciously resonant to the spirit of anti-Semitism that is broadly spread throughout the world.[35]

---

[33] Hayford, "Understanding God's Purposes for Israel," 2.

[34] Hayford, "Allowing the Spirit to Refocus Our Identity," 20.

[35] Hayford, "Seeing Israel and the Jews Through the Eyes of God," 31. Cf. Hayford, "Allowing the Spirit to Refocus Our Identity," 22–23.

Some Christians oppose prophetic promises regarding the restoration of national Israel. There is a line of
teaching called "Replacement Theology."… Replacement
Theology is essentially a theological system that says
when the Jew rejected the Messiah at the time of Christ,
that God broke covenant forever with Israel, and now
His covenant with all mankind is solely through the
church.… Replacement Theology holds then that the
church, only the church, is Israel today.[36]

Hayford has drawn attention to the direct correlation between
anti-Semitism and the growing anti-Zionist movement among Jesus
believers today.[37] What is needed, Hayford has argued, is sincere
repentance, including representative repentance,[38] for the long
history of replacement theology and Christian anti-Semitism that
culminated in the Holocaust. Hayford has called Gentile Christians
to stand on the biblical promises of God's irrevocable covenant with
the descendants of Abraham, Isaac and Jacob, and, *ipso facto*, to
stand with the nation of Israel:

First, I want to predicate everything that follows by
saying that when we speak about our commitment to
stand against anti-Semitism and to take a pro-Israel
stance, it is not because everything is always done perfectly by the Israeli political or military system. Neither is
it because we hold anti-Arab attitudes—we don't.…
From the time of Abraham, the land of Israel (*eretz
Yisrael* in Hebrew) has been given to the Jews as "an
everlasting covenant" (Genesis 17:7–8; 26:3–5;
35:11–15). Deuteronomy 28–30 reveal the conditions of

[36] Hayford, "Seeing Israel and the Jews Through the Eyes of God," 34.
[37] Hayford, "Seeing Israel and the Jews Through the Eyes of God," 31–32.
[38] Hayford, "Seeing Israel and the Jews Through the Eyes of God," 38–39.

obedience, penalties of disobedience, and promises of
forgiveness and restoration regarding the covenant.[39]

Zechariah 12–14 is crystal clear in saying that when all
the nations of the world gather against Israel, then look
up because this thing is closing down.[40]

Jesus had prophesied that the second coming would
relate to the season He would return.… He relates it to
the restoration of the city of Jerusalem—that Jerusalem
would be trodden down by the Gentiles or the nations of
the world, until the time of the fullness of the Gentiles is
being realized [Luke 21:24].[41]

Hayford has served on the board of directors of several organizations that advocate for the Jewish state, including the Fellowship
of Israel Related Ministries (FIRM) and the Israel-Christian Nexus,
of which he was a co-founder. He has traveled to Israel more than
40 times, leading tour groups, and has made a practice of walking
through the length and breadth of the land, marked off by four altars
of stones that he set up in the north, south, east, and west, which
serve as symbols of intercession for the nation.[42] Hayford has given
vision and voice to the importance of all followers of Jesus praying
for the peace of Jerusalem:

The prayer for the peace of Jerusalem (Psalm 122:6) is a
perpetual call to believers.[43]

---

[39] Hayford, "Understanding God's Purposes for Israel," 1.
[40] Hayford, "Understanding God's Purposes for Israel," 5. Cf. Hayford, "Seeing Israel and
the Jews Through the Eyes of God," 32.
[41] Hayford, "Understanding God's Purposes for Israel," 5.
[42] Jack Hayford, "A Pilgrimage to Secure Boundaries" (8 January 2003), 18–32. Online:
http://www.jackhayford.org.
[43] Hayford, "Understanding God's Purposes for Israel," 6.

> Our prophetic intercession … praying for Israel, was based
> on this: the foundational conviction of these two things:
> that the peace of Jerusalem cannot ultimately be found any
> other way than through prayer, which is why God in his
> eternal Word has said, "Pray for the peace of Jerusalem."
> Secondly, that Israel's return, not only to her land, but to
> her God, is essential for peace.[44]

As co-chair of the Day of Prayer for the Peace of Jerusalem, Hayford has encouraged Christians to take the One Percent Challenge, that is, to devote 1% of each day—14 minutes—to pray for the Jewish people and the state of Israel.[45]

The One New Man

A second insight that contributed to Hayford partnering with Messianic Jews has been his vision for the One New Man, made up of Jews and Gentiles in Messiah (Ephesians 2:11–22). For centuries, many Gentile Christians have believed that they did not need Jews. However, Hayford has maintained that there is a relationship of interdependence and mutual blessing between Jewish and Gentile believers in Jesus,[46] the natural and grafted-in branches of the Romans 11 olive tree. The Church needs Messianic Jews to be fully and authentically the One New Man.[47] This means that Gentile Christian leaders should extend the right hand of fellowship and welcome Messianic Jews:

> Every effort should be bent toward helping the whole
> Body of Christ recognize, embrace, and receive Messianic
> Jews with understanding.[48]

---

[44] Hayford, "A Pilgrimage to Secure Boundaries," 22, 24. Cf. Ibid, 28.

[45] Steve Strang, "Hayford Predicts Persecution for Christians Who Stand with Israel," 7 February 2015. Online: http://www.charismanews.com.

[46] Hayford, "Allowing the Spirit to Refocus Our Identity," 28.

[47] Hayford, "Allowing the Spirit to Refocus Our Identity," 18–19, 28–30.

[48] Hayford, "Allowing the Spirit to Refocus Our Identity," 20–21.

Hayford has modeled this hospitality. As mentioned above, since the 1970s, he has been a champion of the Messianic movement in the Los Angeles area by supporting Messianic synagogues and affirming the Jewish identity of hundreds of Jewish believers in Jesus at The Church On The Way. Hayford has consistently maintained that Messianic Jews remain part of the covenant calling and destiny of their people, Israel:

> Galatians 3:28 says that in Christ there is neither Jew nor Greek. Replacement Theology argues that there is not any distinction anymore.... But in Romans 1:16, there the apostle Paul says, "I am not ashamed of the Gospel, for it is the power of God unto salvation ... for the Jew first and also to the Greek (or to the Gentile)." There he is dealing with individuality.... There is equality, but there is still individuality. You don't lose your ethnicity; the integrity of this distinction is maintained in Scripture. But many believers, listen, many believers don't know that this debate exists in the church and some have allowed themselves to believe that Jews are just like everybody else. Well, what is the significance of that? The significance of that posture will be that when God begins to move among the Jews in a unique and distinct way, there won't be any capacity to respond to them in that way because those who regard distinction as lost refuse to recognize that there are covenants and prophecies that are made that have bearing on the Jews, not only as an ethnic people, but as a people of national destiny.[49]

Because of God's ancient and irrevocable covenant with Israel, Hayford has regarded Messianic Jews as "elder brothers and sisters" in the Lord:

---

[49] Hayford, "Seeing Israel and the Jews Through the Eyes of God," 35–36.

["Allowing the Spirit to Refocus Our Identity"] reflects my great love and respect for Jews on any terms. However, I want to convey my distinct desire to honor each Jewish person whom the *Ruach haKodesh* (the Holy Spirit) has brought to faith in Jesus of Nazareth as the Son of God, Savior. They represent the people God chose millennia ago to bear the testimony of the One God, Creator of all, to deliver the Holy Scriptures to the world, and to be the avenue by which the world's Redeemer, the Son of God, would be born. In a very real sense, each of them may well be acknowledged as my "elder brothers and sisters," and thereby I pursue the unity of our fellowship in Yeshua.[50]

One of the most far-reaching ways that Hayford has championed the Messianic Jewish community is through his support for Toward Jerusalem Council II (TJCII), an initiative to pursue repentance and reconciliation between the Jewish and Gentile wings of the Church:

The vision is that one day there will be a second Council of Jerusalem that will be, in an important respect, the inverse of the first Council described in Acts 15. Whereas the first Council was made up of Jewish believers in Yeshua (Jesus), who decided not to impose on the Gentiles the requirements of the Jewish law, so the second Council would be made up of Gentile church leaders, who would recognize and welcome the Jewish believers in Yeshua without requiring them to abandon their Jewish identity and practice.[51]

---

[50] Hayford, "Allowing the Spirit to Refocus Our Identity," 32.

[51] Toward Jerusalem Council II, "Who We Are." Online: http://tjcii.org/about-us. See also Peter Hocken, *The Challenges of the Pentecostal, Charismatic and Messianic Movements: The Tensions of the Spirit* (Burlington: Ashgate, 2009), 111–12; Peter Hocken, *Azusa, Rome, and Zion: Pentecostal Faith, Catholic Reform, and Jewish Roots* (Eugene: Pickwick, 2016), 133–61, 199; Daniel C. Juster, "Messianic Gentiles and the Gentile Christian World," in *Introduction to Messianic Judaism*, 139–42.

Hayford was one of the first to support TJCII. Rabbi Marty Waldman, who had the vision for this initiative, traveled to Israel in March 1995 to seek Pastor Jack's wisdom in the matter. At that time, Hayford was teaching at a Messianic Jewish leadership conference in Jerusalem hosted by Maoz Ministries and funded by The Church On The Way with more than 200 Messianic Israeli leaders in attendance.[52] After one of the sessions, Waldman went up and said, "Dr. Hayford, the Lord has given to me what I believe could be a very important vision. May I share it with you?" Waldman recounts, "His response was, 'Let's have lunch tomorrow.' The next day I had lunch with Jack and his wife and presented him with a written copy of the vision. He read it, then turned to me and responded, 'Marty, this is from God.' We talked about it during lunch and he offered his 100% endorsement … Jack made that commitment to TJCII even before we had formed a TJCII Executive Committee! I returned from Israel feeling confident that the vision of TJCII was indeed a vision from the LORD."[53] A month later, Hayford referred to Waldman and his vision in his teaching "Seeing Israel and the Jews Through the Eyes of God."[54] Hayford was the opening speaker for the first TJCII consultation in 2003. In 2009, through Hayford's leadership as president of the International Church of the Foursquare Gospel, which represents globally more than 66,000 churches (including several Messianic Jewish congregations)[55] in 140+ countries,[56] ICFG became the first larger denomination to

---

[52] "Our congregation made a gift of in excess of $25,000 to assist in making possible that conference that occurred in the middle of March, just a little over a month ago. So you prayed and you gave, and we gave the report last week" (Hayford, "Seeing Israel and the Jews Through the Eyes of God," 7). Cf. Ibid., 5, 19–20.

[53] *Toward Jerusalem Council II: Vision, Origin and Documents* (TJCII, 2010).

[54] Hayford, "Seeing Israel and the Jews Through the Eyes of God," 19–20.

[55] The denomination also has an association for leaders of Foursquare Messianic congregations. "The Foursquare Rabbis Caucus is the voice of the Messianic Movement within the International Church of the Foursquare Gospel. Our mission is to encourage and network messianic leaders and congregations. We facilitate teaching the Jewish roots of Christianity and God's heart for Israel and the Church. Our desire is to expand the awareness of the Jewish Messiah in the world today" (http://foursquaremessianic.wixsite.com/frchome).

[56] See http://www.foursquare.org.

endorse the TJCII "Seven Affirmations" statement. This document declares:

> Consistent with the principle established in the original Jerusalem Council of Acts Chapter 15 regarding respect for diversity in the Body of Christ concerning Jewish and Gentile identity, we do make the following affirmations:
>
> 1. We affirm the election of Israel, its irrevocable nature and God's unfinished work with the Jewish people regarding salvation and the role of Israel as a blessing to the nations.
> 2. We affirm that Jews who come to faith in the Messiah, Jesus, are called to retain their Jewish identity and live as part of their people in ways consistent with the New Covenant.
> 3. We affirm the formation of Messianic Jewish congregations as a significant and effective way to express Jewish collective identity (in Jesus) and as a means of witnessing to Jesus before the Jewish community. We also affirm Jewish individuals and groups that are part of churches and encourage them in their commitment to Jewish life and identity.
> 4. We affirm our willingness as an ecclesiastical body to build bridges to the Messianic Jewish community; to extend the hand of friendship and to pray for their growth and vitality.
> 5. We affirm our willingness to share our resources with Messianic Jewish congregations, mission organizations and theological training institutes so as to empower them to fulfill their God-given purpose.
> 6. We affirm our willingness to be a voice within our own ecclesiastical structures and spheres of influence against all forms of anti-Semitism, replacement theology (supersessionism) and teaching that precludes the expression of Jewish identity in Jesus.
> 7. Finally, we affirm that as Jewish and Gentile expressions of life in Jesus grow organically side by side with distinct

identities that God will be glorified; that the Kingdom of Heaven will be advanced and that the vision of "the one new man" in Ephesians 2 will unfold as part of the original Abrahamic blessing to the nations.

The King's University adopted the TJCII Seven Affirmations statement in 2016 with Hayford's longstanding support for the document being a significant factor. Hayford has also spoken at reconciliation conferences where ecclesial leaders focus on healing the schism between Messianic Jews and Gentile Christians through representative repentance:

> Unforgettable among these is that highlight occasion I shared with more than 1,000 leaders who were at the 2004 conference conducted by *The Road to Jerusalem* ministry led by Bill McCartney and Raleigh Washington. Dr. Bill Hamel and I each spoke, representing the historic and evangelical Christian community of our day, addressing Daniel Juster and Jonathan Bernis of the Messianic Jewish community. Our purpose was to break down all walls that have separated us as brothers within the One New Man. Pastor Hamel and I were humbled to stand as representatives of Gentile believers, as well as Protestant denominational leaders, to pray as intercessory penitents for the violations—unintended or intentional—that have been inflicted by Gentile believers upon both the Jewish people historically and the Messianic Jewish brethren and sisters in recent years. We united on the platform, a large crowd comprising both peoples in near equal numbers. Though a symbolic act to those unaware of the spiritual power of "representative repentance," we invoked God's blessing to multiply our manifest unity of that moment in ever widening circles—among churches, groups, and individual believers globally. In that moment, all who were present saw a living demonstration of the One New Man, Jew and Gentile

grafted together, laying aside their differences, humbly asking forgiveness after centuries of persecution directed towards each other.[57]

In addition, Hayford has played a key role in the development of a Messianic Jewish Bible translation through his endorsement of the Tree of Life Version (TLV). The King's University is a Founding University Sponsor of the version, and Jack Hayford Ministries hosted a TLV Bible Conference at the university in 2015 that addressed Messianic Jewish translation issues. At a special TKU chapel where the TLV was introduced, Rabbi Mark Greenberg, Chairman of the Board of the TLV, expressed the sentiment of many Messianic Jewish leaders when he thanked Pastor Jack for his decades-long commitment to mentoring leaders in the Messianic community and for his support for the TLV:

> The King's University has chosen to stand with the Messianic remnant of Israel to help complete this Bible translation out of our loving bond in Yeshua. The King's University chancellor, Pastor Jack Hayford, has been a spiritual father to many key Messianic Jewish leaders throughout the development of the Messianic Jewish movement. We are going back thirty years or more. His personal commitment to nurture Messianic leaders has been international in scope and multigenerational. Pastor Jack and The King's University have modeled divine service in their love and support for all Israel, and have established their faithful partnership with God as joint blessers of Israel (Gen 12:3).[58]

It is beyond the scope of this essay to survey all the many ways that Hayford has been a champion of the Messianic Jewish community. This notwithstanding, a case can be made that his

---

[57] Hayford, "Allowing the Spirit to Refocus Our Identity," 32.
[58] Mark Greenburg, "TLV & TKU Chapel" (2013). Online: https://www.youtube.com.

greatest gift to Messianic Jews has been in the area of leadership development. Pastor Jack has not only mentored dozens of key Messianic Jewish leaders over the past 45 years, but he also established a Messianic Jewish Studies program at The King's University for the formal training of Messianic rabbis and other leaders who are called to serve as bridges between the Church and the Jewish people.

The story of how this educational program began is a testimony to Pastor Jack's commitment to serve the Messianic movement: In April 2007, Hayford taught a School of Pastoral Nurture for Messianic leaders in Van Nuys that was sponsored by Rabbi Jonathan Bernis of Jewish Voice Ministries International (JVMI). More than 40 Messianic Jewish leaders attended. In the middle of one of the sessions, after talking about the importance of Jerusalem, Pastor Jack turned to Rabbi Bernis and said, "I really do feel Jonathan that we are supposed to be available for ongoing Messianic studies integrated into the things we are doing at The King's.... I feel this profoundly and I don't know its implications."[59] Later he told Rabbi Bernis that it "was a prophetic moment of destiny that must be seized."[60] At the end of the meetings, Hayford gave Dr. Paul Chappell approval to work out the details with Rabbi Bernis and Dr. Wayne Wilks, with the goal of establishing a partnership between The King's College and Seminary (later renamed The King's University), JVMI, and Messianic Jewish Bible Institutes (MJBI).[61] Classes began that fall under the oversight of Dr. Ray Gannon, the first director of The King's Messianic Jewish Studies (MJS) Program.

In 2017, the director of the Messianic Jewish Studies program was Dr. David Rudolph, a second-generation Messianic Jew, and its full-time Coordinator was Tali Snow, also a second-generation Messianic Jew. The program had over 100 degree students and

[59] From Dr. Hayford's teaching on Friday, 27 April 2007.

[60] From an email that Dr. Wilks sent to the MJBI board on April 28, 2007 with the subject heading "MJBI Partnership with The King's College and Seminary."

[61] Subsequent to the conference, Rabbi Dan Juster became a key Tikkun/MJBI leader involved in the formation of the program.

offered several accredited degrees with a concentration in Messianic Jewish Studies that could be completed entirely online or on campus, including a Bachelor of Biblical & Theological Studies, Master of Practical Theology, and Master of Divinity. The university also offered an accredited Doctor of Ministry with a Messianic Jewish Studies track.[62]

Hayford's vision to train Messianic Jewish leaders has led to The King's University becoming an approved school of the Union of Messianic Jewish Congregations (UMJC) and offering the courses needed for *Smikha* (Rabbinical ordination) and *Madrikh* (teacher) certification. Pastor Jack had the foresight to recognize that the Messianic movement would need to raise up hundreds of new leaders to serve the next generation, and that Messianic rabbis and other leaders called to be bridges between the Church and the Jewish people required specialized training.[63] According to Pastor Jack, "The King's University has made a firm commitment to develop an extensive Messianic Jewish Studies program.... By providing this platform for university-level biblical education for both Jewish and Christian students, they are blessing Israel while advancing the kingdom of God and the restoration of the world to God through Messiah Yeshua."[64]

Awakening by the Holy Spirit

A third reason that Hayford has given for partnering with Messianic Jews is that the Holy Spirit awakened him to the importance of this:

> I was "born again" already but was "blind" to the truth of the principle that reveals the *spiritual* indebtedness *all* believers owe to the Jews (see Romans. 15:15–17).

[62] See http://www.tku.edu/messianicstudies

[63] See David Rudolph, "The Rabbi as Pastor Theologian: Torah Scholars Qua Ecclesial Leaders in the Post-Biblical Jewish Context," Center for Pastor Theologians (CPT) Symposium, 12 October 2009. Online: http://www.rabbidavid.net.

[64] Jack Hayford, "TLV & TKU Chapel" (2013). Online: https://www.youtube.com.

Though I had received Christ, as well as having received his call into pastoral ministry before I entered college, I was in pastoral ministry nearly 15 years before I began to see how unaware I was. The implications of my spiritual obligation to prioritize our call to *first* love, honor and thus *reach out* to God's ancient people, the Jews. I was "blind though born again," not even "seeing" the many basic biblical statements that forthrightly reveal that my faith in Jesus Christ had brought me (a) through *their* promised Messiah (see Gal. 3:26–27), (b) into an intended unity *with believing Jews* in the Body of Christ (see Gal. 3:28), (c) uniting us with them in faith first seeded by *Abraham* (see Gal. 3:29) and, (d) by faith in Christ alone, apart from the law, *grafting me* into the single root system through which eternal life flows— from the Messiah (see Isa. 53:2–6).[65]

Hayford concludes that a spiritual "awakening" is necessary to see these truths about the One New Man:

The biblical call to the One New Man will only *ultimately* be received by a Holy Spirit-begotten awakening of a Gentile believer's "inner man." Reasoned teaching is valuable, but prayerful availability to the Holy Spirit, as the One Jesus said would "lead you into all truth," will determine the depth and practical commitment anyone brings to a One New Man lifestyle. This is not because the subject is without intellectual or theological footings, but because it is *spiritual* truth. It will only realize a passionate response in our lifestyle where *hearts* invite the Holy Spirit—as they prayerfully open the Word and openly engage conversation and fellowship with Messianic leaders.[66]

[65] Hayford, "Allowing the Spirit to Refocus Our Identity," 26.
[66] Hayford, "Allowing the Spirit to Refocus Our Identity," 21.

Pastor Jack has fervently maintained for half a century that unity in the Church and the global spread of the gospel will only be realized when we, like Peter in Acts 10–11, are awakened by the Holy Spirit to what God is doing today in forming His One New Man made up of Jews and Gentiles in Messiah. Hayford gives the charge, *"If any one of us—but better, each one of us—will open* [up] to the Lord's purpose to give rise to [the] One New Man, revival will spread and Messiah Jesus will be glorified through His Church."[67]

Conclusion

The modern Messianic movement budded in the early eighteenth century and blossomed in the late twentieth century. Count Zinzendorf and Pastor Jack have made their marks in history as Gentile champions of the Messianic Jewish community during these two key stages in the movement's development. There is a Yiddish saying: *A freint bleibt a freint biz di kesheneh* ("A friend remains a friend up to his pocket"). Count Zinzendorf and Pastor Jack have been more than friends of the Messianic community; they have been true brothers in the Lord. They not only gave what was in their pockets, but they also gave the shirts off their backs. They are shining examples of Gentile Christian leaders who, being awakened by the Holy Spirit and stirred to "love, honor and thus *reach out* to God's covenant people," stoked the flames of Messianic Jewish revival.

---

[67] Hayford, "Allowing the Spirit to Refocus Our Identity," 28–29.

5

The Many Lives of Benjamin Hardin Irwin (1854–1926)

Vinson Synan

ONE OF THE most elusive figures in recent American religious history has been Benjamin Hardin Irwin, a major mover and shaker in the Holiness-Pentecostal Movement of the late nineteenth and early twentieth centuries. He is known mainly as the founder of the Fire-Baptized Holiness Church, which served as a major bridge between the American Holiness and Pentecostal movements. Although much has been known about his early life and ministry, little has been known about the end of his life. In fact, until recently, no one had even seen a photograph of him or knew when or where he died. For over fifty years, I have searched for more data on the last part of his life. Only now do we know more about the life of this important leader.

In his lifetime of some 72 years, Irwin led many lives. This paper will detail Irwin as a Primitive Baptist youth, a lawyer, an American Baptist pastor, a Wesleyan Methodist Holiness preacher, an international evangelist, the founder of an international denomination called the Fire Baptized Holiness Church, an utter failure as a husband and father, and, finally, as a preacher in the Two-Seed-in-the-Spirit Predestinarian Baptist Church.

Benjamin Hardin Irwin was born in Mercer County, Missouri, in 1854. He was raised in an ultra-Calvinist "hard shell (Primitive Baptist) Church."[1] His youth was spent in Tecumseh, Nebraska,

---

[1] This information was in Irwin's paper, *Live Coals of Fire*, June 1, 1900, p. 2. In 2017, Irwin's biography, along with his major writings, will appear as *Fire-Baptized: The Many*

117

where his family moved by covered wagon in 1863. There, he studied law and maintained a mediocre law practice for eight years. In 1876 he married Anna M. Stewart. Together, they had one son, Stewart Toombs Irwin, who was to help him in ministry in later years. In 1879 he was converted in a Primitive Baptist church and afterwards studied for the ministry while serving as pastor of his Baptist congregation. In 1890 he was ordained by the American Baptist Church.[2] During this time, Irwin came into contact with preachers of the Iowa Holiness Association, which had recently been organized by Isaiah Reid as part of the massive and fast-growing national Holiness Association movement. In 1891 after receiving the Wesleyan experience of "entire sanctification," Irwin left the Baptist church to become a "John Wesley Methodist."[3]

After joining the Wesleyan Methodist Church, Irwin began an itinerant evangelistic ministry, in which he soon exhibited exceptional gifts of oratorical preaching, attracting large crowds to his meetings. He also became known as a divine healer who claimed miraculous healings in answer to prayer. His earlier meetings, which were held in Kansas, Nebraska, and Iowa, were conducted in churches, tents, and camp meetings, some of which were held in Brethren in Christ and Mennonite congregations. At this stage of ministry, Irwin was a typical Holiness preacher, emphasizing

---

Lives of Benjamin Hardin Irwin by Vinson Synan and Dan Woods (Lexington, KY: E-Meth Publisher, forthcoming).

[2] The American Baptist Church was also known as a "Missionary" Baptist Church, in contrast to the Primitive Baptists, who opposed foreign missions since everyone was already elected to be saved or lost.

[3] The major contemporary source on Irwin is J. H. King, "History of the Fire-Baptized Holiness Church," *The Pentecostal Holiness Advocate*, March 24, 1921, p. 4. Also see Vinson Synan, *The Old Time Power: A History of the Pentecostal Holiness Church* (Franklin Springs, GA: Advocate Press, 1998), pp. 44–66. Also see Joseph E. Campbell, *The Pentecostal Holiness Church (1898–1948)* (Franklin Springs, GA: Publishing House of the Pentecostal Holiness Church, 1951), pp. 196–200. Also see *American Baptist Yearbook, 1891* (Philadelphia), p. 143. Also James Kerwin, "Isaiah Reid" (masters thesis, Regent University, 2014), pp. 194–204 and 291–300. P. 194 records his IHA membership as appearing in the 1892 minutes.

salvation, sanctification as a second work of grace, divine healing, and the pre-millennial second coming of Christ. At these meetings, one reported, "Irwin employed his brilliant intellectual powers, magnetic personality, ardent nature, and bold disposition" to sway the crowds.[4]

During his transition to the Methodist holiness tradition, Irwin began a deep study of major Methodist sources, including the works of John Wesley and such Catholic mystics as Madame Guyon and Francois Fenelon. He was most impressed, however, with the works of the Anglican John Fletcher, Wesley's theologian and designated successor. In Fletcher's massive work, *Checks to Antinomianism*, Irwin saw the possibility of a "baptism of burning love" after sanctification, with more baptisms to follow. He then began to seek a third blessing, which he called a baptism in the Holy Ghost and fire.[5]

In October 1895 his ministry radically changed when he claimed to receive the experience of baptism in the Holy Ghost and "fire" while holding a revival in the town of Enid, Oklahoma. One night, while he was in bed, he described a burning sensation that made him "literally on fire" in a "luminous seven-fold light" that was "burning, glowing, and blazing" throughout his body.[6]

He soon began to teach this as a "third blessing" that he called "the fire." Soon hundreds of seekers came to the altars to seek this fiery baptism. A typical testimony was that of Benjamin Wesley Young at the 1896 Neosho Valley Holiness Camp meeting in Kansas:

> I felt led to pray to the God of Fire. God got hold of me
> and the mighty cyclone came and I was prostrated. All at
> once the mighty wave struck me.... I rolled in the flames

---

[4] Martin Schrag, "The Spiritual Pilgrimage of the Reverend Benjamin Hardin Irwin" *Brethren in Christ History and Life* 4 (June 1, 1981), pp. 3–29. Also see Craig Charles Fankhauser, "The Fire Baptized Revolt (1895–1911) in "The Heritage of Faith" (masters thesis, Pittsburgh State University, Kansas, 1983), pp. 121–147.

[5] Vinson Synan, *The Holiness Pentecostal Tradition* (Battle Creek: Wm. E. Eerdmans, 1997), pp. 1–60.

[6] Synan, *Old Time Power*, p. 46.

and the flames in me, and the building was a solid mass
of fire. It was brighter than five suns could make it… It
was a sea of glass mingled with fire and it settled into a
white heat.[7]

Irwin's fame spread through reports in several Holiness journals,
and soon invitations poured in for him to preach in other parts of
America and even in Canada. In 1896 he held protracted meetings
in Iowa, Kansas, Oklahoma, and in Winnipeg, Canada. Hundreds
of people came to these meetings to receive the fire. In some cases,
the tents could hold only half the people who crowded in to hear the
fiery evangelist.

Not everyone was pleased with the burgeoning popularity of
Irwin, however. In short order, two Holiness journals, the *Christian
Witness* and the *Christian Journal*, banned any reports of Irwin's
meetings. Others around the nation joined in to denounce what
they called "the third blessing heresy." The most important one
that supported Irwin was the *Way of Faith*, published in Columbia,
South Carolina, by J. M. Pike, an outspoken Methodist supporter
of the Holiness cause. Soon incredible reports of Irwin's meetings
appeared in the paper along with a booklet published by Irwin
called *Pyrophobia* (a morbid dread of fire). Readers all over the
nation, and especially the South, were entranced by these reports,
and soon the intrepid evangelist was invited to bring the fire to the
Old South.[8]

By December 1896 Irwin was in South Carolina preaching in
Wesleyan Methodist churches "in cyclone fashion." In Piedmont,
the pastor A. K. Willis received not only the "fire" but the "holy
dance." Everywhere Irwin preached, the people "jumped, shouted,
screamed, and praised God for the 'fire' baptism."[9] Everywhere
people testified to their experiences with the fire. An observer from

[7] Fankhauser, "The Fire-Baptized Revolt," p. 125.
[8] *The Way of Faith*, October 20, 1897, p. 2.
[9] King, *The Pentecostal Holiness Advocate*, March 24, 1921, pp. 4–5.

North Carolina, G. F Taylor, wrote the following description of Irwin's followers:

> The testimonies on the fire were very interesting. Some said they felt the fire burning in their souls, but others claimed it as burning in their bodies also. It was felt in the face, in the tongue, in the fingers, in the palm of the hand, in the feet, in the side, in the arms, and so on. Then the Bible itself often felt warm to those who had the fire in them. The church would seem to be lighted with fire, the trees of the wood would appear as flames of fire, the landscape would seem to be baptized in the glory of the fire. As some rode from one appointment to another, according to their testimonies, they seemed to be enveloped with the holy fire. The noise of the engine seemed to sound notes of praise to God, and the clatter of the wheels beneath the cars seemed to be saying *Glory to God, Hallelujah!* The coaches themselves were fire-lighted, and the wheels beneath seemed to be wheels of fire. Fire! Fire! Holy Fire!!! was the ring of their testimonies.[10]

With this notoriety, the future looked bright for the fast-rising evangelist who seemed to be taking the South by storm. During these years of barnstorming ministry, Irwin showed a talent for organizing his followers. Beginning at Olmitz, Iowa, in 1896, he led his followers into organizing the "Iowa Fire-Baptized Association" as a split in the older Iowa Holiness Association led by Isaiah Reid. Explaining this action, Irwin said:

> While at the Olmitz Camp Meeting it was clearly opened to us by the spirit of God that the Fire-Baptized saints should unite in a definite organization and an outline for a constitution came to me like a divine revelation. The

---

[10] G. F. Taylor, *The Pentecostal Holiness Advocate*, May 22, 1930, p. 8.

next morning I wrote the organizational constitution and submitted it to some of the brethren. It met with their most hearty approval. A few days later it was adopted and the first Fire Baptized Holiness Association was in existence.[11]

For the next two years, Irwin organized Fire-Baptized Holiness Associations and appointed "Overseers" in the following states and Canada: South Carolina, North Carolina, Georgia, Florida, Oklahoma, Kansas, Texas, Iowa, Virginia, Tennessee, Winnipeg, and Manitoba.[12] With this growing following, he and his friends organized a national denomination in Anderson, South Carolina, in 1898, which was called the "Fire Baptized Holiness Church." Joining the church at this meeting was the young Methodist pastor Joseph King, who later was destined to succeed Irwin as head of the church. Also joining at this time was W. E. Fuller of Mountsville, South Carolina, a black man who not only set out to organize black churches for the group but also was elected to the Executive Board of the new denomination. This was extremely rare at this time in American history.[13]

Irwin was named "General Overseer" for life with the power to appoint state and regional overseers for the rest of the nation and the Canadian provinces. To help spread his new movement, a year later, in 1899, Irwin began publication of a magazine which he called *Live Coals of Fire*, published from his home in Lincoln, Nebraska. In a shrewd decision, he sent copies of each paper to the Library of Congress in Washington, D.C., where they would be preserved forever.

The new church also adopted a governing manual titled the *Constitution and General Rules of the Fire-Baptized Holiness Church*. It was similar to other Holiness manuals with several glaring

[11] B. H. Irwin, "The Central Idea," *Live Coals of Fire*, May 10, 1899, p. 4.
[12] Synan, *Old Time Power*, p. 52.
[13] Ibid.

exceptions. The statement of faith included the following doctrinal paragraph:

> We believe that the baptism in the Holy Ghost is obtainable by a definite act of appropriating faith on the part of the fully cleansed believer. We believe also that the baptism with fire is a definite scriptural experience, obtainable by faith on the part of the Spirit-filled believer.[14]

It also contained one of the strictest Holiness codes ever. Although all this was not in the constitution, Irwin's followers were forbidden to eat pork and required to observe all the dietary restrictions of the Old Testament. Also, the drinking of coffee or tea was forbidden. Irwin also forbade the wearing of neckties for men and all jewelry for women. Like all other Holiness churches, the *Constitution* also forbade the use of all alcohol and tobacco products. Another restriction was the wearing of mustaches and beards on the men of the Church. In some meetings, new male converts were shorn of their facial hair by barbers who were hired to do the job right on the sidewalks.

As to the place of women in the new denomination, Irwin added a statement that was far ahead of its time in giving women full rights to ordination and equal leadership in the church. It read:

> In view of the increasing number and efficiency of women who are evidently called of God into the evangelistic, missionary, and rescue, provision is hereby made for the appointing, ordaining, and sending forth of women thus called of God, exactly the same as men, thus placing fire-baptized women, called of God, upon the same footing with our brethren of the stronger sex.[15]

---

[14] Ibid., pp. 50–52.

[15] *Constitution and General Rules of the Fire-Baptized Holiness Association of America* (1900), pp. 3–4. In fact, Irwin appointed many women as "Ruling Elders" in various parts of the church.

During his preaching tours, Irwin also began to teach doctrines that were then new to the holiness movement. These included the any-moment rapture of the church in the second coming of Christ and divine healing through the laying on of hands. Soon many people claimed instant and miraculous healing in his meetings. One such healing occurred in Mound Valley, Kansas, in 1897:

> The poor woman (was) still sick, and unable to walk, or turn herself in bed. She was also unsaved. Some of the "holy women" went to the wagon, and insisted upon having her carried to the meeting. She did not want to come, but they persisted. Four strong men lifted her from the wagon, and placed her upon a cot, and, like the case in the Bible, "brought her to Jesus." We prayed for her, and the writer preached, and then anointed her with oil in the name of the Lord. The brethren laid their hands upon her and she was not only converted right there but instantly healed of all her diseases. The writer took her by the hand, and said, "In the name of Jesus Christ, rise up and walk," and she did so, running back and forth *across* the platform, and testifying of what God had done for her soul. She testified then and there, "The Lord has healed me, both soul and body." Afterwards (toward the close of the service) she walked, unassisted, to the wagon seventy-five or a hundred yards away. The next day she was sanctified wholly and the same night received the experience of the baptism of fire as a separate and definite experience.[16]

With his fast-growing denomination in place, Irwin took annual preaching tours starting in the Midwest, going through the South, and ending up in Canada. In 1899 he added the baptism of "dynamite" as a fourth blessing, which everyone was expected to receive in his frenzied altar calls. This experience was based on

---

[16] "Brother Irwin's Letter," *Way of Faith and Neglected Themes* (October 20, 1897), p. 2.

Acts 1:8 (you shall receive "Power" or "dunamis" after the Holy Ghost has come upon you). In short order, he also attempted to lead his followers into subsequent baptisms of "oxidite," and "lyddite," explosives that were developed during the 1898 Boer War in South Africa. These new teachings were roundly denounced by the larger and more conservative Holiness movement.[17]

A typical testimony of one receiving the dynamite baptism was that of Jesse Bathurst of Kansas who reportedly got "spiritual hiccups" before his mouth flew open and "in went the little ball of pure irresistible dynamite."[18] A sad testimony of a poor lady who claimed all of these blessings was published in 1898:

> August 1st 1898, I was pardoned from my sins. On the following Sunday at eleven O'Clock, God sanctified me wholly. A few days later I received the Comforter. Later on in October, God gave me the Baptism of Fire. The devil and all the hosts of hell cannot make me doubt this. When my sister Mattie was married, I fell into a trance, and saw a vision. During services a night or so afterwards, God showed me that I needed more power for service, so I made my wants known, and prayer being offered, my faith took hold of God's promises, and I received the dynamite. A few nights after this, I received the definite experience of Lyddite. This gives the Devil trouble, and he wonders what is coming next. Well I am in for all the Lord has for me.[19]

The editor of the paper, A. M. Hills, said that this was "fanaticism," and that the lady should have sought for and received one more blessing, "the baptism of common sense." In later years, G. F. Taylor spoke of these experiences as a "religious rainbow's end."

---

[17] Synan, *Holiness-Pentecostal Movement*, pp. 57–58.

[18] "Jesse Bathurst's Letter," *Live Coals of Fire*, November 10, 1899, p. 5.

[19] Synan, *Old Time Power*, pp. 55–56. A. M. Hills, "Fanaticism Among Holiness People," *The Holiness Advocate*, April 1, 1903, p. 5.

In 1900, in spite of fierce opposition, Irwin began plans for a national headquarters in the town of Beniah, Tennessee, where he planned to have a missionary home and a "school of the prophets." In nearby Cleveland, Tennessee, he planted "satellite" churches, which later became the nucleus of the Church of God (Cleveland, Tennessee). In 1896 it was reported that in a Fire-Baptized Holiness meeting in the Schearer School House over the state line in North Carolina, some 100 persons spoke in tongues, thus presaging the later Pentecostal movement.

To the utter shock of his followers, Irwin was discovered in 1900 to be living in what was described as "open and gross sin" when he was reportedly seen leaving a bar in Kansas City (Omaha), drunken and smoking a cigar.[20] When he was confronted, he resigned as General Overseer and turned leadership over to his young assistant, J. H. King. King then was faced with the task of holding together the fragments of a movement that was fast falling apart.

After leaving the movement he founded, Irwin moved on to Oregon, leaving his wife behind. In these years of wandering, he met and married Mary Lee Jordan, a well-bred young woman in Texas who came from a socially prominent family. He married her, however, without divorcing his first wife, Anna. Thus, he was guilty of bigamy. To this marriage were born three sons and one daughter. The boys were named for three of Irwin's theological heroes: Vidalin, Fenelon, and Pember.[21]

Five years later, on December 25, 1906, Irwin showed up in a Pentecostal meeting in Salem, Oregon, led by Florence Crawford of Azusa Street fame, where he experienced the Pentecostal baptism evidenced by speaking in tongues. In his usual colorful language, he described his experience in *Triumphs of Faith*:

[20] Fankhouser, p. 144. Also see H. C. Morrison, "A Sad Duty," *Pentecostal Herald*, XII, June 20, 1900, p. 8.

[21] Much of this information is from Harold Schechter's *The Mad Sculptor* (New York: New Harvest, 2014), pp. 53–99.

My vocal organs were in the hands and under the
control of another, and that Other was the Divine
Paraclete within me. He was beginning to speak
through me in other tongues... Since that time I have
been used of God in speaking many times in Chinese,
Hindustani, Bengali, Arabic, and other languages
unknown to me.[22]

In later conversations with Charles Fox Parham, Irwin stated that
the tongues-attested baptism was what he had really been seeking
all along.[23] For four years, he carried on a Pentecostal ministry
connected with Crawford's Apostolic Faith Mission in Portland,
Oregon. Interestingly enough, the denomination he had founded
(the Fire Baptized Holiness Church) renounced, under King's
leadership, the multiple baptisms taught by Irwin and joined the
Pentecostal movement in 1908. In 1911, the Fire Baptized Holiness
Church merged with the Pentecostal Holiness Church as a part of
the worldwide Pentecostal movement.[24]

In the meantime, Irwin fell again into immorality. In 1910 he
abandoned his second wife, Mary for a younger woman, leaving
Mary with three young sons and no means of support. According
to Mary, her husband was "definitely immoral" and "a slave to his
passions." His son Fenelon said of him, "He wanted to reform the
world, but he could not reform himself." After leaving Mary, he
seldom saw his wife or children again.[25] After Irwin's departure,

---

[22] B. H. Irwin, "My Pentecostal Baptism—A Christmas Gift." *Triumphs of Faith* (May
1907), pp. 114–117. He also reported his Pentecostal experience in William J. Seymour,
Apostolic Faith, December 1906, p. 4.

[23] Synan, *Old Time Power*, p. 55.

[24] In 1921, King said, "How glad I am that the last vestige of Irwinism has been swept
from the P. H. Church. His life for many years alternated between the pulpit and the
harlot's house. He would go from the pulpit to wallow with prostitutes the rest of the
night. During that time he was preaching fiercely against wearing neckties, eating pork,
and drinking coffee." See J. H. King, "History of the F.B.H.C." in *The Pentecostal Holiness
Advocate*, April 7, 1921, p. 11.

[25] Schechter, *The Mad Sculptor*, pp. 52–64.

Mary joined Florence Crawford's large Pentecostal Church in Portland, where she became a dedicated altar worker. Living in poverty, she raised her boys on the paltry money she made as a washerwoman. The boys ultimately rejected the religion of their parents and as teenagers followed lives of crime, with much time spent in reformatories in Portland.[26]

The one son who made a name for himself was Fenelon, who changed his name to Robert Irwin.[27] An avid sculptor, he eventually made his way to New York City, where he became part of the social scene with his captivating personality and sculptural talent. In the end, he became famous, not for his art, but for murdering three persons in a mad rage and for standing trial in New York City in 1938 in a case that drew national attention. He was ultimately acquitted on grounds of insanity and lived out his life in a mental institution. His story and that of his father are recounted in Harold Schechter's 2014 book, *The Mad Sculptor*.[28]

Little is known about Benjamin Hardin Irwin after 1910. At some point, he left the Pentecostal Movement and became involved with the Two-Seed-in-the-Spirit-Predestinarian Baptist Church, with which he had family connections. This church was an ultra-conservative branch of the Primitive Baptists and was known as the most extreme Calvinist sect in the nation. The "two seeds" were the elect and non-elect, and since everyone was pre-destined anyhow, there was no need to send missionaries. In some places, they were also known as the "forty gallon Baptists" since they accepted the drinking of alcohol among their ministers and members.

---

[26] Robert Irwin's tawdry life was splashed across several New York City newspapers. Among them was: "Robert Irwin's Own Story," *New York Daily News*, April 12, 1937, p. 3., and Harriet Hammond, "Bob Irwin's Secret Life," *New York Daily Mirror*, April 18, 1937, p. 24.

[27] Born in a Pentecostal revival tent in Seco Arroyo, California, he was named Fenelon Arroyo Seco Irwin.

[28] Schechter, *The Mad Sculptor*, pp. 231–308. Also see "Behind the Irwin Murders," *Sunday Oregonian* (Portland, OR), December 4, 1938, p. 3, and the reports on brothers Vidalin and Pember. Also see "Irwin held Hot-Tempered, But not Sex-Mad Criminal" in the *Oregonian* (Portland, OR), April 13, 1937, p. 4.

Eventually, Irwin wound up in a boarding house in a village called Brickhouse, Georgia, in Newton County. He was listed as living in Brickhouse in the 1920 federal census. By 1923, he was living in nearby Social Circle, Georgia, in the home of a Mrs. George N. Miller. Here, he retyped all 419 pages of *A Brief Account of the Life, Experiences, Labours, Struggles, Persecutions, Victories of Elder Daniel Parker*, the memoirs of the founder of the Two-Seed Church. The book was first published in 1931. Thus, Irwin went full circle from the strictest and most radical Holiness perfectionist Arminianism to the most extremely radical predestinarian Calvinism. He was never moderate in anything he did.

During these years, he seems to have divided his time between his home in Georgia and in Indiana and Texas, where he was connected with the Otter Creek and Trinity River Two-Seed-in-the-Spirit-Predestinarian Baptist Associations. Records show that he applied for ordination in Texas in 1917 and was denied because he preached that "everything was predestined, both good and evil." After the refusal, Irwin walked out, saying "By God I will preach." One lady said to him as he left "if you do preach it will be by God." After returning to Georgia, he was ordained by another group of Two-Seed Baptists. Returning to Texas, he was welcomed back since he now preached "sound doctrine." A photo of him with other Texas Two-Seed leaders in 1923 showed that he was then in good standing with the church. Another photo shows Irwin in Texas in 1924, smoking a pipe.[29]

According to records found on Genealogy.com, Irwin's many lives came to an end on January 22, 1926, in Palestine, Texas, the historic stronghold of the Two-Seed Church. Other dates of his death, however, were given by his sons, so it is still not finally certain when and where he died. One son, Pember, said that he died in Los

[29] This information is from the Minutes of the Otter Creek Two-Seed Baptist Association of Indiana in 1924 and 1925 and the Trinity River Regular Predestinarian Baptist Association in Texas in 1923 and 1924, where Irwin was the featured preacher and messenger from the Little Hope Church. These minutes were supplied by Dr. John Crowley of Valdosta State University in Georgia.

Angeles in 1927, while another son, Stewart, reported that he died in 1924. The Palestine, Texas date in 1926 seems to be the most probable one.[30]

Whatever the date, the death of Irwin ended the story of one of the most colorful religious leaders in American history. He was the first Holiness teacher to separate the Wesleyan experience of entire sanctification from the Baptism in the Holy Spirit, a direct precursor of Azusa Street. In the end, his most enduring accomplishment was the founding of the Fire Baptized Holiness Church, which served as bridge between the Holiness and Pentecostal movements.

Two major Pentecostal denominations still exist today that can trace much of their early beginnings to Irwin's ministry. They are the International Pentecostal Holiness Church and the Church of God (Cleveland, Tennessee). Together, they number some 10 million members worldwide.

The task of evaluating Irwin's legacy as a holiness preacher is a difficult one indeed. Was he ever sincere? Was he an opportunist who shamelessly used his spectacular gifts to deceive his followers while leading a double life? Did his followers receive genuine spiritual experiences in spite of the unworthiness of the preacher? These are questions that go back to the early beginnings of Christianity. The supreme case was that of Donatus, a North African bishop who in the fourth century led a schism and declared that if a priest was unworthy, all the sacraments he performed were invalid. Thus, all baptisms, weddings, penances, and Eucharists, etc., performed by such a priest were null and void. This led to a major controversy that engulfed and divided the entire church. In the end, "Donatism" was ultimately rejected as a heresy, and therefore all the questionable sacraments were seen to be valid indeed due to the holiness and faith of the Church and the work of grace in these sacramentals, and not that of the priest who performed them.

---

[30] See the *Sunday Oregonian*, December 4, 1938, p. 3.

Another classic statement on the question of unworthy ministers for Protestant churches is found in the following statement by Martin Luther in one of his "Table Talks" in 1532, in which the topic was the fall of Judas:

> One ought to think as follows about ministers. The office does not belong to Judas but to Christ alone. When Christ said to Judas, "Go, baptize," Christ was himself the baptizer and not Judas because the command comes from above even if it passes down through a stinking pipe. Nothing is taken from the office on account of the unworthiness of a minister.

Another important statement for Protestants was placed in the Articles of Religion of the Church of England. Article XXVI reads as follows:

> Of the Unworthiness of the Ministers, which hinders not the effect of the Sacraments.
> Although in the visible Church the evil be ever mingled with the good, and sometimes the evil have chief authority in the Ministration of the Word and Sacraments, yet forasmuch as they do not the same in their own name, but in Christ's, and do minister by his commission and authority, we may use their Ministry, both in hearing the Word of God, and in receiving the Sacraments. Neither is the effect of Christ's ordinance taken away by their wickedness, nor the grace of God's gifts diminished from such as by faith, and rightly, do receive the Sacraments ministered unto them; which be effectual, because of Christ's institution and promise, although they be ministered by evil men. Nevertheless, it appertaineth to the discipline of the Church, that inquiry be made of evil Ministers, and that they be accused by

those that have knowledge of their offences; and finally, being found guilty, by just judgment be deposed.[6]

Most Protestants have adopted the view that the message and not the messenger is what produces spiritual results. Even if the messenger is flawed, unworthy, or even in error, individual followers can receive genuine grace through the mercy of God, the effectual Scriptures, and the proclaimed Word.

Undoubtedly, thousands of Irwin's followers received genuine spiritual experiences in spite of the preacher's double life. The fact that Irwin resigned as head of the church when his transgressions were discovered, instead of trying to hold on to power, was to his credit. Also, the fact that he abandoned his false teachings in favor of the new Pentecostal understanding of the "third blessing" evidenced by speaking in tongues was to his credit.

Section Three

Theology

6

Girl Talk

A Feminist Re-Imagination of Pentecostal Theological Discourse and Experience

Kimberly Ervin Alexander

Preface[1]

I AM HONORED to have this essay included in a *festschrift* honoring Rev. Jack Hayford, a Pentecostal pastor and leader for whom I've had great respect for so many years. When I first heard of Pastor Jack, it was as the pastor of the Second Chapter of Acts, an early Christian Rock group whose inspired lyrics and harmonies were spiritually transforming for me, a third-generation Church of God girl. As I began to listen to the teachings of Pastor Jack, I always resonated with his understanding of the primacy of spiritual experience. His situating of speaking in tongues in the *affective* arena, as expressions of love and gratitude, had a profound impact on my own understanding and later theologizing. A few years ago, I was told by a friend, New Testament scholar Ayodeji Adewuya, that at the 1989 meeting

---

[1] The idea for this paper was generated out of a roundtable discussion on gender and historical studies, co-sponsored by the History and Religion and Culture Interest Groups at the 41st Annual Meeting of the Society for Pentecostal Studies on March 1, 2012, in Virginia Beach, VA, at Regent University. I am grateful for the insights of the other panelists: Linda Ambrose, Leah Payne, and Abraham Ruelas. An earlier version of this paper was presented at the Holy Spirit in the Christian Life Conference, Regent University, in Virginia Beach, VA, on March 2, 2013; this version was presented at the 43rd Annual Meeting of the Society for Pentecostal Studies in Springfield, MO.

of the Lausanne Conference in Manila, he witnessed Jack Hayford rise to speak at a particularly contentious moment, sharing what I would deem a word of wisdom: "A man with an experience is not at the mercy of a man with a doctrine." It is that emphasis on experience with which this essay resonates and, I hope, builds upon.

Recently, Reformed popular preacher and author John Piper horrified many with his analysis of historic Christianity: "Now, from all of that I conclude that God has given Christianity a masculine feel. And being God, a God of love, He has done that for our maximum flourishing both male and female."[2] As skewed as I believe Piper's reading of the biblical text to be, he has a point: Christianity has been male-dominated and, thus, may be read and analyzed as masculine in affect and expression. Indeed, Piper does us a favor by pointing out that a gendered approach has controlled the interpretation of Scripture as well as Christian experience. This, surprisingly and disappointingly, is no less true in Pentecostal history and theology. Pentecostal theological and doctrinal discourse has been written, primarily, by male leaders and, later, by male scholars. Often these discourses have followed the propositional patterns of Evangelicalism or, in the academy, scholasticism. This has resulted in a particular way of understanding Pentecostal experiences that often fails to convey meaning and significance and disconnects it from the whole of the Christian life.

Consider this case study:

In his 2003 volume, *Thinking in the Spirit: Theologies of the Early Pentecostal Movement*, Douglas Jacobsen set out to explore "how ideas that defined that movement during these formative years [1900–1925] and how a variety of creative Pentecostal leaders rethought the Christian faith in light of their new experience of God."[3] Jacobsen willingly acknowledges, and in some way defends, the idea that Pentecostals' theology may not look like theology

[2] http://www.christianpost.com/news/john-piper-god-gave-christianity-a-masculine-feel-68385/#UA674ry0MBJKv344.99.

[3] Douglas Jacobsen, *Thinking in the Spirit: Theologies of the Early Pentecostal Movement* (Bloomington and Indianapolis: Indiana University Press, 2003), p. ix.

proper, as it is understood in other Christian traditions, while maintaining that difference is really "one of degree, not as radical disjuncture."[4] Nevertheless, Jacobsen's assessment of the criteria for who is really a theologian in this early period is quite revealing, if somewhat amorphous. One primary consideration seems to be that these authors actually wrote a monograph rather than "merely jotting off short articles for publication."[5] He identified twelve authors "who dabbled briefly or at length in theological matters," who were "more reflective and comprehensive in their thinking" than others.[6] The twelve are all male. He explains:

> Even though the Pentecostal movement did allow women certain positions of leadership, women were not for the most part looked to for guidance in the realm of doctrine. This did not prevent some women from doing theology on their own and announcing their results in the form of sermons, letters, and journal articles—and many of these women were creative and insightful—but no women composed book-length theological treatises.[7]

In the words of one colleague, "When men study the Bible it's called theology; when women and children study it, it's called Christian Education."

Jacobsen goes on to explain why one important early leader, A. J. Tomlinson, who *did* write a monograph (*The Last Great Conflict*) was not included: "He had a sharp mind and is often quite quotable, but Tomlinson was not a particularly systematic thinker."[8]

Jacobsen's bias is evident: real thinking and legitimate theologizing must be done in "systematic," book-length ways. So, sermonic material, letters, and journal articles do not represent proper

---

[4] Jacobsen, p. 7.
[5] Jacobsen, p. 13.
[6] Jacobsen, p. 13.
[7] Jacobsen, p. 14.
[8] Jacobsen, p. 15.

thinking or proper theologizing. The point is that, for Jacobson and others, legitimate theologizing is done in a certain way, and that way has, for a variety of reasons, left out the contributions of women.[9]

This understanding of theological discourse is alluded to in George Paul Wood's review of Pentecostal blogger and author Sarah Bessey's book *Jesus Feminist: An Invitation to Revisit the Bible's View of Women*, in which he summarizes his initial problem with Bessey's approach:

> Although Sarah Bessey writes well and although I pretty much agree with her, I found reading the book's initial pages to be a long, hard slog. She tells stories where I would assert propositions. She asks questions where I would offer answers. She assumes conclusions where I would make long arguments. Her authorial voice is so different than mine. I would approach the topic of "the Bible's view of women" in such a different way.[10]

To his credit, he admits:

> Midway through chapter 2 (or was it 3?), I realized what the problem was. It wasn't her, it was me. Here am I, a man, having a hard time listening to a woman make a case in her own voice on an issue where we agree. Let me

---

[9] The discussions surrounding "legitimate theologizing" are not new to Wesleyan scholars who have, for decades, attempted to answer the charge that John Wesley left no real body of theological writing. Thomas Noble offers an assessment of these arguments in "John Wesley as a Theologian: An Introduction," *Evangelical Quarterly* 82, no. 3 (2010): pp. 238–257. Though these apologetics date to at least as early as the 1930s, an early defense offered by Albert Outler may be found in Albert Outler, ed., *John Wesley* (New York: Oxford University Press, 1964), pp. iii-viii. More recently, N. T. Wright has made a case for the inherent theological coherence found within the thoughts and writings of Paul in *Paul and the Faithfulness of God* (Minneapolis: Fortress Press, 2013).

[10] http://georgepwood.com/2014/01/23/review-of-jesus-feminist-by-sarah-bessey/ (Accessed on 1/24/2014).

repeat that for my male readers: I wasn't listening to what a woman was saying *because she was a woman*.[11]

Clearly, Wood has put his finger on the sexism that still exists in twenty-first century Pentecostalism, mirroring the sexism of the larger culture. But I would assert that the bias goes beyond simplistic stereotypes. I believe that the discussion needs to be pushed further, forcing us to again examine what it means to *be* Pentecostal, to bear witness of being filled with the Spirit, in our personal and communal lives in both the church and academy.

It is the thesis of this discussion that this kind of bias can be accounted for because of at least two realities operative in the church and academy and, likely, in larger society: there are still certain ways of thinking and writing that are (1) considered gender-specific and (2) considered the proper or "sophisticated" way of theologizing. The implication of this thesis is that many attempts at constructing Pentecostal theology and experience are construed in "masculine" ways and, more precisely, in forms that betray and ultimately alter the spirituality of Pentecostalism. This has resulted in a rather flat understanding of Pentecostal experience and one that is bereft of its original vitality.

The Gendering of Speech

To have a better understanding of how this near flatlining has occurred in what is normally understood to be a lively expression of Christianity, it is necessary to look at the nineteenth-century views of gender. Scholar of rhetoric Nan Johnson describes the "gendering of conversation in etiquette literature" in Postbellum America. She concludes that this gendering of rhetoric "predisposed American readers to conflate rhetorical behavior with the performance of

---

[11] http://georgepwood.com/2014/01/23/review-of-jesus-feminist-by-sarah-bessey/ (Accessed on 1/24/2014).

gender and thus to remain vulnerable to the cultural anxiety that change in rhetorical conventions necessarily meant a change in gender relations."[12] In other words, if women talk differently, the precious balance of societal roles and spheres will be upset, roles will shift, and morality will collapse. While advising women to maintain and aspire to "grace and discretion," young men were told "to cultivate 'concise-ness and accuracy' in their conversation."[13] Johnson sees this predisposition in the late nineteenth century carrying into the next century.[14]

Betty A. DeBerg's landmark study, *Ungodly Women: Gender and the First Wave of American Fundamentalism*, details the reaction of Fundamentalist leaders and writers in the late nineteenth and early twentieth centuries. Upholding the Victorian-era categorization of the home as the sphere of women, these preachers and writers warned readers and hearers against movements such as women's suffrage that would undermine the sanctity of the home through its contamination by the "strife of politics."[15] Also in view was the rising accessibility of higher education for women. DeBerg concludes, "For the most radical premillennialists of the late nineteenth century, education for women threatened Christian faith itself."[16] DeBerg

---

[12] Nan Johnson, "Reigning in the Court of Silence: Women and Rhetorical Space in Postbellum America" in *Philosophy and Rhetoric* 33, no. 3 (2000): p. 240. See also Nan Johnson, *Nineteenth-Century Rhetoric in North America* (Carbondale and Evansville: Southern Illinois University Press, 1991).

[13] Johnson, "Reigning in the Court," p. 239.

[14] It may be argued that the expectations have also been carried into the twenty-first century. Recent studies of the interactions between men and women in discussions within the online learning environment claim to have shown that "men prefer debate-like learning situations, whereas women are more likely to learn by interacting in a collegial manner." Alfred P. Rovai cites a 1999 study by Blum characterizing male posts "as tending to be confrontational, autonomous, certain, abstract, or consisted of a controlling nature." Those of females "tended to be empathetic, mentioned self, family, or spouse, or had a cooperative tone." Alfred P. Rovai, "Online and Traditional Assessments: What is the Difference?" *Internet and Higher Education* 3 (2000): p. 147.

[15] Betty A. DeBerg, *Ungodly Women and the First Wave of American Fundamentalism* (Minneapolis: Fortress Press, 1990; new edition published in Macon, GA: Mercer University Press, 2000), p. 53ff. Citations refer to the Mercer edition.

[16] DeBerg, p. 55.

builds on the work of Leonard I. Sweet, who examined education and gender in Antebellum America. Sweet noted that certain subjects of study had been considered "masculine," such as the maths and sciences as well as the language studies of Latin and Greek. The designation "masculine study" was made on the basis of a subject's "usefulness" while the criterion for what was a "feminine study" was that it was "ornamental."[17] While "useful" courses began to be included in women's seminary training in Antebellum America, the Fundamentalist backlash against the higher education of women all but guaranteed that biblical exposition and theological discourse would be relegated to the arena of "masculine study."

It is important to remember that these admonitions to women were couched in an understanding of the virtuous woman as the moral compass of society, yielding her influence in her "sphere of ideal womanhood," the home.[18] DeBerg describes the Fundamentalist appropriation of the Victorian notion in a chapter titled "The Divinized Home."[19] Resulting from this was a reclamation of the church for men and an urging toward "manly Christianity."[20]

At the same time, and perhaps not coincidentally, this was an era where women, such as the abolitionists, suffragettes, and temperance leaguers became major shapers of social change and were renowned for their persuasive rhetoric in the public arena. In the Holiness churches, women such as Phoebe Palmer, Catherine Booth, and Amanda Berry Smith defended the rights of women to preach in "mixed assemblies." In this light, it is easy to conclude that the early Pentecostals inherited a mixed bag of expectations with regard to the

[17] Leonard I. Sweet, "The Female Seminary Movement and Women's Mission in Antebellum America," *Church History* 54, no. 1 (March 1985): pp. 45–46.

[18] See Barbara J. MacHaffie's discussion of "The Cult of True Womanhood" in *Her Story: Women in Christian Tradition*, 2nd ed. (Minneapolis: Fortress Press, 2006), pp. 159–163.

[19] DeBerg, pp. 59–74.

[20] See DeBerg, pp. 75–98 and Colleen McDannell, *The Christian Home in Victorian America 1840–1900* (Indiana University Press, 1994).

rhetoric of women. This ambiguity is evidenced in the ecclesiastical struggles over the official status of women beginning within the first five years of the Pentecostal revival.[21]

Dreams and Visions

When surveying the earliest periodical literature published by Pentecostals, however, it is apparent that women were as actively engaged in ministry and were just as likely, if not more likely, to experience Pentecostal manifestations as were their male counterparts, and they were apt to talk about them—even in mixed company. Many of these earliest publications were documentations of the revival as it occurred, replete with the written testimonies of those experiencing "their Pentecost" as well as other Spiritual encounters. There is no evidence of editorial bias toward the writing of women. In fact, women were the editors of many of the major and earliest publications, including *The Apostolic Faith* (Azusa St. Mission; editors: Florence Crawford and Clara Lum) and *The Bridegroom's Messenger* (Atlanta, GA; editor: Elizabeth Sexton).

In the September 1908 edition of *The Pentecost*, Ruth Angstead describes her experience of being filled with the Spirit. In her lengthy testimony, she writes:

> Our union, so sweetly begun, grew to such preciousness and glory as the months and years sped by, with panting hunger that He should manifest His "never failing" love

---

[21] See Kimberly Ervin Alexander and James P. Bowers, "Race and Gender Equality in a Classical Pentecostal Denomination: How Godly Love Flourished and Foundered," in Matthew T. Lee and Amos Young, eds., *Godly Love: Impediments and Possibilities* (Lanham, MD: Lexington Books, 2012), pp. 131–152, and Kimberly Ervin Alexander and James P. Bowers, *What Women Want: Pentecostal Women Ministers Speak for Themselves* (Lanham, MD: The Seymour Press, 2013). Note especially Appendix 1, "Limiting Liberty," by David G. Roebuck.

and almighty power in the vessel He had washed in His own life blood.[22]

She narrates a kind of "vision-quest" in which she travels in the Spirit:

> I tasted of the cup of His suffering. It seemed my very heart would break and the blood oozed from the pores of my body. I then had a glimpse of the Celestial City of Glory. A stream pure as crystal flowed from under the throne, winding about, with trees of life on either side. Oh such wonderful flowers and mansions. No tongue or pen could describe these or the wonderful glory from His radiant countenance which lighted the whole, no, not through the ceaseless ages of eternity. [sic] Then I saw the ascension and His glorious return in the clouds with ten thousand of His angels. Beloved of earth He cometh soon.[23]

After a struggle with Satan, she describes hearing God assure her, "Do not leave the room till I sing through you in tongues."[24] She then describes the fruit of this vision:

> Then I sank out of self in such glorious worship before the Father, far too deep for any utterance. There seemed to be many waters surging through my being, then the Holy Spirit sang through me four songs, such beautiful words and music. I never could sing much. I was a spell-bound listener to the songs just bursting forth from the glorified Jesus through His Holy Spirit. The first three, as I sang them each time—often in English—were new to me, but the fourth was that glorious old song "All glory and praise to the Lamb that was slain:" [sic] Then I spoke

---

22 *The Pentecost* 1, no. 2 (September 1908): p. 1.

23 *The Pentecost* 1, no. 2 (September 1908): p. 1.

24 *The Pentecost* 1, no. 2 (September 1908): p. 1.

in tongues, each time interpreting, magnifying Father, Son and the precious blood.[25]

A similar journey in the Spirit is recounted by Marie Burgess Brown, founder of Glad Tidings Tabernacle in New York City. Brown's experience in 1906 followed a period of tarrying for several days. She describes her vision:

And on the third day of waiting (tarrying) He came just as He came to them in that upper room. He did not make me a Peter or a John, but just a witness, and for five hours He filled and flooded my whole being.

Then He opened my eyes to see the great need of this dark world. It seemed as if I went from one foreign field to another and in each field He would pray through me in the language of that people. I knew it not—but He did. There seemed to be great stone walls about each field and I could hear them cry for Jesus and as the Holy Spirit would begin to pray in the language of each field, I could see the walls begin to crumble and fall. How this cry touched my heart, as every cry of the Holy Spirit will and I said, "Lord, send me, send me," that those who want Jesus may find Him.[26]

For Angstead and Brown, the experience of Spirit baptism is about being given new eyes to see and new ears to hear both the cries of the lost and the voice of God.[27]

Concurrently, across the Atlantic, Jane Vazeille Boddy, the daughter of Anglican vicar A. A. Boddy, described her spiritual experiences in *Confidence*, published in Sunderland, England, by her father:

[25] *The Pentecost* 1, no. 2 (September 1908): pp. 1–2.
[26] Marie Burgess Brown, "A Testimony By Mrs. Marie Burgess Brown," *The Midnight Cry* vol. 1, 2nd edition, no. 1 (March–April 1911): pp. 1–2.
[27] Brown, "Testimony," p. 2.

So we prayed and the Holy Ghost fell upon me in a great way causing me to shake very much and praise His Holy Name. This went on for some time, until a wonderful power seized my tongue and jaws and I spoke in 'an unknown tongue.' Great joy and peace came to me, and power seemed to be passing through my body and shaking it very much. Several messages were given, but it was not me at all, but Christ in me. I was powerless. Once I looked up and saw a wonderful light shining, and although I saw no form I knew it was the Lord, and I praised Him for it. He is so good.

Since then Christ is my one aim, life is not worth living without Him, He is such a wonderful reality.

One day, as I knelt in prayer, I felt coming over me a wonderful sensation; it was like a veil covering every part of my body from head to foot, and the words came, "The Blood of Jesus," and I knew it was His protection from all evil and assaults of the Devil.

Jesus is always with me, silently planning for me, and it is very wonderful and real. When I was confirmed this year He was very present. It [*sic*] was like "The peace of God, which passeth all understanding." My first Holy Communion was a source of great help and filled me with new spiritual life.[28]

After recounting a dream of the Resurrection morning, Sister Dagmar Gregerson urged readers, "When you have your Baptism, go on, seek more. Get deeper into the secrets of God."[29]

In later issues of *Confidence*, the testimonies and exhortations of women most often contain this same emotive, descriptive, and visionary language. Catherine Price testified, "I love Him to manifest

---

[28] Jane Vazeille Boddy, "Testimony of a Vicar's Daughter" in *Confidence*, no.2 (May 1908): pp. 6–7.

[29] Sister Dagmar Gregerson, "World Wide Revival" in *Confidence*, no.3 (June 30, 1908): p. 11.

Himself and to speak through me in other Tongues as the Spirit gives utterance, for at such times there is a wonderful fellowship with Jesus and access into His presence, but if it would cause me to enjoy the manifestations more than *Himself* I should ask Him to withhold them."[30] She goes on to exhort, revealing her understanding of the role of the Spirit in her life, "The words just now come to me as I write—'Dwell deep.' These are days in which we need to be hidden in Christ. 'The flesh profiteth nothing.' Only that which comes down from heaven can ascend into heaven."[31] In this exhortation, Price contends that this experience is both transformative and teleological, and her words are reminiscent of Eastern ideas of *theosis*.

It seems that in these earliest days of this early twentieth-century renewal movement, Pentecostal women, inspired by the Spirit, transcended barriers of speech and place, *not* necessarily by adopting the speech patterns of men, striving to be "concise and accurate." Rather, it seems, the openness to the influence of the Holy Spirit actually served to blur the distinctive spheres, if not to give the church a "distinctive feminine feel."

There is ample evidence that men, when experiencing manifestations of the Spirit, "their Pentecost," also had "vision quests," resonated with the suffering of Jesus, and described the transformation in soteriological as well as mystical terms.[32]

Before traveling from Memphis to Los Angeles, Charles H. Mason had a visionary experience apparently interpreted as an urging to seek the experience of Spirit baptism as it was being manifested at the Azusa Street revival. A "parable" received after his arrival in Los Angeles further confirmed this instruction:

---

[30] Letter from Catherine Price of Brixton, supplement, *Confidence*, no.3 (June 30, 1908): p. 2.

[31] Price, *Confidence*, p. 2.

[32] See also Kimberly Ervin Alexander, "Boundless Love Divine: A Re-evaluation of Early Understandings of the Experience of Spirit Baptism," in S. J. Land, R. D. Moore, and J. C. Thomas, eds., *Passover, Pentecost and Parousia: Studies in Celebration of the Life and Ministry of R. Hollis Gause*, JPT Supplement Series 35 (Blandford Forum, Dorset: Deo Publishing, 2010), pp. 145–170.

I went to the altar and the Lord put a parable before me.
If you were going to marry, would you be sad? I said, no,
when I was going to be married, I was glad. He then
showed me this was wedlock to Christ. If there was
anything imperfect about me, He would make it right
and marry me anyway. Then my faith was settled and laid
firmly hold on the promise.[33]

After leaving the altar area and returning to his seat in the mission,
Mason testifies that he focused on Jesus and experienced a transformation via the work of the Spirit:

> The Holy Ghost took charge of me. I surrendered perfectly
> to Him and consented to Him. Then I began singing a
> song in unknown tongues, and it was the sweetest thing to
> have Him sing that song through me. He had complete
> charge of me. I let Him have my mouth and everything.
> After that it seemed I was standing at the cross and heard
> Him as He groaned, the dying groans of Jesus, and I
> groaned. It was not my voice but the voice of my Beloved
> that I heard in me. When He got through with that, He
> started the singing again in unknown tongues. When the
> singing stopped, I felt that complete death. It was my life
> going out, but it was a complete death to me. When He
> had finished this, I let Him hold my hands up, and they
> rested just as easily up as down. Then He turned on the
> joy of it. He began to lift me up. I was passive in His hands.
> I was not going to do a thing. I could hear the people but
> did not let anything bother me. It came to me, "I charge
> thee, O daughters of Jerusalem, that ye stir not up nor
> awake my Beloved until He please." S. S. 8. 4. He lifted me
> to my feet and then the light of heaven fell upon me and
> burst into me filling me. Then God took charge of my
> tongue and I went to preaching in tongues. I could not
> change my tongue. The glory of God filled the temple. The

---

[33] *The Apostolic Faith* 1, no. 6 (February–March 1907): p. 7.

gestures of my hands and movements of my body were His. O it was marvelous and I thank God for giving it to me in His way. Such an indescribable peace and quietness went all through my flesh and into my very brain and has been there ever since.[34]

Noteworthy is Mason's experience of the *pathos* of Jesus' crucifixion, similar to that of Angstead, and his description of the resulting ontological changes.

A comparable testimony by a noted male leader may be found in the autobiographical description of Ambrose J. Tomlinson's 1908 experience in Cleveland, Tennessee, in his 1913 work *The Last Great Conflict*:

At one time, while lying flat on my back, I seemed to see a great sheet let down, and as it came to me I felt it as it enveloped me in its folds, and I really felt myself literally lifted up and off the floor several inches, and carried in that sheet several feet in the direction my feet pointed, and then let down on the floor again. As I lay there great joy flooded on my soul. The happiest moments I had ever known up to that time. I never knew what real joy was before. My hands clasped together with no effort on my part. Oh, such floods and billows of glory ran through my whole being for several minutes! There were times that I suffered the most excruciating pain and agony, but my spirit always said "yes" to God.[35]

Tomlinson continues describing his vision-quest in the Spirit:

In vision I was carried to Central America, and was shown the awful condition of the people there. A

[34] *The Apostolic Faith*, 1, no. 6 (February–March 1907): p. 7.
[35] A. J. Tomlinson, *Last Great Conflict* (Cleveland, TN: White Wing Publishing House), p. 234.

paroxysm of suffering came over me as I seemed to be in soul travail for their salvation. Then I spoke in tongues as the Spirit gave utterance, and in the vision I seemed to be speaking the very same language of the Indian tribes with whom I was surrounded.[36]

After "traveling" to South America and Africa, he described seeing Jerusalem, noting, "I endured the most intense suffering, as if I might have been suffering similar to that of my Savior on Mount Calvary. I never can describe the awful agony that I felt in my body."[37]

Theology "Proper"

As the Wood confession and the Jacobsen case study reveal, "proper theologizing," "systematic thinking," and doctrinal discourse have been understood as articulated, whether orally or on paper, in a particular way. Perhaps not to be underestimated is the observation that this "proper" way corresponds nicely with the nineteenth-century description of "masculine" speech. Though many early Pentecostals began decrying the exclusivity and non-charitable nature of "creedalism" as, ironically, "*man*-made" (italics mine), within a relatively short time statements of faith or "doctrinal teachings" began to be formulated. Additionally, short monographs of an apologetic or polemical nature also emerged. Because of the concurrent ecclesiastical debates regarding the "place" of women in the burgeoning denominations and the virtual restriction of them from all leadership positions, these statements and monographs were almost exclusively in the purview of men. It is therefore significant that the rise of institutionalization of the Pentecostal movement occurred simultaneously with the rise of male dominance, the adoption of a "masculine feel" to these churches. Along with this shift toward more hierarchy and its supporting

---

[36] Tomlinson, *Last Great Conflict*, p. 234.
[37] Tomlinson, *Last Great Conflict*, p. 235.

infrastructure came changes in views of the role of women and even the nomenclature associated with their ministry credentials.[38]

Important for this study is the change in the discourse or rhetoric utilized to explain the meaning and purpose of Spirit baptism. Some early attempts at doctrinal discourse did take into account the *affective* dimensions of spiritual experience. For instance, J. Roswell Flower and C. J. Quinn warn readers in 1908:

> The baptism of the Holy Ghost does not consist in simply speaking in tongues. No. It has a much more grand and deeper meaning than that. It fills our souls with the love of God for lost humanity, and makes us much more than willing to leave home, friends, and all to work in His vineyard, even if it be far away among the heathen.[39]

Church of God overseer A. J. Tomlinson contended, "The Holy Ghost is given for service not for pleasure. He is to guide into all truth, even into the fellowship of the mystery. The natural man cannot comprehend the things of God, but 'the Spirit searcheth all things, yea, the deep things of God.' Then if you have Him dwelling in your mortal body you may expect to be led deeper and yet deeper until the end is reached."[40]

Nevertheless, most statements of faith expressed, in a shorthand way, tenets that identified Spirit baptism as distinct from sanctification or even distinct from a "work of grace" as a polemic against the Holiness tradition from which they had come and, as further distinction, insisted upon the necessity of speaking in tongues as evidence of the experience.[41] Tellingly, the doctrinal exposition developed by the General Council of the Assemblies of God in 1916 was and is called

---

[38] See Roebuck in Alexander and Bowers, *What Women Want*.

[39] *The Pentecost* 1, no. 1 (August 1908): p. 4.

[40] Tomlinson, *Last Great Conflict*, pp. 76–77.

[41] See Alexander, "Boundless Love," pp. 149–158.

"The Statement of Fundamental Truths." As is the way of creeds, these early Pentecostal tenets, beginning as statements of the "lowest common denominator," soon became definitive and even all-encompassing, no longer "teachings being made prominent," and tests of fellowship.

By mid-century, as more Pentecostals embraced formal education and, following their Evangelical friends, sought to better codify doctrinal belief as well as ministerial training, the affective, emotive, and mystical language was replaced with "reasonable accounts." Donald S. Aultmann, a Church of God educator and administrator, wrote in the preface to James L. Slay's *This We Believe*, "A movement, no matter how vigorous, cannot long survive with a faith based merely on ambiguous mental assent. It must prepare for precise intellectual affirmation."[42] Within the decade, educator Donald N. Bowdle expressed a similar view: "This book is predicated upon the conviction that an intellectually responsible and thoroughly relevant Pentecostalism is our most urgent need."[43] He continues to describe his approach in writing a book "requiring more than a cursory reading," one in which he has "introduced numerous theological terms—always with definition—which represent important biblical concepts, and of which each of us must have some elemental understanding if he is to communicate this 'good news' with clarity and power."[44] Apparently, by this time, Pentecostals viewed narrative as an ineffective way of conveying their Pentecostal message. Fittingly, the *festschrift* honoring Bowdle, published in 2000, was titled *The Spirit and the Mind: Essays in Informed Pentecostalism*.[45]

[42] Donald S. Aultmann, preface to James L. Slay, *This We Believe* (Cleveland, TN: Pathway Press, 1963), p. 7.

[43] Donald N. Bowdle, *Redemption Accomplished and Applied* (Cleveland, TN: Pathway Press, 1972), p. 13.

[44] Bowdle, p. 13.

[45] Terry L. Cross and Emerson B. Powery, *The Spirit and the Mind: Essays in Informed Pentecostalism* (Lanham, MD: University Press of America, 2000).

Lost in Translation

It's not just a matter of semantics. The reduction of Pentecostal experience to a minimalist apologetic set forth in a series of arguments or
principles is, one may argue, antithetical to a spirituality that construes
itself out of the biblical narrative and finds resonance with the stories
within that text. Indeed, it may be argued that the Pentecostal revival
was a move toward the feminization of the Christian movement.

Pentecostal formation, it has been argued, does not take place,
primarily, in the catechetical classroom.[46] Instead, Pentecostals are
transformed in community and in worship.[47] If we are formed in and
through spiritual experience in community, it is incongruent, even
disjunctive, to attempt to express "belief" in prescribed categories or
systems and in lists of tenets or propositions and even more dysfunc-
tional to attempt to form a people or pass down the faith using a
schema more conducive to less experientially oriented traditions.
Pentecostals have found and understood their experience out of the
biblical narrative and out of the story of salvation. Their story of
God's provision of grace and their response to it resonates and is at
home in the larger narrative of God's story. Like Peter in his rooftop
vision and Paul in his visit to the third heaven, they are transformed
in each encounter with God, each encounter anticipatory of the next,
and each encounter shaping their theology and ministerial practice.

Pentecostal scholar Kenneth J. Archer warns, "Doing Pentecostal
theology involves more than simply retrieving and restating or
employing a revisionist historiography; it involves faithfully re-visioning
our tradition in light of the Spirit and the Word."[48] He continues his

---

[46] See Cheryl Bridges Johns, *Pentecostal Formation: A Pedagogy Among the Oppressed*
(Eugene, OR: Wipf and Stock, 2010).

[47] Jerome R. Boone, "Community and Worship: The Key Components of Pentecostal
Christian Formation," *Journal of Pentecostal Theology*, no. 8 (April 1996): pp. 129–142.

[48] Kenneth J. Archer, *The Gospel Revisited: Towards a Pentecostal Theology of Worship and
Witness* (Eugene, OR: Pickwick, 2011), p. 5.

warning against doing the work of theology in a way that is "disembodied from community life and spirituality" where "doctrinal statements take precedence over both communal praxis and communal pathos."[49]

More than just connection to community is to be sought, however. This is more than just a call for a change of the *locus* of theological construction, to reconnect it with the worshiping community. Those are the age-long struggles between the academy and the church. What is at stake here is not just consistency and congruity. In reality, that kind of "fact-checking" belongs to another sphere and is not at home in the Pentecostal community, where spiritual discernment of what "seems good to the Holy Ghost and to us" is understood to be the way forward.

More to the point, the attempt to convey spiritual experience in modalities that are abstractions of the reality, "concise and accurate," informative rather than transformative, easily bulleted, in actuality has the effect of altering the meaning and reducing or minimizing the experience. Critiquing Simon Chan, Archer has argued our failure is not one of being unable to explain the truth. Our failure is in replacing the story with an abstraction, an explanation. Clark Pinnock, a post-conservative Evangelical, who testified to a renewing experience in the Holy Spirit, wrote, "Stories are not just engaging ways of making a point that could really be better made by using abstract propositions."[50] Similarly, Pentecostal philosopher James K. A. Smith well states, "And there is something *irreducible* about this mode of testimony—it cannot be simply reduced to a mere pool of extracting philosophical propositions, nor can it be simply translated into theological dogmas."[51] Smith argues that Pentecostal "spirituality is rooted in affective, narrative epistemic practice" and that "knowledge is rooted in the heart

---

[49] Archer, p. 6.

[50] Clark Pinnock, quoted in Roger E. Olson, *Reformed and Always Reforming: The Postconservative Approach to Evangelical Theology* (Grand Rapids, MI: Baker Academic, 2007), p. 170.

[51] James K. A. Smith, *Thinking in Tongues: Pentecostal Contributions to Christian Philosophy* (Grand Rapids, MI: Eerdmans, 2010), p. xxiii.

and traffics in the stuff of story."[52] Describing humans as "narrative animals"[53] and elsewhere as "loving things" (as opposed to "thinking things" or "doing things"),[54] Smith drives home the point that it is in relating to and with God and others that we *know.*

As Pentecostalism has adapted to a "masculine Christianity," it has, in effect, altered the shape of its spirituality. To paraphrase Smith, if the *feminine* affective "testimony is translated into 'mere'" *masculine* "facts, codified with propositions, distilled into ideas, then we are dealing with a different animal."[55]

If Walter Hollenweger's assessment of Pentecostalism as a spirituality with an "African root,"[56] "expressed in oral/narrative forms and manifested in prayer, dreams, visions, healing, and embodied worship"[57] has merit, then it would seem that narrative accounts of experience, testimony, and accounts of those dreams and visions must be viewed as *first-order*, and not in the sense that later ordering is superior or even more correct. Beyond the narrative formulation Pentecostals refer to as *testimony*, attention should also be given to the role of dreams and visions, as well as embodied worship and experience (including healing), as *first-order* means of expression of faith.[58]

As noted earlier, many of the extended testimonies of early Pentecostals included narrations of dreamlike sequences in which they participated in the sufferings of Christ, worship in the City of God, the sufferings of others, or were immersed in light or water.

---

[52] Smith, *Thinking in Tongues*, p. 43.

[53] Smith, *Thinking in Tongues*, p. 44.

[54] James A. K. Smith, *Desiring the Kingdom: Worship, Worldview and Cultural Formation* (Grand Rapids, MI: Baker Academic, 2009).

[55] Smith, *Thinking in Tongues*, p. 64.

[56] Walter J. Hollenweger, *Pentecostalism: Origins and Developments Worldwide* (Peabody, MA: Hendrickson Publishers, 1997), p. 18.

[57] Henry H. Knight, III, *From Aldersgate to Azusa: Wesleyan, Holiness, and Pentecostal Visions of the New Creation* (Eugene, OR: Pickwick, 2010), p. 203.

[58] Hollenweger notes that the criticism of Pentecostal liturgy in South Africa during *Apartheid* "can be seen as opting for superior 'Western values' in the church." Hollenweger, *Pentecostalism*, p. 47.

These experiences often took the form of the familiar narrative archetype of a journey.

From at least the work of early psychoanalysts Sigmund Freud and Carl Jung until the more recent discoveries of neuroscience, the narrative format of dreams is understood as often providing insight into larger, more complicated, and sometimes subconscious realities of the inner life.[59] Before the prominence of reason and the proclamation of the Word with the advent of the Reformation traditions, dreams and visions were "at the heart of the Christian tradition."[60]

Think, for instance, of the role of dreams and visions in the theologizing of Bernard of Clairvaux[61] and Hildegard of Bingen. Of Hildegard's visions, Barbara Newman writes, they "provided both the material and the authority for her teaching."[62] Newman claims that Hildegard's visions were not only regarded as "direct experience of God" but also as "a source of unmediated truth."[63] Most Pentecostals, even Pentecostal scholars and historians, would not dispute the "direct experience of God" described by early Pentecostal adherents and may even hold that experience in high regard. Few, if any, however, would regard the descriptions of these

[59] See John A. Sandford, *The Kingdom Within: The Inner Meaning of Jesus' Sayings*, rev. ed. (San Francisco: HarperSanFrancisco, 1987); David G. Benner, *Spirituality and the Awakening Self: The Sacred Journey of Transformation* (Grand Rapids, MI: Brazos Press, 2012). See also Michael McGuire, "Enter Imaginings, Beliefs, Uncertainty, and Ambiguity" in *Believing: The Neuroscience of Fantasies, Fears, and Convictions* (Amherst, NY: Prometheus Books, 2013). pp. 143–152.

[60] Isobel Moreira, *Dreams, Visions, and Spiritual Authority in Merovingian Gaul* (NY: Cornell University Press, 2000), p. 3. See also Michael Lodahl, "Dreams and Visions" in Glen G. Scorgie, gen. ed., *Dictionary of Christian Spirituality* (Grand Rapids, MI: Zondervan, 2011), pp. 413–14. John Sanford lamented this "loss" of the significance of the "inner life" in his classic work, *Dreams: God's Forgotten Language* (San Francisco: HarperSanFrancisco, 1968) and in *The Kingdom Within: The Inner Meanings of Jesus' Sayings* (San Francisco: HarperSanFrancisco, 1989).

[61] See M. Burcht Pranger, *Bernard of Clairvaux and the Shape of Monastic Thought: Broken Dreams*, Brill's Studies in Intellectual History 56 (Leiden, The Netherlands: E. J. Brill, 1994).

[62] Barbara Newman, "Hildegard of Bingen: Visions and Validation" in *Church History* 54, no. 2 (June 1985): p. 164.

[63] Newman, p. 164.

visionary experiences as a "source of unmediated truth," though it likely functions in that way for the dreamer. While counselors and spiritual directors seize upon the importance of dreams as windows into a "bigger reality" and "awareness of deeper truths not always apparent in our conscious" state,[64] theologians, even Pentecostal ones, have been reticent to take seriously, in the academic sense, the importance of dreams and visions as a way truth is conveyed.[65]

Conclusions

Pentecostal historians and critics have sometimes situated the restrictions on the role of women as an outcome of Pentecostal associations with Fundamentalism or Evangelicalism. The assumption, often substantiated by research and data, has been that when Pentecostals began looking for models of organization and infrastructure, they borrowed or adopted models of other ecclesial bodies outside of the Pentecostal sphere. The often cited and grieved trajectory has been that this "Evangelicalization" of Pentecostalism has led to a loss of spiritual vitality.

I would propose that the story may be read differently and the present declining state of the North American Pentecostal movement may be traced back to something as elemental to Pentecostal spirituality as "inspired speech." An exchange of Spirit-inspired feminine speech forms ("girl talk") for the ill-fitting masculine speech of the world (what might be understood as "worldliness") has resulted in a "form of godliness, denying the power thereof." How ironic that the demise of the Pentecostal church, where "everybody's a preacher," would be precipitated by a quenching of the Spirit as *She* spoke through *Her* church.

---

[64] Christine Valters Paintner, "Bringing the Arts to Dreamwork" in *Awakening the Creative Spirit: Bringing the Arts to Spiritual Direction*, Christine Valters Paintner and Betsey Beckman, eds. (NY: Morehouse Publishing, 2010), p. 172.

[65] Perhaps what is called for is an interdisciplinary approach similar to what is proposed by Ann Taves, *Religious Experience Reconsidered: A Building-Block Approach to the Study of Religion and Other Special Things* (Princeton, NJ: Princeton University Press, 2011).

7

Jesus, Our Center of Gravity in the Church and the Academy

An Isaiah 61 Declaration for Our Time

John Jackson

I AM GRATEFUL for the opportunity to write for my friends in pastoral ministry leadership and for those in leadership within Christ-centered university (academy) settings. I write as one who has engaged in church leadership for all of my adult life. My involvement in Christ-centered higher education has been as a participant and now as an administrative leader for the past several years. The formative and integrated nature of those streams in my life will be reflected in this essay. While the majority of these comments will be anchored in the domestic US context from which I write, I hope my global friends will be equally ministered to by these reflections.

My longing in this essay is for the church and academy to recover a mutual and passionate commitment to what God's Word says is the fundamental ministry of Jesus and His people on planet Earth. I have long been convinced that the academy is the "child of the church" (more on this later) and that the church and academy need each other to fulfill the Great Commission and Great Commandment. My passionate prayer is for this essay to spur leaders of churches and academies to embrace their mutual assignments in greater levels of partnership and mutual ministry.

Pastor Jack Hayford has been a distance mentor for years, and I consider him a father in the faith. His broad and deep leadership has impacted me greatly, and I am thankful for his grace and truth spoken into my life at a distance and in proximity. I have always appreciated Pastor Jack as being deeply rooted in an experience of the Holy Spirit and as a student of the Word of God, history, and the world in which he has been called to minister. Pastor Jack has been consistently deeper than most and has called us generally, and me specifically, to the deeper things. Even now, we desperately need leadership wisdom that speaks in depth of understanding and discernment. Ours is an age that calls us to be "wise as serpents" (Matthew 10:16) and to "understand the times and know what to do" (1 Chronicles 12:32). In that light, here is a word about how we clearly identify the center of gravity for our season.

Jesus as the Center of Gravity of Church and Christ-Centered Higher Education

What is the center of gravity for the spiritual condition of our age? Is it the church? There are likely a number of metrics that would argue otherwise, most notably the rise of "nones" (persons with no religious affiliation), suggesting the declining influence of organized religion in American life.[1] One might argue for the university as the locus of gravity for spiritual life but would be hard pressed to show evidence that even Christ-centered schools, like the one I lead, are making a dent in the emerging generation's spiritual values. Many have written resources that support this claim, including George Marsden[2] and Robert Wuthnow.[3]

I specifically want to contend that Jesus is the center of gravity, the center of meaning, and the center of hope for our planet, and

---

[1] Michael Lipka, "Religious 'Nones' Are Not Only Growing, They're Becoming More Secular," *Pew Research Center,* 2015, http://www.pewresearch.org/fact-tank/2015/11/11/religious-nones-are-not-only-growing-theyre-becoming-more-secular/.

[2] George Marsden, *The Soul of the American University: From Protestant Establishment to Established Nonbelief* (New York: Oxford University Press, 1994).

[3] Robert Wuthnow, "Can Faith Be More Than a Side Show in the Contemporary Academy?" in *Postsecular College: A New Place for Religion in the University,* eds. Douglas Jacobsen and Rhonda Hustedt Jacobsen (New York: Oxford University Press, 2007).

that the church and Christ-centered academy must work together to ensure that Jesus is the fundamental reality of our experience. The truth of this ought to be so self-evident that I would argue further how anything less than this is sub-Christian. I want to contend in this present and emerging hour that Jesus longs to be revealed in greater measure in His church and in His academy. I also want to argue that Jesus longs to have His presence, His love, His truth, and His grace manifested in every walk of life for the revival He longs to bring. Finally, I want to argue that the Christ-centered academy is a "child of the church" and, as such, must submit to both the Lordship of Christ and the teachings of the church. The church that does not fully partner with the academy is limiting its kingdom reach and influence, and the Christ-centered academy that does not partner with the church is automatically deficient in the fulfillment of its mission. Jesus is the center of gravity for our times and the fulfillment of the Great Commission and Great Commandment, requiring that we press into Him like never before.

In the spring of 2014, the university I lead[4] was pleased to have Pastor Jack as our commencement speaker. This was a bit of a "double blessing" for me, as I had invited him to speak to a gathering of Baptists when I was a young denominational leader in the early 1990s. Not only was Pastor Jack delightful as a commencement speaker, but also our leadership team had the added pleasure of sharing lunch with him and his wife, Anna. During the lunch, Pastor Jack referenced Isaiah 2:2: "Now it will come about in the last days that the mountain of the house of the Lord will be established as the chief of the mountains, and will be raised above the hills" (NASB). We talked about our mutual commitment to the idea that the church is the center of gravity for the body of Christ. Leading churches to be full of the presence of Jesus is a challenge that we, in the church and academy, see as a priority of the greatest magnitude.

---

[4] "Who We Are," *William Jessup University*, accessed March 8, 2017, http://www.jessup.edu/about/who-we-are/.

The very next day, my wife, Pam, was praying and studying the center of gravity, and she particularly enjoyed the notion of a low center of gravity for trucks and cars as she applied it to the church when thinking about Jesus, the Word, and the five-fold ministry as the foundation of the church. Pastor Jack's remarks, my wife's prayer and study, and my experience these last several years leading a Christ-centered liberal arts university caused me to reflect more deeply on the subject of "center of gravity" as it relates to our time. I believe Jesus' declaration in Luke 4, quoting from Isaiah 61, is a clarion call for our time.

Isaiah 61 and the Heart of God for Redemption

The heart of God is redemption. Therefore, we live and walk as redemptive people. We are always looking to share the life-giving message of hope in Christ and are consistently seeking to walk as Jesus did, full of grace and truth. We think that the order of the words *grace* and *truth* is significant. There is no diminishing of truth among us, but we lead with grace. We are seeking to point people to Jesus and not to us. We manifest the life, love, and light of Jesus everywhere we go. We live in a dynamic relationship with the Holy Spirit and bring the salvation, healing, and deliverance of Jesus to a dying and broken world.

Because of our commitment to Jesus as the center of gravity in all we do, we are prepared to live out the announced mission and ministry of Jesus. The lengthier section of Scripture that Jesus quoted from Isaiah 61, in full:

> The Spirit of the Sovereign Lord is on me,
>> because the Lord has anointed me
>> to proclaim good news to the poor.
> He has sent me to bind up the brokenhearted,
>> to proclaim freedom for the captives
>> and release from darkness for the prisoners,

to proclaim the year of the Lord's favor
    and the day of vengeance of our God,
to comfort all who mourn,
    and provide for those who grieve in Zion—
to bestow on them a crown of beauty
    instead of ashes,
the oil of joy
    instead of mourning,
and a garment of praise
    instead of a spirit of despair.
They will be called oaks of righteousness,
    a planting of the Lord
    for the display of his splendor.
They will rebuild the ancient ruins
    and restore the places long devastated;
they will renew the ruined cities
    that have been devastated for generations.
Strangers will shepherd your flocks;
    foreigners will work your fields and vineyards.
And you will be called priests of the Lord,
    you will be named ministers of our God.
You will feed on the wealth of nations,
    and in their riches you will boast.
Instead of your shame
    you will receive a double portion,
and instead of disgrace
    you will rejoice in your inheritance.
And so you will inherit a double portion in your land,
    and everlasting joy will be yours.
"For I, the Lord, love justice;
    I hate robbery and wrongdoing.
In my faithfulness I will reward my people
    and make an everlasting covenant with them.
Their descendants will be known among the nations
    and their offspring among the peoples.

All who see them will acknowledge
    that they are a people the Lord has blessed."
I delight greatly in the Lord;
    my soul rejoices in my God.
For he has clothed me with garments of salvation
    and arrayed me in a robe of his righteousness,
as a bridegroom adorns his head like a priest,
    and as a bride adorns herself with her jewels.
For as the soil makes the sprout come up
    and a garden causes seeds to grow,
so the Sovereign Lord will make righteousness
    and praise spring up before all nations
    (Isaiah 61:1–11).

I believe each of these sentences is life-giving and full of divine mandate. But I also know that ours is not the first or likely the last generation to be confronted by these declarations. How can we respond in this hour to the call of Isaiah 61 that Jesus quoted in Luke 4 at the declaration of His public ministry? In the pages that follow, I will unpack what I believe are primary implications for the church and academy; but first, a word about simplicity and complexity.

Simplicity and Complexity

Former Justice Oliver Wendell Holmes is reported to have said, "I wouldn't give a fig for simplicity this side of complexity, but I'd give my right arm for simplicity on the other side of complexity." That thought has been rolling around in my mind as I think about transformational leadership for our troubled times.

The tension in the United States threatens to overwhelm us with shocking murders in our cities, fast-moving changes in sexual mores, sporadic rioting amid racial tensions, and perpetual and instantaneous reporting of all life by the media and our own contributions of unending social media engagement. The recent presidential transition has heightened this tension so that we now appear locked in a state of continuous disequilibrium. We long for simplicity amid the complexity of our world.

As a leader, I feel the tension of ensuring that my leadership is appropriately complex (robust enough to withstand the reality of our times) and appropriately modeling simplicity (so that it can be catalytic and transferable). Simplicity becomes simplistic when we fail to recognize complexity. This can be dangerous and shallow. Our world calls for a robust and meaningful faith.

The rise of "nones" in recent religious affiliation surveys[5] and the increasing plurality of the American landscape call for recognition of the underlying principles of freedom of religion that we hold sacred in the American founding documents. Religious freedom in a pluralistic present, given a Judeo-Christian dominant past, is a complex exercise, and we do well to acknowledge that fact. People of faith in the United States (still over 90% of the population!) carry a special burden of advocating for religious freedom for others, even those who do not share their specific faith perspective.

Real faith moves toward simplicity when it is lived out in a loving and redemptive fashion, even in the face of undeniable evil. While some continue to deny the presence of evil in our world, most of us see tragic evidence of it every day. This world, this beautiful and evil world of ours, needs faith that is understandable, transferable, and experienced in our everyday reality. As a Christian, I am called to testify to my faith in ways that are understandable and compelling to the culture around me. The tragic events in June 2015 with the Charleston church mass shooting saw yet another redemptive and loving act as Charleston family members offered forgiveness to that gunman, even as they were in

---

[5] "'Nones' on the Rise," *Pew Research Center,* 2012, http://www.pewforum.org/2012/10/09/nones-on-the-rise/.

the midst of their pain. In 2006, the Amish community in Nickel Mines, Pennsylvania, demonstrated complex and simple faith when they forgave and loved the family members of the murderer who killed ten of their young girls.

Our times call for faith that is personally, organizationally, and culturally transformative. Transformative faith will be both complex and simple; it will call forth love into action. Movements occur when complexity is translated into simplicity. Helping others to understand, grasp, apply, and reproduce complex and simple faith is a powerful calling, and it is catalytic. I need to make sure I am daily translating my faith into simplicity through love in action. Those of us who lead churches and educational systems must press into both the complexity and the simplicity of our faith in these times. The people of Emmanuel AME in Charleston and the Amish in Pennsylvania have given us good models that are both complex and simple.

Complexity and simplicity alike require leadership from us that honors the past, honestly assesses the present, and ushers in the future that the Father has prepared for us. This is a time and season where leaders must co-labor with God to bring about His Kingdom here on earth. We are in a season of tremendous creative capacity, and the creation literally groans to see the manifestation of the Kingdom of God (Romans 8:15–25).

Creating the Future

How do we, as leaders, pursue this appropriately complex future in a simple and yet profound fashion? I personally am hardwired as an apostolic leader, so I'm always looking ahead to the future. Dr. John Richardson said that when it comes to the future, there are three types of people: those who let it happen, those who make it happen, and those who wonder what happened.

In a world as fast changing as ours, it is tempting to wonder what happened or merely be a bystander on the road, simply letting it happen. But I believe that people of faith actually have a mandate to create the future because of their hope in God. I believe that people of faith, and particularly followers of Jesus, are called to carry hope into the world and help create a God-honoring future for their world.

People of faith are believers in the future. In the midst of present reality, people of faith are, by definition, those who believe in things we hope for, yet have not seen (Hebrews 1:11). Because of our hope in the future, we lean in when others lean away. The early Christians in plague-stricken Rome were those who stayed when others fled—those who rescued the children left on the garbage heaps of the community. Two millennia later, on September 11, 2001, the first responders who ran up the stairs when everyone else was running down were a testament to this greater hope. Belief in the power of God to change a heart, a home, an organization, and a culture is the core conviction of people of faith. Hope is so central to leadership; I have long believed that a defining role of leaders is that they traffic in hope.

Our belief in the future also engenders a creative capacity within the faith community. The community is creative as an expression of hope in the future and faith to see beauty in the midst of pain. God created the first human beings and each successive generation with unique and redemptive potential so that the world might see His love and grace. Sir Ken Robinson does a glorious work in lifting up the creative capacities of children in his TED talk delivered in 2006, "Do Schools Kill Creativity?" that received close to forty-three million views as I write this.[6]

People in our churches and academies have the creative capacity from the throne of Heaven to birth new Kingdom reality in our time. The birth of new Kingdom realities can be part of allowing the world to see, sense, and experience the goodness of God and be drawn to Him for hope and life (Matthew 5:12–16). My friend Ray Johnston,

---

[6] Ken Robinson, *Do Schools Kill Creativity?* Video, 19:24, 2006, http://www.ted.com/talks/ken_robinson_says_schools_kill_creativity.

author of *Hope Quotient*, says, "Nobody ever gets a dream without hope. I know of many leaders around the world, some blessed with great resources and others who have almost nothing, who have made major impacts on their communities. They all have the one thing that nobody can do without—*hope*."[7]

There are certainly areas of contemporary society that are cause for great despair—racial injustice, economic and educational disparities, global hotspots of terrorism and conflict, to name a few. But none of those despair magnets can overcome the resolute capacity of people of faith to hope for the future and create new life-giving environments. I'm praying and advocating for leaders of faith to keep on hoping in the King who holds the future, creating a world that is both worth living and sacrificing for, on His behalf and through His grace and power being released in our world.

Presence-Filled Ministry: A Personal Confession and an Invitation

If I may, I would like to share a personal part of my own journey in a way that illustrates and magnifies the calling for our time. If Jesus is to be our center of gravity for the church and academy, many of us will need to encounter Him in ways beyond what our formal educational or preparatory process has provided. I share the following in the hope that my story can encourage you on your own journey in leading well in the present hour.

I love Pastor Rick Warren and Saddleback Church, the PEACE plan, and the impact of their ministry around the globe. I have had the occasion to be with Pastor Rick and have tried to honor him each time I have been with him or spoken about him. Pastor Rick and

[7] Ray Johnston, "The Four Things That Only Hope Can Do, Part 3: Hope Sets You Free to Dream," *The Hope Quotient*, May 29, 2014, http://hopequotient.com/blog/four-things-hope-can-part-3-hope-sets-free-dream/#more-111.

Saddleback have shaped my life in many wonderful ways, and the fruit of their impact has been really good. I loved *The Purpose Driven Church* and *The Purpose Driven Life* long before they became international best sellers. Our church in Nevada was a pilot site (one of only 300 in the country) for 40 Days of Purpose before it became a huge, global campaign success. Much of my ministry leadership for over 25 years was purposeful, strategic, and successful, and I am grateful for the impact of purpose driven ministry. I hope I have made that abundantly clear.

What I am about to confess to you is not in any way attributable to Pastor Rick or Saddleback Church. I love and honor them and their ministry. I was a ministry success in many respects during those seasons and am a thankful recipient of great leadership and teaching. But a nagging dis-ease continually gnawed at my soul during those years. It was not until 2006 that I began to understand a basic truth about my life as a follower of Jesus. Back then, the truth would come slowly and progressively over time due to the resistant nature of my spirit. Thankfully, I have increased my sensitivity to the present working of the Holy Spirit in my life and, I think, increased my sensitivity to hearing His voice. Even now, I continue to grapple with the reality of how deeply embedded a subtle deception was, and occasionally is, in my spirit. This truth would unmask me more than once: *I loved the purposes of God more than His presence. I led the people of God to fulfill His purposes but not to enjoy His presence.*

There, I said it. The purposes of God gave me focus and energy and made me part of a crusade. I like overcoming and I like building; I like being strategic and I like galvanizing others. I did not like sitting still. I did not like listening. I did not like waiting, and I still do not. Bible passages like John 15:1–17, where "abiding" is described, were easy to glide right by. When reading Matthew and hearing about the sheep and goats—with those described as sheep following what the Lord commanded— I could easily hear that teaching (Matthew 25:31–46). But when Mary is affirmed for having "chosen what it better" by sitting at the feet of Jesus (Luke 10:42) while her sister Martha worked herself to a frenzy, I was embarrassed by personally relating more to Martha than Mary.

During this period of discovery, I also began to understand something more about the nature of my relationship with God. I related to God as an orphan and not as a son. You can see *Spiritual Slavery to Spiritual Sonship*[8] by Jack Frost for more on this topic. As the discovery of my orphan spirit was made clear to me, I began to understand two formulas: (1) Purpose over Presence = Performance and (2) Presence before Purpose = Power. Thankfully, God was working way upstream for my wife and me. In 2006, Pam and I went through our most intense spiritual experience ever, up to that time, through a ministry called Restoring the Foundations.[9] In 2007, Pam received a special calling to a ministry of presence with the Lord. Through these experiences and a host of others, we began moving to the front edge of life in the presence of God.

The Presence of Jesus is Our Center of Gravity

Today, we are walking every day as son and daughter of the King of Kings. We have been grateful to experience a Jesus-centered life in fresh new ways. Through this process, I have had to confess and repent of the many seasons where people in the churches and ministries we led experienced success in growth, programs, and buildings but never actually experienced the joy of the presence of Jesus. I am deeply burdened that the ministries of our churches and Christ-centered academies do not miss the presence of Jesus as our center of gravity. My prayer is that we will experience the presence-filled life. It is my firm belief that living the presence-filled life is the most purposeful and pleasing invitation we will ever receive from the Father.

[8] Trisha Frost and Jack Frost, *Spiritual Slavery to Spiritual Sonship* (Shippensburg: Destiny Image Publishers, 2006).

[9] *Restoring the Foundations*, Accessed March 9, 2017. http://www.restoringthefoundations.org/.

The Psalmist describes our experience of His presence as the source of joy: "You make known to me the path of life; you will fill me with joy in your presence, with eternal pleasures at your right hand" (Psalm 16:11 NIV). Proverbs 3:5 declares that acknowledging Him in all our ways will make our paths straight. The writers of the New Testament tell us, under the inspiration of the Holy Spirit, that we are the people who carry His presence into the world (1 Peter 2:9) and that our relationship with Him is to be defined by His presence (John 15:1–4).

If experiencing and manifesting the presence of Christ is so clear in the pages of Scripture, then what has happened to the Bride of Christ? Have we lost our center of gravity? I wonder if the center of gravity in our churches and academies is no longer the person and work of Christ but our respective institutional frameworks. My own experience suggests that we are often and rather easily distracted into producing religious programming, more than being and making disciples and manifesting the peace, power, and promises of Jesus. I pray for our churches and academies to manifest the presence of Jesus in our services, programs, classes, events, and activities so that the world may hear, see, and experience the risen Christ. This is not a new challenge. The Apostle Paul himself urged the Colossian people in this: "So then, just as you received Christ Jesus as Lord, continue to live your lives in Him, rooted and built up in Him, strengthened in the faith as you were taught, and overflowing with thankfulness" (Colossians 2:6–7).

But What About Academies?

In his book, *The Outrageous Idea of Christian Scholarship*,[10] historian George Marsden observes that the "contemporary university culture is

[10] George Marsden, *The Outrageous Idea of Christian Scholarship* (Oxford: Oxford University Press, 1997).

hollow at its core." As a Harvard Law School professor once expressed, many professors have become like "priests who have lost their faith, and kept their jobs."[11] At our Christ-centered university,[12] we say *No* to that caricature of academic life. We are unashamed about our commitments. We believe that students can and should become more spiritually thriving during college. We believe that students can and should receive a quality liberal arts education that equips them to think and behave well as followers of Christ. We believe that our students can and will be exceptionally employable and that they are being sent out as transformative ambassadors of reconciliation.

The mission of the church in the Great Commission (to disciple all nations) and in the Great Commandment (to love God with all our heart, mind, soul, and strength and love our neighbor as ourselves) is equally enjoined to the church and the academy. Churches who seek to equip their people will exhort them to participate in appropriate educational pathways to allow them to greater influence and impact their community. Academies will long to partner with such churches to offer "just in time" and "just on target" educational programs to educate and equip men and women for our time. At our university, we are proud of our concise and focused mission statement, "In partnership with the Church, the purpose of William Jessup University is to educate transformational leaders for the glory of God."[13]

Both churches and academies must also release the presence of God and His people so that we experience the reality of what I have called a "Second Reformation." While the Protestant Reformation was a glorious revelation of the grace of God received, I believe this new Reformation will be a glorious experience of a grace distributed. The people of God are the priesthood of all believers. We have declared that now for centuries and yet still have small minorities of

---

[11] Marsden, *The Outrageous Idea of Christian Scholarship*, 63.

[12] "Who We Are." *William Jessup University*. Accessed March 9, 2017. http://www.jessup.edu/about/who-we-are/.

[13] Ibid.

Christ followers actually living activated lives with the presence and power of God in each aspect of their being. This Second Reformation is unleashing the presence and power of God for our time.

The prophet Micah said, "And what does the Lord require of you? To act justly and to love mercy and to walk humbly with your God" (Micah 6:8 NIV). Churches and academies that commit to educating and equipping the saints will see tremendous opportunity in the days ahead. In my role as president of a Christ-centered university, I have said that the future of higher education will be "FDA" (not that FDA!). FDA stands for Flexible-Distributed-Affordable. Learning needs to take place in a student-centered experience that will flex to where the student is encountering life. Teaching, mentoring, coaching, and pastoring will all be distributed in a variety of ways and settings. Finally, we in the Christ-centered higher education community simply must make the cost of college and graduate education more affordable. A partnership between churches, academies, technology, and highly resourced people will be required to provide these pathways to the future.

What About the Real World?

I have now spent almost forty years in some form of pastoral ministry. People still regularly ask me the question, "In the Great Commission, which is more important—evangelism or discipleship?" My answer is always *Yes!* Both are absolutely vital. You can't have discipleship without evangelism, and evangelism without discipleship violates the John 16 exhortation to bear fruit that remains. I think the same way about university education. University education equips students with the ability to think, read, write, and speak well, among other disciplines. The capacity to have a dynamic liberal arts education educates our church and academy students to be part of the transformative landscape.

Hart Research Associates surveyed employers[14] to determine what they were looking for in their employees. The results are below:

Critical thinking and analytic reasoning: 81%
Complex problem solving: 75%
Teamwork skills in diverse groups: 71%
Creativity and innovation: 70%
Information literacy: 68%
Quantitative reasoning: 63%

When I speak with traditional undergraduate students (roughly ages 18–25), I often suggest that they consider these three pathways to becoming exceptionally employable and transformative ambassadors:

Engage their academic pursuits fully; progressively grasp general studies and major focus across the span of their four years.

Engage in a series of increasingly challenging and focused "real world" internships, work experience, and practical settings over their four years.

Engage with a Christ-following community of relationships where they are mentored, encouraged, held accountable, and growing in and over time.

One other value that must be embraced by the church and academy is to ensure that our people are thriving spiritually. As we have said previously, we want to be about Jesus, about His Word, and about His work in the world. Romans tells us that transformation happens when we present ourselves to God as an act of worship, and it occurs through the renewing of our minds by the power of His Spirit (Romans 12:1–2). The commission of God gets lived out and proved by us when we are in submission to Him.

Isaiah 61 is indeed a rich declaration of what needs to be the Jesus-centered point of gravity, and I claim it for our time. I claim

---

[14] "Raising the Bar: Employers' Views on College Learning in the Wake of the Economic Downturn," *Hart Research Associates*, 2010, accessed March 9, 2017, http://hartresearch.com/.

it as from the throne of heaven, and I claim it as being the will of the Father for this earth. I declare it over our churches and our academies. I pronounce it as a divine mandate over the nations in North America and across the continents of the earth. I say *Yes* to the goodness of God. I say it is His kindness that leads us to repentance (Romans 2:4) and that His people will manifest His kindness to the world around us. I say *now* is the time to declare the acceptable year of the Lord for salvation and His favor. I say we will embrace both the mystery of God's sovereignty and the prayer and faith that it will be "on earth as it is in heaven" (Matthew 6:7).

It is the will of the Lord that His followers become oaks of righteousness (Isaiah 61:3). Rebuilding, renewing, and rejoicing are the inheritance we are to receive as we live and move and have our being in Him. I am praying for, believing for, and living and leading this hour for a victorious church that is consecrated to Him and that lives and loves in such a way that righteousness and praise spring up before all nations. Join me in a Jesus-centered experience of the church and academy that transforms people, families, churches, communities, states, nations, and the world we live in for the glory of God. Even so, Lord, *Maranatha!*

© Dr. John Jackson, president of William Jessup University and author of books on cultural transformation, leadership, and spiritual formation (www.drjohnjackson.com).

8

The Discernment of the Spirit(s) in Pentecostal Practice and Theology

Veli-Matti Kärkkäinen

First Words: The Need for and Dearth of Pentecostal Theology of Discernment[1]

Following a typical Pentecostal custom of borrowing from other traditions and using their resources, the entry on "Discernment of Spirits, Gift of" in *The New International Dictionary of Pentecostal and Charismatic Movements* is authored by a Roman Catholic—similar to the entry on "Church, Theology of"![2] No wonder Stephen E. Parker, in what is so far the most important practical-theological study on discernment, *Led by the Spirit: Toward a Practical Theology of Pentecostal Discernment and Decision Making*, laments that there are

---

[1] This essay is a slightly edited version of the (unpublished) presentation given at the second session of the Sixth Phase of the International Dialogue between the Pontifical Council for Promoting Christian Unity and Some Classical Pentecostal Churches and Leaders held in Helsinki (Finland), from 28 June to 5 July 2012. For a recent larger contribution to the topic, including the discernment of the spirit(s) in an interfaith environment, see my *Spirit and Salvation, A Constructive Christian Theology for the Pluralistic World*, vol. 4 (Grand Rapids, MI: Eerdmans, 2016), chap. 5.

[2] F. Martin, "Discernment of Spirits, Gift of," in *The New International Dictionary of Pentecostal and Charismatic Movements*, ed. Stanley M. Burgess and Eduard M. van der Maas, rev. and expanded ed. (Grand Rapids: Zondervan, 2002), 582–84; P. D. Hocken, "Church, Theology of," in ibid., 544–51.

no major systematic studies that deal with the topic.[3] A quick look at defining Pentecostal doctrinal manuals confirms the impression; they usually let it suffice to add a few practical and biblical notes on the "gift of discernment of the spirits" in the context of discussing charisms.[4] Hence, the title for this essay giving primacy to the *practice* before the theology of discernment.

The dearth of focused reflections and writings on the topic, however, should not be taken to mean that among Pentecostals discernment has not been needed. On the contrary, just consider this confession by a leading Pentecostal preacher and TV speaker, Kenneth Hagin: "Everywhere I go there is always somebody who has a 'word' from the Lord for me—sometimes two or three. In all these years, only one or two of them have been correct."[5] Hagin refers to the common Pentecostal custom of claiming to have an inspired message for another person. This has everything to do with the underlying spirituality of the movement: "At the heart of Pentecostal practice is an experience of the Spirit's immediate presence, an experience that often involves claims to direct guidance from the Spirit for decisions and actions."[6] That claim, of course, calls for continuing discernment and assessment as it has hardly been self-authenticating. Walter J. Hollenweger underlines this need with

---

[3] Stephen E. Parker, *Led by the Spirit: Toward a Practical Theology of Pentecostal Discernment and Decision Making* (Sheffield: Sheffield Academic Press, 1996), 31.

[4] See, for example, the widely-used Guy P. Duffield and N. M. Van Cleave, *Foundations of Pentecostal Theology* (Los Angeles: L.I.F.E. Bible College, 1983), 336–37; the space devoted to the topic is less than one page in a book of over 600 pages! A delightful exception is from my homeland, a fairly short manual of Pentecostal doctrines (200 pages), which devotes no less than almost six pages to the discussion of this particular gift. Mauri Viksten, *Terveen opin pääpiirteitä* (Vantaa: RV-Kirjat, 1980), 142–47. Another widely used Finnish doctrinal presentation devotes merely one paragraph to this theme: Juhani Kuosmanen, *Raamatun Opetuksia* (Vantaa: RV-Kirjat, 1993), 157.

[5] Kenneth Hagin, *How You Can Be Led by the Spirit of God* (Tulsa: Kenneth Hagin Ministries, 1979), 108; I am indebted to Cecil M. Robeck Jr., "Discerning the Spirit in the Life of the Church," in *The Church in the Movement of the Spirit*, ed. William R. Barr and Rena M. Yocum (Grand Rapids, MI: Eerdmans, 1994), 35.

[6] Parker, *Led by the Spirit*, 9.

his striking observation, based on a wide study of practices among Pentecostals in various global locations: "We have known marriages arranged, church business conducted, personal fellowship dissolved, family matters dealt with, money matters handled" on the basis of prophetic words and "messages."[7] Talk about the need to discern!

Christian tradition at large is of course well familiar with the practice and theology of discernment; there is no need to delve into that rich discussion here.[8] The distinctively—although not exclusively—*Pentecostal* take on the topic has to do with its focus on "the gift of discernment of spirits." This centering of discussion tells us two things. First, in keeping with the underlying charismatic spirituality, Pentecostals primarily see the capacity to discern as a "supernatural" gifting and empowerment of the divine Spirit. Second, while not necessarily ruling out other aspects of the discernment process, particularly in the beginning of the movement, it had much to do with the (biblically guided intuition of) discerning the *spirits*, often in terms of judging what is the (ultimate) source of the utterance, effect, or action. In recent years, particularly among the Pentecostal academicians and ecumenists, some important work has been done in both clarifying and expanding the Pentecostal notion of discernment. These contributions will be noted later in the essay.

---

[7] Walter J. Hollenweger, *The Pentecostals*, trans. R. Wilson (Minneapolis: Augsburg, 1972), 345.

[8] A useful and accessible brief overview of biblical, historical, and contemporary global perspectives can be found in Amos Yong, "Discernment; Discerning the Spirits," in *Global Dictionary of Theology*, ed. William Dyrness and Veli-Matti Kärkkäinen; assis. ed., Simon Chan and Juan Martinez (Downers Grove, IL: InterVarsity Press, 2008), 232–35. The Pentecostal church historian Dale M. Coulter rightly notes that there have been shifting patterns and foci during the history of the church regarding discernment: "Within the Egyptian monastic tradition, discernment of spirits and moral discernment were two sides of the same coin because the 'principalities and powers' tempted the believer to commit sin. In the thirteenth century, it came to be associated with prudence (*prudentia*), and ultimately became part of the analysis of conscience to encompass the practice of moral, spiritual, and psychological discernment." Coulter, "'Discerning' the Spirit of the Charismatic Movement," *Renewal Dynamics: The Official Blog of Regent Divinity School & The Center of Renewal Studies*, Friday, March 21, 2010, n.p., http://renewaldynamics.com/2010/05/21/discerning-the-spirit-of-the-charismatic-movement/.

The purpose of this essay is to take stock of the current place of contemporary Pentecostal reflection and theology of spiritual discernment. That goal involves two interrelated tasks. First, I will try to provide a report of typical practice and teaching among Pentecostal churches, based on some representative doctrinal manuals and other relevant writings. Second, I will look at the rich reporting and discussion of the theme of discernment done by Pentecostal ecumenists—as representatives of their communities—in engaging other Christian traditions. In this task, we are well served by two major international dialogues, namely, with Roman Catholics and the Reformed, which have devoted some quality time to the topic. At the end of the chapter, instead of conclusions, I will seek to discern "Whither Pentecostal Theology of Discernment?" by looking at some current Pentecostal scholarly works relevant to the topic as well as identifying some common tasks for mutual consideration with other Christian traditions.

Discernment in Pentecostal Practice and Teaching

The history of the modern Pentecostal movement offers numerous examples of the use of the gift of discernment—or safer to say: a *claim* to that effect—regarding various kinds of important decisions, moves, and negotiations. Speaking from the African context, the Pentecostal theologian D. A. Adasanya has noted that his community may engage in discernment through what he calls "spiritual enquiry," concerning, for instance, the calling of leaders and the solemnization of marriages.[9] Leadership and related ministry issues among Pentecostals are often linked with the use of the gift of discernment— at times with conflicting conclusions. Typical also are breaks in relationships in situations where the church has discouraged more entrepreneurial leaders who find it difficult to work in and through

---

[9] D. A. Adasanya, "Sources of Authority in our Churches at Present, Reflections from Where We are Now," Presentation at the Faith and Order Meeting, 27 June–2 July 2011, Moscow, Russia, unpublished MS, pp. 7–8.

established structures, as a result of which new ministries and networks have been established.[10] Disputes over doctrinal decisions, particularly in the beginning phase of the Pentecostal movement, were at times occasions for claiming the gift of discernment.[11] Recent Pentecostal history also knows a few instances where a fallen Pentecostal leader has disagreed with the movement's requirement for rehabilitation on the basis of a claim to discernment.[12]

Pentecostals routinely note that among several New Testament passages that speak of discernment, the key biblical passage is 1 Cor 12:10–11: "To one is given through the Spirit [v. 8] … prophecy, to another *the ability to distinguish between spirits*.… All these are empowered by one and the same Spirit, who apportions to each one individually as he wills" (ESV, my emphasis). In keeping

---

[10] Cecil M. Robeck, "Tradition and Traditions: Sources of Authority for the Church; The Authority of the Holy Spirit in Pentecostal Churches: A Response to Professor David Adasanya," Presentation at the Faith and Order Meeting, 27 June–2 July 2011, Moscow, Russia, unpublished MS, pp. 9–10. Robeck refers to the sociological study by Margaret M. Poloma, *The Assemblies of God at the Crossroads: Charisma and Institutional Dilemmas* (Knoxville: The University of Tennessee Press, 1989), 130–34, which discusses Loren Cunningham's "Youth with a Mission" work (see www.ywam.org) as well as the ecumenical work of David du Plessis as case studies.

[11] Robeck, "Tradition and Traditions," 10n.2: "One can look at the 1916 break between the Trinitarian majority in the Assemblies of God and the proponents of the Oneness position, who formed the Pentecostal Assemblies of the World, as an event during which a group of pastors rejected the decision based upon the 'discernment' and vote of the majority." See William W. Menzies, *Anointed to Serve: The Story of the Assemblies of God* (Springfield, MO: Gospel Publishing House, 1971), 120–21, who claimed simply that "the doctrinal statement as adopted militated against the Oneness views, which resulted in the loss of some of the brethren"; while Talmadge L. French, *Our God Is One: The Story of the Oneness Pentecostals* (Indianapolis: Voice and Vision Publications, 1999), 72, described the same incident as a "stunning blow" that resulted "from the expulsion from the Assemblies of God."

[12] Robeck, "Tradition and Traditions," 10n.26: "Jimmy Swaggart is a prime example of this. The Assemblies of God discerned the need for him to resign from ministry and undergo a process of confession, healing, and restoration in keeping with the constitution and bylaws he had long affirmed. His refusal to accept their judgment and participate in the prescribed disciplinary and restoration process resulted in his expulsion altogether from ministry in the Assemblies of God under discipline. He subsequently reorganized as an independent ministry known as Jimmy Swaggart Ministries, see www.jsm.org."

with Pentecostal intuitions, this passage makes a close connection
between prophecy and the gift of discernment. Hence, it is best to
think of these two as pairs, something similar to speaking in tongues
and interpretation of tongues mentioned in the same context (v. 10).[13]

On the basis of relevant New Testament passages, an influential Pentecostal doctrinal manual defines and describes the gift
of discernment in a way typical of the movement's view: "Quite
clearly, the gift of discerning of spirits is the capacity to discern the
source of a spiritual manifestation, whether it is the Holy Spirit,
an evil spirit, or merely the human spirit…. [S]omeone with the
gift of discernment should be present when the gift of prophecy is
used." With reference to 1 Corinthians 14:29, the manual states:
"Apparently, in Corinth the gift of discernment was as common as
that of prophecy ('let the others [pl.] judge [discern]'). All Spirit-
filled believers are, in a measure, able to judge vocal gifts operations
on the basis of whether they are spiritually edifying the body." That
said, it is noted that the exercise of the gift is not infallible, and hence
the one who happens to use the gift of discernment in a way that
appears to miss the mark should learn how to be humble and possess
a teachable spirit. Finally, the manual says that "the gift of 'discerning of spirits' is not that of judging people, but the spirit behind
the manifestation, whether Holy, evil, or human."[14] The important
observation about this lesson is the point noted above, namely, that
in Pentecostal intuition—based on the biblical teaching—the term
discernment primarily relates to (the use of) the specific charismatic
gift of discerning a spiritual utterance, usually a prophetic word. The
manual cited above limits the discussion of "discernment" to that one
aspect of discernment alone. That is not an exception but a norm
in standard traditional Pentecostal teaching manuals which, not
surprisingly, are mainly expositions of biblical theology.[15] The widely

---

[13] Robeck, "Discerning the Spirit," 32.

[14] Duffield and Van Cleave, *Foundations of Pentecostal Theology*, 337.

[15] So also Kuosmanen, *Raamatun Opetuksia*, 157, and Viksten, *Terveen opin pääpiirteitä*,
142–45, particularly. For typical doctrinal pamphlets that consider discernment mainly

used authoritative Finnish doctrinal manual follows suit and adds that, usually, people who can properly use the gift of discernment are those who know the Scriptures well and those "who have their faculties trained by practice to distinguish" (Hebrews 5:14).

That Pentecostal intuitions and basic teaching aids have this stated focus does not mean that Pentecostals wouldn't know and reflect on the wider aspects of the category of discernment—if not for other reasons, then for the kinds of practical reasons related to the examples listed in the beginning of this section (the various types of decision-making and choices) as well as assessment of the authenticity and genuineness of issues other than just a prophetic utterance. Two terms are used in the New Testament to speak of discernment: *diakriseis* (*pneumatōn*), in the passage above (and 1 Corinthians 14:29), and *dokimazō*, as in 1 Thessalonians 5:19–21: "Do not quench the Spirit, do not despise prophesying, but test [*dokimazete*] everything; hold fast to what is good" (RSV). Significantly, here again the connection of discernment with prophesying can be seen. In 1 John 4:1–6, the "testing" has to do with Christological confession and shows us that the domain of discernment, while often linked with prophetic gifts, is not limited to it. Rather, discernment may include doctrinal, ethical, and other similar issues.[16]

Typical criteria for discernment in Pentecostal teaching include the alignment with Scripture, the hallmark among all criteria; the spiritual and moral quality of the person giving the utterance, making a decision, or doing the act; and what can be called "transrational criterion," that is, something that "may appear almost as an existential, intuitive sense that all is not as it may otherwise appear. It is a

---

(although not exclusively) in the context of prophetic words, see D. Basham, *A Handbook on Tongues, Interpretation and Prophecy* (Monroeville, PA: Whitaker Books, 1971); S. Horton, *Tongue Speaking and Prophecy* (Springfield, MO: Gospel Publishing House, 1972).

[16] Behind the New Testament admonitions to "test," "weigh," "critique," and "discern" is of course the wide and varied Old Testament history of the people of God who constantly were faced with such challenges, particularly regarding the capacity to follow the right God and reject self-appointed "prophets" (as in Deuteronomy 18).

divinely given sense which enables the detection of the source from which the prophetic word arises."[17] Based on an ethnographic study, Parker also confirms the intuition common among Pentecostals that "[o]ne criterion that Pentecostals used to discern the Spirit's leading was retrospective judgment; if things worked out for the good, then it was the Lord's leading, if they did not, it probably was not."[18]

Cecil M. Robeck summarizes the wider context of discernment in Pentecostal spirituality, along with the charismatic gift of discerning the spirits:

> [T]he discernment process that Pentecostals use may go beyond the limits of a charism which may be linked specifically to prophetic words. Discernment within the Pentecostal community may follow rational lines of thought (Matt. 7:20; Acts 13:1–3; 15:6–21; 1 Thess 5:19–22; 1 John 4:1–3) or it may be more trans-rational or intuitive in nature (Acts 16:16–18). It appears to be done by groups such as in 1 Cor. 14:29; when someone prophesies, the others are enjoined to weigh what is said. Similarly, in 1 Thess. 5:20–21, the congregation to whom the Apostle writes is instructed not to quench the Holy Spirit or to despise prophesying but to test everything, holding what is good but abstaining from that which is evil…. Many times the discernment process, especially at the local level, is accomplished in helpful and redemptive ways within the community of faith. It may take place within the context of oral prayer requests, times of shared prayer, personal testimonies, charismatic manifestations especially in prophecy, words of wisdom, words of knowledge, even in tongues and the interpretation of tongues, in personal times of prayer around the altar, reading and discussing the Bible

---

17   C. M. Robeck, "Written Prophecies: A Question of Authority," *Pneuma* 2, no. 2 (1980): 38. For the listing and discussion of the criteria mentioned above and some others, based on a comprehensive scrutiny of Pentecostal sources, see Parker, *Led by the Spirit*, 31–37.

18   Parker, *Led by the Spirit*, 105.

together, preaching the Word of God, as well as hearing the Word of God preached. It should be apparent, then, that while a word or action may be discerned to have the authority of the Holy Spirit in such situations, it is typically viewed as possessing an *ad hoc* kind of authority.[19]

An important platform in recent decades for Pentecostals to share about their distinctive practice and theology of discernment, as well as learn from others by comparing notes, has to do with important ecumenical dialogues.

Pentecostals in Dialogue about Discernment

Discernment in Catholic-Pentecostal Perspective

Already, in the first dialogue, Pentecostals and Catholics mutually affirmed the scriptural mandate for spiritual discernment.[20] It was commonly agreed that there are both "supernatural" (coming directly from the Spirit) and "natural" (human experience, wisdom, and reason) aspects of the discerning process.[21] Discernment was hence

---

[19] Robeck, "Tradition and Traditions," 20; reference is given to Shane Clifton, *Pentecostal Churches in Transition: Analyzing the Developing Ecclesiology of the Assemblies of God in Australia*, Global Pentecostal and Charismatic Studies 3 (Leiden, The Netherlands: Koninklijke Brill, 2009), 130.

[20] For a theological and ecumenical analysis of the topic of discernment during the first three quinquennia, see Veli-Matti Kärkkäinen, *Spiritus ubi vult Spirat: Pneumatology in Roman Catholic-Pentecostal Dialogue (1972–1989)*, Schriften der Luther-Agricola Gesellschat 42 (Helsinki: Luther-Agricola Society, 1988), 406–12.

[21] *FR I*, 38: "The New Testament witnesses to the charism of the discerning of spirits (1 Cor 12:10), and also to a form of discernment through the testing of the spirits (1 John 4:1), and the proving of the will of God (Romans 12:2), each exercised in the power of the Spirit. There are different aspects of discernment of spirits which allow for human experience, wisdom and reason as a consequence of growth in the Spirit, while other aspects imply an immediate communication of the Spirit for discernment in a specific situation." *Final Reports*

seen as "essential to authentic ministry" as a way to finding "the mind of the Spirit." At the same time, discernment was also "understood as a diagnostic gift which leads to the further manifestation of other charismata for the edification of the body of Christ and the work of the gospel. The operation of this gift in dependence upon the Spirit develops both in the believer and community a growth in a mature sensitivity to the Spirit" (FR I, 39). To be useful, the discerning must take place in a loving atmosphere to care for God's people and not to quench the genuine moving of the Spirit; this kind of attitude is of special importance during times of spiritual renewal when new impulses are coming into view.[22]

Importantly, the first Final Report devoted a whole section to "Discernment of Spirits" (FR I, 38–41). Other issues in need of discernment include renewal and the miraculous element usually linked with it (FR I, 17). An important joint statement on discernment was issued:

> The Holy Spirit gratuitously manifests himself in signs and charisms for the common good (Mark 16:17–18), working in and through but going beyond the believer's natural ability. There is a great variety of ministries in which the Spirit manifests himself. Without minimizing the importance of these experiences or denying the fruitfulness of these gifts for the Church, the participants

---

abbreviated as FR I, FR II, etc. They are readily available, e.g., on the Vatican's website (www. vatican.va). The two position papers on discernment read during the first quinquennium are John Mahoney, "Discernment of Spirits," One in Christ 13 (1977): 64–77 (Catholic); Larry Christenson, "Revelation and Discernment," One in Christ 13 (1977): 84–86 (charismatic Lutheran; in the first phase, the Pentecostal side also included charismatics from other churches).

22 FR I, 17: "During times of renewal when charismatic elements are more manifest, tensions can arise because of prejudice, lack of mutual understanding and communication. Also, at such times as this the discerning of spirits is more necessary than ever. This necessity should not lead to discernment being misused so as to exclude charismatic manifestations. The true exercise of the charism takes place in love and leads to a greater fidelity to Christ and his Church."

wished to lay stronger stress on faith, hope and charity as sure guides in responding to God (1 Cor 13:13–14:1; 1 Thess 1:3–5). Precisely out of respect for the Spirit and his gifts it is necessary to discern between true gifts and their counterfeits (1 Thess 5:22; 1 John 4:1–4). In this discernment process the spiritual authority in the Church has its own specific ministry (1 John 4:6; Acts 20:28–31; 1 Cor 14:37, 38) because it has special concern for the common good, the unity of the Church and her mission in the world (Romans 15:17–19; Acts 1:8). (*FR I, 15*).

In later encounters, other topics discussed included the need for the community to discern an individual's spiritual experience (*FR II, 17; FR III, 66*) and the role of discernment through the Holy Spirit in the interpretation of Scripture in relation to the role of the community and tradition (*FR II, 20, 51–52; FR III, 24, 26, among others*). The mutual conversations sought to identify central criteria of discernment, such as the scriptural foundation of the incarnation (referring to 1 John 4:1–6), the lordship of Christ, the building up of his church, and the common wisdom of the community, "walking and living in the Spirit." The last one, the community criterion, was underlined.[23]

The disagreements or differences of orientation had less to do with discernment *per se* and everything to do with the foundational differences among these two ecclesiastical families, particularly regarding the personal-communal dimension, the role of tradition, and the openness—or perhaps better, expectancy—towards the manifested presence of the Spirit among the believers and in the

---

[23] *FR I, 40*: "The important element of community criteria involves the common wisdom of a group of believers, walking and living in the Spirit, when, led by those exercising the ministry of discernment, a mature discipline results and the group is capable of discerning the mind of God." *FR II, 17*: "No matter how vivid or powerful the individual's spiritual experience may be, it needs to be discerned and judged by the community. Love, which is the normative bond of community life, is the biblical criterion of all spiritual experience (crf. 1 Cor. 13)." The Catholic dialogue paper by Mahoney, "Discernment of Spirits," discussed the community criteria and some of the major difficulties related to its use; we will exposit the paper later in this section.

church. Pentecostals also tended to stress the importance of the charismatically endowed gift of the discernment of the Spirit, though not exclusively at all, while Catholics expressed a wider scope in the category of discernment.

Discernment in Reformed-Pentecostal Perspective

The topic of discernment in the International Dialogue between the World Alliance of Reformed Churches and Pentecostals has played an important role in both the first and second phases so far completed (started in 1986). The first Final Report, "Word and Spirit, Church and World" (1996–2000), has a long section titled "Spirit, Proclamation, and Spiritual Discernment" (FR 1, 22–35).[24] An even more extensive discussion appears in the second report, which covered the first decade of the third millennium.[25] There was an acknowledgment that, notwithstanding a long and rich history among various churches, neither the subject nor its meaning are well known today, nor is there any commonly established set of criteria for discernment. Questions such as the following wait for clarification: "How does the Church view discernment with respect to the use of the various charisms or gifts of the Holy Spirit that it has received? How does the Church discern whether a claim that one speaks on behalf of God is genuine or not? How does the Church discern which concerns it should heed and which ones it can rightly or safely

---

[24] "Word and Spirit, Church and World: The Final Report of the International Dialogue between Representatives of the World Alliance of Reformed Churches and Some Classical Pentecostal Churches and Leaders," Pneuma: The Journal of the Society for Pentecostal Studies 23, no. 1 (Spring 2001): 9–43. This document was also published in the Asian Journal of Pentecostal Studies 4, no. 1 (2001): 41–72; and as "Word and Spirit, Church and World: Final Report of the International Pentecostal-Reformed Dialogue," Reformed World 50, no. 3 (September 2000): 128–56. The first and second Final Reports are abbreviated FR 1 and FR 2.

[25] "Experience in Christian Faith and Life: Worship, Discipleship, Discernment, Community, and Justice," The Report of the International Dialogue between Representatives of the World Alliance of Reformed Churches and Some Classical Pentecostal Churches and Leaders 2001–2011, Cyberjournal for Pentecostal-Charismatic Research 21, January 2012, http://www.pctii.org/cyberj/cyberj21/WARC_2011d.html.

ignore? Furthermore, the question of who is empowered to exercise
discernment in and on behalf of the community of faith is one that
brings various responses." Yet another continuing question that arises
among both communities has to do with the relationship between
individual and communal discernment (FR 2, 73, 74).

These two ecclesial families affirm that "[t]hrough the Holy
Spirit, the Bible speaks the Word of God.... The Bible nourishes
the People of God and enables them to discern the spirits." With the
Reformed, Pentecostals "stress the mutual bond of the Word and
the Spirit" (FR 1, 22). "Each Pentecostal community, formed by the
outpouring of the Spirit and shaped by the Spirit's gifts, discerns
what the Spirit is saying to the Church through the Word and is
thereby shaped by the Spirit in conformity to the Word" (39).[26]
Because for Pentecostals "the anointing of the Spirit" and a "Spirit-
empowered proclamation" of the biblical message is central, and they
therefore also cherish "multiple gifts ... to channel God's presence
and to communicate God's will," discernment is an essential task.
Honestly, they acknowledge that there have been instances in which
for some Pentecostals the gifts have trumped the written Word.
That said: "The locus of discernment tends to be distributed in many
Pentecostal churches among the entire congregation, so that whether
gathered in worship or dispersed in society, all members are called to
exercise their gifts in ministry.... Discernment, then, requires active
participation by all the members of the community. They listen for
the Spirit to speak through the Word communicated by preaching,
teaching, testimony, and action" (FR 1, 25, 49). This is not to elevate
the community over the Spirit but to "recognize the Spirit's leadership in the Church" (FR 1, 42). Trusting the Spirit's continuing

---

[26] Similarly, FR 2, 92: "All ... words must be tested to see whether they conform to
Scripture. No prophetic word is accepted that contradicts the word of God that we find
in Scripture. No prophetic word is accepted as providing a normative revelation for all
Christians, whether by addition or deletion. These gifts most often bring to remembrance
those things that Jesus taught, in keeping with Jesus' promise of the Holy Spirit's role (John
14:26) and applies them in ways that are consistent with Paul's teaching in 1 Corinthians 14."

overseeing and guidance, the Pentecostal team made this important statement:

> Ideally, spiritual discernment plays an essential role in Pentecostalism. The practice of Pentecostal spirituality collectively prepares congregations, ministries, and denominations to discern God's will in concrete situations. Functioning within many dimensions of the Church as community, the discernment dynamic relies upon the Spirit's assistance and leadership for an authentication of communal prayer. This is manifested in a collective inner witness that is consistent with Scripture. Prayerful deliberations or conversations enable the local church to arrive at consensus about its response to an issue or situation. Included in the communal discernment is the interaction between Pentecostals and society (FR *1*, 47).

Among the many biblical texts studied together, a programmatic one for Pentecostals is the passage from Acts 15:1–35, often preached on and referred to among them. This "graphic example," concerning whether the Gentiles should be included fully in the Church of Christ or not, shows us that even though opposing and differing sides had been drawn after a fierce debate, the Apostle Peter appealed to the reception of the Holy Spirit by the Gentiles as the "evidence" of the divine work, including "signs and wonders that God had done" through the apostles (v. 12b). The obvious conclusion was that this was in keeping with the Scriptures and that therefore the Gentiles should be included. The summative statement is that this "seemed good to the Holy Spirit and to us" (v. 28a) (*FR 2*, 78, 79).

Regarding the classic New Testament passage in 1 Corinthians 12:10, it was mutually concluded that "Paul provides a clear link between the Spirit-given ability to speak in various kinds of tongues and the charism of interpretation (verse 10). In the same way, there appears to be a link between those who are given the charism of prophecy and those who are used in the discernment of spirits. This link is more explicit in 1 Corinthians 14:29 when Paul instructs the Corinthians that when they gather for worship they may 'Let two or three prophets speak, and let the others weigh [literally: discern (*diakrinetōsan*)] what is said.'" (FR 2, 81).

In my understanding, some of the ecumenically most far-reaching common affirmations in this discussion have to do with three important broad principles concerning discernment. First, "Sometimes discernment requires interpretation," as can be seen in the biblical encounter between the prophet Agabus and Paul in Acts chapter 21. While Agabus' prophecy—claimed under the authority of the Holy Spirit—about Paul's fate if going up to Jerusalem, was taken by the audience as a warning against the trip, Paul, "bound by the Spirit" to make this journey (20:22; 21:13), did go there (FR 2, 97). Second, "Sometimes discernment takes time," as evident in several biblical passages, including the promise of God to Abraham (Gen 12:1–3). Even though Abraham died long before God's promise came to pass, in hindsight the promise could be discerned to be authentic. In addition to several other biblical instances, the Final Report significantly notices that "Similarly, the *Kairos Document* played a prophetic role in the abandonment of apartheid in South Africa, though it continues to seek fulfillment to this day" (FR 2, 98). Third and related, "A prophetic word is ultimately considered to be valid when it is fulfilled.… This point of discernment is important to remember in light of recent claims by some that the Lord would return by a specific date (Matthew 24:36; 25:13)" (FR 2, 99).

Along with these significant common affirmations, there were also issues that brought some discomfort due to differences in understanding and orientation. Going back to the two major New Testament passages discussed above, discomfort had to do with the Reformed preference for the Acts 15 paradigm over 1 Corinthians 12 vis-à-vis Pentecostals' equal weighing of the two (FR 2, 84). Other noteworthy differences had to do with issues that are also relevant to the Catholic-Pentecostal dialogue, such as the Pentecostal comfort with speaking of discernment as a charismatic gifting and Reformed stress on discernment primarily in terms of a decision-making process:

> Reformed Christians think of the primary locus for decision-making being the legitimate exercise of discernment, undertaken in light of the Scriptures and especially within the community of faith. But many Reformed Christians have difficulty understanding why Pentecostals insist on discerning spirits, prophesying, or exorcising demons as a result of a discernment process, and they have many questions about the value and exercise of some of the charisms listed in Paul's charismatic catalogues. They worry about what they view as the subjectivity of Pentecostal actions and experiences in these things (FR 2, 85).

A related issue is the differing understanding of the category of "prophetic speaking," which for the Reformed has primarily do with speaking to the social issues while Pentecostals usually (although not exclusively) understand it in terms of charismatic utterance (FR 2, 88).

Yet another topic in need of long-term comparing of notes and mutual consultation has to do with the use of the gift of discernment in relation to other living faiths, a topic that so far has not occupied much of the Pentecostal agenda: "The Church is called to discern the spirits through the charism of the Holy Spirit informed by the Word of God (1 Corinthians 12:10, 14:29; cf. 1 Thessalonians 5:19–21; 1 John 4:2–3)." Pentecostals took up the challenge, acknowledging that they, "like many of the early Christians, are sensitive to the elements in other religions that oppose biblical teaching. They are, therefore, encouraged to receive the guidance of the Holy Spirit" (FR 2, 73). Understandably, no consensus was reached, particularly in light of the fact that the various Reformed traditions articulate no official position regarding the theology of religions and that Pentecostals are not used to applying the gift of discernment to the question of other religions (apart from the limited question of whether it has a demonic influence). Some contemporary Pentecostal theologians, however, have recently taken up this issue.

As a summary observation, it can be said that Pentecostals share important common affirmations with the Reformed, particularly concerning the biblical mandate, basic meaning(s) of the subject, and its diverse contexts of application. That said, as with the Roman Catholics, some of the differences have less to do with the topic of discernment *per se* and more with the overall differences of spirituality and ecclesiastical culture. It has been a great asset to Pentecostals to have these mutual dialogues with both traditions. It has given them an opportunity to consider widely different aspects of discernment that have not been so much unknown among them as in need of intentional reflection. At the same time, the encounter with Pentecostals has allowed both Catholics and Reformed to consider with great urgency the role of the Holy Spirit in discernment, including the charismatic endowment of the gift of testing the spirits.

In Lieu of Conclusions: Promises and Tasks for the Future

Rather than a comprehensive account of Pentecostal practice and theology of the discernment of the spirits, I consider this essay as an interim report. Interim reports do not yield neat conclusions. By definition, they are open-ended. Instead of the final word, I wish to add a few remarks, first on "Whither Pentecostal Theology of Discernment?" by taking a brief look at some promising work done by scholars of the movement. Thereafter, I seek to identify some common tasks for further reflection and consideration.

The contemporary generation of academically trained Pentecostals have ventured into areas rarely walked by their forebears. The biblical scholar Chris Thomas has considered the role of discernment in relation to sickness and demon possession in an important study titled *The Devil, Disease, and Deliverance.*[27] A careful exegetical study, it seeks to clarify the many occurrences of the terms "discern," "test," and so forth—for example, in relation to "discerning the body" or discerning sin in one's life in relation to sickness—and to offer pastoral and spiritual guidance. The above-mentioned comprehensive study by Parker, *Toward a Practical Theology of Pentecostal Discernment and Decision Making,* including an ethnographic survey of a group of Pentecostal church members, has highlighted the complex interplay of divine and human elements in diverse decision-making experiences. A multidisciplinary project, it has also utilized psychological resources as well as the Lutheran theologian Paul Tillich's ideas about decision-making. As is well known, in the third volume of his systematic theology—focusing on the Life in the Spirit—Tillich sought to acknowledge the genuine experience of the Spirit linked with the Word and sacrament but not imprisoned by them any more than by ecclesiastical and hierarchical structures.[28] Some other Pentecostals have similarly drawn on psychological resources, particularly in relation to counseling. David F. Cartledge's recent essay not only seeks to provide guidelines for such an enterprise but also to correct and balance the excesses of some of the (mostly charismatic rather than Pentecostal) "inner healing" and "spiritual warfare" approaches and their way of using the category of discernment.[29]

The leading Pentecostal theologian of religions, Amos Yong, has labored for a number of years in the field of religious pluralism, interfaith encounters, and comparative theology. His published dissertation, *Discerning the Spirit(s),* works towards a pneumatologically

---

[27] John Christopher Thomas, *The Devil, Disease, and Deliverance: Origins of Illness in New Testament Thought* (Sheffield: Sheffield Academic Press, 1998).

[28] Parker, *Led by the Spirit.*

[29] David F. Cartledge, "A Pentecostal Approach to Pastoral Counselling: Applying Gifts of the Spirit & Revelation Knowledge," *webjournals.alphacrucis.edu.au* (2012), http://webjournals.ac.edu.au/journals/aps/issue-4/a-pentecostal-approach-to-pastoral-counselling-app/.

loaded Pentecostal theology of religions through the lens of
discernment. His several subsequent publications continue the
trend, including a close engagement of Buddhist traditions from
the perspective of the Spirit.[30] These are all enterprising projects
whose full promise in terms of dissemination among and embrace
by churches and grassroots Pentecostals is yet to come and to be
appraised. These are indications of the ever-widening, vibrant
scholarly investigation of an essential topic for Pentecostals.

To put in perspective the topic of discernment, whether in its
traditional grassroots form among the churches, its exploratory
form among the academicians, or its dialogical form in relation to
other confessions, the obvious yet often ignored observation is that
when speaking of the charismatic gift of discerning the spirits, it
is not only about discerning the prophetic word or other message
or action or choice itself but also about the charismatic gift itself!
Parker rightly notes:

> [I]t would be erroneous to assume that Pentecostals have
> been unequivocal in their endorsement of charismatic
> manifestations as the means for discerning the leading of
> the Spirit. The relationship of charismatic manifestations
> to discernment and decision making is more subtle than
> a one-to-one identification of charismatic manifestations
> as the leading of the Spirit. Charismatic manifestations
> might better be conceived as not only a means for dis-
> cernment in some circumstances, but also as the very
> thing that needs to be discerned in other circumstances.
> Charismatic manifestations may be evidence of the

[30] Amos Yong, *Discerning the Spirit(s): A Pentecostal-Charismatic Contribution to Christian Theology of Religions* (Sheffield: Sheffield Academic Press, 2000); Idem, *Pneumatology and the Christian-Buddhist Dialogue: Does the Spirit Blow through the Middle Way?* Studies in Systematic Theology 11 (Leiden and Boston: Brill, 2012). See also Tony Richie, "The Wide Reach of the Spirit: A Renewal Theology of Mission and Interreligious Encounter in Dialogue with Yves Congar," ch. 2 in *The Wide Reach of the Spirit: Renewal and Theology of Mission in a Religiously Plural World* (Lexington, KY: Emeth Press, 2011).

Spirit's presence, yet they are not sufficient in and of
themselves for discerning the Spirit's leading.[31]

In this job of discerning regarding discernment, Pentecostals have
been greatly helped in their contacts with other Christians. That said,
a too-often-neglected common question is this: What kind of criteria
have non-Pentecostals used—and are still using—when seeking
to discern whether Pentecostalism is a genuine Spirit-movement
or not?[32] This goes back, of course, to the wider question of how
the Spirit-movements throughout history, beginning from the
Montanists, have been evaluated.

When considering the nature and value of the gift of discernment, one must be mindful that even in its most charismatically
endowed mode, it is still a robustly human enterprise. All human
discernment is just that—*human*—and hence liable to mistakes and
misuse. Continuing and patient mutual assessment of discernment,
both within the Pentecostal communities and outside, in tandem
with other Christians, is thus badly needed. The *human* nature of
the discernment process notwithstanding, it is also important to
note that "Pentecostal discernment and decision making cannot be
separated entirely from the deeply held conviction that God is at
work in these activities; decision making is not a human endeavor
only." Far from being an attempt to "engineer divine intervention,"
this statement is "an acknowledgment that Christian decision
making participates in realities wider than the egos of the decision
makers themselves."[33]

---

[31] Parker, *Led by the Spirit*, 34.

[32] Robeck opens his essay "Discerning the Spirit" (pp. 29–30) with a newspaper clip from
the San Francisco *Chronicle* of 1989, in which a writer bluntly lumps Pentecostals and New
Agers together under the pejorative nomenclature "Great Awakening." He also provides striking early responses in newspapers to the newly founded Pentecostal Church of Azusa Street,
Los Angeles, CA, in 1906 (pp. 31–32). For a fuller account, see his *The Azusa Street Mission
and Revival* (Nashville: Thomas Nelson, 2006).

[33] Parker, *Led by the Spirit*, 205.

9

An Expanding Light?
Pentecostals and the Protestant Reformation
Frank D. Macchia

THE CHURCH CATHOLIC has the opportunity this year to reflect on Luther's hammering his 95 Theses to the door of the castle church at Wittenberg. We are now 500 years from that momentous occasion. Luther could never have anticipated at that time that this simple act of dialogue (and defiance) at that relatively small chapel would create the firestorm that would follow. In an analogous manner, little did those who participated in that relatively small mission on Azusa Street in Los Angeles anticipate that it would become the hub of an expanding global movement. Perhaps Pentecostals could pause this year to consider how they fit into the larger Protestant movement. As a Pentecostal leader, Jack Hayford has represented for many of us an ecumenical figure. It is thus fitting that I offer as part of this collection of essays a reflection on Pentecostalism as a Protestant movement.

Locating the Pentecostal movement within the larger Protestant landscape is no easy task since the movement is vast and diverse. The central place of origin for the Pentecostal movement at the turn of the twentieth century was the *Apostolic Faith Mission* on Azusa Street in Los Angeles. Many stories came from the revival of apostolic power for mission that was said to occur there over the months of the Mission's global popularity. Though this Mission in Los Angeles was the central hub of the early Pentecostal movement, Pentecostalism globally has many roots that may be traced back to a variety of Holiness, Pietistic, and Higher Life movements. The ethos of these movements has influenced the diverse fabric of Pentecostalism to this day. I will attempt to describe this fabric as I relate the Pentecostal witness to the larger Reformation heritage.

Deeds over Creeds

The Founder of the Apostolic Faith Mission, William J. Seymour, wrote in his Mission's paper, *The Apostolic Faith*, that the new Pentecostal movement "stands for the restoration of the faith once delivered to the saints."[1] He stood in line with the larger desire of Protestantism to restore something vital to the faith that came to be neglected in the expanding tradition of the Church. Christ alone or faith alone, as witnessed to by Scripture alone, were accents that brought a laser focus on what was neglected or perhaps shrouded to some extent in confusion. The Pentecostals had similar commitments but focused instead on the experience and life of this faith that centered on Christ and Scripture, not on the reality of Christ as a thing of the past as testified of in dead letters, but rather on the living Christ who is present in the reality and power of the Spirit to be experienced and lived. There was an effort to return to the biblical text to hear with fresh ears and to see with fresh eyes. The Pentecostals and their Protestant forerunners were *restorationists* in some ways, meaning that, in a sense, they understood the best way *forward* as a *return* to that which was vital to the founding of the Church.

The broader details of what was needed to be restored, however, were varied in the larger Protestant landscape. The Pentecostals highlighted the power of the Holy Spirit in the life of faith, so one could say that they largely followed the radical wing of the Reformation by stressing the restoration of the *life* of faith as needed to properly fulfill and unify the church in the midst of its

---

[1] William J. Seymour, "The Apostolic Faith Movement," *Apostolic Faith*, 1:1 (September 1906): 2.

diversity. This renewed life in the Spirit for the Pentecostals was centrally oriented around an experience of Jesus Christ as Savior (and Sanctifier), Spirit Baptizer, Healer, and Coming King.[2] The experience of Spirit baptism or a life-transforming renewal and empowerment of the Spirit was focused on Christ, on a deeper involvement in his latter-day mission in the world, with all of the signs and wonders that attend the magnification of grace in the world as the time of deliverance draws near.[3] Their worship involved body and soul and followed closely the narrative of Jesus as the one who is alive today because in imparting the Spirit he imparts his own life to us.[4] In general, the power of the Spirit in bringing the Church more deeply into the communion and mission of Christ in the world was thought to be most powerfully felt in a deep sense of God's presence in worship, in an expectation of power in overcoming the hold of sin and sickness, and in a vibrant involvement in world missions.

This renewed life in the presence of the Spirit was thought to unify the people of God and to deliver them from the sterility and divisiveness of an otherwise "merely confessed" orthodoxy. But the Pentecostals were also sometimes sensitive to the extremes of spiritual fanaticism without biblical or Christological discernment and guidance. Seymour thus wrote in the preamble of his Mission's paper: "We are not fighting men or churches, but seeking to displace dead forms and creeds and wild fanaticisms with living, practical Christianity. 'Love, faith, unity' are our watchwords."[5] As with the

---

[2] I am obviously dependent here on Donald W. Dayton, *Theological Roots of Pentecostalism* (Grand Rapids, MI: Zondervan, 1988).

[3] The central thesis of David William Faupel, *The Everlasting Gospel: The Significance of Eschatology in the Development of Pentecostal Thought* (Sheffield: Sheffield Academic Press, 1999). See also my eschatological development of Spirit baptism in Frank D. Macchia, *Baptized in the Spirit: A Global Pentecostal Theology* (Grand Rapids, MI: Zondervan, 2006).

[4] Walter J. Hollenweger accented the holistic and narrative aspects of Pentecostal spirituality. See his "Flowers and Songs: A Mexican Contribution to Theological Hermeneutics," *International Review of Mission*, 60.238 (April 1971): 232–244.

[5] William J. Seymour, "The Apostolic Faith Movement," *Apostolic Faith*, 1:1 (September 1906): 2.

Reformers, Seymour saw the Pentecostal renewal as for the entire Church and not as the founding of a particular sect within it.

Within the winds of spiritual renewal, most Pentecostals did not want to eliminate widely held creedal affirmations. However, they wanted to rediscover the original purpose of church creeds and forms as occasions for the free and overflowing work of the divine Spirit. They wanted confessional affirmations that arose from an authentic participation in the life of faith. Interestingly, the Pentecostal desire to stress "deeds over creeds" was difficult to maintain in the long run. The occasion soon arose that demanded creedal affirmation. Within two decades of the movement's history, Pentecostalism was embroiled in doctrinal controversies that threatened the unity of the young movement. Most significantly, the Apostolic (sometimes called Oneness) Pentecostals maintained that baptism was to be practiced in Jesus' name only rather than in the name of the Father, Son, and Holy Spirit (cf. Acts 2:38). They then sought to harmonize this Jesus-name baptism with the triadic baptismal formula of Matthew 28:19. They concluded from this effort that Jesus' name is precisely the name of the Father, the Son, and the Holy Spirit, these three being titles (and not names) or modes of operation of the one God who is centrally and decisively revealed in Jesus Christ and under the banner of his name alone. They ended up becoming what may be termed Christocentric modalists in their understanding of the Trinity.

The Trinitarian Pentecostals who were in communion with the Apostolics engaged in conversation with them for more than a year before acting to exclude them. This act of exclusion cut against their grain, for they were a movement centrally devoted to the practical way of Christ through the renewing power of the Spirit in the world. Their confidence that this renewal would protect them from division was being severely put to the test in ways that they at that moment may not have fully realized. Both sides felt compelled to disrupt their unity in life and service in favor of faithfulness to the scriptural witness to Christ. Their conviction remained that theirs was not a dead or divisive creed but one that expressed a living faith in Christ. The Apostolics presently make up about twenty-five percent of the global Classical Pentecostal movement. Ecumenical conversations between them and Trinitarian Pentecostals are ongoing, and both sides take comfort in the fact that they both affirm the full deity of Christ and the worship of Christ as Lord of all. They both stress the power of the Spirit in our living communion with Christ and our participation in his mission for the world.[6] Efforts by more fundamentalist Pentecostals to view Apostolics as a "cult" or to view Trinitarian Pentecostals as polytheists are therefore to be avoided. Both sides are heirs in their own way of the orthodox faith that was inherited by the Reformation. Bear in mind that the great Athanasius joined with Marcellus of Ancyra (a Christocentric modalist) in affirming together the Nicene Creed.[7] The Pentecostal accent on experience, worship, and mission could, if followed, represent an example of a far-reaching Protestant ecumenism that joins with other church families in a common witness to the world.

Filled with the Spirit

Some think that the struggle between the Trinitarians and the Apostolics over Christology and the Trinity was inevitable since a focus on the life of the Spirit inevitably raises larger questions about Christ and God. Indeed, Pentecostals have always cultivated a Christological focus in their spirituality. Christ's atonement and resurrection were always highlighted as the powerful victory that became the wellspring of the Spirit's saving and healing work in the

---

[6] I was privileged to chair the Trinitarian side of the Oneness-Trinitarian Pentecostal dialogue. For my analysis of the dialogue's final report, see Frank D. Macchia, "The Oneness-Trinitarian Pentecostal Dialogue: Exploring the Diversity of Apostolic Faith," *Harvard Theological Review*, 103:3 (July 2010): 329–349.

[7] See Joseph Lienhard's excellent *Contra Marcellum: Marcellus of Ancyra and Fourth Century Theology* (Washington DC: Catholic University of America Press, 1999).

church. We drink from Christ's fullness in being filled with the Spirit, and we are thereby shaped in his image. Seymour thus wrote: "Let us lift up Christ to the world in all his fullness . . . in healing and salvation from all sin."[8] Yet, the overwhelming emphasis of the Pentecostals was still on the reality and experience of being filled with the Holy Spirit. Faith in their view was not a mere confession or intellectual belief but rather a response to the gospel enabled by the transforming work of the Spirit. Their stress was on the *experience of faith* first and foremost. Their battle was thus not exactly the same as Luther's or Calvin's. The Pentecostals were not seeking to discover the objective and certain foundation for faith in the midst of the uncertainties and ambiguities of Christian piety. Pentecostals sought instead the *experience* of faith in the midst of an overly intellectual understanding of faith as a mere confessional stance. They were pietists of a sort.

This accent on the experience of faith was not entirely foreign to the roots of the magisterial Reformation. Both Luther and Calvin understood faith as a transformative union with Christ.[9] This experiential emphasis took many forms among the movements that most directly influenced Pentecostalism. The Wesleyans emphasized the transformation of the affections into passions for holy love. Among the pietists, attention was placed on the priority of new birth through the Word of God. The higher life movements highlighted spiritual awakenings involving repentance and new life. The Pentecostals were blessed by all of these spiritual accents but focused uniquely on the infilling and empowerment of the Holy Spirit for the expanding witness of the Church to the reality of Jesus Christ. Of course, many within the orbit of these movements felt that they were preserving the original assumption of the Reformers that faith is a living response to God that partakes of Christ in all his fullness. Those involved later in the "traditions of the heart" saw themselves

---

[8] William J. Seymour, "River of Living Water," *Apostolic Faith* 1:3 (November 1906): 2.

[9] See, for example, Tuomo Mannermaa, *Christ Present in Faith: Luther's View of Justification* (Minneapolis: Fortress Press, 2005).

as fulfilling this assumption by making it explicit and by highlighting its significance. They were expanding the Reformation desire to restore to the churches something neglected in the living faith of the Apostolic witness.

The Pentecostals traced the message concerning the infilling and experience of the Holy Spirit to the promise of the Spirit in Joel chapter 2 and to its penultimate fulfillment at the Day of Pentecost in Acts chapter 2. Allow me to illustrate how this was done by looking briefly at the work of the Pentecostal evangelist Aimee Semple McPherson. According to McPherson, the promise of the Spirit in Joel and the fulfillment with power in Acts is the reality that must be restored to the Church. She notes that the vision of the Pentecostal movement from the beginning was to bring the Church back to the original apostolic experience of the Spirit, which is meant for everyone in the Church. One cannot regard the apostolic experience of the Spirit as unique, as though the Apostles were spiritual elites whose experiences of the Spirit were inaccessible to ordinary Christians. The goal was thus to make the Church once again aware of the power of the Holy Spirit as an indwelling and overflowing presence. According to McPherson, this recovery of the apostolic experience of the Spirit is especially needed to deliver the Church from the decay of mere confessionalism. McPherson wrote that the God of Pentecost is not merely to be "confessed" or "professed;" God is also to be "possessed."[10] She did not mean with this term "possession" that we can master or control God's Spirit. Her overarching theme was rather the mighty outpouring of the Spirit by which God takes hold of us and transforms us into living witnesses of his presence in the world. Still, in God's possessing us, we come of our own choice to bear the Spirit.

---

[10] Aimee Semple McPherson, *This Is That: Personal Experiences, Sermons, and Writings of Aimee Semple McPherson, Evangelist* (Los Angeles: The Bridal Call Publishing House, 1919), 390–406, esp. 392.

McPherson's idea of willfully becoming a vessel of the Spirit was a common theme in early Pentecostal preaching. Pentecostals held that God has drawn near to us, not only because God has come to us in the person of Jesus Christ but also (and especially) because God is now present in power as a flowing river of life into which human persons and communities are to be taken up and transformed into Christ's image. The work of the Spirit is for the Pentecostals, therefore, a neglected part of the "full gospel." In accepting the gospel, Christ is not only to be believed; he is also to be taken hold of in the Spirit so that we become like Him, partake of His fullness, and join Him in His mission. Consequently, participation in Christ through the life of the Spirit was not for the Pentecostals merely supplemental to the gospel or the means by which the gospel is affirmed. The Spirit's outpouring is rather vital to the substance of the good news itself. Indeed, the gospel means that, through the Spirit, a sinful and alienated human life becomes the dwelling place of God, a living temple for God's glory, and a witness of that glory before the world.

This pneumatological focus meant that Pentecostal preachers were most preoccupied with the issue of how one becomes the dwelling place of the Spirit. There were doctrinal differences among the Pentecostals, but they all held in common this passion for living in conscious awareness of the presence of the Spirit. As Walter Hollenweger noted, "Talk of 'the doctrine' of the Pentecostal churches is highly problematical. What unites the Pentecostal churches is not a doctrine but a religious experience, and this can be interpreted and substantiated in many different ways."[11] James Dunn has described well the ecumenical challenge of this emphasis on the experience of the Spirit as an indwelling presence. In his significant study on the baptism in the Spirit, in which he was critical of Pentecostal teaching, he also had this to say in its defense:

[11] Walter J. Hollenweger, "From Azusa Street to the Toronto Phenomenon" in *Pentecostal Movements as an Ecumenical Challenge*, *Concilium*, Jürgen Moltmann and Josef Kuschel (London: SCM Press, 1996), 7.

It is a sad commentary on the poverty of our own immediate experience of the Spirit that when we come across
language in which the NT writers refer directly to the
gift of the Spirit and to their experience of it, either we
automatically refer it to the sacraments and can only give
it meaning when we do so . . . or else we discount the
experience as too subjective or mystical in favor of a faith
which is essentially an affirmation of biblical propositions,
or else we in effect psychologize the Spirit out of
existence.[12]

By way of contrast, Dunn notes that "in earliest days of Christianity, possession of the Spirit was a fact of immediate perception . . . a conscious experience."[13] Of course, Pentecostalism is not the only renewal movement to point us to the experiential reality of life in the Spirit. But their witness does add force to those in other wings of the Church catholic attempting to make this point.

Stages of the Spirit

Dunn's statements do expose a problem. How one comes to receive and experience the Spirit is difficult to define, as the Pentecostals were to discover. How did the Pentecostals come to wrestle with this problem? Can one's journey into the life of the Spirit be mapped? Though Pentecostals believed that faith begins with the work of the Spirit, they also inherited from the Holiness Movement the belief that the Holy Spirit is received and experienced in precise "stages." In their search to describe this process of infilling, the Pentecostals borrowed from established nomenclature in the area of soteriology. Terms like regeneration, sanctification, and Spirit baptism were transformed into stages in faith's reception of the Spirit. Among the earliest Pentecostals who came from the Holiness Movement,

---

[12] James D. G. Dunn, *Baptism in the Holy Spirit* (London: SCM Press, 1970), 225–226.
[13] Ibid., 149, 105.

regeneration was viewed as an experience of new birth and sanctification as an experience of total cleansing and consecration unto God. The culmination of one's initiation into the full presence and power of the Holy Spirit, however, was termed the "baptism in the Holy Spirit." Here is where the Pentecostals reached for a term that was somewhat neglected in the history of theology. Usually held by the Pentecostals as distinct from the experiences of regeneration and sanctification, Spirit baptism was viewed as the full reception of the Spirit, resulting in deeper participation in God's supernatural power for witness.

Typical for Wesleyan Pentecostals is Seymour's "three-stage" description of how the sinner becomes the vessel of the Spirit:

> The Lord has mercy on him for Christ's sake and puts eternal life in his soul, pardoning him of his sins, washing away his guilty pollution, and he stands before God justified as though he had never sinned . . . Then . . . Jesus takes that soul that has eternal life in it and presents it to God for thorough cleansing and purging from all Adamic sin . . . Now he is on the altar for the fire of God to fall, which is the baptism with the Holy Ghost. It is the free gift upon the sanctified, cleansed heart.[14]

Notice how Seymour attempts to trace the phases through which the sinner becomes the dwelling place of the Spirit. First, there is the moment of faith, which is described as a new birth experience, a reception of eternal life into the soul. One is justified within this embrace of the Spirit. Implied here is that regeneration involves justification because justifying faith is itself a transforming experience. Then comes total cleansing and consecration, through which the believer is placed on the altar of sacrifice. One is consecrated wholly unto God and God's purposes in the world. But more is needed, according to Seymour. The believers require the power to fulfill these divine purposes. They must be filled with divine love so as to become a channel of that love to others. To fulfill the

---

[14] William J. Seymour, "The Way Into the Holiest," *Apostolic Faith* 1:2 (October 1906): 4.

experience of faith, the fire from heaven comes streaming down, which is viewed as the gift of power for the Christian life, especially the life of witness in the world. This is the good news of the full gospel according to Seymour: The sinner is fully taken up into the embrace of the Holy Spirit of God and is turned into a mighty witness of Christ in the world. Our initial "conversion" from the world to God is now fulfilled through a "second conversion" from God back to the world for Christ's sake. The "fullness" of the Spirit thus resulted for Seymour in the formation of a called and spiritually-gifted community that functions as a witness before the world of the coming Kingdom of God. The Church as a communion in the Spirit is the missional church, the church for "others."

Seymour's vision of initiation to the Spirit was popular in the earliest years of the movement. But not all Pentecostals came to accept every detail of Seymour's journey from regeneration to sanctification to Spirit baptism. As might be expected, controversy over these stages erupted within the first decade of the movement's history. Pentecostals who came into the movement from Reformed backgrounds did not view sanctification as concentrated on a single crisis experience subsequent to regeneration. Sanctification, for them, was rather a lifelong process that begins with regeneration. Entry into the life of the Spirit was thus described by them as having only two major steps: regeneration and Spirit baptism (as empowerment). This difference from Seymour, however, is not as great as it may first appear. These Reformed Pentecostals were still influenced by the Wesleyan Holiness Movement to a degree since they also emphasized consecration of life and often assumed that sanctification as a process does include dramatic breakthroughs in the holy life. Moreover, within this Reformed (or "finished work") Pentecostal wing, the Apostolic Pentecostals (described above as modalistic in their view of the Trinity) were strongly oriented towards a holiness way of life.

Interestingly, the Apostolics arrived very early at an integrated understanding of initiation to the life of the Spirit in which not even Spirit baptism was viewed as separable from regeneration. The Apostolics reduced initiation to the life of the Spirit to one complex step: The infilling of the Spirit was said to culminate a process of transformation involving repentance, faith, and water baptism. The Apostolics, however, agreed with all Pentecostals that the reception or infilling of the Spirit culminates in an empowering experience that turns the community of Christ into a living witness. I agree with William Faupel here that the early Pentecostal focus on Christ as the center of all experiences in the Spirit moved Pentecostals towards an integrated notion of initiation into the life of the Spirit.[15] Their accent on the Spirit opened them up to a complex initiation that can be described in experiential phases, but their Christocentrism was a counterbalance to this, orientating them towards viewing the entire initiation process as dimensions of a living faith in Christ. Thus, one may view the complex but single initiation process of the Apostolics as the quintessential Pentecostal soteriology.[16]

The Wesleyan Pentecostal way illustrated by Seymour, the Reformed Pentecostal way, and the Apostolic Pentecostal way were not the only ways of mapping one's journey into the Spirit among the Pentecostals. But I have described these three in order to grant some idea of the variety of options among Pentecostal groups for understanding our reception of the Spirit. Despite this variety, however, all Pentecostals accented the good news that sinful human beings can become bearers of the Spirit. All of them emphasized that the reception of the Spirit is life transforming from beginning to end. All Pentecostals stressed that the reception of the Spirit culminates in an experience of power for witness in the world. The focus on power was meant to involve the whole person—body and soul, mind and the subconscious depths. Spiritual gifts involve us on every level

---

[15] Faupel notes this in his *Everlasting Gospel*.

[16] See Frank D. Macchia, *Justified in the Spirit: Creation, Redemption, and the Triune God* (Grand Rapids, MI: Eerdmans, 2010), 75–102.

of our being. Interestingly, such attention to these gifts is becoming a prominent part of the expansion of Christianity in the global South. As Philip Jenkins has noted:

> The Christianity that is flourishing in the global South is a Christianity that looks very strange to Western eyes. It takes prophecy and spiritual healing very seriously. Dreams, visions, trances are all notions that carry a good deal of currency in the countries in which Christianity is succeeding very dramatically.[17]

Especially in the United States, speaking in tongues was highlighted historically as the characteristic sign of this culminating experience of power for witness, though not all Pentecostals made this sign a necessary accompaniment of the experience. The challenge as many of us see it is in appreciating the gift of tongues and its sign value without making this gift exclusionary of those who do not articulate it in ways that may be recognized as glossolalic. Most importantly, it is vital that this focus on spiritual power does not eclipse a prior emphasis on love. The power of the Spirit is the power of divine love. A number of early Pentecostal authors did refer to the experience of Spirit baptism as a baptism in divine love.[18] In fact, Seymour was clear that love was the chief sign of the presence of the Spirit in the Pentecostal church. Speaking in tongues was for Seymour of subordinate status. The many tongues of Pentecost functioned for Seymour to symbolize the fact that divine love crosses all boundaries of human existence in order to form a diverse community in which everyone is accepted, called, and empowered.

---

[17] See interview with Jenkins at: http://www.carnegiecouncil.org/resources/transcripts/136.html. See also Philip Jenkins, *The Next Christendom: The Coming of Global Christianity* (New York: Oxford University Press, 2011).

[18] See, for example, author unknown, "The Old Time Pentecost," *Apostolic Faith*, 1:1 (September 1906): 2, and "Tongues as a Sign," *Apostolic Faith*, 1:1 (September 1906): 2.

It is clear that our ecumenical conversation partners, Protestant and Catholic, have helped us to search our own tradition fruitfully for insights in all of the above areas of concern. In recent Pentecostal/Reformed conversations, for example, the Pentecostals recognized that they must take care not to use one single gift or cluster of gifts referred to in the New Testament as superior to the others. The Reformed participants recognized in response that they have historically been too "casual" about the extraordinary gifts of the Spirit described in the New Testament and perhaps present among a growing number within the membership of their own churches.[19]

The fact that many Pentecostals attempt to describe regeneration, sanctification, and Spirit baptism as distinct "stages" in one's reception of the Spirit is potentially problematic in that this could lead to elitism. Those who participate in Pentecostal power can end up thinking that they occupy a higher stage in the life of the Spirit. At any rate, the Spirit is a living person and not a substance that can be received in separately measured portions. A careful reading of Pentecostal sources will reveal that such ideas were in most cases not their intention. Ecumenical conversation partners who have written on the topic of Spirit baptism, such as Kilian McDonnell (from a Catholic perspective), have helped many of us to see that these "stages" should more appropriately be viewed as "dimensions" of life in the Spirit, all of which are potentially present in the life of the Spirit and may be experienced or "released" in life in different ways. I have specifically proposed viewing Spirit baptism as a kind of "root metaphor" of the entire life of the Spirit in which we participate by faith. We are born anew, justified, sanctified, and empowered in the Spirit from the depth and horizon of the Spirit poured out abundantly upon us in Christ and received in faith.[20]

---

[19] See the Final Report: "Word and Spirit, Church and World, The Pentecostal Reformed Dialogue, 1996 2000," http://www.warc.ch/dt/erl1/20.html.

[20] The central thesis of my *Baptized in the Spirit: A Global Pentecostal Theology*.

Pentecostals and the Reformation:
An Expanding Light

The above description of Pentecostalism is enough to show that the movement was a diversely unique expression of Protestant faith (as were all branches of Protestantism). The Pentecostals attempted (somewhat clumsily) to capture this continuity and uniqueness by viewing their movement as part of an expanding Protestant light in history. The phases of their experience of the Spirit were writ large into an interpretation of Protestant history. Pentecostals commonly saw themselves as participating in a long line of "Reformers" who sought to rediscover neglected features of these phases. Luther and Calvin were credited with restoring to the Church the great power of the atonement as the foundation for the justification of sinners. Wesley was then praised for writing about the great significance of consecration by the Spirit in which the believer totally yields to God. The Pentecostal movement was then viewed as the culmination of this trajectory by accenting the baptism in the Holy Spirit as that power that turns the Church into a living witness for Christ in the world.

McPherson illustrates this tendency well. She gives us a prominent example of this reading of the gradual restoration of the apostolic witness in history. She wrote that the prophet Joel not only foretold of the outpouring of the Spirit at Pentecost, but he also foresaw the erosion of a proper attention to the filling and power of the Spirit. The locust plague in Joel foreshadowed the erosion of attention to the Spirit in the history of the Church. As a result, the experiences of justification, sanctification, and Spirit baptism, along with the full spectrum of fruits and gifts of the Spirit, began to wane in the Church during the "dark ages" or medieval period. Concerning this spiritual erosion, she wrote bluntly: "The gifts and fruits of the Spirit gone, the baptism of the Holy Spirit gone, separation and Holiness gone, justification by faith gone."[21] According to McPherson, the outpouring of the Spirit in the latter days will bring the needed restoration from this spiritual erosion. This restoration began with Martin Luther. When Luther grasped the powerful victory of Christ's atonement, it was as if "a great light fell from heaven."[22] Through his message, "life again began to surge through the trunk and limbs of the tree."[23] William Booth of the Salvation Army and John Wesley are then praised for their emphasis on consecration and holiness.[24] Lastly, the experience of Spirit baptism, especially as signified in gifts like speaking in tongues, brings the restoration of the damaged plant to completion. The healing of the church from the damage of the locust plague is now finding completion in this latter-day outpouring of the Spirit upon the church.

Of course, there are obvious limitations to this classical Pentecostal reading of church history and of the place of Pentecostalism within the expanding Protestant witness in history, as many Pentecostals involved in ecumenical discussions would readily conclude. The Catholic and Orthodox witness cannot be made invisible in this way or reduced to a period of "dark ages" or locust-plague erosion. And the location of Pentecostalism at the pinnacle of the Protestant witness in history is by implication triumphalistic. Of course, Pentecostals are not the only ones who have read theological history in ways that highlight their own self-importance. But the mere fact that others are guilty of a similar limitation is no justification for our own limitations. As might be expected, more recent Pentecostal authors are seeking to locate the winds of Pentecostal renewal within a more expansive understanding of the work of the Spirit in history and in the world today. We are not the only Christian communities that have drawn attention to the presence and power of the Spirit in the Christian life. With

---

[21] McPherson, *This Is That*, 393.
[22] Ibid., 390–406, esp. 396.
[23] Ibid., 396.
[24] Ibid., 398–399.

all of this having been said, we cannot ignore the problem of the *Geistvergessenheit* in the history of theology in the West, and I appreciate the fact that Pentecostal men and women gave so much in helping us to remember!

Conclusion

One could say that from the moment God breathed into the nostrils of Adam, we were made for the Spirit, to be the Spirit's dwelling place and to move in the Spirit's liberty and power. All of the great preachers of the Pentecostal movement have tried to stress this point. Though they appropriately highlighted the victory of Christ as at the core of spiritual renewal, they always managed in some way to come back around to the need to live in this victory ourselves by the power of the Spirit. I appreciate this Pentecostal emphasis on receiving and living by the power of the Spirit. Allow me to say why. First, the Pentecostals remind us that all soteriological categories have to do with the renewal of life in the Spirit, including justification by faith, sanctification, and, ultimately, glorification. I mention justification because, as Paul Tillich reminds us, the justified discover unambiguous life through the Spirit in the midst of ambiguous experience, and this is the "in spite of" affirmed in the Reformation.[25] I include glorification because Paul writes that those who are justified are glorified (Romans 8:30). The resurrection body will be the *pneumatic* body that fully participates in the powerful liberty of the Spirit (1 Corinthians 15:44; Romans 8:18–23). The life of faith is from beginning to end a reaching for that liberty in the Spirit of the crucified and risen Christ.

Second, the church is called to strive continuously for more of God, for an experience of the Spirit's presence in all dimensions of

---

[25] Paul Tillich, *Systematic Theology*, vol. 3 (Chicago: University of Chicago Press, 1963), 124–131. See my development of justification in the Spirit in Frank D. Macchia, *Justified in the Spirit: Creation, Redemption, and the Triune God* (Grand Rapids, MI: Eerdmans, 2010).

the life of faith. Though the soteriological terms used by Pentecostals are more than experiences, they still point to aspects of life in the Spirit that can and should be experienced or "released" in life. Third, the church is called to discover the fullness of power precisely in its worship, its spiritually-gifted ministries, and its missionary life, or in its transformation into a gifted and mutually-edifying community that is called to bear witness of Christ in the world. And this power is full because it claims us in every dimension of our existence. If our hearts are restless until they are filled with the Spirit and moved by the Spirit, then we must continue to yield so as to receive, again and again. Pentecostals join with a host of other Protestants and, indeed, with Christian families everywhere, in insisting that we return to the voices of the Scriptures again and again to hear and respond to such challenges afresh in our times and places with hope for the renewal of all flesh in Christ.

10

Presence, Providence, and the Calling of God

Susan L. Maros

THE ROLE OF pastor is the archetypical role to which a person is called by God in the Pentecostal/charismatic community.[1] Pentecostal and charismatic believers may embrace other life roles as constituting a "calling,"[2] yet the role of pastor retains a special status distinct from other vocations. Concerning the call of God to pastors, Jack W. Hayford reflects this sense of the uniqueness of the role when he writes, "As shepherds who have been 'called of God,' we have answered an inescapably insistent summons; we are committed to serve a cause that pursues values earth can't quantify, and offers hope unto an era when earth will have vaporized."[3]

---

[1] Writing as a Pentecostal theologian, Terry Cross states, "I have *never* heard anyone speak of their 'non-clergy' career as a calling." Terry L. Cross, *Answering the Call in the Spirit: Pentecostal Reflections on a Theology of Vocation, Work and Life* (Cleveland, TN: Lee University Press, 2007), 33, emphasis in the original. Cross continues, "Everywhere in the literature of early Pentecostals 'calling' means to preaching or full-time ministry." Ibid., 46. In this historical context, pastor, evangelist, and missionary were all valued roles. This essay focuses particularly on the pastoral role.

[2] Ultimately, this is what Cross argues for, writing, "When we 'work in the Spirit,' we offer to God our lives in response to the grace given to us already.... Work, then, is cooperating with God's goals in the universe by offering our hands for God's service by the power of the Spirit." Cross, *Answering the Call in the Spirit*, 84. In this, Cross echoes Miroslav Volf, who writes, "Since the whole life of a Christian is by definition a life in the Spirit, work cannot be an exception, whether that work is ecclesiastical or secular. *Work in the Spirit is one dimension of the Christian walk in the Spirit.*" Miroslav Volf, *Work in the Spirit: Toward a Theology of Work* (New York: Oxford University Press, 1991), viii, emphasis in the original.

[3] Jack W. Hayford, *Pastors of Promise* (Ventura, CA: Regal Books, 1997), 21–22.

Beyond esteem shown for the role of pastor in general, stories of pastors living faithful to God's call—particularly those faithful across a lifetime of service—are the hero stories of the community. These faithful heroes are the community's exemplar—the model, example, and pattern the community uses to understand what it means to live as a person called by God. The stories told by these heroes shape the community's understanding of God's nature and character. As the community listens to the narratives of encounters with God, the community learns how God speaks and acts in the world. As the heroes tell of their responses to God, the community learns what God desires of their own responses. The stories of heroes of the faith are the narrative lessons that embed biblical and theological truths deep in the heart of the community. These stories move and motivate the community to live faithful to the call of God.

This essay explores the ways in which narratives shape understanding of the nature of God's call, particularly around the themes of presence and providence. The model of faithful pastors constitutes a resource the faith community draws from to understand God and the world, and to make sense of its communal life. The way stories are told reflects the assumptions the community makes about the nature of God's presence and God's providence. These assumptions in turn impact whether a person interprets life experiences as symptomatic of a call to be a pastor. This essay examines these dynamics, looking at three narratives of encounters with God in the life of Jack W. Hayford and the call stories of two men in The King's University community. It argues for a need to embrace the stories of faith heroes like Dr. Hayford that testify to God's dynamic presence and the need to embrace those stories that embody the quiet work of God's providence, lest people learn to disregard God's providential leading.

Narratives as Resources for Meaning-Making

The model of pastoral heroes and the stories of their encounters with God contribute narrative resources the community uses to make sense of life, individually and collectively. The community observes pastors' lives as exemplars of what it means to be a person called by God. The narratives of heroes shape the mental models that people will use to think about their own calling. Individuals use these narrative resources to understand their experiences, interpreting their lives in light of the stories of the leaders they esteem and follow.[4]

The stories of heroes of faith serve to form the mental models of the community.[5] Leadership theorist Peter Senge defines mental models as "deeply held internal images of how the world works."[6] These mental models are "the images, assumptions, and stories which we carry in our minds of ourselves, other people, institutions, and every aspect of the world."[7] For the Pentecostal/charismatic community, as has been noted, the dominant mental model of a "called person" is that of a pastor. This mental model embodies the

---

[4] This essay explores the power of narratives to frame an individual's understanding of God's call, taking a cognitive anthropology perspective as a starting point. A similar case could be made from the standpoint of practical theology, considering the ways in which the community works to read and interpret Scripture, to draw from theological and historical resources, to make sense of the world, and to discern what would be faithful engagement with God's mission in that world. This latter approach was taken in a conference paper presented at the Society for Pentecostal Studies by the author in March 2017. The work in this present essay leans heavily on the author's earlier work looking at understanding of calling in adult students at The King's University. Susan L. Maros, *Knowing My Call: A Cultural Model of the Experience of Call in a Pentecostal/Charismatic Context* (Ann Arbor, MI: UMI, 2014).

[5] The mental models demonstrated by the structure of heroes' stories are themselves shaped by the community's assumptions. The story structure reflects a template already in place, governing what elements of the story get told. Stories model what is valued by the community. This dynamic of how stories are framed by the values and assumptions present in a group is a key aspect of narratives and mental models but not the focus of the present essay.

[6] Peter Senge, *The Fifth Discipline: The Art and Practice of the Learning Organization*, rev. and updated ed. (New York: Doubleday/Currency, 2006), 163.

[7] Ibid., 235.

assumptions and expectations of the community concerning the nature of God's call and how one comes to know this call. Calling is imaged primarily in terms of the call to preach or the call to ministry.

Anthropologist Bradd Shore refers to mental models as "salience-enhancing templates."[8] People attend to experience and ideas, filtering input through their mental models. Experiences that fit the model are deemed relevant and thus remembered and recounted. Experiences that do not fit the model are discarded as irrelevant. Thus, the mental models prominent in a given context very much impact how a person interprets and makes sense of life.

Individuals examine their calling through the lens of the mental models shaped by the hero stories of their community.[9] They have expectations about how God calls people and to what roles God calls people. Those expectations impact what life experiences the individual will consider as being related to knowing God's call. Experiences that fit the model of "calling" are remembered and recalled; life experiences that do not fit the model are disregarded.

Mental models are cultural constructs utilized by a community for the purpose of making sense of life. Writing about leadership as meaning-making activity, Charles Drath and Wilfred Palus define meaning-making as "the process of arranging our understanding of experience so that we can know what has happened and what is happening, and so that we can predict what will happen; it is constructing knowledge of ourself and the world."[10] In a Pentecostal/charismatic context, the stories told by heroes of the faith—recount-

---

[8] Bradd Shore, *Culture in Mind: Cognition, Culture, and the Problem of Meaning* (New York: Oxford University Press, 1996), 315.

[9] Sociologist Ann Swidler includes stories as part of a cultural "tool kit" that members of the community use "in varying configurations to solve different kinds of problems." Ann Swidler, "Culture in Action: Symbols and Strategies," *American Sociological Review* 51 (2):273. For members of a Pentecostal/charismatic community with the "problem" of knowing their calling, the stories of esteemed community members become elements of their cultural tool kit to make sense of their own lives.

[10] Wilfred H. Drath and Charles J. Palus, *Making Common Sense* (Greensboro, NC: Center for Creative Leadership, 1994), 2.

ing how God has worked in their lives, guiding and directing them toward their calling—are meaning-making resources for the community seeking to understand calling. What pastors tell as their own story of making sense of God's call becomes the sense-making resource for the community to identify the nature of a call of God and to know how that call may be received.

To summarize: the experience of being called by God is fundamentally a process of meaning-making. An individual seeks to discern God's purposes for his or her life and, having discerned, to respond with faithfulness. The narratives of heroes of faith offer frameworks for determining what a person expects the nature of calling to be and how God's calling is discerned.

Presence and Providence

Within The King's University community, a common model of calling is that an individual hears directly from God what task or role God has assigned and then acts on the basis of that certain knowledge.[11] This model of calling presupposes certain things to be true about the nature of God's presence and the nature of God's providence. To experience God's presence in the form of God speaking directly and clearly is valued over and above God's quiet providential work of ordering the ordinary circumstances of life.

Scripture offers examples of both God's providential care and supernatural presence. God providentially causes the rain to fall on the just and the unjust (Matthew 5:45) and supernaturally caused the rain to fall in response to Elijah's prayer (1 Kings 18:41–44). As Ancient Israel battled her many enemies, God worked both providentially—as when God blessed David and David won many battles (1 Samuel 18:5; 2 Samuel 8:1–14)—and supernaturally—as

---

[11] Maros, *Knowing My Call*, 139. The model is applied in this context to the role of pastor but also to other life roles and occupations.

when the army of Jehoshaphat went out singing, "Give thanks to the Lord, for his love endures" (2 Chronicles 20:21 NIV), and God caused the armies of Moab, Ammon, and Mount Seir to battle among themselves. Gamaliel studied the law and was a wise teacher and counselor (Acts 5:34) while Peter and John—with no formal education—were empowered by God to teach with authority (Acts 4:13). God is clearly at work in the lives of people both in ways that exhibit providential care and supernatural presence.

If God's presence and God's providence are evident in Scripture, why then would an individual in a Pentecostal/charismatic community prefer one over the other as indication of calling? To examine this dynamic, this essay turns to consider three stories in the life of Dr. Hayford and how the community values reflected in these stories are also reflected in the call narratives of two community members.

Presence and Providence in the Ministry of Jack Hayford

Multiple examples of God's presence and God's providence at work in the life and ministry of Jack W. Hayford could be offered at this juncture. Dr. Hayford, affectionately called "Pastor Jack" by the many he has pastored and led, has demonstrated faithful service across a lifetime of ministry. He is an exemplar of a man who consistently seeks to attend to the voice of God and respond with faithfulness.[12]

In *Pursuing the Will of God*, Pastor Jack recounts an event that occurred when he was in high school. This event represents the culmination of a long series of experiences in Dr. Hayford's childhood that he and his family interpreted as clear indication of

---

[12] Tim Stafford opens his article about Jack Hayford, referring to him as the "Pentecostal gold standard," with a story of hearing from God, and notes that Dr. Hayford tells many such stories. Tim Stafford, "The Pentecostal Gold Standard," *Christianity Today* (July 2005), 25–29.

his call to pastoral ministry.[13] The young Jack enjoyed success in his studies and considered applying to university to study to become a pharmacist. At a youth conference, the speaker "gave the appeal for those who would surrender everything about their lives to the Lord." Teenaged Jack Hayford responded, walking to the front of the auditorium. "And just like that," he writes, "my life plans changed forever."[14]

In *Glory on Your House*, Pastor Jack narrates a story that took place in his mid-thirties and became a meaning-making resource for the community of The Church On The Way (TCOTW). On a Saturday in January 1971, after finishing his sermon preparation, Pastor Jack was preparing to leave the church building when he saw the visible glory of God in the empty sanctuary. Pondering this experience, Pastor Jack sensed God's affirmation, "I have given My glory to dwell in this place."[15] Prior to that weekend in 1971, Sunday morning attendance was about 100 people; that Sunday, 160 people attended TCOTW. By the early 1980s, when the story was first published, attendance had reached 4,300 gathered for Sunday morning service.[16] By the 1990s, aggregate weekly attendance at The Church On The Way averaged 10,000 people.[17]

Similarly, the story of Dr. Hayford's encounter with God in February 1996 became a central narrative in the founding and growth

---

[13] Many of the stories of events of Dr. Hayford's early life have been gathered together in a single narrative in David Moore, *Jack W. Hayford Jr.: A Spiritual Biography* (Ann Arbor, MI: UMI, 2008). See Chapter 2, noting especially the narratives of divine healing and revelation. Early Pentecostal testimonies often included the theme of supernatural healing leading to a surrendering to God's calling. The founder of the Foursquare movement, Sister Aimee Semple McPherson, offers a classic call story in this regard: she was at the point of death before surrendering to God's call to "go." Aimee Semple McPherson, *This is That* (Los Angeles: Foursquare Publications, 1996). In this way, Dr. Hayford's narrative demonstrates how the assumptions and expectations of the Pentecostal community shaped his interpretation of life experiences.

[14] Jack W. Hayford, *Pursuing the Will of God* (Sisters, OR: Multnomah, 1997), 8.

[15] Jack W. Hayford, *Glory on Your House* (Tarrytown, NY: Chosen Books, 1991), 16.

[16] Jack Hayford, *The Church On The Way* (Old Tappan, NJ: Chosen Books, 1982), 31.

[17] Moore, *Jack W. Hayford Jr.: A Spiritual Biography*, 18.

of The King's University (TKU). Now in his early 60s, Dr. Hayford was flying back to Los Angeles from speaking at a conference in another part of the country. Early into the flight, as he looked out the window, Dr. Hayford heard God say "Found a seminary."[18] Dr. Hayford had a long history with education. Bible classes were offered for the members of the congregation of TCOTW starting in the 1970s, growing into an institute by the end of the 1980s. This new step would require growing the institute into a full-fledged college, which was accomplished in 1997. The King's Seminary was then founded in 1999.

In each of these narratives, Dr. Hayford models the Pentecostal certainty of God's active presence. The import of these narratives goes beyond the specific point of direction embodied in each one. The significance of these stories lies in their power to frame the meaning-making process of the two communities—The Church On The Way and The King's University. The stories reflect a Pentecostal understanding of the supernatural presence of God, actively engaged in the world, giving clear and unmistakable direction.

Dr. Hayford's stories reflect a clear sense of God's presence and active engagement. The story of the encounter with God's glory on that Saturday in 1971 is all about presence—presence at that moment and God's promised presence in the church. That presence of God was viewed as the reason the church grew so much and so fast. Dr. Hayford would tell from time to time of being asked to speak at church growth conferences and turning down the requests because the growth of TCOTW was not due to a church growth method but due to the presence and work of God.[19] Dr. Hayford's

---

[18] Ibid., 204. This story is recounted in greater detail on The King's University website: http://www.tku.edu/about-tku/history/.

[19] In 1982 Dr. Hayford wrote about the burgeoning growth of the church, stating, "Trained leaders efficient in church work tend to disbelieve the words that follow here, but they are true: We have done nothing to promote, produce or program for this growth.... Without any notable plan, other than seeking to be faithful to those principles the Holy Spirit has made alive in our hearts, The Church On The Way has grown: but His glory gift was the

story of the call of God to found the seminary is a clear case of inner certainty as to God's direction. The expectation within the broader community is that leaders, especially pastors, will know with this level of certainty that the actions they take are guided by God.

The story of the encounter with the glory of God in 1971 became a central meaning-making resource for the congregation of The Church On The Way. As the story was told over and over again, repeated by Pastor Jack and others,[20] this narrative shaped the imagination of the congregation. "I have given My glory to dwell in this place" became the framework for understanding the growth of TCOTW. Similarly, the story of Dr. Hayford's encounter with God on an airplane in 1996 references clear and unmistakable revelation by God of God's instructions. This story was a foundational narrative for the members of TKU's community in the formative years of the institution.

Dr. Hayford's ministry call story is less widely known or referenced in either the church or university communities as compared to the "glory" story and the airplane story. The call story reflects distinctive Pentecostal expectations concerning pastoral calling, yet it is also a narrative that rests on multiple years of God's work. The moment of Dr. Hayford's response to God's call is a singular, identity-defining event, but it does not include a specific instance of God's direct voice. The narratives that focus on God's supernatural presence over and above the work of God's providence in the circumstances of life receive more attention.

The stories of Dr. Hayford's experiences with God constitute a guiding framework for the community. From the stories come a sense of mission and a sense of assignment from God. People take action, commit to participation, pray, give, and act in faith, all based

---

key to this release." Jack Hayford, *The Church On The Way* (Old Tappan, NJ: Chosen Books, 1982), 31.

[20] Dr. Hayford did not tell anyone of this experience at the time. Hayford, *Glory of Your House*, 18. In subsequent years, though, this story became widely known and repeated. Moore, *Jack W Hayford Jr.: A Spiritual Biography*, 2.

on the perception that God is actively engaged with the community. These stories form a meaning-making framework that establishes for the community their identity as the people of God with an assignment from God.

Impact of Presence and Providence in Call Stories

With the examples of God's presence in Dr. Hayford's life in mind, consider the call stories of two members of the TKU community: Tanner and Marquis.[21] Tanner attended a charismatic church and completed a degree in theology at TKU. Marquis was a pastor when he enrolled at TKU and tells the story of an event that took place while he was on a short-term mission trip with a team from his church. Note in the following examples how each of the stories reflects a prioritization of God's supernatural presence over God's quiet work of providence.

Tanner narrates his story of developing in pastoral ministry in the following manner:

> I fell backward into leadership. I was sixteen or seventeen when I started playing on the worship team for the youth group. The worship leader left suddenly so some other people and I stepped in to fill the leadership gap. Then the church wanted to hire some interns. I was recommended and thought, "Hey, I get to do music and get paid for it. How cool!" When the worship pastor left, the church needed someone and I felt responsible so I filled in. I just kept falling up in layers of ministry.

---

[21] "Tanner" and "Marquis" are two of the individuals who participated in research discussed at length in Susan L. Maros, *Knowing My Call: A Cultural Model of the Experience of Call in a Pentecostal/Charismatic Context* (Ann Arbor, MI: UMI, 2014). The personal stories referenced in this essay come from this research. In all cases, pseudonyms have been used and identifying personal details removed.

Tanner's story is suggestive of God's presence recognized by the community, offering Tanner opportunities to step into positions of pastoral leadership. This can be viewed as God's providential work, opening doors and creating opportunities for the gifts and capacities God had given Tanner to be developed and utilized. However, Tanner does not have "an event" in which he specifically received direction from God to be a pastor. Nor does Tanner have a "surrender everything to Jesus" story like Dr. Hayford's to tell. This absence becomes central to Tanner's interpretation of his life and his decision not to pursue pastoral licensing. He continues,

> There was a low-level sense of calling in terms of doing music and leading worship but no landmark call. By this time, I had graduated from Bible College. It would have been easy to fill out the paperwork and take some classes and become a licensed pastor. But when I considered the paperwork, I just never felt comfortable signing my name. I felt like I was committing to something I wasn't going to be able to back up.
>
> The lack of a landmark call is the reason I went back to school to get my MBA a few years ago. I had gotten married and realized the only way onward and upward in the church meant becoming a licensed pastor. I didn't feel comfortable doing that, and I needed to take care of my family. I needed a paying job. I figured I can still lead worship. You know, probably as much as I want to, the church would be glad to have me [lead worship]. So then, I think of my life as a two-track life: engaging in my vocation in business and doing worship ministry in the church.

The evidence of the providential work of God in Tanner's life is strong. His leadership ability is noted early. He repeatedly rises into positions of leadership, much as the young Joseph gained prominence in each position he entered (Genesis 39:2–3, 21–23).

Further, Tanner has a sense of call. What Tanner is missing is what he refers to as a "landmark call." Without such an event, he does not consider himself to be called as a pastor. For Tanner, and for his community, God's providential work is inadequate as the basis for discerning a pastoral call.

Contrast Tanner's story with the narrative Marquis offers. The presence of God is the key to Marquis' interpretation of this experience as a pastoral call. Marquis was a young adult with a successful business when he participated in a short-term mission trip with members of the church he was attending at that time. During this trip, Marquis had the following experience:

> Walking through the jungle, I felt the tangible presence of God. What made it so significant to me is that I hadn't been fasting. You know, some people say, "I have been fasting, seeking the Lord, tarrying for the Lord." I didn't have any questions. I just knew I was supposed to go on this trip, and he literally met me there that morning. I knew that it was God: the peace that overcame me, the comfort that I had, as well as there seemed to be a suspension of all things natural. I instantly knew that it was God. I knew something was being asked of me. I was not thinking God was saying, "I am calling you," just something being asked of me.

Marquis proceeded to a meeting of the team. The individuals were gathered there in prayer and worship. During this intercession time, the following event took place:

> Pastor Ramon came to me. He just says to me simply, "God has called you to preach. He wants you to preach the gospel. Eat the word, devour the word, for you have been so insecure." And then he just moved onto the next person. Well! That gave me clarity: God wants me to preach. But it raised other questions also. I didn't stick

around to see what else he had for everybody else. I walked off, and I began to really cry. Now I began to *really* cry. Okay, [God] wants me to preach.

The stories Tanner and Marquis tell are different, and yet the stories reflect shared expectations. In particular, both men expect that a legitimate calling from God will be experienced, in the term Tanner used, as a "landmark call." Marquis had just such an experience in the jungle; Tanner did not have such an experience. Marquis considers himself called to be a preacher and pastor; Tanner does not view himself to be called to be a worship pastor. How each man interprets his life experience to indicate he is or is not a "called" person to a particular role reflects a view of calling in this context that emphasizes the individual hearing their call directly from God.

Tanner and Marquis share an assumption that to be a pastor requires a level of clarity in calling not required of other roles. This perspective on pastoral calling is reflected in Tanner's musings on his life in ministry. Because of a lack of a "landmark call," Tanner interprets his sense of responsibility, his desire to serve in worship, and his skill in this area as a "low level call." Even though Tanner has "fallen upward" in ministry repeatedly, indicating an acknowledgement by his community of Tanner's capacities in service as part of God's providential work, this dynamic is not viewed by Tanner as being related to calling. In other words, the providential work of God is, for Tanner, unrelated to God's calling. Tanner expects what Marquis experiences: the presence of God clearly indicating a person's calling.

What a person learns through the stories of the community about the supernatural work of God's presence and the providential work of God in ordinary circumstances of life shapes how that person interprets their life experiences. That God works in a variety of ways to call people can be demonstrated from biblical narratives. This diversity of God's work in a person's life today can be overlooked and devalued when experiences do not fit a person's contextually-shaped expectations for how God works. Expectation of God's presence is an essential element for a person knowing their call, especially a call to pastoral ministry. To the centrality of "knowing," this essay now turns.

Providence, Presence, and Knowing Your Calling

Tanner, Marquis, and others in this community place a premium on "knowing" one's call.[22] Not knowing—not being certain or deeply convicted—means a person cannot move forward in a role as a calling. This is particularly true for the pastoral role. A person must know with certainty that God has called them to be a pastor for their engagement in this role to be valid.[23]

Further, individuals must know God has called them so they can respond and make good choices. Indeed, this population demonstrates a great deal of anxiety over the possibility of "missing" their call due to wrong choices caused by a lack of clear knowing. This perspective demonstrates two important theological issues for the community: a weak theology of providence and an inadequately developed understanding of discernment.

The anxiety to "know" demonstrates a theological conviction that human beings have free will and may therefore choose for and against God. At the same time, human beings are responsible to act in accordance with God's purposes. There seems to be an unspoken assumption among members of this community that God may not take any action, may not work with mistakes, and

---

[22] In research with students from The King's University, this element of "knowing" was shown to be central to their understanding of the nature of calling. See particularly Chapter 5: A Cultural Schema of the Experience of Call in Maros, *Knowing My Call*, 139–145.

[23] This emphasis is so strong in this population that people who pastor without a clear sense of call from God are viewed with suspicion and even condemnation. As one member phrased it, "We know some [pastors] that aren't called. They are wolves in sheep's clothing." Maros, *Knowing My Call*, 124.

may not bring a person through to their God-given purpose unless that person perfectly discerns (i.e., knows) God's intention and perfectly obeys. People fear God will allow a person to choose poorly, even if the consequence is missing God's intended path for their life.

Fundamentally, this anxious certainty about the need to know is grounded in limited understanding of and confidence in God's providence.[24] The assumption here is that God does not work in the ordinary events of life to reveal His purposes. Hearing God directly is legitimate reception of God's word, but circumstances are just ordinary circumstances. To know one's call through the work of God's supernatural presence is legitimate knowing; to know one's call through the quiet work of God's providential ordering of circumstances is not considered a legitimate possibility.

This perspective on providence is related to limitations in a Pentecostal understanding of the nature of the world and of the role of the church in the world. Regarding this dynamic, Cross suggests, "Pentecostals have possessed a radical openness to God's presence, but have lacked a theology of creation in which humans can understand their place in the world." If the emphasis of the community is on God's active engagement with the world, how do we understand the role of the human person? Cross continues, "In addition, Pentecostal emphasis on eschatology has overridden the need for such an understanding. This tended to devalue the role of work in the present world."[25] What the community values most is God's active presence, bringing people to faith in Jesus, and the role of the individuals God calls to be involved with this work.

---

[24] Cross comments on this issue in his own Pentecostal context, suggesting, "Perhaps some doctrine of providence needs to be rehabilitated for Pentecostals so as to help us think in these broader terms about life, the world, and nature." Cross, *Answering the Call in the Spirit*, 126.

[25] Cross, *Answering the Call in the Spirit*, 5.

From a Pentecostal/charismatic perspective, God is the only legitimate source of calling.[26] A person cannot be in a role because they want to, because they enjoy it, because that's where circumstances led them, and refer to this role as a "calling."[27] The role is only a calling if God calls. Thus, knowing God's call is essential. But how can a person "know"?

For many in The King's University community, "knowing" is defined as a deep inner certainty clearly articulated with reference to specific experiences and circumstances.[28] The sense of deep inner certainty is an essential element of "knowing" for this population. People long for, crave, seek, and angst over having that deep inner certainty. Such certainty is viewed as being essential to knowing and living out God's call. If a person cannot articulate a certainty in their sense of knowing, then they may have a call, but they certainly do not live it fully.

The key here is that the inner certainty resides in the individual. If a person is able to articulate an inner certainty, they are more likely to perceive themselves as having received God's call, as is the case with Marquis. The circumstances and experiences referenced in the person's narrative favor those instances of God's supernatural presence in a person's life leading to that inner certainty.

The experiences are not considered evidence of calling when they involve quiet and ordinary circumstances of life, as is the case in Tanner's story. A person's gifts and capacities, particularly if they are innate talents, may be viewed as coming from God as Creator, but

---

[26] In research with members of TKU's community, God is the only origin and source of a call. The call is initiated by God who singles out and selects an individual for the particular role. Maros, *Knowing My Call*, 123–124.

[27] A sense of call based on the community's identification or the expectations of important people in a person's life such as parents or a pastor was not considered a legitimate call. As one respondent put it, "There are pastors that never sensed a calling and just took it on as a vocation without a sense that that was actually God's plan for their life." Ibid., 125. This population expects the individual to have a personal sense of certainty that God has called them. Once they have this certainty, then the knowing is expected to be confirmed by their pastor or the community. Ibid., 130.

[28] Maros, *Knowing My Call*, 142.

not as indicative of God's call. For a person's giftedness to be considered a sign of calling, those gifts need to be evidence of God's supernatural power.[29]

The evidence of Scripture suggests that God works in the ordinary and God supersedes the ordinary. Based on the evidence of Scripture, it is reasonable to suspect God can work in both ways in every life. It is the individual's expectations that determine whether they will discern God at work.

The concept of "discernment" is problematic in this community, however. Some members seem to believe that "discernment" is a human attempt at a wise choice based on human knowledge because that person has not heard directly from God. With an emphasis on God's presence, a person expects to hear clearly and directly from God. In a community with a strong theology of providence, discernment is a means of recognizing the aspects of ordinary life God has sovereignly ordered for a person. For the community focused on presence, a person cannot "discern" their calling; a person can only hear from God, receive, and respond.

Conclusion

God's presence and providence at work in the life and ministry of Jack W. Hayford has been a model and inspiration for many. As we celebrate the work of God in and through this extraordinary pastor, we need also to embrace and celebrate God's presence and providence at work in ways both great and ordinary in the life of every Spirit-formed follower of Jesus. The task of pastors, educators, and leader-formation practitioners is not to teach people the "right" way

---

[29] Church historian Grant Wacker notes of early Pentecostals, "The possession of Holy Spirit gifts facilitated leadership status." Grant Wacker, *Heaven Below: Early Pentecostals and American Culture* (Cambridge, MA: Harvard University Press, 2001), 148. This was particularly true when the gifts included healing. Something of this dynamic seems to remain in the community, although the emphasis on healing is no longer as strong for this population.

to discern their calling but to help them to recognize and respond to the work of God in their lives, in all the forms that work takes.

Pastoral call stories in the Pentecostal/charismatic community tend to emphasize personal encounters with God. Testimonies recount a clear supernatural encounter with God that shapes in the individual a deep inner knowing, a deep certainty of God's direct assignment to them. Listening to these narratives, the community comes to value evidence of God's presence as an indicator of a person's call. In that context, when an individual seeks to discern and follow the calling of God, they look primarily for evidence of God's presence.

What a person expects impacts what that person perceives. If a person expects God to work through presence, those experiences of God's presence are noticed and counted as part of the process of discernment. If a person expects God to work through presence, then they may fail to notice or value God's providential work.

The strength of narratives such as Dr. Hayford's stories of the glory of God present in the sanctuary of The Church On The Way and the direction of the Lord to found TKU is that they emphasize the engagement God has with the people of God in the world for the sake of God's mission in the world. Individuals in this community learn by modeling to expect that God is present and active and intimately engaged in the choices and actions of their lives. They learn to anticipate God's at work and are therefore more likely to recognize the work of God's presence for what it is.

This way of thinking becomes a problem in a Pentecostal/charismatic context when individuals expect they must have a supernatural encounter or a specific hearing of God's voice and do not receive it. Like Tanner lacking his "landmark call," they assume they are not called. Instead of recognizing God's providential work as a legitimate and significant part of God's work in the world, they interpret their lives and their calling as lacking.

God is present and at work. God calls His people to be engaged with Him in His work in the world. Every individual can anticipate an active role in the mission of God. Every individual can anticipate

God's clear revelation and direction around issues that are central to or crucial for their participation in God's mission in the world. God will work quietly in the ordinary circumstances of life as part of God's providential work and God-act, demonstrating His engaged presence with and through His people.

How many women and men with God-given responsibilities have failed to understand their roles as their assignment from God because that assignment came in a form they did not view as a valid revelation? How many men and women with God-given capacity have failed to recognize God's call because it did not fit the expected narrative? Spirit-formed followers of Jesus need both to discern God at work in the quiet and ordinary circumstances of life and anticipate God's ongoing presence, speaking and leading with clarity, so that they may walk all the days of their lives obedient to God's call.

11

Kings, Nations, and Cultures on the Way to the New Jerusalem

A Pentecostal Witness to an Apocalyptic Vision

Amos Yong

ALTHOUGH FEW WOULD reject the multinational and multicultural character of the church in an era of world Christianity, and particularly now that its center of gravity has definitively shifted to the majority world, what that means has been and remains heavily contested (not least in the age of Brexit and Trump).[1] This essay presents some very preliminary reflections on a theology of culture by looking at the Book of Revelation from a pentecostal perspective.[2] As the justification for our focused analysis will be generated over the course of the argument, it needs to be said up front only that our goals are modest: to tease out some implications for contemporary

---

[1] Thanks to S. David Moore for inviting my contribution to this work. Jack Hayford's legacy as a pentecostal leader and statesman is secure. This essay is intended to be my own humble contribution to a book that seeks to recognize and honor that renown, and even then, his achievements precede me given his own treatment of the Apocalypse: Jack Hayford, *E-Quake: A New Approach to Understanding the End Times Mysteries in the Book of Revelation* (Nashville: Thomas Nelson, 1999). Jack's emphasis almost two decades ago that this last book of the biblical canon is fundamentally about the sustaining power of worship during difficult times remains in need of re-articulation, and the following can be read, particularly in the section at the end, as doing little more than echoing aspects of this important message for the purpose of empowering a multicultural church in a hostile world.

[2] David Rhoads, ed., *From Every People and Nation: The Book of Revelation in Intercultural Perspective* (Minneapolis: Fortress Press, 2005), leads the way at this point.

multicultural belief and practice from the book's eschatological images. We will begin by looking at the promise and challenges of the Apocalypse when approached with questions for theology of culture, continue by proposing a pentecostal hermeneutic for this final canonical book, and conclude by reconsidering the message of Revelation from this interpretive site. In brief, we will argue that the apocalyptic rendition of the nations, kings, and peoples of the world will not encourage any cheaply obtained multiculturalism but instead demands performative commitments with potentially prohibitive costs, apart from a fresh Pentecost.

Two caveats before we proceed. First, I am neither a biblical scholar nor an expert on Revelation. However, I have gradually waded into the newly emerging field of theological interpretation of scripture and have recently proposed a pentecostal intervention in this area.[3] The following extends my efforts in this direction, albeit focused on the book of Revelation. Even with my prior work on theology of culture and political theology,[4] there is still a great need to root such reflections deeper in the biblical traditions. Second, then, it is important to realize that any attempt to lift a coherent view of *culture* off the biblical pages is anachronistic since this notion is itself of later development rather than embedded within the Bible's concepts and notions.[5] Our approach will be to work primarily with Revelation's references to the nations and kings of the world and to

---

[3] See Amos Yong, *The Hermeneutical Spirit: Theological Interpretation and the Scriptural Imagination for the Third Christian Millennium* (Eugene, OR: Cascade Books, 2017).

[4] See Amos Yong, *In the Days of Caesar: Pentecostalism and Political Theology – The Cadbury Lectures 2009*, Sacra Doctrina: Christian Theology for a Postmodern Age series (Grand Rapids, MI: Eerdmans, 2010), ch. 5 of which is a theology of culture.

[5] William Edgar, *Created and Creating: A Biblical Theology of Culture* (Downers Grove: IVP Academic, 2017), 53–54 and 226–31, are especially relevant in this regard, with the former pages denoting that the word *culture* does not appear in scripture (so that Edgar's dominant approach is to develop a Reformed version of the so-called cultural mandate via the salvation history narrative), and the latter considering images in the Apocalypse to suggest that the activity of human cultural creation and creaturely creativity will persist in the New Jerusalem.

extrapolate from these implications for thinking about the cultural realm.[6] I hope to show there is much to be gained from hovering over the Apocalypse with regard to these matters.[7]

Nations and Kings in Apocalyptic Perspective: Revelation and Theology of Culture?

Let us begin with an image from the New Jerusalem, unfolded (21:9–22:5) within a broader vision of the new heavens and new earth (Revelation 21–22). We start at the end, not only of Revelation but also of the Christian canon, because of our conviction that our eschatological hopes—for good or ill, both being live options, as we shall see—inevitably shape our aspirations and commitments in the present life.[8] While we will later develop this notion further, for now let us see how John depicts the kings and nations of the world *vis-à-vis* the New Jerusalem:

> I saw no temple in the city, for its temple is the Lord God the Almighty and the Lamb. And the city has no need of sun or moon to shine on it, for the glory of God is its light, and its lamp is the Lamb. The nations will walk by its light, and the kings of the earth will bring their glory into it. Its gates will never be shut by day—and there will be no night there. People will bring into it the glory and the honor of the nations. But nothing unclean will enter

---

[6] For a missiological perspective on *culture*, see Amos Yong, "Culture," in John Corrie, ed., *Dictionary of Mission Theology: Evangelical Foundations* (Nottingham, UK, and Downers Grove, IL: InterVarsity Press, 2007), 82–87.

[7] I also outline a political reading of the Apocalypse in Amos Yong, "Revelation and the Political in the 21st Century: A Review Essay," *Evangelical Review of Theology and Politics* 4 (2016): RA1–10. http://www.evangelicalreview.com/ter_vol_4_contents_2016.html, so here we attempt a theology of culture.

[8] Thus I begin my one volume systematic theology with eschatology; see Amos Yong, *Renewing Christian Theology: Systematics for a Global Christianity*, images and commentary by Jonathan A. Anderson (Waco, TX: Baylor University Press, 2014), ch. 2.

it, nor anyone who practices abomination or falsehood, but only those who are written in the Lamb's book of life (Revelation 21:22–27 NRSV).[9]

A few remarks are in order by way of launching the discussion. First, God is at the center in every respect. The temple that is central to the biblical traditions now is displaced by the Lord God the Almighty and the Lamb, and the sun and the moon that have "governed" the world (e.g., its rhythms) since the primordial creation also defer to and give way to the deity. Hence, whatever we might want to say about nations and kings in this text ought to recognize that their role has also been a subordinate one. John only mentions them here since their role is to lift up divinity; the nations enter into the temple which is the divine presence, and whatever glory kings possess in any conventional reckoning here contributes to God's gloriousness.[10] Hence our takeaways from this passage for any political theology or theology of culture should be decidedly *theological*, recognizing that the Apocalypse is concerned not first and foremost with nations or kings but with the God who is creating all things new.

Second, we also should not underestimate the way in which these images herald the universal rule and reign of the Lord God Almighty. The *nations*—consistently rendered as such from *ethne* in the original Greek—refer indiscriminately to all the peoples of the earth who were not-Jews: Gentiles, in first-century and even present-day idiom.[11] The image announces the fulfillment of the post-exilic prophecy of Isaiah: "The Lord will arise upon you, / and his glory

[9] Unless otherwise noted, all biblical quotations will be from the New Revised Standard Version.

[10] Brian K. Blount, *Revelation: A Commentary*, The New Testament Library (Louisville: Westminster John Knox Press, 2009), 393, suggests that here the contrast is with "the gifts and treasures [brought] to demonstrate homage and fidelity to Rome."

[11] See Vernard Eller, "How the Kings of the Earth Land in the New Jerusalem: 'The World' in the Book of Revelation," *Katallagete—Be Reconciled: Journal of the Committee of Southern Churchmen* 5 (1975): 25.

will appear over you. / Nations shall come to your light, / and kings to the brightness of your dawn" (Isaiah 60:2b–3 NRSV).[12] The Abrahamic promise, "in you all the families of the earth shall be blessed" (Genesis. 12:3b), episodically revived in Israel's history but mostly languishing across the millennia, here finds its fulfillment. Yet this is not any simplistic universalism either, as those who remain excluded outside the New Jerusalem are also clearly identified.[13]

The point to be made is that God's glory receives from that of the nations and kings of the earth. The final consummation thus sanctifies and purifies the contributions of all those who were not-Israel so that the new and final people of God includes the distinctive attainments of the world's nations and kings. Theologies of culture, understood broadly in terms of the polis to include peoples and nations and their leadership, hence can do no better than to build on this eschatological vision. The New Jerusalem includes, rather than negates, the donation of the nations and their cultural achievements to the glory and honor of God's reign.

However, the well-known obscurity of this final book of the Bible will not allow us to leave things as simple as the above discussion suggests. The question that immediately emerges is how to understand the presence of nations and kings in the New Jerusalem when the final battles in the preceding chapters clearly depict their apocalyptic destruction. The rider on a white horse is unveiled with "a sharp sword with which to strike down the nations" (Revelation 19:15) and proceeds to prepare the "great supper of God"

---

[12] Richard J. Mouw, *When the Kings Come Marching In: Isaiah and the New Jerusalem*, rev. ed. (Grand Rapids, MI: Eerdmans, 2002), is a beautiful meditation of the intertextual connections between Isaiah 60 and Revelation 21–22.

[13] Any universalistic implications—argued strenuously, for instance, by Bradley Jersak, *Her Gates Will Never Be Shut: Hope, Hell, and the New Jerusalem* (Eugene, OR: Wipf & Stock, 2009)—are better understood vis-à-vis Israel's salvation history than with reference to the totality of individual persons, much less to the entirety of ethnicities, nation-states, or people groups; see J. du Preez, "Exegetical Notes: People and Nations in the Kingdom of God according to the Book of Revelation," *Journal of Theology for Southern Africa* 49 (Dec. 1984): 49–51.

(19:17) from "the flesh of kings, the flesh of captains, the flesh of the mighty, the flesh of horses and their riders—flesh of all, both free and slave, both small and great" (19:18). Indeed, the final celebration, the great banquet of divine triumph, arises out of the annihilation (19:21a) of "the kings of the earth with their armies" (19:19a). And just so that there is no mistake, after the millennial reign,

> Satan will be released from his prison and will come out to deceive the nations at the four corners of the earth, Gog and Magog, in order to gather them for battle; they are as numerous as the sands of the sea. They marched up over the breadth of the earth and surrounded the camp of the saints and the beloved city. And *fire came down from heaven and consumed them* (20:7b–9 NRSV, italics added).

There are no survivors from among the nations, neither from the pre-millennial conflagration nor assuredly from the post-millennial apocalypse. If the kings of the earth and their nations will be abolished in this way, from whence do they arrive into the New Jerusalem?[14]

But there are deeper issues. It is not just that the kings and nations mysteriously resurface in the New Jerusalem, but that, by and large, they repeatedly appear in the apocalyptic revelation as opposed to the divine rule and thereby as deserving of obliteration. Most pervasively, the kings and nations of the earth have eagerly embraced the impurities and immoralities of "Babylon the great, mother of whores and of earth's abominations" (17:5b).[15] It is with

---

[14] Thus the "salvation" of the nations and the "damnation" of all that is impure "stand in some tension with one another and are never fully reconciled in the Apocalypse"; see John Christopher Thomas, "New Jerusalem and the Conversion of the Nations: An Exercise in Pneumatic Discernment (Revelation 21:1–22:5)," in I. Howard Marshall, Volker Rabens, and Cornelis Bennema, eds., *The Spirit and Christ in the New Testament and Christian Theology: Essays in Honor of Max Turner* (Grand Rapids, MI: Eerdmans, 2012), 228–45, at 244.

[15] Hence, as Matthew Charles Baines, "The Identity and Fate of the Kings of the Earth in the Book of Revelation," *Reformed Theological Review* 75:2 (2016): 73–88, argues, the kings of the earth symbolize those caught in the grips of socially and culturally sinful accommodation.

the worldly (Babylonian) system that "the kings of the earth have committed fornication, and with the wine of whose fornication the inhabitants of the earth have become drunk" (17:2; cf. 18:3, 9). But not only is Babylon "the great city that rules over the kings of the earth" (17:18b), she also "has made all nations drink of the wine of the wrath of her fornication" (14:8), and her demonic trinity—the dragon, beast, and false prophet—has gone "to the kings of the whole world, to assemble them for battle on the great day of God the Almighty" (16:14). John writes that, deceived by Babylon's sorcery (18:23), "The nations raged" (11:18a, here alluding to Psalm 2:1), not only acting in utter disregard for Jerusalem—they "trample[d] over the holy city for forty-two months" (11:2b)—but also devastating the creation: the nations are those "who destroy the earth," and thus John sees in turn that they will be destroyed by the divine wrath (11:18b). No wonder, then, the kings and nations of the earth are so easily deceived and mobilized against God and the Lamb in the two final great battles that sandwich the millennium.

The challenges for theology of culture are now more clearly decipherable. If nations and kings are to be present in the New Jerusalem, they not only will need a miraculous preservation through the final carnage but will require remarkable redemption and transformation. Revelation suggests that their historical arc is aligned not with, but against truth, beauty, and goodness. More comprehensively, the whole world lies under the deceptive power of the Satan (12:9; cf. 20:3, 10a), even as "the whole earth followed the beast" (13:3b) and "all the inhabitants of the earth will worship it" (13:8). It is unlikely, impossible even, for the world and its cultures, historically opposed to God and his people, to be eschatologically reoriented in the New Jerusalem.

Whither then theology of culture in this apocalyptic scenario? Or perhaps more accurately: whither theology in a culture of apocalypse?[16] Even as the final redemption suggests that nations and kings

---

[16] See Marina Warner, "Angels and Engines: The Culture of Apocalypse," *Raritan* 25:2 (2005): 12–41.

will honor and glorify God, the predominant narrative in the book of Revelation announces otherwise: of their dishonoring the divine and exalting themselves. The world left on its own, it seems, will be galvanized for any purposes except those intended by its Creator. The kings and nations of the earth, representative of its peoples and cultures, appear in these eschatological times to be resolute in their rejection of the truth, tenacious in their resistance to his ways, and steadfast in opposition to his people. The cultures of this world, from this apocalyptic perspective, would appear to be irretrievably corrupted by all that is divergent from the divine reign and rule.

The Spirit Says "Come!": De-Apocalyptisizing the Nations after Pentecost

Commentators have responded variously in their efforts to render a more coherent account of the presence of the nations and kings in the New Jerusalem, ranging from suggestions that although the nations and kings "likely include some who have persecuted God's people," here "they have repented and will be allowed entrance to the city,"[17] to arguments that rather than any conversion of pagan or idolaters at the end, the final vision concerns only those with prior allegiance to the Lamb's will.[18] Without presuming the invalidity of these suggestions,[19] the approach taken in the rest of the essay will be a more decidedly pentecostal one. We will suggest a reading of the nations and kings in the book of Revelation—and by extension of their peoples, tribes, and languages—from a post-Pentecost perspective. This is less a reference to the pentecostal sensibilities of the modern

---

[17] G. K. Beale, *The Book of Revelation: A Commentary on the Greek Text* (Grand Rapids, MI: Eerdmans, 1999), 1097.

[18] See Ekhard J. Schnabel, "John and the Future of the Nations," *Bulletin for Biblical Research* 12:2 (2002): 243–71.

[19] Allan J. McNicol, *The Conversion of the Nations in Revelation*, Library of New Testament Studies 438 (New York: Bloomsbury, 2011), has a complete discussion.

revival and renewal movement (although there is no intention here to exclude such stances) than it is to the vantage point provided by the Day of Pentecost narrative. In other words, while my own pentecostal hermeneutic cannot be easily dissociated from the modern pentecostal-charismatic movement within which I have been raised and have been in lifelong dialogue, I seek to ground the interpretive moves made here first and foremost in the Acts narrative.[20]

What, however, does it mean to adopt such a pentecostal posture? I suggest that Luke's Pentecost account invites a universal (not universalist) horizon appropriate to our tasks. Three interrelated considerations are germane in this regard. First, the promise of the Spirit empowers messianic witness "in Jerusalem, in all Judea and Samaria, and to the ends of the earth" (Acts 1:8b). And while Acts shows that the gospel does arrive in Rome—considered to be the "ends of the earth" from the apostolic Jerusalem-centric perspective—in the book's final chapter, the initial response to the promise was on the Day of Pentecost when there were both Jews and proselytes (2:10b) "from every nation under heaven living in Jerusalem" (2:5b). The listing of those from the gathered crowd who heard the apostles speaking to them in their own languages from around the Mediterranean world is a selective and partial one drawing from the universal enumeration of the seventy (or seventy-two) nations in the Old Testament.[21] Second, then, Luke records Peter confirming initial fulfillment of the pentecostal promise to and from the "ends of the earth" by resorting to the prophet Joel: "'In the last days it will be', God declares, 'that I will pour out my Spirit *upon all flesh*'" (2:17a, italics added; cf. Joel 2:28a). If there were any doubts that the divine witness would extend to the farthest horizons of the apostolic

---

[20] My previous efforts in biblical scholarship have focused on Luke and especially Acts—see, e.g., Amos Yong, *Who is the Holy Spirit? A Walk with the Apostles* (Brewster, MA: Paraclete Press, 2011)—but here I apply the hermeneutical approach developed in that venue to Revelation.

[21] See Amos Yong, *The Spirit Poured Out on All Flesh: Pentecostalism and the Possibility of Global Theology* (Grand Rapids, MI: Baker Academic, 2005), ch. 4.

imagination, this Lukan-Petrine clarification was that yes: the promise of the Spirit belonged just as well to those who derived from the regions of despised Romans, dishonest Cretans, and estranged Arabs—these three mentioned in Acts 2:10–11 (among those from other regions)—regardless of how local Palestinian populations might have felt about these peoples.[22] Last but not least, shortly thereafter, Peter again, this time in his sermon in Solomon's Porch after the healing of the lame man at the Beautiful Gate, emphatically pronounced that the universal salvation of God was being fulfilled as anticipated by the prophets of old:

> Repent therefore, and turn to God so that your sins may be wiped out, so that times of refreshing may come from the presence of the Lord, and that he may send the Messiah appointed for you, that is, Jesus, who must remain in heaven until the time of universal restoration that God announced long ago through his holy prophets (3:19–21 NRSV).

Jesus is the promised Messiah, and his gift of the Spirit (2:35) brings about the restoration of Israel, the benefits of which are not just for Jews but for the whole world.[23]

The universality of the Spirit's outpouring does not translate into any blanket universalism, at least not yet. Contingencies are clearly involved—for instance, that hearers (those listening to the Spirit-filled Peter in Solomon's Porch for example) would repent. "Everyone who calls on the name of the Lord shall be saved" (2:21) is

---

[22] Recall that it was well-known regarding the Cretans: "It was one of them, their very own prophet, who said, 'Cretans are always liars, vicious brutes, lazy gluttons.' That testimony is true" (Titus 1:12–13 NRSV).

[23] See Max Turner, *Power from on High: The Spirit in Israel's Restoration and Witness in Luke-Acts*, Journal of Pentecostal Theology Supplement Series 9 (Sheffield: Sheffield Academic Press, 1996); cf. also Göran Lennartsson, *Refreshing and Restoration: Two Eschatological Motifs in Acts 3:19–21* (Lund: Lund University Center for Theology & Religious Studies, 2007).

how the text of Joel's appropriated prophecy concludes. Hence, also at the end of his Day of Pentecost message, Peter reiterates: "Repent, and be baptized every one of you in the name of Jesus Christ so that your sins may be forgiven; and you will receive the gift of the Holy Spirit. For the promise is for you, for your children, and for all who are far away, everyone whom the Lord our God calls to him" (2:38–39). The response of listeners also presumes a prior occurrence: that recipients of the Spirit bear witness as empowered to do so (1:8). Thus are the eschatological promises of God to be fulfilled in the "last days" (2:17a): the outpouring of the Spirit enables witness to the Messiah to the ends of the earth and draws forth repentance for the messianic time of deliverance. The Lukan eschatological vision of God's salvation is thus comprehensive, even as it involves human participants in proclaiming and heralding in the present time the arrival of the divine reign.

Such a pentecostal eschatology is therefore far removed from any dispensational emphasis on futuristic or otherworldly developments.[24] Rather, the Day of Pentecost inaugurates the eschatological time, the "last days," of the Spirit. God's eschatological salvation thus accomplishes divine redemption in the present era, not just in the life to come. In that respect, apostolic eschatology is as much about our contemporary response to and participation in the last days' work of the Holy Spirit.[25] Acts not only describes what happened two thousand years ago but invites readers to experience the pentecostal gift that still is available to all and then to live into that apostolic way of life charted by the Spirit's enablement. So, if the Spirit's outpouring "on all flesh" is not intended literally on the Day of Pentecost, then the continued reception of the Spirit among all generations and

---

[24] See also the final chapter on eschatology in Amos Yong, *In the Days of Caesar: Pentecostalism and Political Theology—The Cadbury Lectures 2009*, Sacra Doctrina: Christian Theology for a Postmodern Age series (Grand Rapids, MI: Eerdmans, 2010).

[25] For a similar stance, albeit argued from an other-than-pentecostal site, see Karl Rahner, "The Hermeneutics of Eschatological Assertions," in Rahner, *Theological Investigations*, vol. 4, trans. Kevin Smyth (Baltimore: Helicon, 1966), 323–46.

the responses of such Spirit-filled believers to the ends of the earth since may yet anticipate the universal restoration of the imminent divine reign.

What does it mean, then, to read Revelation not just after Good Friday, Easter, and the ascension but after Pentecost? Revelation summons a Christological and incarnational hermeneutic, grounded in the "revelation of Jesus Christ" (Revelation 1:1). However, John the seer also calls his book a "prophecy" (1:3) and explicitly says that "the testimony of Jesus is the spirit of prophecy" (19:10), thus bidding readers to approach this as a Spirit-inspired text. There are innumerable other references to the divine breath (*pneuma*) that serve as cues to reading Revelation pneumatologically. The letters to the seven churches each conclude with a pneumatic invitation: "Let anyone who has an ear listen to what the Spirit is saying to the churches" (2:7; also 2:11, 17, 29, 3:6, 13, 22), even as the narrative trajectory of the prophecy is segmented by charismatically-charged events. The manifestation of Jesus in the prologue was given to John while he was "in the spirit on the Lord's day" (1:9), even as John's seeing of the throne room and the events that "must take place after this" is facilitated while he "was in the spirit" (4:1–2). Later, the final destruction of Babylon is also unveiled to John "in the spirit in the wilderness" (17:3a), anticipating the unfolding of the New Jerusalem in the final vision (21:9).[26]

Pentecostal New Testament scholar and Revelation expert Robby Waddell suggests that there are additional warrants, of the intertextual variety, for understanding the book pneumatological-ly.[27] If readers are repeatedly urged to hear from the Spirit, then how might the Apocalypse's words resonate, in particular with

---

[26] Not surprisingly, pentecostal exegetes have approached the Apocalypse as divided at least in part by these pneumatological references; see, e.g., Rebecca Skaggs and Priscilla C. Benham, *Revelation*, Pentecostal Commentary Series (Blandford Forum, UK: Deo Publishing, 2009), 14–15, and John Christopher Thomas, *The Apocalypse: A Literary and Theological Commentary* (Cleveland, TN: CPT Press, 2012), 2–6.

[27] See Robby Waddell, *The Spirit of the Book of Revelation*, Journal of Pentecostal Theology Supplement Series 30 (Blandford Forum, UK: Deo, 2006).

regard to the upwards of 500 allusions to the Old Testament canon
prevalent across the prophecy?[28] More specifically, granting for the
moment Waddell's discerning the vision of the two witnesses in
Revelation 11:1–13 as being at the heart of the major vision of the
book (4:1–16:21),[29] he urges that the resonances between the "two
olive trees and the two lampstands" in John's apocalypse (11:4)
and Zechariah's fifth vision (Zech. 4:1–14) are unmistakable and
that the latter's clear pneumatological—perhaps more accurately
ruah-logical—reference thereby marks the former as well. So, when
Yahweh says to Zerubbabel, "Not by might, nor by power, but by
my spirit," (Zech. 4:6b) such carries over to the capacities of the two
witnesses in Revelation 11. More expansively, given that John's vision
is mediated by the "spirit of prophecy," (19:10) the call is not only
to attend to what the Spirit says but to carry out the witness of the
Spirit. Hence, Waddell concludes, Revelation 11 "enables John to
express richly the role of the Spirit in the prophetic ministry of the
church, whose primary task is to bear witness to Jesus in the world."[30]
Even if we might want to argue about various aspects of Waddell's
proposal, our colleague makes an important point that the witness of
the Spirit is, even in Revelation, to inspire and enable the witness of
its readers.[31]

My claim is that reading Revelation after Pentecost invites
embrace of the eschatological promise of Christ in the Spirit. If a
pentecostal hermeneutic applied to the book of Acts urges readers
to receive the Spirit and live into the apostolic way, then such an
interpretive perspective brought to Revelation similarly prompts

[28] Steve Moyise, *The Old Testament in Revelation*, Journal for the Study of the New
Testament Supplement Series 115 (1995; reprint, London and New York: Bloomsbury T&T
Clark, 2015), 16; see also G. K. Beale, *John's Use of the Old Testament in Revelation*, Library
of New Testament Studies 166 (1998; reprint, London and New York: Bloomsbury T&T
Clark, 2015).

[29] See Waddell, *The Spirit of the Book of Revelation*, 148–50.

[30] Waddell, *The Spirit of the Book of Revelation*, 190.

[31] See also Michael J. Gorman, *Reading Revelation Responsibly: Uncivil Worship & Witness
Following the Lamb into the New Creation* (Eugene, OR: Cascade Books, 2011).

readers to attend and embody the apocalyptic Spirit of prophecy. The closing verses of this book say as much: "The Spirit and the bride say, 'Come.' / And let everyone who hears say, 'Come.' / And let everyone who is thirsty come. / Let anyone who wishes take the water of life as a gift" (Revelation 22:17). Hence, Revelation as a pneumatic and pentecostal text involves a response, indeed opens up space and creates an occasion for entry into the work of the Spirit that stretches back toward the beginning of time.[32] As such, even if "what is to take place after this" (1:19b) at least in part concerns what is future from our contemporary perspective, it certainly relates to the eschatological "last days" initiated on the Day of Pentecost. The fulfillment of Revelation's prophetic visions thereby depends in that sense on the response of those listening to and filled with the Spirit of prophecy as much as they are conditional on the final saving works of God.[33]

From this perspective, the redemption of the nations and kings and the salvaging of their cultural glory and honor are less eschatological pronouncements than they are contemporary tasks. What John sees apocalyptically, with all the ambiguity surrounding the fate of the nations and their kings, can be received as a mandate for faithful messianic witness: the hope of the nations, rooted as such in the revelatory promise, nevertheless involves Spirit-invited witness and persistence.[34] Hanging in the balance may be the destruction, or the salvation, of the nations, kings, and cultures of the world.

---

[32] As also signified by development of themes from the First Testament that culminate in Revelation's epilogue; see William J. Dumbrell, *The End of the Beginning: Revelation 21–22 and the Old Testament* (Grand Rapids, MI: Baker Book House, 1985).

[33] The basic thesis here is not new. As Ronald Herms, *An Apocalypse for the Church and for the World: The Narrative Function of Universal Language in the Book of Revelation*, Beihefte zur Zeirschrift für die neutestamentliche Wissenschaft und die Kunde der älteren Kirche 143 (Berlin and New York: Walter de Gruyter, 2006), argued, the universalistic language in the book is hortatory, consistent with the apocalyptic genre, and is designed to encourage the faithful in anticipation of a final vindication. Whether universalism—of persons or, in our case, of nations and kings—is finally true or not is not a real question for John at this narrative and literary level.

[34] As pentecostal scholars Chris Thomas and Frank Macchia put it: "A case can be made that the Spirit in Revelation is mainly directed to the conversion of the nations to the Lamb

Many Tribes, Languages, Peoples, and Nations: Performing an Eschatological Pneumatology of Culture

Our modest goal is elaboration of a theology of culture that can inspire our own efforts to work for a multicultural church. Toward this end, we have hedged our bets that an eschatological imagination provides normative orientation for such a vision: what is finally promised to be, we have suggested, ought to guide what should be in the meanwhile. Although the nations and kings of the world bringing their glory and honor into the New Jerusalem are potent images of a multicultural people of God, the overall ambiguity of these symbols across Revelation provides a less than coherent message for our purposes. We therefore turned to resourcing our task from a pentecostal perspective, exploring particularly how the universal horizon of the book of Acts in general and the Day of Pentecost narrative in particular invited not just a theoretical appreciation for the inclusion of the ends of the earth within the restoration of Israel but also practical commitments to enter into and embrace the inspiration and empowerment of the Spirit for universal witness. Will this more performative approach provide the needed recalibration for understanding apocalyptic kings and nations for contemporary multicultural praxis?

If what I am suggesting is a performative response to Revelation, however, then we must confront one important set of concerns before proceeding any further. The issue is that any call to enact the Apocalypse risks not just condoning but advocating its violence as well. Especially worrisome is that the violence is inflicted by the sword of the Lamb (19:15, 21) and consummated by heavenly fire

---

of God.... The Spirit is the global Spirit, who takes the blessings of God's grace beyond the borders of Israel to the nations," see John Christopher Thomas and Frank D. Macchia, *Revelation*, The Two Horizons New Testament Commentary (Grand Rapids, MI: Eerdmans, 2016), 494–95.

(20:9b).[35] The problem is that even if Revelation clearly depicts the divine overthrow of the sinful systems of this world, this seems to happen precisely through the violent mechanisms undergirding what will soon be swept away. Hence, to advocate a kind of living into the message of the Apocalypse is to commend a divine imperialism that mimics (even if it is also indicated to do away with) the imperial violence of the nations and kings of this world.[36] If such performance is inconceivable for those on the margins of history, then the larger history of Christendom warns us of how such perceptions of divinely-sanctioned authority and exemplarity can be lethal when wielded by those at the centers of power.

Hence, any pentecostal performance of Revelation will have to be discerning, not naively universalistic. Such particularism will have costs within the current neo-imperial and neo-colonial context of global capitalism. On the one side, considering that those interested in maintaining the status quo can resort to (now divinely underwritten) violence to keep the revolutionaries in their proper places, on the underside of empire, for instance, the question will inevitably need to be asked: toward what are Spirit-inspired and empowered practices directed? On the other side, then, if Revelation can also comfort those who are persecuted, oppressed, and marginalized with promises of divine vindication in the coming inferno, is it

---

[35] That the violence of Revelation has long been a concern of its readers is evidenced in Joseph Verheyden, Tobias Nicklas, and Andreas Markt, eds., in cooperation with Mark Grundeken, *Ancient Christian Interpretation of "Violent Texts" in The Apocalypse*, Novum Testamentum et Orbis Antiquus/Studien Zur Umwelt des Neuen Testaments 92 (Gottingen: Vendenhoeck & Ruprecht, 2011).

[36] "To construct God or Christ, together with their putatively salvific activities, from the raw material of imperial ideology is not to shatter the cycle of empire but merely to transfer it to a transcendental plane, thereby reifying and reinscribing it … creating an imperial divine 'essence' that is extremely difficult to dismantle or dislodge…. Revelation, locked as it is in visions of empires and counter-empires, emperors and counter-emperors, seems singularly powerless to provide: a conception of the divine sphere as other than empire writ large." Stephen D. Moore, "The Revelation to John," in Fernando F. Segovia and R. S. Sugitharajah, eds., *A Postcolonial Commentary on the New Testament Writings*, The Bible and Postcolonialism 13 (London: T&T Clark, 2009), 452.

possible for such consolation to be translated into praxis that works simultaneously for justice in this present world?[37] These are not merely theoretical or abstract questions since the Apocalypse itself explicitly narrates that the vindication of the disinherited of history involves the overturning of the social and economic mechanisms of the powers that be (Revelation 17–18). As such, the final welcoming of the gifts and glory of the nations of the world follows from, rather than uncritically baptizes, their socio-economic achievements and accomplishments, and it is from out of recognition of the life-denying and destroying character of the imperial regimes of this world that divine judgment is pronounced. From this perspective, then, it is crucial to ask how the voice of the Spirit might enable faithful discipleship when it is just as possible for those of us who are now on the so-called "upper side" of history to appeal to this apocalyptic text for sanitizing the world of its impure elements as a way of preserving a more monocultural status quo, rather than embracing a more multicultural community that simultaneously requires a resistant praxis toward the systems that support our way of life, even as it welcomes the coming reign of God.

Revelation itself recognizes that not every voice echoes the salvific message of God. In fact, even at the heart of the book (if we followed Waddell), "members of the peoples and tribes and languages and nations" (11:9a) gloat over the death of the two divine witnesses as part of their revelry in their iniquities. Not surprisingly, then, the beast "was allowed to make war on the saints and to conquer them. It was given authority over every tribe and people and language and nation, and all the inhabitants of the earth will worship it, everyone whose name has not been written from the foundation of the world in the book of life of the Lamb that was slaughtered" (13:7–8). The many tongues of humankind, indeed all flesh, are just as capable of worshipping the beast as of witnessing to the Lamb (cf. 17:15).

---

[37] As we see for instance in Allan Boesak, *Comfort and Protest: The Apocalypse from a South African Perspective* (Louisville: Westminster John Knox Press, 1987).

Yet there is hope for the multitude, consistent with and expanding on the Pentecost miracle of the end-time gathering of the ends of the earth as the new people of God. John sees "another angel flying in mid-heaven, with an eternal gospel to proclaim to those who live on the earth—to every nation and tribe and language and people" (14:6; cf. 10:11). It is "from every tribe and language and people and nation" that saints have been redeemed for God by the blood of the Lamb (5:9),[38] and it is "from every nation, from all tribes and peoples and languages" that they stand, "before the throne and before the Lamb, robed in white, with palm branches in their hands" (7:9). Richard Bauckham's analysis of these seven formulaic references to the many nations, et al., is that for John, "the nations which now serve Babylon will become, through the witness of the martyrs, God's peoples with whom he will be present in the New Jerusalem."[39] As "seven spirits of God [are] sent out into all the earth" (5:6b), so also will the nations—and their peoples and kings—be drawn into the new heavens and earth.

From this perspective, then, we can comprehend that the Apocalypse suggests perhaps two contrasting ultimate possibilities for the nations and their kings: damnation or salvation. "Both futures remain open; the question is how the world will respond."[40] More pointedly, this same question is posed for the churches: "Do these competing visions suggest divergent potentials for the future, that the nations may be either converted or destroyed, depending on the faithfulness of Christ's church?"[41] Put another way: Revelation's

---

[38] On the saving blood of the Lamb, see also Amos Yong, "'To Him Who Loves Us and Freed Us from Our Sins by His Blood …': A Pentecostal-Canonical Interpretation of Apocalyptic Love," in Blaine Charette and Robby Waddell, eds., *Festschrift for John Christopher Thomas* (Cleveland, TN: CPT Press, 2019), forthcoming.

[39] Richard Bauckham, *The Theology of the Book of Revelation* (Cambridge: Cambridge University Press, 2003), 336.

[40] Craig R. Koester, *Revelation: A New Translation with Introduction and Commentary*, The Anchor Yale Bible 38A (New Haven: Yale University Press, 2014), 833.

[41] Craig S. Keener, *The NIV Application Commentary: Revelation* (Grand Rapids, MI: Zondervan, 2000), 506.

admonitions are not just for believers struggling against persecution or attempting to remain faithful amidst the seductions of the world, whatever the *Sitz im Leben* of the original writing turns out to be. Rather, there are cosmic implications at stake: faithfulness has consequences beyond individual lives and extends to many nations and peoples, along with their kings.[42]

Read pentecostally, I suggest the presence of nations and kings in the New Jerusalem, whatever else such might signify, also acts as a prod for messianic faithfulness. Traced across the apocalypse, the tension between national and regal judgment and salvation is retained in full force rather than absolved.[43] The point is practical rather than theoretical: not if and why the nations and kings are there but *how* did they get there. Answering the latter question implicates each reader—from every nation and ethnic group—in all his or her existential situatedness and cultural embeddedness.

Hermeneutically, then, such a pentecostal angle searches for other textual cues that can inspire supportive praxis for the deity's redemptive works. Hence the already mentioned worship of the saints, drawn from the ends of the earth (5:9, 7:9), ought to be foregrounded: "every creature in heaven and on earth and under the earth and in the sea, and all that is in them, singing, 'To the one seated on the throne and to the Lamb, be blessing and honor and glory and might for ever and ever!'" (5:13).[44] The multicultural worship of the eschatological community is thereby not just an image to be yearned for but a call for enactment. Similarly, John envisions, in a recapitulation of Moses's song (cf. Exodus 15:1–18):

---

[42] See also David Mathewson, *A New Heaven and a New Earth: The Meaning and Function of the Old Testament in Revelation 21.1–22.5*, Journal for the Study of the New Testament Supplement Series 238 (Sheffield: Sheffield Academic Press, 2003), 174–75, who notes that this rhetorical tension is indicative of the Apocalypse's hortatory design.

[43] See Dave Mathewson, "The Destiny of the Nations in Revelation 21:1–22:5: A Reconsideration," *Tyndale Bulletin* 53:1 (2002): 121–42.

[44] The centrality of worship is also unpacked by J. Nelson Krabill, *Apocalypse and Allegiance: Worship, Politics, and Devotion in the Book of Revelation* (Grand Rapids, MI: Brazos Press, 2010).

"Great and amazing are your deeds,
　　Lord God the Almighty!
Just and true are your ways,
　　King of the nations!
Lord, who will not fear
　　and glorify your name?
For you alone are holy.
　　All nations will come
　　and worship before you,
for your judgments have been revealed"
　　(Revelation 15:3–4 NRSV, italics added).

The question for us is then this: how might such trans- or inter-national worship be facilitated on this side of the eschaton? Can multinational and multicultural worship in the Spirit be fostered, anticipating the final salvation? Can contemporary Pentecostalism, as a global and multinational worshipping communion, find inspiration in the Spirit through such a performative reading of worship in the book of Revelation so as to embrace, develop, and promote appropriate multicultural practices that can, in turn, underwrite a biblically and eschatologically oriented theology of culture for the twenty-first century?[45]

But authentic worship involves the divine shalom, which is peace with justice. Multinational worship in a post-colonial world will require justice, not just between the nations but also between the haves and the have-nots. This is not to say that justice precedes worship but to enter into the hermeneutical circle that sees worship heralding justice and justice precipitating worship. Hence, the haves

---

[45] Melissa L. Archer, *'I Was in the Spirit on the Lord's Day': A Pentecostal Engagement with Worship in the Apocalypse* (Cleveland, TN: CPT Press, 2015), shows how early Pentecostals read Revelation in ways that also shaped their eschatological affections and worshipful experience of God; my claim is that contemporary Pentecostals in their second century need similar apocalyptic reorientation in order to further ecclesial thinking and practice in our multicultural world.

will not be able to read Babylon and eschatological worship merely spiritually, just as the have-nots will inevitably read Babylon socially, politically, and economically as the spiritual powers and structures of persecution and oppression.[46] Yet the Spirit's outpouring was also on "slaves [*doulous*], both men and women," (Acts 2:18a) and this prompted both mutual sharing and common worship in the Spirit (Acts 2:42–47). Such a pentecostal approach to the Apocalypse ought to engender nothing less: a mutuality that bridges the gaps between kings and subjects, between governors and the governed, between those at the center and those on the historical underside of nations and peoples.

John surely recognized the audaciousness of the vision that involved the redemption of nations and kings so committed otherwise in pursuit of the sinfulness of Babylon. Perhaps for this reason he understood that the New Jerusalem would have to include the "tree of life with its twelve kinds of fruit, producing its fruit each month; and the leaves of the tree are for the healing of the nations" (22:2b).[47] Apart from their deep-rooted transfiguration and transformation—salvific reparation, no less—the new heavens and earth would be narrowly construed rather than constituted by the ends of the earth. It might be that even with the revelation of Jesus Christ in the Apocalypse we are still no less in need of a fresh Pentecost, a continual pentecostal revival that allows the many tongues to sing, the many languages to proclaim, the many nations to glorify God, the many kings to honor the deity, and the many cultures to live into and achieve their creational promise.[48]

---

[46] E.g., Humphry Waweru, "Postcolonial and Contrapuntal Reading of Revelation 22:1–5," 2 parts, *Churchman* 121:1–2 (2007): 23–38 and 139–62.

[47] This text structures the argument of Justo L. González, *For the Healing of the Nations: The Book of Revelation in an Age of Cultural Conflict* (Maryknoll: Orbis Books, 1999).

[48] Thanks to Dale Coulter for the invitation to give one of the plenary presentations at the 46th Annual Meeting of the Society for Pentecostal Studies, Florissant, Missouri, 9–11 March 2017, devoted to the theme "Pentecostalism and Culture." I appreciate Melissa Archer for her constructive comments on a previous version of this paper. Any errors of fact or interpretation remain my own responsibility.

Section Four

Worship

12

"Magnify, Come Glorify . . ."
Some Thoughts About Throne Room Worship
Richard J. Mouw

IN THE UNITED States, one of the most widely read academic books in recent decades was written by a team of sociologists headed by Robert Bellah. Bellah taught for many years at the University of California in Berkeley. The book had the title *Habits of the Heart*, and its subtitle highlighted the theme that is relevant to the church shopping topic: *Individualism and Commitment in American Life*.

The Bellah team conducted many extensive interviews with people and, on that basis, gave a detailed account of the individualism that has, in recent years, come to characterize American culture at large. They offered as an example of this individualism their much-cited story of a woman named Sheila Larson who told the interviewers that she follows the dictates of a religion that she described as "Sheilaism"—a religion centered on her own needs and desires. The basic teaching of this religion is, as Sheila put it, "just try to love yourself and be gentle with yourself," and building on that foundation, Sheila also saw a need to love and be gentle with those who were closest to her.[1]

Bellah and his colleagues saw this kind of individualism as standing in sharp contrast to more traditional ways of viewing the individual's relationship with the larger world. They advocated an understanding of reality wherein the individual is obligated to subordinate individual interests to the well-being of the larger community

---

[1] Robert Bellah et al., *Habits of the Heart: Individualism and Commitment in American Life* (Los Angeles: University of California Press, 1985), 221.

and especially in the obligation to devote one's life to the greater glory of God.

The Bellah team observed that the ways in which the persons whom they interviewed described their lives provided clear evidence that the older language of commitment and self-sacrifice was diminishing, being replaced by two other languages. One is the language of "cost-benefit analysis," in which a person decides what to do on the basis of what will bring them the most personal pleasure or profit. The other is the language of "self-actualization," in which people talk about becoming more authentic, emphasizing the need for a continuing "personal growth."

In one of their case studies, the Bellah team described a man, Brian, who was in a second marriage, the first having ended in a divorce. He expressed regret about the way he had treated his first wife. He had been so committed to advancing his career, he said, that he had neglected his relationship with her. In his new marriage, however, things were very different. In this relationship, he was concentrating on his own growth as a well-rounded human being. He talked about how much he enjoyed being with his wife, about how he was now feeling more fulfilled in this marriage.

Brian had difficulty finding the proper language for the change that occurred, however. While he was clearly now employing "expressive" concepts, his actual talk still made use of utilitarian vocabulary. Brian's case, the interviewers observed, offers an example of how individuals in our culture "frequently live out a fuller sense of purpose in life than they can justify in rational terms."[2]

The man had a difficult time expressing himself at this point. It was clear that he wanted to say that he would stay committed to his wife under difficult conditions, but he lacked the language to express that commitment. Talking in terms of a personal "cost-benefit analysis" did not allow him to express his commitment. Neither was it helpful simply to talk about "personal growth."

---

[2] Bellah, *Habits*, 4–6.

What the sociologists were getting at is that commitment to a relationship with another person often requires us to stay faithful even when there are not individual benefits or chances to have "fun" with that person. Real commitment often requires categories that go beyond self-interest, beyond the meeting of personal needs. The man they had interviewed somehow knew this in his deep places, but he lacked the language to express himself. This led the Bellah team to make an important observation. One of the few places in our culture where the older ways of speaking are preserved, they said, is in places of religious worship. Our worshipping communities, they argued, serve today as "communities of memory."[3] They are places where traditional worldviews, reinforced by the language of commitment and the larger purposes of our individual lives, continue to be an important cultural influence.

To be sure, the Bellah team's focus on worship was primarily motivated by a concern for what it can produce for a healthy civic consciousness. But those of us who care for the broader patterns of biblical fidelity can be grateful for their reminder that our worshipping communities must be sustained "traditions that tell us about the nature of the world, about the nature of society, and about who we are as a people."[4]

Much has changed, of course, in the patterns of worship since the Bellah team offered those observations several decades ago. Christian worship has increasingly come to employ the language of the very individualisms criticized by the Bellah team. The vocabulary of much of the newer hymnody and preaching in evangelical churches frequently echoes an individualism of the "expressive" variety. Nor are things any better in more "mainline" contexts where, for example, any mention of an atonement that satisfies the demands of divine justice is often eliminated in favor of references to God's unconditional love for the likes of us.

---

[3] Bellah, *Habits*, 152–155.
[4] Bellah, *Habits*, 281–282.

Fortunately, though, not all is lost. This book of essays honors the ministry of someone who has done much to preserve a profound sense that true worship means looking beyond ourselves to the love and service of a divine "Majesty" that saves us through the blood of Christ and promotes the kind of human growth that can only be found through the power of the Holy Spirit. My reflections here on the worshipping life of the church are meant as expressions of gratitude for how Jack Hayford has both inspired and taught me.

—•—

Critics of contemporary patterns of worship—particularly patterns in the evangelical community—frequently complain about the prevalence of a "consumerist" approach to congregational affiliation. They observe that Christians no longer attend churches out of loyalty to a tradition or a doctrinal system but make their choices instead by identifying what they "need" from a worship service or a religious community. And then they "shop around" until they find something that satisfies their felt needs.

I heard someone draw an analogy recently, in criticizing this trend in congregational affiliations, to preferences in soft drinks. The person who leaves a Presbyterian church for a more charismatic congregation, it was said, is like a longtime Coca Cola drinker who tires of the taste of that soft drink and switches to Pepsi Cola. He finds that his new brand has a taste that is a little more stimulating. Thus, religion has become much like tastes in foods, the critic suggested. We no longer have brand loyalty in our religious life. We keep shopping around until we find something that—for a while at least—satisfies our needs.

There is obviously some legitimacy to this concern about a consumerist spirit in religion, and I will point out the dangers of "shopping around" a little further on. But first I want to caution against drawing too close a parallel between changing religious affiliation and switching brands in our tastes in food.

Religion and physical hunger are certainly alike in that each of them is grounded in very real human needs. Without food, we starve. And without spiritual nourishment, we also starve. In the well-known words of the first question and answer of the Westminster Shorter Catechism, our "chief end" as human beings "is to glorify God and to enjoy him forever." When we cut ourselves off from a vital relationship with God by ignoring the means of grace that God has made available to us in the life of the Christian church, we become less than what we have been created to be. We try to find our ultimate satisfaction in the wrong places, and eventually, this is a path that leads to spiritual death.

Interestingly, the Bible itself draws a parallel between our spiritual needs and our need for food and drink. Jesus talks about those who "hunger and thirst after righteousness." And in Psalm 42, the Psalmist describes his own longing for God as like a desperately thirsty deer that is panting as it searches for a stream from which it can drink.

The difference between our physical needs and our spiritual ones, of course, is that our spiritual longings are much more basic to who we are as human beings. They have to do with our "chief end," the fulfillment of our created nature. It should not surprise us, then, if people today would think at least as much about what they are "consuming" in their spiritual lives as they do in the decisions they make about what they will eat and drink.

The main reason why decisions about "consuming" have come to dominate our lives today is that we now live in a world in which we are surrounded by choices. Think about what life was like for a teenage girl in a Pennsylvania village in the early nineteenth century. She would seldom have reason to wonder what kind of food would be consumed in her next meal. The daily diet was relatively unchanging. Nor would she think much about what kind of work she would be engaged in for the rest of her life. Chances are she would not even be confronted with a lot of choice about who her husband might be or whether she would bear children or not. And it is very unlikely that she would think deeply about which religion she would affiliate with.

A girl of her age today, living in Pittsburgh or some other major city, would be faced with a wide range of options about these matters. If she confines herself to a rather consistent daily diet, there are still food choices that she regularly makes. She will likely think about the issues of when and whether to marry and bear children. She will consider various vocational goals and available programs for the training that leads to those goals. She will give some thought to where she will live eventually—and that might even involve deciding whether she will remain in Pennsylvania or live elsewhere.

Needless to say, she will also be faced with choices about religious affiliation. Unlike her counterpart of two centuries ago, she has many possibilities to choose from—different religions, different groups, and different denominations within various religions. Of course, she also has the possibility of no religious affiliation at all.

It does no good simply to criticize all of this as "consumerism," as if that is a bad thing. Many young people today think much, for example, about where they will pursue their university studies. In a sense, that is a choice about what kind of education they will "consume." But that kind of choice can be exciting, one of the blessings of living in our contemporary world.

Of special concern for theological exploration, of course, is the array of religious choices with which we are now confronted. From a biblical perspective, our choice about the rather lifeless term "religious affiliation" is in fact about the most important area of our human lives. It is a choice about how we are to fulfill our deepest needs as persons who are created in God's image and likeness.

For many Christians, therefore, our choices about where to worship are profoundly important from a family perspective. Many parents, for example, may be content with their own traditional patterns of worship, but they know that their children are turned off by those patterns. So, they look for something to which their whole family can commit. They are struggling to find resources that will help them deal with some of the most significant issues of their lives.

— • —

It is understandable why some observers dislike the language of "shopping around" in describing choices about worship. But we must not allow the use of that image to demean what is often happening in that process. Some of our "shopping" choices have to do with matters that are crucial for our well-being. "Shopping around" for a life partner, for example, can be a way of taking marriage very seriously. We want to be sure we make the right choice because once we make that choice, we know we have to stay committed, for better or for worse, in sickness and in health.

Looking for a church should also be seen as an extremely serious matter. Here too, commitment is an important part of the picture. And that is often what is missing when Christians simply go from one church relationship to another, changing brands at the first sign that staying committed will require a serious effort on their part.

It is precisely because commitment to a worshipping community is so important that it is incumbent on those who are responsible for planning and sustaining our worship to think deeply about what is required for how we enter into the presence of God in our congregational gatherings. The Bellah team's reference to the importance of "communities of memory" provides us with one important lesson in this regard. The worshipping church must be a place of remembering. In our culture of self-actualization and self-indulgence, it is important that entering the church serves as a place where we are reminded of other times and other places where people have sought to be faithful to the cause of the Gospel.

A few years ago, I read a story on the religion page of a newspaper about a pastor who organizes his services around popular secular show tunes. He would use these as a springboard for a dialogue with the gathered worshippers about various lines in the songs. The pastor admitted that some worshippers were not happy with this approach. They wanted some traditional hymns sung in their worship services, and they would ask him, "How's this got anything to do with religion?" To which he would respond: "If you are sitting in church for an hour, reciting words and singing hymns you hardly know, what's that got to do with religion?"

This pastor was confused. The hymns of the past are the shorthand poetic records of the spiritual and theological memories of the Christian church. We should certainly encourage new generations of Christians to compose and sing new hymns, ones that preserve their own spiritual and theological experiences. But we cannot ignore the riches that are readily available in those hymns that record the memories of those who have walked the paths of discipleship in the past.

But singing the thoughts of the church must also be accompanied by the preaching and teaching of the Word of God. To be sure, we must find new ways of bringing our message to a new and challenging culture. We must be "all things to all human beings, so that some might be saved." In doing so, however, we cannot forget what we have learned in the past about what it means to together "grow up in every way" into the fullness of what Christ offers to all of us.

I cannot help but add that this growing up in Christ means that we should leave a worship service with a clear sense of our identity as agents of God's work in the world. One of the most exciting discussions taking place these days about the church is the idea of the "missional church." We come to church to encounter the living God. And that God sends us forth from the church back into the world to serve him. The worship service must also be a place where we receive instructions for that sending-out. And this is another way in which sensitivity to the culture around us must be present in our times of worship.

I must quickly add here, though, that worship should not simply be seen as preparation for action. Gustavo Gutierrez wrote what many consider to be the classic text in "liberation theology," but he made it very clear in that book that worship must not be reduced to an occasion for activist training. He wisely insists that the Christian life must be "filled with a living sense of *gratuitousness*. Communion with the Lord and with all men is more than anything else a gift."[5] Furthermore, he contends, prayer, as the means by which we engage in our communion with God, "is an experience of gratuitousness." Properly understood, prayer is entering into God's presence with no agenda, with no list of causes that we insist on promoting. Prayer, he says, is a "'leisure' action"; it is a "'wasted' time, [that] reminds us that the Lord is beyond the categories of useful and useless. God is not of this world."[6]

Jack Hayford would agree. Worship is first and foremost the opportunity to enter into the throne room: "Majesty! Worship His majesty!" The Spirit-filled life of service requires times when we lift up Jesus' name and "waste" our time in his presence.

In a book published over two decades after the Bellah team's *Habits of the Heart*, another sociologist, Stephen Ellingson, made significant use of the "community of memory" theme but this time in a study focusing specifically on worship patterns. Ellingson provided in-depth accounts of the ways in which nine Lutheran congregations in the San Francisco area have responded to new challenges for the church's life and mission. While each of the congregations exhibited its own unique character, Ellingson saw two very different patterns being explored, with one group attempting to be "communities of memory" and the other promoting a model associated with "communities of interest."

[5] Gustavo Gutierrez, *A Theology of Liberation: History, Politics, and Salvation* (Maryknoll, NY: Orbis Books, 1973), 206.

[6] Gutierrez, *A Theology of Liberation*, 206.

As Ellingson sets forth his typology, the differences between the two approaches to worship are clear. The community of interest pattern sees the local congregation as utilizing music, stories, and concepts that are much like what characterizes their surrounding culture. All of this is a part of a deliberate strategy for encouraging persons attending worship to receive the Christian message in terms that are very familiar to them. This is what we have come to know as "seeker-sensitive worship." This stands in contrast to a community of memory church where worship embodies traditions that are not well-known in the larger culture.

The community of interest model is often harshly criticized by defenders of traditional modes of worship. They argue that the integrity of the Gospel requires that people who come to church be invited into an active worshipping community, one that takes the teachings and practices of the Christian tradition seriously, and that our worship spaces must feature symbols that foster an experience of transcendence.

While many of the criticisms are legitimate, I am convinced that we need to be willing to learn some lessons about ministry from the community of interest model. For me, as one steeped in the Reformed tradition, I see some good theological reasons for taking more seriously the emphasis on "seeker-sensitive" patterns in our church life. I find encouragement in this regard from John Calvin. The great Reformer introduces in his *Institutes of the Christian Religion* two concepts for understanding the indelibly spiritual character of human existence, even in its fallen condition: the sense of divinity (*sensus divinitatis*) and the seed of religion (*semen religionis*). All human beings, Calvin says, have a sense of the divine, whether they consciously acknowledge it or not. This is because God has planted the seed of religion in every human heart. Human beings, even sinful human beings, yearn for God.[7] As St. Augustine

---

[7] John Calvin, *Institutes of the Christian Religion*, ed. John T. McNeill, trans. Ford Lewis Battles (Philadelphia: Westminster, 1960), bk. 1, 43–44.

put it in the form of a prayer at the beginning of his *Confessions*: "Thou hast made us for thyself and our hearts are restless until they find rest in Thee."[8]

A more popular spiritual formulation of this same point is captured in this wonderful line in the Christmas carol, "O Little Town of Bethlehem": "The hopes and fears of all the years are met in thee tonight." This is what both Augustine and Calvin are encouraging us to think about: the ways in which the basic hopes and fears of the human heart, even the sinful human heart, are in some way fulfilled in the redemptive ministry of Jesus Christ.

At the same time, of course, the longings of the unredeemed human heart are fundamentally misdirected. But it is precisely because we are created for fellowship with the Living God that our yearnings are not satisfied when we direct them to something less than our Creator.

Working diligently, then, at being "seeker sensitive" can conform well to solid traditional theology. The experienced "needs" of the unbelievers whom we want to reach with the Gospel are themselves expressions of deep, although certainly misdirected, yearnings that are planted by God in their hearts. This does not mean, of course, that we simply take at face value the ways in which those persons describe their needs. We must identify the real nature of those needs by probing beneath the surface for the underlying God-implanted yearnings that give rise to what appears on the surface.

I once heard a speaker quote a Roman Catholic writer as saying that the man who knocks on the door of a house of prostitution is looking for God. At first, I was shocked by this suggestion, but the more I thought about it, the more I realized that it was a profound observation. Obviously, the statement should not be taken as meaning that the man who approaches the house of prostitution

---

[8] Saint Augustine, *Confessions and Enchiridion*, trans. Albert C. Outler (Grand Rapids: Christian Classics Ethereal Library, 2006), 13.
http://www.ccel.org/ccel/augustine/confessions.iv.html.

hopes that God will be the one who opens the door. The real message is that people are looking for ultimate fulfillment in the quest for sexual pleasure or wealth or power. Nothing brings genuine fulfillment to the human spirit other than an obedient relationship with our Creator.

When we think, then, about the experienced "needs" of unbelievers in our own day, it is important that we recognize that those needs, those quests and longings, are not wrong in themselves. Rather, they are misdirected. People who are trapped in sinful lives are looking in the wrong places to find ultimate meaning and true satisfaction.

Properly understood, we do not have to choose between communities of memory and communities of interest in establishing God-honoring patterns of worship. To cultivate our memories of the Christian past is to see how previous generations of believers have been sensitive to the ways in which human beings are—to use Carol Zaleski's apt phrasing—"hunted down by the God who instills transcendent longing" in all of us.[9]

―•―

I have expended much energy in my career in arguing for the importance of the kind of evangelical activism that takes seriously the Bible's call for us to promote the causes of justice, peace, and moral righteousness in the larger society in which we find ourselves. Jack Hayford has on numerous occasions been an inspiration to me in this regard since he has voiced similar concerns while also exhibiting a deep devotion to promoting and nurturing a Spirit-filled, worshipping life in the local church.

While Jack has held these two aspects of the Christian life together in a marvelous way, I have been less than diligent in my own efforts in paying close attention to the worship element. In

---

[9] Carol Zaleski, "Case for the Defense," Christian Century (June 26, 2007), http://www.christiancentury.org/article_print.lasso?id=3462.

recent years, however, I have come to see the supreme importance of focusing intensely on the relationship between worship and activism. And to hold them together, I have come to see, is not simply a matter of acknowledging a both-and. They need to be *integrated*.

In our efforts at integration, however, we must avoid the impression that worship is all about equipping God's people for service. In a profound sense—and here I repeat the kind of emphasis I insisted upon earlier in citing the views of Gustavo Guterierrez—a good part of our worship requires setting aside any social activist agenda in order simply to *be* in the presence of the Lord. Indeed, to set aside an activist agenda for a portion of our worship is the best thing we can do for the sake of a faithful activism. We must spend time cultivating an awareness of the character of the One in whose presence we are "wasting time." He is surely our Savior, the divine Lover of our souls. But he is also a King who wants a deep awareness of his "kingdom authority [to] flow from his throne unto his own."

We have been learning many new lessons in recent years about how our worship of the Living God must be "contextualized" for the complex challenges of discipleship in our contemporary world. The Apostle Paul sets the right example for us in this: "I have become all things to all people so that by all possible means I might save some. I do all this for the sake of the gospel, that I may share in its blessings" (1 Corinthians 9:22–23 NIV). And those blessings certainly include the satisfaction of knowing that in our worshipping life we have welcomed people into the throne room of the King of Kings and the Lord of Lords.

13

Authenticity and Attractiveness in Christian Worship

Kenneth C. Ulmer

THIS FESTSCHRIFT HONORS Dr. Jack Hayford, a friend of mine who has modeled a life of worship for the forty years that I have known him.

In this article, I identify what I believe to be a fundamental tension in contemporary Christianity and a problem faced by many pastors. The tension is that which exists between the proclamation of the truth of the gospel on the one hand and the desire to engage the surrounding culture in a relevant and appealing way on the other hand. It is a tension between what I describe as the authenticity of the gospel in proclaimed worship and the attractiveness of praise in expressive worship. The answer to this tension, I believe, is rooted in the statement Jesus made to His disciples prior to His crucifixion: "And I, If I be lifted up from the earth, will draw all men to me" (John 12:32 KJV). When we "lift up" Christ in our proclamation of God's love while, at the same time, we create an inviting atmosphere that accommodates the "drawing" ministry of the Holy Spirit, we will see the transformative power of God in the lives of His people.

A Defining Story of Prayer and Friendship

The sanctuary of Hollywood Presbyterian Church was crowded with hundreds of local pastors and church leaders. We had gathered to pray for our city of lost angels, our leaders, and for one another at a critical time.[1] "Shepherds Love LA" was a prayer meeting. We had no preaching, no lectures, no Sunday school lessons. Just prayer. There were musical prayers, congregational prayers, and intercessory prayers. There were prayers with words understood, prayers prompted by the Spirit of God, and prayers of silent meditation. It was a pastor and preacher prayer meeting.

I sat on the front row of the well-known Presbyterian church with the expectancy of a young pastor recently appointed to one of the historic African American churches in the city. As the gathering divided into small groups to pray, I soon found myself on my knees with two men who would become gifts of God to my life and two of my closest friends: Dr. Lloyd Ogilvie, pastor of the host church, and Dr. Jack Hayford, pastor of The Church On The Way. I had heard these men speak, read their books, and drawn on their teachings over the years. That day changed my life as God gave to me the gift of friendship—a friendship that began on our knees in prayer.

Experiencing Authenticity and Attractiveness at TCOTW

As a result of my friendship with Jack Hayford, I became familiar with The Church On The Way (TCOTW) and saw that, on any given Sunday, a predominantly Anglo but multi-colored tapestry of worshippers would gather in celebration of God, often raising their hands spontaneously in response to the message from the pulpit or in response to the message of one of the songs that filled the air. Having grown up in black congregations, my experience at TCOTW was the first with a mixed congregation that I had ever enjoyed. In fact, at one time TCOTW had about 1,200 African American members. That meant, on average, Pastor Jack stood before more black worshippers than the average black pastor in the average black church in Los Angeles. It was

---

[1] Unknown to us at the time (1989), Los Angeles would erupt in rage, racial strife, and riots just a few years later in April 1992.

and is a testament to the submission of a leader whose only commitment throughout his ministry has been to hear God and obey His word
with a boldness that extends beyond traditional models, experiences,
and lines of demarcation.[2] My experience at TCOTW was also a
defining encounter with the synthesis of authenticity in the teaching of
the Word of God and attractiveness in the worship of God in song.

Yadah Worship

The worship I experienced at TCOTW was substantial in meaning
and rich in style, with priority given to the expositional presentation
of the Word of God. It was attractive and authentic at the same time.
I was impressed by the frequent, comfortable, and non-ostentatious
display of lifted hands as part of the worship and moved by the
unabashed response to the presence and power of God. I knew that
such worship with the lifting of hands was and is biblical and could
cite many passages in support of it.[3]

The Hebrew *yadah* captures the special significance of this type
of biblical worship. The singular nature of this term has to do with

---

[2] I was 30 years old at this time and did not know there were Africans in the Bible. I had
not heard that there were Jewish worshippers from African countries present in Jerusalem
on the Day of Pentecost. One might think it was universally understood that Egypt, Libya/
Cyrene, and Ethiopia were and are North African countries, and therefore their people would
be North African, but it was a revelation to me that the man who helped Jesus carry the cross
was from Cyrene in North Africa (Matthew 27:32), and that two of the leaders on the council
described in Acts 13 (Lucius of Cyrene and Simeon called Niger) were North Africans, and
that Simeon himself was a black man (*Amplified Bible, Complete Jewish Bible, God's Word
Translation, Good News Translation, The Living Bible*). This information was and is significant
for people who at one time were told they were three-fifths human and created inferior by
God to be slaves of the dominant culture. It was remarkable to me that my people were in the
Bible. This was my background and understanding as I experienced the multiracial, multicultural worship at TCOTW.

[3] The psalmists exhort God's people to give joyful praise in a manner appropriate to Him
(Genesis 29:35; 2 Chronicles 7:6; Psalms 28:6; 30:4; 49:18; 67:3, 5; 71:22; 86:12; 88:10;
89:5; 97:12; 99:3; 138:2, 4; Isaiah 25:1).

the method of praise it signifies. A common word, it is used by the psalmists more than 70 times as an expression of both personal and public praise in response to the move of God among His people, sometimes miraculously, sometimes providentially.

The root of the word (*yad*) is the word for *hand*. One way to think of *yadah* praise is as hand praise: "*Yadah* . . . is to throw out the hands, or extend the hands in the giving of thanks as part of our worship experience. *Yadah* praise is one in which we raise our hands in an outburst of spontaneous gratitude for what God has done. Our hands are used as an extension of our expression of thanks."[4]

Hands may be raised in one of two ways: lifted and extended to God with palms up, or lifted and extended to God with palms down. Hands raised with palms up signifies our desire to receive the attention and favor of God. Such a posture acknowledges our need for God and our sincere desire to receive His blessing and favor. Hands raised with palms down or extended out is a prayer posture of supplication and petition. It signifies the release of praise to God for receiving what we release to Him. When we raise our hands to the Lord with our palms down, we show surrender and submission to Him and affirm His superiority over our life. We show our desire to exchange that which is in our hands with what He has in His hands.[5]

---

[4] Orlando Figueiredo, "Praise—Yadah and Towdah," Global Word Ministry, https://www.globalwordministry.org/worship/praise-yadah-and-todah/.

[5] One of the most moving demonstrations of hand praise and worship occurred in a board meeting of The King's University. The agenda was filled with items requiring difficult decisions by the board. As is our custom, we began with worship. That day there came a powerful, unplanned anointing of God in the board room. The atmosphere was thick with the presence of God. As we worshiped, I noticed Pastor Jack, who was standing next to me, gingerly get on his knees. He had not been well and was attending the meeting against the requests of several board members. I could not help but shift my attention from the Spirit-filled atmosphere in the room to the struggle my brother was having getting on his knees. He was in such a blissful attitude of worship, however, that I dared not interrupt him, even to give him assistance. It took a minute or so, but he finally positioned himself on his knees with the glow of God resting on his face while continuing to sing, his hands uplifted to the Lord. What I had witnessed in that moment was *yadah* praise. I had witnessed hand worship!

Attractive African Influence in Pentecostal Worship

Such expressive hand gestures, along with verbal expressions of honor, praise, and dependence on God are common in traditional Pentecostal worship settings and represent a type of historic praise born out of the exuberant praise and worship initiated by a one-eyed, black, ex-Baptist preacher, William J. Seymour, at the beginning of the Pentecostal movement. As Daniel Albrecht remarks, "The ritual expressions, attitudes, and sensibilities—even the values and convictions [of Pentecostal worship]—draw from historical sources."[6]

Even though the theological roots of Pentecostalism can be traced to the radical evangelical and holiness traditions, its liturgical substance, seen in practices like hand worship, grew out of African tradition and culture. To this point, Walter Hollenweger has observed that "'Black' or 'African' worship has been a primary influence in Pentecostalism" since its beginning.[7] And, as David Daniels III has noted, this influence is evident in the practice of "tarrying," the self-initiated shutting off or locking in of people for prayer until God visits with His presence.[8] Hollenweger goes on to emphasize that "the vitality and transferability of Pentecostal liturgy are mainly due to the oral (and kinesthetic) qualities of the Pentecostal worship practices and experience," insisting that "'Black' (oral) sources and influences first helped to develop, and continue to sustain, Pentecostal liturgy around the world."[9] Cecil Robeck adds, "Some of the Black influences were mediated through the revivalist

---

[6] Daniel Albrecht, "Worshiping and the Spirit: Transmuting Liturgy Pentecostally," in *The Spirit in Worship-Worship in the Spirit*, eds. Teresa Berger and Bryan D. Spinks (Collegeville, Minnesota: Liturgical Press, 2009), 226.

[7] Ibid., 227.

[8] Ibid.

[9] Ibid., 228.

camp meetings of the times. The camp meeting formed the religious, cultural, and liturgical practices of both Black and white churches."[10]

Robeck goes on to observe that Pentecostalism at its founding was compelling because of the experiences people were having with God. People from as far away as India and Scandinavia were attracted to "the little Apostolic Faith Mission at 312 Azusa Street in downtown Los Angeles" because of "the distinctive experience and the developing theology of that movement" they found there.[11] It was the experience people had with God at Azusa Street that was the spiritual magnet, drawing worshippers from the north, south, east, and west, that particularly resonated with men and women in the African American community.

> Unlike the Western-oriented Christian, whose theology is rooted in Greco-Roman concepts and culture, African peoples tend to seek to know God personally rather than to know about God from doctrines and creeds. Traditional Africans, whose entire existence is a religious phenomenon, would become immersed early in the idea that God "is," not because they had been told about God's existence, but because God can be experienced in all of creation. This is summarized in the Ashanti proverb: "No one shows a child the Supreme Being," which means in essence that everybody, including children, knows God almost as if by instinct.[12]

People from many diverse backgrounds were attracted to the love and unity they experienced at Azusa. As Daniel K. Norris, one of the leaders in the Brownsville Revival, notes:

---

[10] Ibid.

[11] Cecil M. Robeck, "The International Significance of Azusa Street," *Pneuma* 8:1 (Spring 1986).

[12] Melva Wilson Costen, *African American Christian Worship* (Nashville: Abingdon Press, 1993), 7.

There is something to be learned from Azusa that offers
hope for us today, if we are willing to take notice.
Consider for a moment just how unique this move of
God truly was. This was the turn of the 20th century.
Racism ruled supreme in all corners of the country.
However, at Azusa those lines of separation vanished.
William Seymour was overseeing something that defied
reason. People from all different walks of life were
coming together to participate in this revival. It is one of
the truly remarkable and uncelebrated phenomena of
Azusa. In many ways it could be considered the first civil
rights movement of the 1900s and it started in a
multi-racial prayer meeting![13]

Of course, experience can lead to excess, especially when that experience is deeply moving, uplifting, and healing, and people desire as much
of it as possible. In addition, not only did the revival give way to excess
in certain experiences, but by many accounts it succumbed to the very
racism that its multiracial community was confuting. The revival was
peopled by a historic racial mix of blacks, whites, Latinos, and Asians
of all ages at the turn of the century when racism was still the unwritten
law of the land and only 40 years after the Emancipation Proclamation
had become law. Nonetheless, as Phillip Chan comments:

[While Azusa] began as a movement of the Spirit as well
as one which broke many different social boundaries
erected by men, *it ultimately was destroyed by the very
thing it was trying to rid of—racism.* The revival meetings
were ended by three successive conflicts all of which dealt
with issues of race. The results were startling:
Pentecostalism, while starting off as a multiethnic phenomenon ended as one of the most racial divisive

[13] Daniel K. Norris, "The Frontlines," *Charisma News*, September 10, 2016, accessed May 2017, http://www.charismanews.com/opinion/from-the-frontlines/60462-how-azusa-street-exposed-mdash-and-overturned-mdash-racism-in-the-church.

denominations for the next decades. The walls of racism were denominationally erected as white churches would reject and frown upon black ministers, churches, and mission that would take years and years to reverse.[14]

The expressive worship of TCOTW was attractive in its physical expression of supplication and appreciation and represented an extension of the worship experienced at the beginning of the Pentecostal movement with its roots in African American celebration. And, as the Azusa revival teaches us, within a healing, reconciling move of God, there is no place for excess that seeks experience for the sake of experience rather than the experience of God Himself, even as there is no place for anything that leads to division, such as selfishness or racism. Attractive worship is worship that binds up, heals, reconciles, and unifies.

The Tension of Authenticity and Attractiveness

It is providential that western expository preaching and teaching has been fused with African experiential expression within the Pentecostal movement, and it is not inconsequential that the traditions passed down from the Azusa revival continue to cross-pollinate both western and African culture that can be seen especially in the ongoing attempt to balance the authenticity of the Word and the attractiveness of experiential worship.[15]

The spiritual bond between the authenticity of the Word and the attractiveness of experience brings us to one of the tensions

---

[14] Phillip Chan, "The Azusa Street Revival and Racism," June 12, 2011, *The Phillip Chan Blog*, accessed May 2017, http://phillipchan.org/the-azusa-street-revival-and-racism/.

[15] As implied above, such cross-pollination of the Word and experience was and remains a distinctive feature of the culture at TCOTW. Through the teaching and leadership of Jack Hayford, the worship at the church was founded on strong exegesis of God's Word and, at the same time, open to the experience of God's Spirit for the spiritual welfare of everyone within the congregation.

with which the church continues to grapple. It is not too strong to say that the church seems to be fighting "worship wars" that are, in essence, struggles over the tension between authenticity and attractiveness. Authenticity is related to one's commitment to the biblical revelation of Christ while attractiveness is related to the culture in which said authenticity is practiced. Such was the challenge of the early church in its response to Jesus' mandate to take the gospel to the ends of the earth. At its inception, the commission required significant adjustments in the practice of the followers of Jesus while also challenging them to remain true to the principles and truths of their faith. The sequence of the guidelines of Jesus required a progressive crossing of boundaries: Jerusalem, Judea, Samaria, and the utmost parts of the earth all demanded traversing established cultural restrictions. Jesus spoke His words in Jerusalem, which was their starting point. From Jerusalem to Judea required crossing geographical boundaries; Judea to Samaria required crossing ethnic boundaries; Samaria to the uttermost parts of the world required crossing political lines into the outlying territories of the Roman Empire. As Jesus' followers crossed these boundaries, their challenge would be to maintain a balance between the authentic gospel and the attractiveness of that same gospel as it was shared in different cultural settings.

The challenges posed by Jesus' commission remain today and are present in the worship that the multicultural, multiracial, multigenerational church gives to God. If possible, the challenges are even greater given the micro-digitized culture that impacts all of us. The contemporary church wrestles with the tug of traditionalism on one hand and the promises of innovation that appeal to the tastes of an ever-evolving society on the other hand. And in response to the promises of innovation, contemporary church worship has taken on a distinctive appearance in the hope of being attractive. It has done this by (1) using contemporary language, (2) addressing contemporary concerns, (3) targeting specific groups of people, (4) drawing upon contemporary musical styles, (5) expanding the time given to congregational singing in church services, (6) giving prominent place to musicians in church services, (7) encouraging physical expressions of worship, (8) allowing for informality, and (9) making use of cutting-edge technology.[16]

The attractiveness of contemporary worship, as indicated by these characteristics, is held in tension with the authenticity of the proclamation of good news. Some churches address this tension by offering multiple services with different worship styles. Other churches retain traditional forms of worship. No one is surprised that those who prefer more traditional worship often regard contemporary worship as inauthentic. Nonetheless, it must be recognized that the style of worship (attractiveness) has become definitive for many people and takes precedence over doctrinal commitments (authenticity). As Greg Scheern comments:

> Denominational loyalty has all but eroded, replaced by music style. It used to be that a family would move to a new town and look for the nearest Baptist or Episcopal Church, but now they look for the nearest 'contemporary,' 'blended' or 'emerging' church. And how do they know that the Methodist church down the road is an Evangelical boomer community? Because it advertises a 'contemporary' service.[17]

The pull to be attractive is strong. Pastors who prefer traditional worship styles quote "where two or three are gathered in my name, there I am in the midst of them" and conclude that as long as they have met the irreducible minimum of two or three, they have succeeded in garnering God's presence and blessing. All the while they keep a close eye on the church down the street that has more members, a larger building, and boasts all the bells and whistles that appeal to people.

---

[16] Michael Lee, "Research, Worship, Music; The Diffusion and Influence of Contemporary Worship; How Does Worship Music Style Relate to Congregational Growth?" *The Exchange*, March 18, 2017, accessed April 2017, http://www.christianitytoday.com/edstetzer/2017/march/diffusion-and-influence-of-contemporary-worship.html.

[17] Ibid.

Pastors in the Middle of Authenticity and Attractiveness

It appears that pastors and their churches often opt for authenticity *or* attractiveness. On the one hand, in an attempt to be solidly authentic, they make no place for the prophetic word of God; there is no "in season" word for the people of God. On the other hand, in an attempt to be relevantly attractive, more times than not the authentic gospel of Jesus is compromised for fear of being politically incorrect, too hard, or lacking compassion.

The landscape of modern culture is less and less populated with churchgoers. "More Americans than ever are not attending church. Most of them did at some point and, for one reason or another, decided not to continue."[18] David Kinnaman of the Barna Group remarks, "This fact should motivate church leaders and attenders to examine how to make appropriate changes—not for the sake of enhancing attendance numbers but to address the lack of life transformation that would attract more people to remain an active part."[19]

The response of many pastors to these changing times has been to sacrifice authenticity for attractiveness. The goal of filling seats within the walls of the church often replaces the presentation of a savior who came to deliver people from the problem of sin and its eternal consequences. As a result, worship gatherings all too often cater to those who are preoccupied with everything from personal grooming to iPhones in their quest to look good and stay connected. Thus, pastors resort to sophisticated technology and give less attention to biblical teaching.

Pastors fill their quiet hours, when no one else is listening, with questions like: "Are we growing?" "What can we do to infuse new life and growth into this house?" And as they ask these questions, they

---

[18] *Barna Trends 2017* (Grand Rapids: Baker Book, 2016), 148.

[19] Ibid.

lean into the wind of either authenticity or attractiveness, hoping that one or the other will lead to growth and life. There may be days when pastors don't count attendance numbers, but ultimately the average pastor is always concerned about whether or not the church is growing. He or she is aware that what goes on inside the church impacts who comes in from the outside. And since worship style is the primary variable that swings a congregation in one direction or the other, pastors are attracted to the style that is more attractive to the potential worshipper. It is a reality that just as authenticity must be balanced with attractiveness, style must be balanced with substance. The challenge for the pastor of a local congregation is to find that formula of authenticity and attractiveness that issues in health and growth.

The pastor who is driven by the intoxication of success is more likely to seek church growth by any means necessary and will be influenced in his or her desire to "do good and look good." He or she will do almost anything or try almost anything to resurrect a dead or dying congregation. This pastor will raise the flag of invitation saying, "Come here and give us a try. We are like nothing you have ever seen." Such a pastor will likely experience frustration, discouragement, and even anger over the lack of growth or the lack of life in the growth they see.

This pastor's sincere desire to please and honor the Lord often leads him or her to do whatever they can to grow the church—even if it means compromising their integrity or the integrity of the Gospel. The temptation to dilute the message of Christ and disguise the identity of Christ is real. It is easy to make Jesus merely one of the biblical prophets, a loving historical figure who speaks positive blessings of prosperity, success, and unqualified health. As the pendulum swings more and more toward success, Jesus becomes one of the paths to a loving God. Sins are described as mistakes, heaven becomes an earthly utopia, and salvation is more existential than spiritual. Heaven becomes more a universal reality rather than a universal potentiality based on repentance from sin and "call[ing] upon the name of the Lord" (Romans 10:13). False promises of earthly blessings at best distort biblical truth and, at worst, present a Christless salvation where a relationship with God is attainable by being a good person or by choosing any one of the multitude of optional ways to relationship with Him.[20] Such attempts at attractiveness value political correctness more than sound biblical hermeneutics, exposition, and declaration of the truth that Jesus is "the way, the truth, and the life" (John 14:6).

Finally, if pastors are not motivated by church growth, then they are motivated by their own psychological need for significance. The man or woman who has done his or her best and who has refused to compromise the authenticity of biblical revelation often becomes discouraged and frustrated when preaching alone does not draw people into the church. They might even become angry as they see the seeker generation passing by their "authentic house" on their way to one down the street with the bells and whistles of attractive messages and methods. They are painfully aware of how long it has been since anyone was saved in their church, and they grow weary of doing funerals and memorials for the faithful few who come to their regular seats in the sparsely populated sanctuary. They feel limited by the routine calendar of activities that recycle the same people doing the same things season after season and feel trapped by those faithful few who have become the self-appointed program police, making sure the church does not turn to the left or to the right but is committed to the status quo.

Holding Together Authenticity and Attractiveness

The way forward for pastors and their churches as they attempt to hold together the authenticity of God's Word with the attractiveness of an expressive worship of God involves three steps. It involves

---

[20] Several years ago, the marquee outside a Los Angeles church promoted the title of an upcoming Sunday message: "Many Paths up the Same Mountain."

understanding what worship is. It requires heartfelt calling upon the Holy Spirit. And it is based on a clear engagement with Jesus' promise to draw all men to Himself when He is lifted up (John 12:32).

Definitions of worship vary and range from the theological to the practical. This speaks more about the multidimensional dynamics of worship than disagreement on what it is. A. W. Tozer defines worship as "the normal employment of human beings,"[21] while Robert Webber says that "worship is a dramatic retelling of the relationship between God and ourselves."[22] Andrew Hill leans toward mutual love as the basis of his definition when he writes, "Worship is the expression of a loving relationship between God and His people,"[23]and, in agreement with this, Jack Hayford offers that "worship is our primary ministry."[24] All would agree that worship defines men and women created in God's image.

Principles and practice must come together under the power of God in order to perform the divinely intended purpose of worship to transform people into His image. Whether two or three people gather together or thousands, the presence of God by His Spirit among His people is the goal of worship. Principles of the truth of God (authenticity) and practices under the anointing of God (attractiveness) need not be estranged from one another. And they are not estranged as long as welcome is given to the Spirit.

This is not always the case, however, and Albrecht cites N. T. Wright, who has observed a division in work done on the Spirit and that done on worship:

> At first sight, it appears strange that those who have written about the Holy Spirit in the New Testament have not usually given much attention to worship, and

---

[21] Andrew Hill, *Enter His Courts with Praise* (Baker Books: Grand Rapids, 1993), xvii.

[22] Ibid., 113.

[23] Ibid., 134.

[24] Jack Hayford, *Explaining Worship* (Lancaster, UK: Sovereign World, 2012), 56. Kindle edition.

those who have written about worship in the New Testament have not usually given much attention to the Holy Spirit. Gordon Fee's massive book on the Spirit in Paul has precisely three pages on worship. Paul Bradshaw's splendid book on the origins of Christian worship doesn't have either Spirit or Holy Spirit in the index. These may be unrepresentative, but I don't think so. Even the Westminster/SCM *Dictionary of Liturgy and Worship* has no entry under Spirit or Holy Spirit. You might have thought it would at least advise us to look under "Pentecost" instead, but it doesn't.[25]

Over time, there has been a drifting from worship "in spirit and in truth" that Jesus speaks of to the woman at the well (John 4:23–24). We have removed the Spirit from our engagement with God's truth in our worship. The antidote to this separation is to call upon the Spirit once again who, according to Matthew Boulton, "intervenes in Christian worship, conspiring with it by subsuming our malformed prayers into her own better singing, lifting up our words into her own wordless breath of life." The Holy Spirit not only addresses our inability to pray by interceding with and for us but also responds to our spiritual need of not knowing how to worship.[26]

On our own terms and by our own lights, our liturgies and lives only too closely resemble that mythic, presumptuous attempt to "make a name for ourselves" by building "a tower with its top in the heavens" (Gen 11:4). So when the Spirit joins her voice and presence to this insolent work, conspiring with it and incorporating it into her own mission, she thereby simultaneously conspires

[25] N.T. Wright, "Worship and the Spirit in the New Testament" in *The Spirit in Worship-Worship in the Spirit*, eds. Teresa Berger and Bryan D. Spinks (Collegeville, Minnesota: Liturgical Press, 2009), 3.

[26] Matthew Myer Bolton, "The Adversary: Agony, Irony, and the Liturgical Role of the Holy Spirit" in *The Spirit in Worship-Worship in the Spirit*, eds. Teresa Berger and Bryan D. Spinks (Collegeville, Minnesota: Liturgical Press, 2009), 73.

against it, covers its shamelessness, transforms its preten-
sion, bridges its divisiveness—in short, she "intercedes" in
and for Christian worship. ... We Christians cannot
accomplish this transformation on our own; in every
Christian worship service the Spirit must come again
and accomplish such transformation afresh."[27]

Recalling Karl Barth's view of the Spirit and worship, Boulton writes:

For Barth a governing mission of the Holy Spirit is to
expose and oppose religion, and in particular to expose
and oppose Christianity. In this sense the Holy Spirit
acts as Christianity's divine Adversary. And for Barth,
since the epitome and "very best" of Christianity is
Christian worship, the Adversary's work is paradigmatically liturgical. In and through Christian worship the
Spirit wrestles and struggles and works – toward the
"abolition" of Christian worship."[28]

It is precisely this ministry of the Spirit that is needed today to
fuse together authenticity and attractiveness in Christian worship.
Barth's use of the word "abolition" speaks of the Spirit's necessary
radical adjustment to worship in the life of the church that rids it of its
formulas and rigid, lifeless, impotent structures. Once again, Boulton:

The outpouring of the Holy Spirit involves a threefold
engagement with religion generally, and above all with
Christian worship: the Spirit (1) elevates worship to a
new level by participating in it subsuming or raking it up
into the divine mission; (2) preserves and works with
worship insofar as it is subsumed and not merely van-
quished or eliminated; and (3) ends or abolishes worship
insofar as this subsumption radically refigures and

---

[27] Ibid.
[28] Ibid., 74.

transforms it. ... And thus does Christian worship
become "true worship," and Christianity, "true religion."[29]

The church needs to be reminded that people have been created
for and called to worship that tenaciously holds to the truth of God's
Word and vibrantly celebrates who He is. In addition to this, the
church needs to call upon the Holy Spirit to show God's people how
to worship in a radical, truthful, and transformative way.

To Lift Up Jesus So He Might Draw People

As we have already observed, pastors, worship leaders, and worshippers of all stripes are caught in a tension. How are they to abolish
worship and, at the same time, enter into true worship? It is suggested here that they are to do so by lifting up Jesus from the earth:
"And I, if I be lifted up from the earth, will draw all men unto me"
(John 12:32 KJV).

The lifting of which Jesus speaks is the lifting of the cross in
crucifixion—a method of slow painful death—that also recalls
the lifting of the serpent in the wilderness for Israel's healing
(Numbers 21:7–9). Jesus understood that He was the incarnation
of the revelation that God gave to Moses when He promised that if
anyone looked upon the serpent on the raised pole, they would be
healed and live. Jesus was saying, "If I am lifted up on the cross like
that writhing serpent, as a sin-bearer, I will draw all who believe in
me to myself." What draws people to Jesus is His being lifted up as
our atonement for our sins.[30] This truth is beautifully expressed by
the hymnist William A. Ogden when he wrote: "'Tis recorded in
His word, hallelujah! It is only that you 'look and live.'"[31]

---

[29] Ibid., 74–75.

[30] R. K. Hughes, *John: That You May Believe* (Wheaton, IL: Crossway Books, 1999), 307.

[31] *The New National Baptist Hymnal* (Nashville: National Baptist Publishing Board, 1977), 136.

There is theological meaning attached to the idea of lifting up as well, as D. A. Carson observes:

> [It] is quite certain that the verb used here has been chosen because it is ambiguous. Jesus is not only 'lifted up' on the cross, he is 'lifted up' (*i.e.* 'exalted') to glory. The notions of 'being lifted up' and 'glorification' come together in Isaiah 52:13, where 'being lifted up' refers to the exaltation of the Servant of the Lord, though the context lays emphasis on his sufferings. In the New Testament, Jesus' atoning death and his exaltation come together, with various degrees of explicitness, in Philippians 2:9; 1 Timothy 3:16; Hebrews 1:3 and possibly Luke 9:51.[32]

Jesus will draw all men to Himself when He is "lifted up from the earth."[33] When we do the lifting and show His glory in our worship and in how we live our lives, He will do the drawing. Just as Roman soldiers lifted Jesus in crucifixion, we lift Him in exaltation as the risen, soon coming King. Yes, the verb *lifted up* is ambiguous and refers to the lifting of Jesus in crucifixion as well as to His lifting in exaltation. Both meanings are present in Jesus' prophetic words. The elevation of Jesus onto the cross is to be understood as the exaltation of Jesus as the one who reigns[34]

"I will draw everyone to me" may be rendered as "I will cause everyone to come to me."[35] A. T. Robertson provides insight on this when he writes:

[32] D. A. Carson, *The Gospel According to John* (Grand Rapids/Leicester, England: William B. Eerdmans Publishing Company/Inter-Varsity, 1991), 443–444.

[33] William Hendriksen, *Exposition of the Gospel According to John*, vol. 2 (Grand Rapids: Baker Academic, 1983), 203.

[34] Bruce Milne, *The Message of John* (Downers Grove, IL: IVP, 1993), 190–191.

[35] Unfortunately, some translators attempt to reproduce literally the meaning of *draw* and produce translations like "I will drag everyone to me."

Jesus had already used this verb of the Father's drawing power (John 6:44). The magnetism of the Cross is now known of all men, however little they understand the mystery of the Cross. By "all men" (παντας [*pantas*]) Jesus does not mean every individual man, for some, as Simeon said (Luke 2:34) are repelled by Christ, but this is the way that Greeks [communicated].[36]

Jesus' declaration that He will draw all people to Himself speaks of the power the love shown at the cross will exert on those who hear this good news without prejudice. To "draw all men" is meant to include even His Gentile enemies who put Him on the cross. Hence Jesus speaks of their ignorance when He says they do not know what they are doing. It was the very lifting of that cross that effected salvation for all people, even those who were His enemies.

Jesus' words may be interpreted in yet another way, one that offers hope and possibility for worship in our churches today. The juxtaposition of lifting and drawing may be seen in relation to what Paul declares in 1 Corinthians 2:2: "For I determined not to know anything among you, save Jesus Christ, and him crucified" (KJV). Paul only knew the cross—he only lifted up the crucified and glorified Jesus—among the Corinthians in his preaching and teaching. His example becomes our practice. If we only know Jesus and His crucifixion by making that message the heart of the good news we proclaim, then we lift up Jesus, and He will draw all people to Himself. If we do the lifting, He will do the drawing. Therein lies the tension—and the connection—between lifting and drawing. Both point to action related to Jesus. If Jesus is lifted, He will draw. Jesus will draw to Himself people, without force, through the attraction of the message of God's great love.

In the gospel, we experience the tension of sacrifice and attraction. There is first the lifting of Jesus who is the essence of the authentic

---

[36] A. T. Robertson, *Word Pictures in the New Testament* (Nashville, TN: Broadman Press, 1933).

gospel. The true gospel is only authentic if it is the proclamation of the One who hung on the cross. However, due to His salvific death, Jesus is also attractive. He will draw, He will attract people to Himself. Hence the tension between lifting and drawing is the tension between authenticity and attractiveness. If the authentic Jesus is lifted up in proclamation, then Jesus will attract people to Himself through our worship by means of His Spirit. The variable is with the lifting, not with the drawing. If He is lifted, He will draw. Not either-or but both-and. Authentic and attractive. Therein lies the challenge and the resolution of contemporary worship.

A Call to Authenticity and Attractiveness

Attractive worship welcomes people from all backgrounds. In the Pentecostal tradition of which TCOTW was a part, expressions of worship from the African American community were welcomed and contributed to the powerful move of God's Spirit in that tradition over the past century. Such worship is *yadah* worship. It is worship that gives and receives. It gives to God the honor that is His due, and, at the same time, it receives the blessing of His presence in response. This giving and receiving is possible when it is founded upon the authenticity of God's Word and the proclamation of the Gospel. At the heart of the good news, at the very center of the message we declare to others even as we declare it to ourselves, is Jesus who lived, who died on the cross, and who was raised to life again. To lift up the name of Jesus in our preaching and in our praising is to draw people to Him with authenticity and attractiveness.

When we lift up Jesus in the Word and in our worship, He will draw all people by His Spirit to Himself. This is one of the most vital lessons we can learn from the pastoral ministry of Jack Hayford. When we teach the Word in humility and faithfulness and lead in worship with sincerity and compassion, people will be drawn to the Jesus that they see in such teaching and worship. It is certainly what we all experienced and learned during Shepherds Love LA when we gathered from all the corners of Los Angeles to lift Jesus above our city in humility and love. With the help of the Holy Spirit and a commitment to the Holy Scriptures, let us continue to lift our hands to our God. Let us lift our hands in *yadah* worship. Let us lift up Jesus. When we do, the pressure to succeed according to false standards will lift as well, and the burden of chasing success based on numbers will be removed by the one who runs for the joy of the cross. *We* will then be drawn to Jesus in a fresh way, renewed in our lives, and strengthened in our ministries. And as we are drawn, others will follow in their desire for the authenticity and attractiveness they see being formed in us.

Section Five

Jack Hayford

14

Discerning The "Spirit" of the Word

The Holy Spirit in the Hermeneutics and Preaching of Jack W. Hayford Jr.[1]

S. David Moore

Introduction[2]

As JACK HAYFORD tells the story, he had just returned to his The Church On The Way office in Van Nuys, CA, after sharing a cordial and enjoyable breakfast in John MacArthur's Grace Community Church office in Panorama City. Hayford and MacArthur were pastoring congregations that not only were growing remarkably fast, but both men were gaining national attention because of their successful pastorates. The two had started the practice of meeting together at least annually for fellowship and collegiality. Their church campuses were less than two miles apart in the Los Angeles San Fernando Valley suburbs. Their backgrounds were dramatically different: Hayford was Classical pentecostal, closely associated with the charismatic renewal, while MacArthur was a strict cessationist

---

[1] The narrative style of much of this essay reflects my orientation as an historian and as Hayford's biographer. Although I do occasionally teach graduate hermeneutics, it is not my specialization. I welcome, therefore, the perspectives from my biblical studies colleagues in critiquing this mostly descriptive presentation of Hayford's approach to the Bible and preaching.

[2] This chapter is an edited version of a paper presented in March 2014 at the 43rd Annual Meeting of the Society for Pentecostal Studies held in Springfield, MO.

291

and fundamentalist.³ Nevertheless, they enjoyed the friendship they shared.⁴

As Hayford sat down in his office, he began to scan MacArthur's newly published book, *The Charismatics: A Doctrinal Perspective*. MacArthur had given Hayford a signed copy as he left MacArthur's office that morning. The very first pages Hayford opened to caught him completely off guard. The section was addressing MacArthur's concerns over charismatic Bible teachers' "gimmick" of teaching whatever they wanted to say by "spiritualizing" or allegorizing from biblical texts. Hayford was even more surprised by what he read next.

> They say marriages are made in heaven. Here was a marriage made in allegory and a silly one at that! But this kind of interpretation has gone on since the early days of the church, and it continues today, especially in the Charismatic movement. A well-known Charismatic preacher, whom I have talked with often, did a series on Nehemiah. As he taught, just about everything in the book represented something else or meant something symbolic. These were among his main points:
>
> "Jerusalem's walls were in ruin, and that speaks of the broken-down wall of the human personality. Nehemiah represents the Holy Spirit who comes to rebuild the walls of the human personality. When he got to the King's Pool (Neh. 2:14), he said this meant the baptism of the Holy Spirit, and from there he went on to teach the importance of tongues."
>
> The book of Nehemiah has nothing to do with the Spirit, or tongues; but a preacher can allegorize all that

---

³ In this essay, I generally follow James K. A. Smith and others in using "small p" pentecostalism to refer to the broad and diverse Spirit movements of renewal in the twentieth and twenty-first centuries. James K. A. Smith, *Thinking in Tongues; Pentecostal Contributions to Christian Philosophy* (Grand Rapids: Eerdmans, 2010), xvii.

⁴ Jack W. Hayford, interview with the author, December 30, 2013.

into the story, and some people think it is marvelous Bible teaching. I say it isn't. *It is huckstering the Word of God* to teach what we want in place of what God really intends to say [emphasis mine].[5]

"He was talking about me, and I was flabbergasted!" Hayford immediately phoned MacArthur. "John, I wasn't even looking for this section," which Hayford then read to MacArthur. "John, you are writing about me, and you didn't even talk to me first." MacArthur acknowledged Hayford was right and apologized. Hayford went on to challenge MacArthur that he had written these things without seeking any clarification or further understanding. Hayford told MacArthur that as an author, especially given their personal relationship, he had a responsibility to verify and be certain of facts before making public assertions about another leader's teaching or ministry. At the very least, MacArthur could have let Hayford know his concerns before writing about them publicly.

What concerned Hayford, apart from its strain on the relationship he shared with MacArthur, was that his Nehemiah teaching series was, by 1978, a "landmark" set of messages that thousands of people nationally and internationally had heard—it would later become one of Hayford's best-selling books.[6] The Nehemiah messages had been videotaped and broadcast twice on the Christian Broadcasting Network (CBN) and three times on the Trinity Broadcasting Network (TBN). Still in the heyday of the audio-cassette, tens of thousands of copies of the Nehemiah series had been sold and were in many charismatic and Pentecostal churches and ministries' tape lending libraries, multiplying their distribution. While MacArthur had not specifically named Hayford as that

---

[5] John F. MacArthur Jr., *The Charismatics: A Doctrinal Perspective* (Grand Rapids: Acadamie Books/Zondervan, 1978), 43. MacArthur provided no citation in his book for his assertions about this "Charismatic preacher."

[6] Jack W. Hayford, *Rebuilding the Real You: God's Pathway to Personal Restoration* (Ventura: Regal Books, 1986).

"Charismatic preacher," many would know exactly to whom he was referring.

Hayford and MacArthur would continue to meet annually, and MacArthur would continue to criticize Hayford. In 1992, when MacArthur published a significantly revised edition of the book retitled *Charismatic Chaos*, he once again wrote of the "Charismatic preacher," this time calling Hayford's teaching on Nehemiah "hucksterism," only slightly modifying his original words.[7] In the 1992 edition, MacArthur also criticized Hayford, this time by name, for a vision he shared at a Pentecostal Fellowship of North America gathering, arguing that in doing so Hayford was advocating ongoing revelation.[8]

However one defines hucksterism, it was hardly an appropriate descriptor for Hayford's Nehemiah interpretation. Although nothing I say will likely change MacArthur's opinion—his latest book, *Strange Fire*,[9] continues his unrestrained assault on charismatics—this essay will explore Hayford's Nehemiah series as an example of his "Spirited"[10] hermeneutic and passion for "prophetic" preaching. I will argue that the way Jack W. Hayford Jr. interpreted Nehemiah is part of his passionate quest to "discern the spirit of the Word" and to see his preaching transform the lives of his hearers. The Nehemiah messages will serve as my starting place, and I will then explore Hayford's apologetic for his approach to Scripture and preaching, in which he uses his interpretation of Luke's Annunciation narrative as a case study. Together, these two examples provide a lens through which we may view a noted pentecostal pastor/practitioner, arguably one of the movement's most respected leaders, at work commu-

---

[7] John F. MacArthur Jr., *Charismatic Chaos* (Grand Rapids: Zondervan, 1992), 91.

[8] Ibid, 48–50. The Pentecostal Fellowship of North America (PFNA) has since been renamed as the Pentecostal Charismatic Churches of North America (PCCNA).

[9] John MacArthur, *Strange Fire: The Danger of Offending the Holy Spirit with Counterfeit Worship* (Nashville: Thomas Nelson, 2013).

[10] Describing Hayford's hermeneutics as "Spirited" comes from my King's University colleague, Dr. Jon Huntzinger.

nicating the Bible in a way that he feels is true to God's purposes. Continued reflection is needed on the actual practice of ministry within pentecostalism today and ongoing engagement with the issues raised by these practices. Given the scope of Hayford's influence, especially to pastors, his approach to biblical interpretation and preaching serves as a helpful case study. My observations and engagement with the contemporary scholarly conversation will mostly be reserved for the footnotes.

Discerning the "spirit of the Word" and Prophetic Preaching

Appreciated broadly in both Evangelical and pentecostal/charismatic circles for his balanced and sensible teaching and preaching, Jack Hayford is not viewed as someone on the fringe of Christianity in North America; to the contrary, he has been called a "statesmen almost without peer" and someone known for his "theological depth."[11] His self-effacing and articulate communication style, coupled with the fruitful 30-year pastorate of the 10,000-member The Church On The Way, have helped Hayford become a pastor of pastors, speaking annually to over 20,000 pastors and Christian leaders for 25 years.[12] Hayford is known and praised for his integrity and ecumenicity. The evangelical magazine *Christianity Today* illustrated the broad respect Hayford has garnered, calling him on its cover the "Pentecostal gold standard."[13] Although Hayford does not consider himself an academic, he is a strong advocate for theological education, having served his alma mater, Life Bible College (now Life Pacific College) in

---

[11] Tim Stafford, "The Pentecostal Gold Standard," *Christianity Today* (July 2005), 26.

[12] For a detailed perspective on Hayford, see my Ph.D. dissertation: S. David Moore, *Jack W. Hayford: A Spiritual Biography* (Virginia Beach: Regent University, 2008). For a brief biographical sketch, see S. D. Moore, "Jack Williams Hayford Jr.," in Stanley Burgess, ed., *The New International Dictionary of the Pentecostal Charismatic Movement* (Grand Rapids: Zondervan, 2002), 692–93.

[13] *Christianity Today* (July 2005): Cover.

various roles as professor, dean of students, and president for five years. Hayford founded The King's University in 1997, where he presently serves as Chancellor.[14]

As a pastor and practitioner in the Pentecostal tradition, Hayford's take on Nehemiah was not unusual. He was practicing something that is the warp and woof of the pentecostal conviction—that God continues to speak through the Scriptures in ways that directly engage contemporary hearers and readers. In the early 1970s, Hayford was strongly identified with the charismatic renewal with its emphasis on creative and lively biblical interpretation.[15] This identification is largely why MacArthur labeled him as a "charismatic preacher." Nevertheless, what MacArthur was missing with his caricature was that Hayford was increasingly becoming known for his more careful and nuanced approach to teaching and preaching. Hayford took great care to root his teaching first in exegesis of a biblical passage with sensitivity to a text's historical and cultural context. At the same time, and important to keep in mind, Hayford was unflinching in his conviction that God wanted to speak prophetically through the text to the people he pastored (or his broader audience), and this often meant seeing texts imbued with new and fuller meaning.[16]

[14] While holding several honorary doctorates, Hayford has not earned an advanced degree but does hold two bachelors degrees, one from Life Bible College and one from Azusa Pacific University. He can be quite apologetic about his lack of advanced training, and he holds those who have done so in high regard. He is proficient in *Koine* Greek.

[15] During the early years of Hayford's ministry at The Church On The Way, Jack Hayford was known nationally more as a charismatic than for his participation in his Classical Pentecostal denomination, the International Church of the Foursquare Gospel. Even some people who attended his Van Nuys church were unaware that its legal name was actually the First Foursquare of Van Nuys.

[16] Some prefer to follow E.D. Hirsch and others in arguing for meaning being confined to the biblical author's intention to the original audience and to refer to a text's contemporary meaning as its significance. I prefer to think of meaning encompassing both authorial intention and a text's contemporary voice. This remains a significant hermeneutical issue for evangelicals and many pentecostals. See Millard Erickson, *Evangelical Hermeneutics* (Grand Rapids: Baker, 1993), 11; Kevin J. Vanhoozer, *Is There a Meaning in This Text* (Grand Rapids:

Moreover, while always concerned not to diminish the place of grammatical-historical exegesis, Hayford believed the Bible pointed beyond itself to Jesus Christ, the living Word, and that bibliolatry must be avoided at all cost. Finally, for Hayford, the aim of biblical teaching and preaching[17] was not first about doctrine but transformation.[18] With these preliminary observations, I want to consider more closely the Nehemiah messages.

The Nehemiah teaching series was born the way so many of Hayford's landmark teachings are born: he believed God spoke to him.[19] By early 1972, Hayford had pastored the Van Nuys church for almost three years and had witnessed the church grow over the last year from an attendance of 100 to 400. While ministering at a February pastors conference in Illinois, Hayford went out for an early morning walk in the snow and cold, something he couldn't do in sunny Southern California. As he walked, he heard in his mind these words: "I want you to begin to gather men and to train them. As you do, I will raise up strong leadership for the future of this church."[20] As he pondered this in the days that followed, he thought about the broken condition of so many he was pastoring in his California

---

Zondervan, 1998); For a pentecostal discussion on the issues of where to locate meaning, see Kenneth J. Archer, *A Pentecostal Hermeneutic for the Twenty-first Century* (London: T & T Clark International, 2004); Bradley Truman Noel, *Pentecostal and Postmodern Hermeneutics* (Eugene: Wipf & Stock, 2010); Kevin L. Spawn and Archie T. Wright, eds., *Spirit & Scripture: Examining A Pneumatic Hermeneutic* (London: T & T Clark, 2012).

[17] In this essay, I am following Hayford's practice of using "teaching" and "preaching" interchangeably.

[18] Hayford is fond of quoting Titus 2:1 and pointing out that, for Paul, sound teaching was fundamentally more ethical than propositional. Jack Hayford, *The Manifestation of the Word: A Proposition* (Van Nuys: The Soundword Tape Ministry, 1984 Pastors Seminar), audiocassette.

[19] The way Hayford believes God speaks to him is not through audible voices outside himself or through unusual mystical experiences; rather, God speaks through impressions and thoughts that may come to him and that he discerns to be God's voice. When he speaks, Hayford endeavors to make the idea that God speaks a normal and matter-of-fact affair that all believers should expect. Moore, *Hayford: A Spiritual Biography*, 240–45.

[20] Jack Hayford, *A Man's Starting Place* (Van Nuys: Living Way Ministries, 1992), 9–10.

church.[21] The church had burgeoned with many young people converted to Christ through the Jesus People movement; not a few of these young people bore the scars of drug use and promiscuous sex. The men in the Los Angeles music and film industry, of which Van Nuys was a suburb, attended The Church On The Way and were new converts to Christianity, many struggling to find wholeness in their lives.

Around that same time, Hayford was reading large portions of the Bible that included the book of Nehemiah. Hayford began to "see" analogies in his repeated readings of Nehemiah that pointed to God's redemptive, restoring work in the lives of his children. As he thought about the name Nehemiah, he discovered that "'Nehemiah—the consolation of God—derived from *nacham*, to breathe strongly, to pity, to console; and from *Yah*, the sacred name of the Lord.' In short, Nehemiah means 'the consoling breath or spirit of God.'"[22] Hayford continues:

> In it all, Nehemiah was not only beginning to appear as a picture of the Holy Spirit, his name was virtually synonymous with His. The first whispers of a parallel study in the ministry of the Holy Spirit unfolding in this book had hardly prepared me for the amazing discovery I made in the meaning of Nehemiah's name! And it was on these grounds that I began to proceed more boldly, with deepening conviction.
>
> Could it be that centuries before the coming of Jesus— long before the gift of the Holy Spirit—God had implanted in His own Word a coded message about the Holy Spirit's ministry of recovery? Could it be that

---

[21] Not long before this "word from the Lord," an elder of Hayford's congregation spoke to him about the brokenness he observed in so many of the men attending TCOTW. Hayford, interview, December 30, 2013: Hayford, *Rebuilding the Real You*, 7.

[22] Hayford, *Rebuilding the Real You*, 36. Hayford's book is popularly written and contains no footnote or lexical citation for these definitions.

forecast in this piece of Israel's history, just as other spiritual truths were prefigured [in] Old Testament events, a message of salvation's fuller provisions was foreshadowed? Could it be that the historical person, Nehemiah, without realizing it himself, was living out a picture being filmed for all times? Are we viewing a photograph of God's Spirit assisting us in our weakness and the recovery of all those ruined parts of our lives which sin has disintegrated? Was it all happenstance? Coincidental?

I became convinced that the book of Nehemiah had at least a three-fold message:

1. Facts of Israel's post-captive history.
2. Principles for cooperation among God's people at work together.
3. Lessons in the Holy Spirit's processes of recovery in our personalities.[23]

Although Hayford's emphasis in teaching Nehemiah was more on analogies and parallels[24] for contemporary application, he was careful in both his spoken and written expositions to state the historical and cultural context of the Book of Nehemiah. In his book on Nehemiah, *Rebuilding the Real You*, Hayford devotes an appendix section to explaining his approach, acknowledging that much of the book is essentially historical and that his analogies are drawn from less than half the book's content.[25]

---

[23] Ibid., 36–37. It is important to note the rationale Hayford had for reading Nehemiah this way. In his thinking, if it is readily acknowledged that there were types in the OT for Christ, why not then for the Holy Spirit as well? Hayford, interview, December 30, 2013.

[24] Under closer scrutiny in interviews, what Hayford synonymously calls analogies or parallels in Nehemiah describe a Gadamerian fusion of horizons where there is an experiential "this is that" interpretation, something John McKay has called a "shared experience." I plan to explore this more closely as I continue my work on the interpretative biography. John McKay, "When the Veil is Taken Away: The Impact of Prophetic Experience on Biblical Interpretation," *JPT* 5 (1994): 26.

[25] Hayford, *Rebuilding the Real You*, 243–247.

Hayford initially preached the Nehemiah messages at The Church On The Way in 1972 with considerable appreciation and affirmation from the congregation. The messages in audio and written form went on to impact the lives of countless thousands over the last 42 years, attested by the letters and testimonies received of renewed hope that God was at work, not only reconciling sinners to himself through Christ but also that people were experiencing substantial healing and recovery in their lives.[26] For Hayford, this was confirmation of his interpretation and resulting preaching.[27]

Hayford believes the series has been so fruitful because he discerned a prophetic word that captured the "spirit"[28] of the Word.

---

[26] On a personal note, I'm hardly objective in this essay regarding Hayford's take on Nehemiah. During my years of pastoring, I regularly recommended Hayford's audio and video Nehemiah messages or his book on Nehemiah, *Rebuilding the Real You*, to several hundred people I counseled or felt could be helped by the material. Without exception, the fruit was positive. I witnessed people experience transformation through Hayford's teaching, experiencing new wholeness in their lives and marriages. Many began following Christ with deeper devotion. In my own life, I experienced refreshed perspective on the nature of spiritual warfare as Hayford addressed the accusations and disdain from Sanballet of the Jews' initial efforts in rebuilding Jerusalem's broken and ruined walls. Hayford paralleled Sanballet's frustration regarding his loss of control over Jerusalem and his mocking assaults on the people rebuilding the walls. Sanballet chides the Jews for their weaknesses and slow progress in rebuilding; he demeans their worship and poor building materials, all with the intent to discourage their progress. I realized this was exactly what Satan tries to do to Christians, like myself, whom he can no longer control. Having experienced spiritual warfare that similarly seeks to discourage my faithfulness to Christ, something within me answered with a resounding "YES!" to Hayford's analogy drawn from Nehemiah 4. See Hayford, *Rebuilding the Real You*, 175–204.

[27] In a discussion on the Wesleyan Quadrilateral, Richard Hays addressed the community's role in confirming the validity of a given interpretation. He said, "Private revelatory experiences may prove edifying, but they can claim normative status in the interpretation of Scripture only insofar as they are received and validated by the wider experience of the community.... Experience serves not just to illuminate the meaning of the text but also to confirm the testimony of Scripture in the hearts and lives of the community." Richard B. Hays, *The Moral Vision of the New Testament: Community, Cross, New Creation* (San Francisco: Harper, 2013), 211. See also James K. A. Smith, "The Closing of the Book: Pentecostals, Evangelicals, and the Sacred Writings," *JPT* 11 (1997): 69; Amos Yong, *Spirit-Word-Community: Theological Hermeneutics in Trinitarian Perspective* (Eugene: Wipf & Stock, 2002).

[28] When addressing his approach to preaching, Hayford does not capitalize "spirit" in the phrase in his written handouts. In a recent interview, he explained the reason was his hope

In using the term *prophetic*, he means "the ability to 'see' spiritual things; gain insight into God's Word with an eye not only to discerning truth [facts, propositions, concepts] but also discerning its direct applicability to a speaker's constituency (1 Peter 4:11)."[29] Hayford believes that the "contemporary pastor/teacher may expect God to give 'direct promptings' ... concerning what he should preach ... [and] that the Holy Spirit will respond and assist with insight into how a specific text speaks specifically to the present moment."[30] This, he believes, is prophetic preaching. Hayford is careful to affirm that any prophetic word discerned in Scripture "must be measured against the whole of the Scriptures as to its truthfulness and relative worth and is subject to evaluation thereby by the leadership of the Body (1 Corinthians 14:29; 1 John 4:1–3; 1 Thessalonians 5:21)."[31] While Hayford may not articulate it this way, in practice, he roots meaning in the text neither solely in the author or the interpreter or the Spirit. Hayford recognizes that the study of Scripture brings about a dialogue with all three, but it is a dialogue that does privilege the revelatory and illuminating work the Holy Spirit gives to the text.

Another series of messages Hayford preached is a window into his approach to Scripture and preaching.[32] In December 1973, and

---

to express the dialogue the interpreter has with (1) the words of the text, (2) the interpreter's own pre-understanding and pre-suppositions, and (3) the insight of the Holy Spirit. Hayford, interview, 12/30/13.

[29] Dr. Jack Hayford, *Preaching and Teaching: The Holy Spirit's Intended Means to Transmit and Incarnate God's Living Word*—workshop notes. (Van Nuys: The King's College and Seminary, 2010), 3. These updated notes are used for a King's University preaching module at which Hayford speaks and represent a reworking of the original notes Hayford used at the 1986 COBE event. I cite this more readily available note for the purposes of this paper.

[30] Clark Pinnock's words resonate here with what Hayford is saying. "The biblical text is quantitatively complete (that is, not requiring additions) but can always be more deeply pondered and grasped at a deeper level. The Spirit is always able to cause what has been written to be revealed in a new light." Clark H. Pinnock, "Biblical Texts—Past and Future Meanings," *JET* (March 2000): 80.

[31] Hayford, *Preaching and Teaching*, 6.

[32] Portions of the following sections first appeared in my 2008 dissertation but are presented here with considerable revision and editing.

again with greater detail in 1975, Hayford preached on the Lukan passage (1:26–38) in which the angel Gabriel announces to Mary that she will conceive and give birth to the Savior of the world. These messages, like the Nehemiah series, became among Hayford's most widely distributed audio/video messages and remain a major theme in his public ministry.[33] In 1994, he wrote *The Mary Miracle*, based on those messages and other Gospel texts associated with Mary's annunciation and advent.[34] As with Nehemiah, Hayford believed he was capturing the "spirit" of the Lukan text, and his interpretation was another example in discerning a "prophetic word" that could be applied to the contemporary hearers' lives. For Hayford, the advent narratives in Luke's Gospel provide an analogy of what God wants to do in each believer. Just as Mary conceived by the Holy Spirit the physical Christ in her womb and delivered the baby, God wants to "conceive" and "birth"—to "form," in other words—his Son in the hearts of believers through the living presence of the Holy Spirit.[35] Hayford believes this idea is at the heart of NT teaching; evident, for example, in the Pauline passion for the Galatians that Christ might be "formed in you" (Gal 4:19) and the call to all believers to be conformed to Christ's image (Romans 8:29).

While Hayford clearly acknowledges the narrative character of the Lukan passages, his primary focus is to use the story in Luke 1:26–38, as he did with Nehemiah, as a "picture" or analogy. This time he focuses on how God not only forms believers through his promises but also brings forth his purposes through ordinary people. Hayford says:

---

[33] Jack W. Hayford, *I Wish You a Mary Christmas* (Van Nuys, CA: Living Way Ministry, 1973); Hayford, *The Conceiving and Bearing of Life* (Van Nuys, CA: Living Way Ministry, 1975); Hayford, *Having a Baby Will Stretch You* (Van Nuys, CA: Living Way Ministry, 1975).

[34] Jack W. Hayford, *The Mary Miracle* (Ventura, CA: Regal Books, 1994). The book is now distributed under the title *The Christmas Miracle*.

[35] Steven Land has mentioned this same analogy as it relates to a Pentecostal understanding of the function of Scripture. Steven J. Land, *Pentecostal Spirituality: A Passion for the Kingdom* (Sheffield, UK: Sheffield Academic Press, 1993), 100.

The God who chose a virgin girl as the avenue through whom He would miraculously give mankind His greatest gift is still working that "Mary" kind of miracle today. That is to say: What the Almighty did then in the physical/biological realm—supernaturally begetting life, promise and hope where none existed—He is fully ready and able to do now in virtually any realm.

He does this same kind of thing today—in marriages, in businesses, in hearts, minds, and souls. Where life or love, hope or strength, promise or patience have disappeared—or never been present at all—He comes to offer the Mary miracle. It's a timeless kind of wonder that is still being worked by our changeless heavenly Father.[36]

In saying this, Hayford does not downplay the unique and "astounding physical reality of the supernatural conception Mary experienced," but he is suggesting that "the Mary miracle holds the promised potential of heaven's entry into all our life circumstances."[37]

Significantly, Hayford defended his interpretation of the Lukan passage and, in doing so, indirectly gave a rationale for his Nehemiah interpretation and his hermeneutical approach in general. In 1986, Jack Hayford was invited to speak at the Congress on Biblical Exposition (COBE), an evangelical event held in Anaheim, California, whose thrust was encouraging expository biblical preaching. The congress was nationally promoted in Christian media at the time, and though the event was highly focused on the preaching task, attention was also given to hermeneutical issues and concerns.[38] Plenary session speakers included the likes of Charles Swindoll, John MacArthur, James I. Packer, and other pedigreed evangelicals. Still feeling the sting of MacArthur's critique, Hayford

[36] Hayford, *The Mary Miracle*, 18.
[37] Ibid., 20–21.
[38] Brian Bird, "Biblical Exposition: Becoming a Lost Art?" *Christianity Today* (April 18, 1986), 34.

used the event to defend, in his own carefully nuanced way, his approach to interpretation and preaching.

There was another motivation for his defense. It centered on his concern that too many pentecostal pastors, and for that matter evangelical pastors, were hesitant to practice prophetic preaching and to give room for the Holy Spirit's role in "seeing" passages in ways that more directly apply to a preacher's audience. Hayford was concerned that an overemphasis on a prescribed and restrictive hermeneutic and a preoccupation with expository preaching (defined for Hayford as aimed solely on teasing out authorial intent) could too easily lead to an erosion of "a passion for or expectation of the prophetic revelation and release of the Word."[39]

Hayford spoke at two workshop sessions.[40] In addressing the issue of how he understood biblical interpretation and preaching, one can hear him speaking to an imagined critic/interlocutor,[41] saying rather defensively, "I think you would gather that if it wasn't generally trusted that I was committed to the absolute authority of Scripture, a closed canon of Scripture, and to exegesis of Scripture that I wouldn't have been asked to be here."[42] He went on to say that he was aware that there may be some "resistance to what I would say is the spiritual side of preaching the word."[43] The accusation of "spiritualizing" the text was still very much in Hayford's mind.

Using the Annunciation narrative in Luke, Hayford told the session attendees—a packed room—that his goal in biblical exegesis and exposition was seeing God's "word being 'incarnated' lest …

---

[39] Hayford, *Preaching and Teaching*, 1.

[40] Jack Hayford, *Capturing the Spirit of the Word: Parts One and Two* (Portland: Multnomah Ministries, 1986), two audiocassettes.

[41] In my most recent interview with Hayford, he said this was exactly the case. In many ways, he was speaking to John MacArthur even though he was not present. Hayford, interview, December 30, 2013.

[42] Jack Hayford, *Capturing the Spirit of the Word: Part One*, message transcript, private holding, 3.

[43] Hayford, *Capturing the Spirit of the Word: Part One*.

preaching become solely conceptual, theological, or doctrinal."[44] He argued for "God's word being incarnated," that biblical truth must be internalized and integrated into one's behavior and lifestyle, as opposed to mere comprehension of propositions and facts. He contended that the "incarnated Word [word?]"[45] is the work of the Holy Spirit communicating the "spirit" of the text, not simply the "letter" of the text.[46] This is not sloganeering but an expression of his concern that "[f]acts without force (i.e. Without anointing) at best will only bring inspiration, not transformation."[47] Hayford boldly shared his perspective that many evangelicals are too easily suspicious of anyone who claims that God has spoken to them. Consequently, because of the fear of ridicule, many pastors give way to an interpretive methodology that effectively shuts out the Holy Spirit in biblical interpretation and exposition.[48]

To further address any accusation as to whether he was "spiritualizing"[49] the Luke 1:26–38 passage—his subject text in the

---

[44] Jack W. Hayford, "Capturing the Spirit of the Word," workshop notes, n.d.; Jack W. Hayford, *A Passion for Fullness* (Dallas: Word, 1990), 90. The word being internalized is a familiar theme for Hayford. Jack W. Hayford, *The Manifestation of the Word: A Perspective* (Van Nuys: The Soundword Tape Ministry, 1984 Pastors Seminar), audiocassette; Hayford, *The Manifestation of the Word: A Proposition* (Van Nuys: The Soundword Tape Ministry, 1984 Pastors Seminar), audiocassette; Hayford, *The Manifestation of the Word: A Process*, Parts One and Two (Van Nuys, CA: The Soundword Tape Ministry, 1984 Pastors Seminar), audiocassette.

[45] At times in Hayford's audio presentations, it is unclear whether he is using "word" in reference to Christ or to the Bible as the word of God. This is important to note because Hayford does not believe the Bible is the sum total of God's word. Jesus Christ alone can be called, in the fullest sense, the Word of God.

[46] Hayford, *Capturing the Spirit of the Word: Part One*, manuscript, 4.

[47] Hayford, *Preaching and Teaching*, 1.

[48] Ibid.

[49] I do not think it is completely inaccurate to suggest that Hayford is spiritualizing biblical passages in his Nehemiah or Annunciation interpretations, although he would prefer to describe it differently. Hayford does not read the scholarly discussions on hermeneutics and makes no attempt to describe fully in more academic language what he is doing. He admits this is the case and has acknowledged to me that he is unaware of any detailed understanding of the history of biblical interpretation beyond the level of an introductory hermeneutics text. This makes it all the more remarkable that he has intuited his approach primarily from his

workshop—Hayford affirmed the essential starting place for all interpretation is exegesis that examines genre, grammar, historical context, and so on. This, he said, was the gateway for the interpretive process.[50] With this fundamental commitment clear, Hayford again argued for the quest for prophetic insight, "an approach to study that helps us capture the life and breath of things within the text." Without this essential element for interpretation, "meaning can become very academic and our sermons finally distill to only academic presentations, however lucidly and graciously they are delivered."[51]

In the years since COBE, Hayford has continued to argue for a "Spirited" approach to biblical interpretation and preaching in his School of Pastoral Nurture: Consultation II (SPN II) and in courses on preaching at The King's University. In these presentations, he has been more specific in his assertions. For example, in a 1998 SPN II, he argues for what clearly seems to be a *sensus plenior* or spiritual sense interpretation. "We cannot say something else than what the text says, but we can say something more."[52] He went on to reference how New Testament writers took liberties with Old Testament passages both by rewording them to suit their purposes and by interpreting texts quite differently from apparent authorial intention.[53] For Hayford, interpreters need to be "herme-

---

spirituality and ministry experience. His primary concerns regarding biblical interpretation center more in how it informs his preaching and teaching ministry.

[50] Ibid., 4–5. The term "gateway" is another descriptor of Hayford's hermeneutic that I borrow from my King's University colleague, Jon Huntzinger.

[51] Hayford, *Capturing the Spirit of the Word: Part One*, manuscript, 6.

[52] Jack W. Hayford, School of Pastoral Nurture: Consultation II, King's Seminary, June 1998, audiocassette.

[53] Though it is beyond the scope of this paper, I have little doubt that Hayford practices a *sensus plenior*, whether it is more precisely a *pesher* exegesis, a midrash, or a "spiritual sense" interpretation. At this point, I'm not exactly certain what to call it. It is, however, not just an *application* of authorial intent, even though his language may sometimes suggest so. When Hayford speaks of the "prophetic," he is talking about meaning in texts that unquestionably goes beyond the intention or perception of the Scriptures' human authors. I find Richard Hays' perspective helpful. He says, "Theological exegesis thereby is committed to the discovery

neutically sound without being hermeneutically bound," going on to say that "in our efforts to be hermeneutically precise we must not limit or restrict the Holy Spirit's prophetic insight.[54] It cannot be much clearer.

In summary, Jack Hayford affirms and has modeled the importance of a thorough understanding of a text's original meaning and context as the important interpretive starting place. This is, at least in part, why he has gained such a large hearing among non-Pentecostals. Most of Hayford's preaching does not stir much debate. That said, he believes that all Scripture must be interpreted with an "ear to hear"

---

and exposition of *multiple senses* in biblical texts. Old Testament texts, when read in conjunction with the story of Jesus, take on new and unexpected resonances as they prefigure events far beyond the historical horizon of their authors and original hearers." Richard B. Hays, "Reading the Bible with the Eyes of Faith: The Practice of Theological Exegesis," *Journal of Theological Interpretation* 1.1 (2007): 14. See also Joseph Byrd, "Paul Ricoeur's Hermeneutical Theory and Pentecostal Proclamation," *Pneuma* (Fall 1993): 203–214; Timothy B. Cargal, "Beyond the Fundamentalist-Modernist Controversy: Pentecostals and Hermeneutics in a Postmodern Age," *Pneuma* (Fall 1993): 163–187, especially 175; Matthew W. I. Dunn, "Raymond Brown and the *sensus plenior* Interpretation of the Bible," *Studies in Religion* (2007): 531–551; Andrew L. Minto, "The Charismatic Renewal and the Spiritual Sense of Scripture," *JPT* 27.2 (Fall 2005): 256–272; Mark Stibbe, "This is That: Some Thoughts Concerning Charismatic Hermeneutics," *Anvil* (1998): 181–193; Archie T. Wright, "Second Temple Period Jewish Biblical Interpretation: An Early Pneumatic Hermeneutic," in Spawn & Wright, *Spirit & Scripture*, 93–98.

[54] Hayford, School of Pastoral Nurture: Consultation II audiocassette. Hayford finds plenty of support for his emphasis on the role of the Holy Spirit from scholars in biblical interpretation, including the late Clark Pinnock. Clark Pinnock, "The Work of the Holy Spirit in Hermeneutics," *JPT* 2 (1993): 491–97; Pinnock, "Biblical Texts—Past and Future Meanings," 76; Pinnock, "The Work of the Holy Spirit in Hermeneutics," *JPT* 2 (1993): 3–23; Pinnock, "The Work of the Spirit in the Interpretation of Holy Scripture from the Perspective of a Charismatic Biblical Theologian," *JPT* 18 (2009); Frank D. Macchia, "Theology, Pentecostal," in Stanley S. Burgess, ed., *The New International Dictionary of Pentecostal and Charismatic Movements* (Grand Rapids: Zondervan, 2002), 1122. A number of more recent articles add to the discussion of a distinctively pentecostal approach to hermeneutics: Kenneth J. Archer, "A Pentecostal Way of Doing Theology: Method and Manner," *JPT* 9.3 (July 2007): 301–314; Clayton Coombs, "Reading in Tongues: The Case for a Pneumatological Hermeneutic in Conversation with James K. Smith," *Pneuma* 32 (2010): 261–268; Andrew Davies, "What Does It Mean to Read the Bible as a Pentecostal?" *JPT* 18 (2009): 216–219.

the Holy Spirit's voice.[55] With all passages, he pursues "prophetic insight," his quest at "capturing the spirit of the Word within the Word" in order to communicate biblical truth that will transform lives.[56] Sounding almost Barthian, Hayford expresses a desire to see the Bible set free and enlivened by the same Spirit who inspired the text and who is still speaking through it today, especially through anointed preaching.[57] Finally, as already mentioned, he openly confronts what he calls "bibliolatry" among many evangelicals—and some Pentecostals too—with its attendant over-literalizing and its restrictive focus on authorial intent.[58] Though he does not term it this way, he is, in essence, resisting the reductionist tendencies of modern hermeneutics so prevalent in conservative evangelicalism.[59] He recognizes that many Pentecostals have been seduced by evangelical/fundamentalist ideas and that this has limited their grasp of

---

[55] Hayford, "The Manifestation of the Word: the Process," Audiocassette.

[56] Jack W. Hayford, School of Pastoral Nurture: Consultation II, Kings Seminary, March 2007, digital audio recording 2.10; Jack W. Hayford, School of Pastoral Nurture: Consultation II, Kings Seminary, March 2007, digital audio recording 2.11. I again refer to Clark Pinnock, who said, "By means of historical exegesis we encounter the world of the text and behind the text. In the Spirit by faith we enter a world in front of the text where the goal is to get beyond mere reading and to undergo transformation." Clark Pinnock, "The Role of the Spirit in Interpretation," JETS 36/4 (1993): 494.

[57] Simon Chan has suggested that this Pentecostal orientation beyond the written words of the biblical texts to the "Spirit-illuminated, spoken Word" has kinship with Barth. Simon Chan, Pentecostal Theology and the Christian Spiritual Tradition (Sheffield: Sheffield Academic Press, 2000), 21–22. Hayford may state it differently, but he believes that through anointed preaching the listeners are being "addressed" by God. Barth's well known threefold Word of God—the written Scriptures, the preached word, and Jesus Christ, the Word of God—also finds resonance in Hayford.

[58] Hayford, School of Pastoral Nurture: Consultation II, 2.11. For example, Hayford does not interpret the Genesis 1 narrative as literally depicting 24-hour days. Rather, he sees the passage as figurative. Jack Hayford, Scott Bauer, and Jack Hamilton, How It All Began: An Overview of Genesis (Van Nuys: Living Way Ministries, 1996); Jack W. Hayford, Genesis 1 & 2 (Van Nuys: Soundword Tape Ministry, January 9, 1975), audiocassette.

[59] For a definition of conservative evangelicalism as I see it, see: Roger E. Olson, Reformed and Always Reforming: The Postconservative Approach to Evangelical Theology (Grand Rapids: Baker Academic, 2007), 22–26.

the full breadth of Scripture for the preaching and teaching task so central to pastoral ministry.[60]

It is also worth noting that Hayford has avoided getting caught in the debate over inerrancy. He is more concerned about the Bible's transforming influence in the life of the church. In this regard, he has written:

> We affirm our convictions regarding the *accuracy* of the Scriptures, but still there are some who debate and divide over exactly how this conviction ought to be asserted. Preferring to avoid this arena of scholarly debate, may I suggest we at least receive one another on these terms: *We believe the Bible record about Jesus—His life, His death and resurrection?*[61]

What is most important to Hayford is not whether the term is inerrancy or infallibility; his concern is that "the reliability" of Scripture be acknowledged.[62] The Holy Spirit comes to make the written Word "live" in the life of the believer. This is for Jack Hayford the aim of incarnational preaching.

---

[60] Kenneth Archer has provided perspective on the seduction of Pentecostals by modern hermeneutic trends. See Archer, *A Pentecostal Hermeneutic*, 94–126. Having taught many years at an undergraduate Classical Pentecostal Bible College, I have witnessed the impact of an overemphasis that makes authorial intention the sum total of a text's meaning. In my Bible classes, students regularly treated the text as an object to be exegetically mastered and struggled to let the text directly address their lives. The fear of reading the Bible devotionally or spiritually became an obstacle to what Hayford calls an "ear to hear" the Spirit-enlivened text. Rickie Moore, Cheryl Bridges Johns, and others have freshly reminded pentecostal Bible students that Scripture is more than an object and is essentially "a living Word which interprets us and through which the Spirit flows in ways that we cannot dictate, calculate, or program. This means our Bible study must be open to surprises.... Rickie D. Moore, "A Pentecostal Approach to Scripture" in Lee Roy Martin, ed., *Pentecostal Hermeneutics: A Reader* (Leiden: Brill, 2013), 15. See also the excellent critique by Cheryl Bridges Johns, "A Disenchanted Text: Where Evangelicals Went Wrong with The Bible," in David P. Gushee, ed., *A New Evangelical Manifesto: A Kingdom Vision for the Common Good* (St Louis: Chalice Press, 2012), 17–25.

[61] Hayford, *Passion for Fullness*, 93.

[62] Ibid., 92.

Whatever one's opinion of Hayford's interpretation and preaching, what he argues and practices raises issues that still are hotly debated, particularly so given the contributions in general hermeneutics in the last century and the postmodern collapse of fixed meanings. Several pentecostal scholars continue to privilege the grammatical-historical method affirmed by most conservative evangelicals.[63] Others have cautiously embraced aspects of more postmodern views that see interpretation as less rigid and grant more liberty to interpreters.[64] Hayford is in neither camp. For him, it is a simpler and more fundamental matter: God continues to speak dynamically to his people today through the Bible—and, I should add, through other, multifaceted means.

Concluding Observations

It would be a mistake to conclude this essay without noting that Jack Hayford's approach to the Bible and his preaching flow out from his deep commitment to worship, prayer, and a life of integrity. Hayford has often said that the insights he receives in his study of Scripture are not the result of his own creative or interpretive skills but come from insight God gives, convinced his ability to "see" is fundamentally tied to his obedience and openness in his personal pilgrimage with Christ. Hayford is not arguing for some kind of peculiar or special holiness on the part of preachers. Instead, he believes that the ability to "see" and "hear" God speak comes from living openly and honestly before God. He describes it this way: "My commitment to walk with integrity of heart calls me to refuse to allow the most minor deviations from honesty with my *self*, with the *facts*, and most of all, with *the Holy Spirit's corrections*."[65]

---

[63] Two notable examples are Gordon Fee and Robert Menzies.

[64] Noel, *Pentecostal and Postmodern Hermeneutics*.

[65] Jack Hayford, *Pastors of Promise* (Ventura: Regal, 1997), 138; Hayford, *"DayBreak:" Integrity, Infilling, Insight* (Van Nuys, CA: Soundword Tape Ministry, November 1985); Jack Hayford, "All My Earthbound Senses," *Ministries Today* (May/June 1993), 8–9.

Integrity is essential to the development of one's character, and that process depends

> on how willingly I permit His Spirit to continually refine my imperfect capacities for receiving and responding to His will in the moment-to-moment details of my life. My character is not shaped by the sum of my *information*, but by the process of *transformation* that is as unceasingly needed in *me* as God's word is unchanging with *Him*.
>
> There is more to my character formation than having learned a set of ideas—even if they are God's. I not only need to *turn to the Bible*, but I must keep *tuned to the Holy Spirit*, for with the "grid" of values His Word gives me, He provides His Spirit as the ultimate umpire who comes to apply that Word to my living.... The purpose of His monitoring is not to produce a mystical brand of supposed "holiness," but a dynamic quality of whole-hearted, clear-eyed people.[66]

This understanding of the importance of integrity is the main aspect in his "journey of daily opening [his] heart to [God] for scrutiny." Hayford has described his devotional pilgrimage "not as an exercise in self-flagellating or berating introspection, but a practice of maintaining sensitivity to His Spirit's 'voice,' keeping integrity with His dealings with my heart."[67] Consequently, he has lived his life with a sometimes-brutal honesty. He has also regularly practiced confession with close confidants and fellow pastors for many years.[68] Integrity of heart is the bedrock of his

---

[66] Hayford, *Pastors of Promise*, 137. For other perspectives from Hayford on integrity and character, see: Jack W. Hayford, "Practicing What We Preach," *Ministries Today* (November/December 2003), 22–23; Hayford, "It's Not About 'Office'—It's About Character," *Ministries Today* (January/February 2004), 86, 85.

[67] Hayford, *Pastors of Promise*, 135.

[68] Hayford, "*DayBreak:*" Integrity, Infilling, Insight.

spirituality, and Hayford believes this "way of repentance" not only leaves his heart open to "see and hear" the spirit of a text more clearly but also makes it possible for God's transforming word to flow through him to transform those who also "see and hear" through his preaching.[69]

Hayford's life resonates with the spirituality of the Bible that is remarkably childlike. His approach to the Bible and to preaching are founded on a complex of practices that include his prayers, his worship, his obedience to God, his study of the Bible, and, just as importantly, his praxis as a local church pastor who is thoroughly embedded in his community—his "situatedness."[70] His love for the congregation and an awareness of their needs are front and center as he comes to the Bible to prepare to speak. Hayford sees the Christian life as radically Christocentric and actuated, empowered, and directed by the Holy Spirit.[71] Known and loved for his emphasis on worship, Hayford's life affirms "the aim of all true theology is doxology." These convictions are evident in his nearly 60 years of public ministry.[72] He is not a man concerned with abstractions or speculations *about* God but is all about his relationship *with* God.[73] Reminiscent of early Pentecostalism, he seeks a "dynamic

---

[69] What makes Hayford's emphasis on "integrity of heart" distinctly Pentecostal is the role he gives to the Holy Spirit in the "affairs of the heart." Ibid., 136. It reflects what Steven Land calls "the epistemological priority of the Holy Spirit in prayerful receptivity." Land, *Pentecostal Spirituality*, 38.

[70] Wherever possible, I have avoided using the term "method" in relationship to Hayford's hermeneutics and his consequent preaching because he is not consciously applying "a method," but living out a way of life that regularly engages the Scriptures in order to hear God speak prophetically to his own life and the people he leads. Hayford's "take" on the Christian life is integrative and pre-critical. Like many pentecostal practitioners, he intuits his way theologically more than he critically determines it.

[71] Fee says that "True spirituality … is nothing more or less than life by the Spirit." Gordon Fee, *Listening to the Spirit in the Text* (Grand Rapids: Eerdmans, 2000), 5.

[72] Hayford turns 80 this June and is finally beginning to reduce his travel and ministry schedule after being urged to do so by trusted friends and colleagues.

[73] I contend that Hayford's approach to theology is reminiscent of John Wesley's theologizing. Kenneth J. Collins, *Theology of John Wesley* (Nashville: Abingdon, 2007), 3–5. See also

and progressive" openness to a God who is active in the world.[74] Perhaps Hayford's own words about how he encounters the Bible in preparing to preach, spoken recently at BIOLA University, provide the best summation:

> For me it has to do with the belief that what I am doing is interfacing with the one who breathed this book.... And as I pray in the Spirit, my prayer is really somehow Lord you who long ago, not on this printed page, but upon someone with pen and a parchment or some animal skin began to write as they were borne along by your Holy Spirit ... and your word was faithfully transmitted from generation to generation ... I ask you Lord to let me breathe in what you breathed on. I want that life in what I am going to give these people next week.[75]

Jack Hayford's Bible is not a closed, static repository of facts and propositions but a living instrument of the Holy Spirit that mediates God's presence as the text continues to speak today. In this sense, his stance calls for a recovery of an "enchanted text," as Cheryl Bridges Johns has argued in her essay lamenting the way many evangelicals have allowed a "disenchantment" of the Sacred Scriptures.[76] Although Hayford might not prefer the term "enchanted" to describe the Bible, there is little doubt that he would agree completely with Johns' longing "to see the Holy Spirit using the Word to sweep us into the ecstatic life of God."[77]

Donald W. Dayton, "Yet Another Layer of the Onion," *Ecumenical Review* 40, no.1 (January 1988): 87–110.

[74] Douglas Jacobsen, *Thinking in the Spirit* (Bloomington: Indiana University Press, 2003), 357.

[75] Jack Hayford, "Context, Constraints, and Convictions," transcript, Evangelical Homiletics Society Conference, 2013 (Los Angeles: BIOLA University, October 2013).

[76] Johns, "A Disenchanted Text," 22–25.

[77] Ibid., 25.

15

The Peacemaker

Lloyd John Ogilvie

ONE DAY, WHILE driving along an old country road in the Highlands of Scotland, I passed a stone quarry with a shed beside it. Outside the shed was a sign that read, "A.J. McIntyre, Stonemason. Expert in building and replenishing of walls."

I thought to myself, *I know a lot more people than A. J. McIntyre who know how to build and replenish walls. Only these walls separate people, denominations, congregations, theological persuasions, and racial backgrounds.*

Then my mind turned in a more positive direction. *Who would I say is one of the best demolition experts in tearing down walls that separate Christians?*

I thought of the Church of Christ polarized into the fundamentalists, evangelicals, charismatics, social activists, and denominational separatists. Then I thought of the political division between conservatives and liberals. Each group shouts from behind its own walls, "I've got the truth!" And each misses the point that we need each other.

We become experts at building walls. If we are fundamentalists, we scrutinize what others believe about the Bible. Evangelicals check to hear their own language about being born again. Those involved in soul-sized social issues look with disdain at those who avoid the plumb line of social justice. Some charismatics think a person is a true Christian only if he or she speaks in tongues. And in many congregations and some denominations, personal piety and social action often are separated with an emphasis on one to the exclusion of the other.

As I reflected on these walls separating Christians, I tried to think of a leader who was really effective at breaking down walls. I tried to picture a person who exemplified running with the Master on a two-legged gospel: dynamic, grace-rooted, and joyous, with personal faith, contagious evangelism, passionate preaching, and a life-changing ministry; plus faithfulness and obedience to the biblical mandates of social justice and righteousness expressed in care for the poor, disadvantaged, and disaffected of society through the programs of a local church.

Sadly, my list of leaders who met these qualifications was not very long. However, at the top of my list was one of the truly great Christian leaders of our time.

His name is the Rev. Dr. Jack Hayford. Allow me to share with you the reason this remarkable man topped my list. I knew Jack personally as one of my best friends and my prayer partner for many years. He was Pastor of The Church On The Way in Van Nuys, California, and I was Pastor of the First Presbyterian Church of Hollywood, California.

Our friendship began by meeting occasionally over breakfast, sharing the adventure of discipleship, mutual challenges we both had in leading our churches, and personal needs we were confronting. We both had large churches, radio and television ministries, wrote books, and tried to keep up with very demanding speaking and preaching schedules. A vital part of our time together was spent in prayer for each other.

Sometimes we laughed about our very different denominational backgrounds. When people would say to Jack, "Why don't you wear a clergy robe, recite the Apostles Creed, and sing more traditional hymns?" Jack would respond without any defensiveness, "Go see Lloyd!" When people asked me why I didn't speak in tongues in the worship services, raise my hands in praise, and sing more contemporary songs, I would say with enthusiasm, "Go see Jack!"

As our friendship grew, the walls that might have separated us came tumbling down. We shared a biblical, Christ-centered, Holy

Spirit-inspired, and gifted faith. Both of us loved to study, preached expository sermons, and took great delight in introducing people to Christ and enabling them to receive the indwelling power of the Holy Spirit. We were also deeply concerned about the city of Los Angeles, growing racial tensions, the poor, and the suffering in our sprawling megalopolis.

At this crucial time, Jack Hayford became a leading peacemaker who brought Christian leaders out from behind their theological and denominational walls. A small group of us began meeting for breakfast under Jack's inclusive leadership. We were an interracial group of pastors from high and low churches, rich and poor churches, traditional, evangelical, and charismatic churches. We had two powerful things in common that became sledgehammers in breaking down any walls between us: our commitment to Christ and our deep concern for our city, its people, and its problems. We came together with no other agenda than to encourage each other's ministries and pray for Los Angeles.

When we first met together, sharing our needs and praying for one another, again, I saw the walls come tumbling down. Pastor Jack, the peacemaker, was used by the Holy Spirit to help us grow in a profound love for each other as brothers and sisters in Christ.

Then a vision was birthed among us. Why not become an invitation committee to call together for a prolonged time of prayer all the pastors, church workers, and leaders of missions working in the inner city? A list of over five hundred was assembled, and invitations were sent out. The date set was February 14, 1989—Valentine's Day.

The proposed four-hour prayer time was called "Shepherds Love L.A." Our small group, with Jack's encouragement and example, fell on our knees and then prostrated ourselves with our faces in the carpet, humbly and passionately asking the Lord to inspire a great response from those who would receive the invitations. During the prayer time, Jack tapped me on the shoulder and shared that he felt the Spirit's guidance to suggest that the meeting should be held at my church because of its access for both suburban and inner-city pastors.

I remember the excitement and anticipation I felt when I drove to my church in Hollywood that February 14th morning while it was still dark. *Would anyone come? What would be the attitude of people from so many different backgrounds?* I wondered with a mixture of anxiety and expectation.

My heart leapt with joy as I saw the headlights of cars streaming into Hollywood Presbyterian Church's parking lot. When I reached the fellowship hall where my church elders and deacons were serving breakfast for the pastors and leaders, it was already full. *But how would the prayer time go?* I thought to myself as I talked to many over breakfast.

Just before the prayer meeting was due to open, I met with Jack. As was customary for him, he expressed his confidence that the Lord provides supernatural power for the accomplishment of what He guides. After urgent prayer that the Lord would use us, especially Jack for his opening message, he said with enthusiasm, "Let's go!"

At 7:00 a.m., we moved into the sanctuary and began the four-hour prayer time. The size of the crowd stunned me. The sanctuary was over-crowded. More than 1,300 pastors and church workers had gathered to pray! The late Fred Bock led a hundred-voice choir in a stirring anthem of praise and then served as song leader for the rest of the morning.

It was a pleasure to welcome everyone and introduce Jack to give the opening message on Jeremiah 29:7, 11–13, a passage of Scripture so salient and applicable as a basis for our call to pray for our city: "Seek the peace of the city where I have caused you to be carried away captive, and pray to the Lord for it; **for in its peace you will have peace** … 'For I know the thoughts that I think toward you,' says the Lord, 'thoughts of peace and not of evil, to give you a future and a hope. Then you will call upon Me and go and pray to Me, and I will listen to you. And you will seek Me and find Me, when you search for *Me* with all your heart'" (NKJV bold type added).

As I watched Jack, it was obvious that he was receiving a fresh anointing of the Holy Spirit for the opportunity of communicating the peace that was offered to us and our city if we would break down any walls between us and claim our oneness in Christ.

It was evident that Jack knew many of the pastors and church workers. I observed them carefully. They were all over the crowded sanctuary. Then I noted that the Mayor, Tom Bradley, had slipped into one of the pews. Also, I noticed that a woman Episcopal priest was there with several of her staff. Scanning the faces of the crowd, I identified large numbers of pastors representing black, Hispanic, Filipino, and white congregations. It was encouraging to see Roman Catholic priests present. Many of the leaders of inner-city missions were in attendance. It was stunning!

And here was one of the truly great charismatic leaders speaking to men and women of every imaginable denominational and theological persuasion.

Jim Rayburn, the founder of Young Life, used to tell his youth leaders that they had to earn the right to be heard.

Obviously, Jack had earned the right to be heard that morning because of his magnanimous, inclusive spirit and the witness of his own ministry throughout the city, beyond his own congregation.

Jack, the gentle giant, Christian leader, with his winning, winsome way, was touching the two raw nerves in all of us: our need for a deepening of our personal relationship with the Lord and our growing concern over the growing tensions and unmet needs of our city.

After Jack's opening message, we spent the next hour in guided prayer for our own needs as leaders. We affirmed that nothing can happen through us unless it first happens to us. Pastors have been given the most demanding, challenging, and, at times, lonely calling given by God. They have been chosen to be communicators of the most stupendous good news entrusted to humankind. In turn, they know that they are to be bold, brave, passionate preachers and shepherds who not only care for their flocks but also carry the responsibility of helping their people accept their calling into the ministry of the laity to lead others to Christ and become involved in ministry to the lost, lonely, and marginalized people in the city. Many pastors live with a smarting sense of missing the mark in enabling their churches to be dynamic in both evangelism and mission. Some lose the verve and vitality of their calling. Courageous pastoral leadership is not a solo flight. We need each other to experience affirmation, encouragement, and accountability.

This is the reason, after Jack's message, why we asked everyone to become part of a small group of four for mutual sharing and intercession for each other. The walls between us crumbled as we opened ourselves and shared honestly our hurts and hopes for our lives as persons and as leaders. Graciously, the Holy Spirit moved over the groups, liberating us to be honest and open with each other and then bold in our prayers for each person's confessed needs.

Jack and I started to form our small group. Suddenly, as if by divine prearrangement, a third person joined us. The magnetic power of the Holy Spirit immediately drew the three of us together in what was the beginning of a joyous triumvirate that remains as strong today as it was when it began that morning.

The man who joined us was Bishop Kenneth Ulmer, the now famous Pastor of the Faithful Central Baptist Church. Since that morning, we have met consistently to share the delights and difficulties of city ministry.

We would all three say that we have not faced a personal need, a crushing problem, an overwhelming decision, a physical illness, a time of heart-wrenching grief, or a victory or triumph without profound sharing and prayer together for the Lord's healing, guidance, and hope.

I really affirm what Jack later wrote about Ken Ulmer:

"Ken Ulmer is one of America's new voices, rising with a penetrating call to pragmatic spiritual dynamics. As a Christian leader, he stands tall; as a servant to society, he stands out; as a friend, he stands trustworthy; as a man of God, he stands close—in touch with our Father, that he might be in touch with Him whose touch can change the world." That generous affirmation is characteristic of Jack's desire to turn the spotlight on other leaders. I saw that magnanimity expressed repeatedly over the years.

The friendship in Christ that began that morning between Jack, Ken, and me during the first of the four hours of prayer there in the sanctuary of the Hollywood Presbyterian Church was one of the many wall-demolishing, interracial, multiple denominational, mixed cultural miracles taking place all over the sanctuary.

The next hour was spent praying for our churches. The mutual trust established by the personal sharing freed us church leaders to confide our concerns and boldest dreams for our churches. These became the basis of prayers of intercession for the specific needs and challenges we all faced in leading our churches. Most important of all, the bonds of love and acceptance became the basis of a subsequent outpouring of spiritual and material sharing during the upheaval of the riots that occurred in our city.

It was natural in the next hour of prayer that we turned the focus of our prayers to the gigantic needs of our city. Microphones had been placed in the aisles on the main floor and the balcony in the sanctuary so we could hear the prayers of one another. The church leaders lined up at the microphones and, one by one, led the great assembly in prayers for the gripping needs of our city—the problems of the street people, the street gangs, runaway teens, prostitution, pornography, poverty, hunger, homelessness, and a new wave of prejudice then surging across our city. These are only a few of the many needs brought to the attention of the group and then brought to the Lord in fervent prayer.

Several times the prayers called us to repent for our lack of involved caring and commitment to Christ's agenda of reconciliation and healing. Often, many confessed, they had been part of the problem and too seldom part of the Lord's solution. Tears were shed as we all cried out for Christ to revive His church with new passion and committed involvement to solve the suffering in our city.

The final hour was spent praying for vision and power to get us and our congregations moving as a united church without walls. Again the prayers flowed with intensity interspersed with spontaneous singing as someone would begin a hymn or prayer chorus, and the whole group would join in.

The meeting ended at 11:00 a.m. with the singing of "All Hail the Power of Jesus' Name." The heartfelt recommendation of a large group of the pastors that we meet again was unanimously approved. "Shepherds Love L.A." was launched and continued meeting for several years. A oneness in Christ had been forged among us. We became an interracial, intercultural, interdenominational fellowship without walls.

It was profoundly relevant that these meetings enabled the suburban and inner-city churches to face together the upheaval of the 1992 riots I mentioned earlier. And I think it is significant that one of the churches that responded most generously with truckloads of food and necessities of life for inner-city neighborhoods was a church in Van Nuys called The Church On The Way! Countless other churches whose pastors were part of "Shepherds Love L.A." were part of an outpouring of love in the following weeks and months. Equally important were the regional meetings of pastors that sprang into action.

For Jack Hayford, the peacemaker, this was a contemporary application of Ephesians 2:13–14: "But now in Christ Jesus you who once were far off have been brought near by the blood of Christ. For He Himself is our peace, who has made both one, and has broken down the middle wall of separation" (NKJV).

Paul was writing about the wall of division between Jews and Gentiles in the Temple, but the imaginary walls separating Christians in Los Angeles were no less formidable. In keeping with Jesus' seventh Beatitude, I observed that, for Jack, being a peacemaker was being about his heavenly Father's business among pastors and their churches.

As Jack, Ken Ulmer, and I continued to meet, I was constantly impressed by the impact of Christ, the Prince of Peace, on Jack's calling as a peacemaker seeking to break down walls. Wherever Jesus went, He obliterated the historic walls that separated people from one another. The Savior called not rabbis or priests but twelve laymen to be His disciples. Then He taught them that their ministry was not only to the Jews but also to the Gentiles. Instead of skirting Samaria, Jesus always traveled through it, ministering to those who were called half-breeds and hated by Israel. He ministered to women, caring for them as persons. His forgiving love was offered to tax collectors and prostitutes. Then He went to the cross. As He shed His blood, Christ destroyed the walls that separate people from the Father, from each other, and from their own deep, inner selves. Jack Hayford claimed this stunning example of peacemaking as the mandate of the Master for him.

I have often reflected on what has made Jack the man in Christ that he is and what equips him to be so very effective as a leader of leaders. My answer is that it is his intimacy with the Trinity. Let the word *intimacy* stand. It is that wondrous closeness when the real Jack meets and experiences the tri-splendored Persons of the gracious Father, the risen Savior, and the indwelling power and spiritual gift-giving inspiration of the Holy Spirit.

Jack is a man of prayer. He rises very early every morning to experience a quality of in-depth prayer that is really a conversation with God. We all know from his messages and writings the emphasis he places on praise and adoration in his prayers. Praying in the Spirit draws him into the heart of the Father. In his lifelong quest to claim and realize prevenient sanctification and maturity in Christ, he receives an ongoing character transplant issuing in the fruit of the Spirit.

And from profound sharing with Jack, I have learned of his yearning prayers for all of the gifts of the Spirit. He really believes that the Holy Spirit will provide the gift from within him for the need that is before him.

His prayers of intercession include the long list of people about whom he is concerned. I've been amazed at how many pastors have shared that Jack promised to pray for them and followed up to learn how the Lord had answered his prayers by providing supernatural strength and courage.

I sense that everything Jack attempts has been instigated and bathed in long periods of prayer.

All through the years I have known him, he always is on some new edge of adventure in the kingdom. The word *impossible* is not in his lexicon because of his friendship with the Lord of the impossible.

Jack's time with that Lord explains his remarkable leadership in passionate preaching; evangelism and mission; church growth and expansion; media ministry reaching the nation and portions of the world; authorship of many biblically sound, personally stirring, and inspiring books; commitment to theological education, including the founding of a university and seminary; and impact on the lives of national leaders.

All this and so much more, I think, is because Jack longs to "walk humbly with God." He understands that Micah's use of the Hebrew word, *hatzne`ya*, translated as humility, really means secret, solitary silence, modest listening, and attentiveness with God. It is like *devekut*, clinging to the Lord in an intimate dependence.

From this quality comes the conviction that there is no limit of the grace of the Father, no diminishing of Christ's unifying peace, and no exhaustion of the power of the Holy Spirit. The essence of the exchange between the Lord and the psalmist in Psalm 27:8 most certainly is expressed in his prayer life: "You have said, 'Seek my face.' My heart says to you, 'Your face, Lord, do I seek'" (ESV). And the admonition of verse 14 has become his motto, "Wait on the Lord; be of good courage and He shall strengthen your heart; Wait, I say, on the Lord" (NKJV).

By way of postscript, it is now 2017, and as I write this, Jack, Ken, and I continue to meet. At our last meeting, we focused on gratitude as the antidote for Jack's grief for Anna Hayford, his wife of 64 years, who recently graduated to heaven. With customary dependence on the Lord, Jack expressed fresh courage to press on with the many assignments given to him.

Ken Ulmer shared his deep concern for high school students in the inner cities of America and asked for prayer for raising funds for the Ken Ulmer Institute to bring spiritual, moral, educational, and material aid to them.

I received encouragement in my efforts to raise support for the Ogilvie Institute of Preaching, a ministry to pastors across the country that provides a venue for them to meet monthly to share their needs and vision and to pray for their calling to be passionate preachers.

And so, Jack Hayford, the peacemaker, continues his Holy Spirit ministry. He has exemplified the biblical truth that to whom much is given, much is required, and to whom much is required, much is given!

Section Six

Reflection

16

A Life and Ministry
of Pressing Toward the Mark

Michael Lynch

For over six decades, Jack W. Hayford has sought to cultivate a mindset in believers that God has enfranchised them to be fully qualified, ministering agents of His Kingdom wherever they go—equipped with the keys of the Kingdom, ignited by the Word of God, and empowered by the Holy Spirit—to radiate the warmth of His love, to replicate the ministry of His life, and to penetrate the darkness of a broken and hurting world. And in response, many global leaders in the body of Christ have called him the Apostle Paul of our generation.

Though he dedicated his life to Jesus when he was ten years old, it was in high school when God permanently imprinted the words of Philippians 3:14 on Jack Hayford's soul: *I press toward the mark for the prize of the high calling of God in Christ Jesus"* (KJV). Prompted to cultivate his heart's growing passion for ministry, Jack set aside his career goal of becoming a pharmacist. While attending LIFE Bible College, he met Anna Marie Smith and was, in his own words, "smitten." In 1954, he and Anna were married. "I would not have a ministry without her," says Dr. Hayford. They first pastored in Ft. Wayne, Indiana, from 1955–1960, then returned to California, where he became National Youth Director of the International Church of the Foursquare Gospel (ICFG) from 1960–1965, followed by positions as Dean, then President, of LIFE Bible College from 1965–1969.

Affectionately known as "Pastor Jack," he is the beloved Founder and Pastor Emeritus of The Church On The Way (TCOTW). His service to TCOTW began in 1969 as a temporary assignment to pastor 18 people. Two years into that assignment, he encountered the radiant, visible, *shekinah* glory of God in the church's sanctuary on a Saturday evening. And the Lord spoke to his heart, "I have given My glory to dwell in this place." The very next day, church attendance was 170 while the typical service was at most 100, and the church continued to have dynamic, healthy growth. There was a breakthrough in worship and God's presence that would change the congregation and impact many believers around the world. With worship to God a priority at TCOTW, he continued to minister fruitfully there for more than three decades, and under his leadership, the congregation grew to 12,000 active members, many churches were planted, and many international self-sustaining ministries were birthed.

In addition to ministering on tough topics such as suicide, fractured families, and divorce/remarriage among believers, Pastor Jack boldly led his congregation through the traumas of local, national, and global crises such as the 1991 Gulf War, the 1992 Los Angeles riots, the murder of a congregation member, the Northridge earthquake, and the attacks of September 11, 2001. As one church member noted, "If something major happened in the world, you knew for sure that Pastor Jack would minister to us about it at the next service."

In the same way that Pastor Hayford addressed difficult subjects with his congregation, so also did he minister in his books with truth and tenderness. These tough topics include the loss of a child through miscarriage, stillbirth, abortion, or early infant death (*I'll Hold You in Heaven*), and sexual integrity as seen in his three-book series, *Why Sex Sins Are Worse Than Others, Sex and the Single Soul,* and *The Anatomy of Seduction.* Hope is a recurring theme, and none more poignant than *Hope for a Hopeless Day*, which was released the same week as the 9/11 attacks. While serving as the Executive Editor of *The Hayford Bible Handbook*, he also served as Executive Editor of the *Spirit-Filled Life Bible* since its first publication in 1991, which has now sold more than two million copies.

Each of Jack Hayford's 60-plus published books reflects the practical application of Scripture working in tandem with the companionship and power of the Holy Spirit. A few titles include: *Glory on Your House, Praying is Invading the Impossible, The Key to Everything, The Reward of Worship, Pursuing the Will of God, The Beauty of Spiritual Language, Living the Spirit-Formed Life,* and his groundbreaking study of the Holy Spirit's work in a believer, *Rebuilding the Real You.*

Aside from his prolific writing accomplishments, Pastor Jack's love for God continued to overflow into tangible acts of worship as he penned more than 600 hymns and worship choruses, including the widely-sung "Majesty." It was 1977, the same year as the 25th anniversary of HM Queen Elizabeth II's coronation; symbols of royalty were in abundance everywhere. As Pastor Jack and Anna were driving through the northern parts of Scotland, the opening lyrics and melody simply came to his heart. This Spirit-born song that describes the glorious, kingly, regal, and delivering nature of Jesus captivated hearts around the world. "Majesty" is among the top 50 all-time sung worship songs worldwide.

Pastor Jack's giftings and insight as a leader and his desire to see people come to unity with one another led him to seek reconciliation across denominational, cultural, and ethnic lines and to minister to other spiritual leaders. This began with his Pastors' Seminars at TCOTW in the 1970s and led to his becoming known as a "bridge builder" and "pastor to pastors." Highly significant was his participation in the 1989 Lausanne II Conference on World Evangelism in Manila, where his message about the power of the Holy Spirit in evangelism became one of his most important books, *A Passion for Fullness.* In 1994, he took part in a historic meeting in Memphis of black and white Pentecostal/Charismatic leaders seeking mutual forgiveness, reconciliation, and unity as the Body of Christ. This brought healing among different races and denominations in that widely attended meeting and helped form the Pentecostal/ Charismatic Churches of North America (PCCNA).

A sought-after speaker in the Promise Keepers movement, Pastor Jack served as moderator of the 1997 event on Capitol Mall, attended by over one million men. That same year, while on a plane after having just preached to approximately 42,000 pastors in the Georgia Dome in Atlanta, the Lord spoke to him to found a seminary, which became The King's University (formerly The King's College and Seminary, est. 1997). The King's is a vibrant, Spirit-filled university that fosters servant leadership for the next generation of global leaders. The school has graduated over 1,000 men and women, crossing many denominational and geographical boundaries. He also focused his attention on leadership advancement with his School of Pastoral Nurture (SPN), where, for over 25 years, thousands of pastors from over 100 denominations around the world attended weeklong small group sessions. The concept of "multiplying ministry" now extended beyond the ministry at TCOTW into a global audience who watched on TV and listened to radio broadcasts that aired on over 300 stations, and into the pulpits of the thousands of pastors who received weekly messages by tape/CD, with approximately 150,000 copies distributed annually and over three million in total distribution. While Pastor Jack often spoke to over 20,000 pastors annually, he also hosted the annual Autumn Leadership Conferences at The King's, which was attended by thousands of pastors from around the world.

Pastor Jack's dedication to biblical truth is evident in his deep and abiding love for the land and people of Israel, his passion to teach Christians about their relationship with the Jewish people, and his unwavering commitment to stand with Israel as a nation. For over forty years, he and Anna led groups of believers to tour the Holy Land. In 2002, the Lord called Pastor Jack to be a man who would build a wall of prayer and "stand in the gap" for Israel (Ezekiel 22). So, he built four prayer altars, one in the north, south, east, and west, where many have gone to pray for the nation and people of Israel. A former Minister of Tourism in Israel stated, "Pastor Jack was a force that God used to help preserve the State of Israel."

From 2004–2009, Pastor Jack served as the fifth President of the Foursquare Church (ICFC), the movement that has undergirded his entire life and ministry. He faithfully served his five-year term and brought stability at an important time. In 2005, *Christianity Today* named him the *"Pentecostal Gold Standard,"* saying, "After 50 years in ministry, Jack Hayford continues to confound stereotypes—all to the good."

Today, Jack Hayford Ministries continues to equip and serve the global body of Christ. Last year we provided resources to people from almost every nation and territory through our website (www.jackhayford.org). In 2017, the Jack Hayford Digital Library was launched (www.jackhayfordlibrary.com). This is an online library of 60 years of teachings that are dynamically searchable by keyword, topic, or scripture. The same teachings and ministry that changed so many lives are available as audio recordings, sermon summaries, entire transcripts, and study guides. This tool will ensure that Pastor Jack's transformative teachings will be available to everyone from anywhere at any time.

Jack Hayford's life continues to rise to its true dimensions in the recognition that following Jesus is not about religious achievements but about walking in a lifestyle of dependency upon Him. As he has said, "Over the years, I came to terms with the recognition that—no matter how many years of seasoned service to Christ I accumulated, or how much wisdom or respect I gained—before the Ancient of Days, I am always a child."

Michael V. Lynch
Director, Jack Hayford Ministries
www.jackhayfordlibrary.com
www.jackhayford.org

Name Index

Adams, Jim, *xvii*, *3*
Adasanya, D. A., *177*
Adewuya, Ayodeji, *135*
Albrecht, Daniel, *272, 281*
Alexander, Kimberly, *xviii*
Ambrose, Linda, *135*
Anderson, Robert, *68n*
Angstead, Ruth, *142, 144, 147*
Archer, Kenneth, *152, 153, 309n*
Archer, Melissa, *251n*
Athanasius, *198*
Atteberry, Thomas, *86*
Augustine, *264, 265*
Aultmann, Donald, *150*
Baines, Matthew, *236n*
Barth, Karl, *283, 308n*
Bartleman, Frank, *69, 71, 75, 76, 86*
Bathurst, Jesse, *125*
Bauer, Scott, *xv*
Bellah, Robert, *255, 256, 257, 261, 263*
Bernard of Clairvaux, *155*
Bernis, Jonathan, *111, 113*
Berquist, Jon, *42n*
Bessey, Sarah, *138*
Block, Fred, *319*
Blount, Brian, *234n*
Blum, *140n*
Blumhofer, Edith, *72*
Boddy, A. A., *144*
Boddy, Jane, *144*
Booth, Catherine, *141*
Booth, William, *209*
Boulton, Matthew, *282, 283*

Bowdle, Donald, *151*
Bradley, Tom, *318*
Bradshaw, Paul, *282*
Brown, Colin, *45n, 46n, 47n, 48, 52*
Brown, Marie, *143, 144*
Burdette, R. J., *74, 81, 83*
Calvin, John, *199, 208, 264, 265*
Campbell, Ivey, *89*
Carothers, Warren, *76, 80, 81*
Carson, D. A., *29n, 285*
Cartledge, David, *191*
Chan, Phillip, *274*
Chan, Simon, *153, 308n*
Chappell, Paul, *xv, 113*
Constantine, *93*
Cook, Glen, *78, 79, 83, 85, 86, 87, 90*
Coulter, Dale, *176n, 251n*
Crawford, Florence, *126, 127, 142*
Cross, Terry, *212n, 226*
Crowley, John, *129n*
Cullis, Charles, *77*
Cunningham, Loren, *178n*
Daniels, David, *272*
Daube, David, *54n*
DeBerg, Betty, *140, 141*
Donatus, *130*
Drath, Charles, *215*
Duffield, Guy, *16, 17, 19, 22*
Dunn, James, *3, 8, 9, 10, 11, 15, 24, 25, 26, 30n, 34, 37, 201, 202*
du Plessis, David, *178n*
Edgar, William, *232n*
Ellingson, Stephen, *263, 264*

Scripture Index

About the Editors

Jon Huntzinger

Jon Huntzinger is the Distinguished Professor of Bible and Ministry at The King's University, where he has taught since its founding in 1997. During his years at the school, he has instructed classes in New Testament, biblical Greek and Hebrew, Christian theology, and discipleship. At various times, Dr. Huntzinger has worked as the dean of students, dean of graduate studies, and director of the TKU campus in Los Angeles. While in LA, he and his family were members of The Church On The Way, and he served as an assisting minister there. He currently attends Gateway Church in Southlake, Texas, and teaches in Gateway's Equip program.

Dr. Huntzinger also has taught in Europe and Asia, specializing in the Gospels of Mark and John. His PhD is from Fuller Theological Seminary (1999), and he has taught at FTS as well as at Oral Roberts University. He speaks regularly and has lectured on such topics as Jesus and the wisdom of God, the requirement of biblical confession, and the importance of biblical metaphor.

Dr. Huntzinger was the New Testament editor for the *New Spirit-filled Life Bible* (Thomas Nelson) and author of the commentary on *John* for the Spirit-Filled Life Commentary series (Thomas Nelson). His other writings include an article in *The Holiness Manifesto* (Eerdmans), entitled, "Goodness and Worship: A Perspective on Old Testament Holiness."

He and his wife Penney have two children, both of whom are graduates of Baylor University, and they live in the Dallas/Fort Worth.

S. David Moore

S. DAVID MOORE IS the M.G. Robertson Professor of Pneumatology at The King's University. He served as Professor of Theology at Life Pacific College before joining the King's faculty in 2013. Dr. Moore was the executive director of the John Perkins Center for Christian Community Transformation and Associate Professor of Church Leadership at Patten University in Oakland, California for three years. He was the founding pastor of New Hope Foursquare Church in Manteca, California. Dr. Moore planted the church in the fall of 1978 and was senior pastor for 25 years. He currently serves as the lead pastor at Jackson Avenue Church in Escalon, California.

He teaches nationally and internationally, emphasizing the history and theology of the modern Pentecostal and Charismatic movements. In addition, Dr. Moore is a frequent lecturer on the missional character of the church, pastoral ministry, Christian leadership, and personal & congregational spiritual formation. He holds two earned doctorates (DMin 1999; PhD 2008) from Regent University School of Divinity, where he taught four years as a visiting professor. He also teaches as an adjunct professor for Regent University, Life Pacific College, and Pentecostal Theological Seminary.

Dr. Moore authored *The Shepherding Movement: Controversy and Charismatic Ecclesiology* published in 2003 by T & T Clark, now in a second printing. Dr. Moore was the senior editor of *Renewal History and Theology: Essays in Honor of H. Vinson Synan*. He co-wrote with Jack Hayford *The Charismatic Century: The Enduring Impact of the Azusa Street Revival*, published by Warner Faith in 2006. Dr. Moore is a contributor to many other publications, magazines, and journals. He and his wife Patty have three children, seven grandchildren, and four great grandchildren (he is much too young for great grandchildren!). The Moore family was recently adopted by a cat they have creatively named "Kitty."